Marriage, Duty, & Desire
in Victorian Poetry and Drama

Richard D. McGhee

Marriage, Duty, & Desire
in Victorian Poetry and Drama

THE REGENTS PRESS OF KANSAS
LAWRENCE

Library of Congress Cataloging in Publication Data
McGhee, Richard D., 1940–
Marriage, duty, & desire in Victorian poetry and drama.

Includes bibliographical references and index.
CONTENTS: Tennyson.—Browning.—Arnold and Clough.—
Rossetti and Meredith.—Swinburne and Hopkins.—[etc.]
1. English literature—19th century—History and criticism.
2. Marriage in literature.
3. England—Social life and customs—19th century.
I. Title.
PR469.M35M3   822′.009′354   80-11962
ISBN 0-7006-0203-8

for Marie

Contents

Preface

Victorian literature in Britain is far too various to classify simply or to evaluate with sweeping generalizations. Its complexities and its beauties are as obvious as those of any preceding era of literature. Nevertheless, there are certain ideas, images, metaphors, and words that recur often enough in the works of so many writers to mark the literature by stylistic and thematic idiosyncrasies. I have explored one of those idiosyncrasies in Victorian poetry and drama: a preoccupation with the words—and ideas of—*duty* and *desire*. These words represent the hopes of Victorian writers to keep in balance certain qualities of life that seemed threatened by environmental and historical forces over which individuals had little or no control. What seems particularly Victorian about this preoccupation is the writers' frequent resort to the institution of marriage for subjects and metaphors to keep the notions of duty and desire in balance. The best writers did not use marriage merely for aesthetic purposes, however; they explored its limits as a binding force, often showing its failure as a metaphorical device as well as a social or religious institution.

The focus of Wendell Stacy Johnson's book, *Sex and Marriage in Victorian Poetry*, differs from mine. While Johnson is mainly interested in the "sexual attitudes" involved in Victorian ideas about marriage, I am interested in the symbolic function of marriage in particular poems and dramas by ten Victorian writers. The first half of Johnson's book primarily analyzes sexual attitudes and the idea of marriage in Victorian poetry, while the second half considers Tennyson and Browning. My study, like Johnson's second half, concentrates on the works of particular writers, examining those poems or dramas which best illustrate their authors' use of the subject, or metaphor, of marriage. The most important difference between my approach to the subject and that of Johnson is my interest in the specific function of marriage as a means to unite the sometimes conflicting values of duty and desire.

Part of Chapter 2 appeared earlier in an essay published in *Studia Neophilologica* 47 (1975), and part of Chapter 3 appeared earlier in an essay published in *Browning Institute Studies* 5 (1977). For permission to reprint these portions I am grateful to Lars Hermodsson, editor of *SN*, and to William S. Peterson, editor of *BIS*. I am also grateful to Robert F. Kruh and the Kansas State University Bureau of General Research for several grants supporting my research. I am particularly grateful to William L. Stamey for a leave from teaching and administrative responsibilities, allowing me time to do some extensive revising of the manuscript. For their skill and patience in dealing with my frequent requests for typing, I am grateful to Mildred Iyengar, Karen Caffrey, and Luann Bell; for her many secretarial skills and warm understanding, I am especially thankful to Billie Tunison, without whose help I could not have finished this project.

I am obliged to several colleagues for their advice and encouragement. Michael Timko and Wendell Stacy Johnson made several suggestions for improving the manuscript, and for their encouragement I am very grateful. W. David Shaw was generous with his time, helpful with many parts of my argument and organization, and most gracious in his criticism. Shaw and my friend Mary Schneider did most to make me believe in the value of what I was trying to do; Mary Schneider read the manuscript twice, leaving me obliged to her for many suggestions and insights. She called my attention to *Aurora Leigh* as an appropriate subject for the book, and because of her suggestion I have discovered the poetry of Elizabeth Barrett Browning which earlier I had ignored or was accustomed to scorn (without understanding). Finally, I am forever grateful to my wife, Marie, for allowing me to understand why Victorians could believe in marriage as an identity of desire with duty.

1
Introduction

Joseph Mazzini, one of many Italians exiled in Victorian England, called upon the readers of his book, *The Duties of Man*, to "sanctify the Family in the unity of love [to] make it a temple in which you may sacrifice together to the Country."[1] Mazzini was directing this call particularly to his Italian compatriots, but his English readers would also have understood his fervor and his assertion that "there is an angel in the Family who, by the mysterious influence of grace, of sweetness, and of love, renders the fulfilment of duties less wearisome, sorrows less bitter." He was making the point that any social and political order in the state would have to derive from the model of order and the values that exist in the family; it "contains an element of good rarely found elsewhere, constancy. Its affections wind themselves slowly around you, . . . when you lose them . . . you wander restless and uneasy."[2] Although it did not fall into the political chaos of Italy, England did know the chaos of intellectual anarchy and spiritual wandering.

Indeed the family was a last refuge of emotional and spiritual order. In a handbook typical of its kind, Mrs. Sarah Ellis addressed the young women of England to define their "relative duties" as *The Wives of England*. She explains how important it is that wives should lean only upon the strong love of God to support them, because they in turn will be supporting the lives of their families: "While engaged with all her energies in this first duty [working out her own salvation], she will be more occupied with anxiety to draw others along with her, than with disappointment at their being less perfect than she had imagined."[3] Mrs. Ellis is referring especially to the husbands whom their wives will have to help along to salvation. She explains further that "the perfect identity originating in the marriage bond [is] that identity which gives a spiritual

1

nature to an earthly union"; the result is that the family "is something almost heavenly."[4]

Because "the marital union is the center point of Victorian life, where all is 'combined' and 'concentrated,' where 'every intellectual, every moral element,' every 'organ and function' is 'united' totally and for all time in view of the angels, in the 'image and likeness of God,'" it is no wonder, as Stephen Kern has suggested, that "by the end of the century the Victorian family became an explosive unit, poised in a tenuous solidity that was already beginning to decompose as the very forces that held it together became too much for its individual members to bear."[5] A kind of neurosis attends the Victorian preoccupation with conflicts of love and duty, wifehood and family. According to C. S. Lewis, "Idolatry both of erotic love and of 'the domestic affections' was the great error of Nineteenth Century literature."[6] Kern puts it in a more clinical manner: "The European family of the late nineteenth century . . . was often a source of anxiety and conflict" that resulted in an "emotional tone . . . of explosive intimacy."[7] To call this an "error," as C. S. Lewis does, requires a standard of truth few others can assume so easily, but certainly *something* happened in Victorian literature giving it that special "emotional tone." It is especially visible in the poetry and drama of the age when the critical focus centers upon the myth of family, the ritual of marriage, and the symbols of love and duty.

THE SIGNIFICANCE OF MARRIAGE and family as a symbol for balance and order is clearly present in late sixteenth-century literature, consummately so in the poetry of Spenser and in the drama of Shakespeare. For example, *A Midsummer Night's Dream* is framed by the wedding festivities of Theseus and Hyppolyta, whose previous conflicts are to be resolved by a wedding of their differences. Within this drama are three other plots to harmonize differences through marriage. From the moment Theseus demands that Hermia obey her father's will, the iron law of duty begins to conflict with the stubborn demands of desire; the ideal is suggested by the words of Egeus to his king, "With duty and desire we follow you" (1.1).* Not everyone in this kingdom is an Egeus, however; for duty to become reconciled with desire, several marriages must be made or repaired. When the crosses of love are sorted out, Hermia has her Lysander, Hellena her Demetruis, and Thisby yields to her Oberon. The world that had been filled with discord recovers its lost concord, and the "mazed world" recovers its balance of reason and imagination. The

* References are to act and scene.

2

one world that remains amazed and imbalanced, the world of inept artifice practiced by Bottom et al., represents the failure of a courtship to be fulfilled in marriage.

In Shakespeare's comic world, the strength of marriage to unite duty and desire made it a credible symbol of cosmic harmony. In *Antony and Cleopatra* the world is divided for Antony between his Roman duty and his Egyptian desire; his marriages, first to Fulvia and then to Octavia, were alliances for duty, while his pleasures and affection belonged to Cleopatra. This drama hangs upon the increasing tension of Antony's failure to achieve through his marriages the political—and even cosmic —balance between a public duty and a private affection. When finally he makes a true marriage, it is through death, an ironic minister that binds Antony with Cleopatra: suicide is the clear means for identifying stoical Roman duty with passionate Egyptian desire. When Antony falls upon his sword, he becomes "a bridegroom in [his] death" (4.14), and Cleopatra, nursing her "baby at [her] breast," dies with her call to Antony, "Husband, I come" (5.2). In life or in death, then, Shakespeare's drama turns upon the secure metaphor of marriage, functioning in a universe that insists upon its efficacy.

When John Dryden rewrote Shakespeare's play as *All for Love*, he retained the marriage metaphor to symbolize harmony, but he so diminished its domain that it lost its cosmic or political force. Dryden's version is very much a tragedy of merely domestic proportions, lacking the scope and grandeur of Shakespeare's. It is a clear sign of the increasingly domestic focus in modern literature, leading to a fate deplored by Robert Louis Stevenson: "Marriage, if comfortable, is not at all heroic. It certainly narrows and damps the spirits of generous men."[8] Something like this is already evident in Dryden's play, where his most singular invention for the story occurs in act 3 when Ventidius brings in Antony's Roman family, Octavia and their two daughters, to appeal for Antony's return to his duty. Thus, when Octavia sends her children to kneel before their father to "pull him . . . from that bad woman," Dryden is previewing much of the domestic tragedy to come in British literature. The world of power and domestic ethics, represented by Antony's Roman family, fails to secure the hero's allegiance, however, and duty (law) yields to desire (love) at the price of life itself. For Dryden, the tragedy is that marriage cannot hold together these opposing values, that "passion changes its face and becomes duty,"[9] and so the world is left with the cold calculations of Octavius Caesar and the heated imaginations of hypocritical priests like Serapion. When Dryden rewrote *Paradise Lost* as the "opera" he called *The State of Innocence*, he focused his attention on the relationship of Adam and Eve, excluding as much as he possibly

3

could of the supernatural events and especially of God and Christ. In effect, Dryden did with *Paradise Lost* what he had done with *Antony and Cleopatra*: he domesticated Adam's and Eve's sublimity, in part by reducing the scope of their actions from the cosmic to the family order.

Opera as a serious art form is an important factor in the cultural history of the eighteenth century. Indeed, Eric Bentley has suggested that "Mozart's three operatic masterpieces are the greatest achievement of the eighteenth-century theatre."[10] Opera librettos are useful examples of the continuing importance of marriage as a metaphor of psychological and social—even religious and cosmic—harmony; librettos display in clear ways the major themes of "Western culture in operatic terms and in their widespread philosophic and cultural import."[11] Opera might very well be the clearest "projection of the power, wealth, and taste of the society which supports it"; thus, the study of opera "may illuminate broad cultural developments in any period."[12]

Gluck's *Alceste,* Mozart's *Magic Flute,* and Beethoven's *Fidelio* suggest the range of interests by these masters of the form in using librettos constructed from conventions of marriage. The librettos show how the ideals of reconciliation and harmony contained in marriage were becoming more and more secular and thus being used in psychological and social contexts. The librettos illustrate Freud's point that "the ascetic tendency of Christianity had the effect of raising the psychical value of love in a way that heathen antiquity could never achieve."[13] The narrow base of the self (or, subjective experience) was increasingly relied upon to bear the weight of cosmic importance; and so the pyramid of faith, with marriage at the base and God at the apex, was being turned upside down.

In these operas the very lives, if not the souls, of the men depend upon the strength of their women's love and duty toward them. The hero's rescue from death is a function of female desire (echoing a similar theme in Spenser's adventures of Britomart and Scudamour), but female desire is given direction by the special form of marriage. Denis De Rougemont could well have drawn upon these operas to support his indictment of "the whole middle-class youth in Europe." They were "brought up to regard marriage with respect; and yet at the same time all young people breathe in from books and periodicals, from stage and screen, and from a thousand daily allusions, a romantic atmosphere in the haze of which passion seems to be the supreme test that one day or other awaits every true man or woman, and it is accepted that nobody has really lived till he or she 'has been through it.'"[14] De Rougemont was referring to pre–World War II Europe, not to an audience for grand opera, but the cultural malaise he describes was the product of many

4

generations of aesthetic and moral conditioning that began at least as early as the seventeenth century (if not earlier, as he suggests). The cultural outlook represented by *Alceste, The Magic Flute*, and *Fidelio* prepared the way for such vulgarized advice as that given by Mrs. Ellis to the young wives of Victorian England: "The high and holy purpose" for a wife in marriage is to soften "the harder and more obdurate nature of man, so as to render it capable of impressions upon which the seal of eternity might be set."[15] And to be able to do that, the wife must learn "to bring down [her] every selfish desire, and every rebellious thought, to a due subserviency in the general estimate we form of individual duty."[16] In their own ways, Alceste, Pamina, and Leonore all carry out "the high and holy purpose" described by Mrs. Ellis.

Gluck's *Alceste* concentrates upon marriage at the expense of both Heracles and the theme of hospitality, which were central in the play by Euripides. Alceste has volunteered to sacrifice her life for her husband—not so much because he is needed as king of his people as that she loves him too much to live without him. The opera is a lyrical outpouring of adoration for married love. Without her husband, Alceste imagines the emptiness of all life, and she maintains that "only the heart of wife or mother could comprehend [her] suffering."[17] She is the consummate "wife in tears" (1.1). Her love is chaste and her desire is innocent (1.2). Her eagerness to die for Admetus is exemplary: "I go, most gladly to fulfill my duty" (1.2). And to die for desire and duty is to be filled with exaltation, to be invaded with power:

> To die for one you love,
> for one you love, 'tis but an easy task!
> And I am filled with exaltation.
> I am invaded with new force,
> I go where love calls me.   [1.2]

When Admetus insists on dying with his wife, Gluck and his librettist celebrate these devotees in act 2 as "tender lovers, happy pair," joined by "Eros and Hymen." For man and wife to join in mutual self-sacrifice is to realize, as nearly as any of the literature in modern times ever does, a union of duty with desire. The rescue of this couple from death is not a result of Heracles's actions, but rather of their own perfected passion. No wonder Apollo points to them in act 3 as examples for all married couples to imitate: "Live, happy pair! May mortals, bound / by Hymen's laws, your perfect love commend!" Earlier, in act 2, when Alceste was preparing herself for death, she asked to be remembered as "wife and Queen and mother," and this identifies her—in the order of roles important to her, to the opera, and to the artists, as well as to their audience.

Alceste is above all "a dutiful wife and mother," as Irving Singer has described her.[18]

The close connection of passion with death is a point often developed in the conventions of drama and opera, reflecting the notion that Eros is, as Joseph Bernhart says, "always *Eros thanatos*."[19] Alceste's passionate love brings her to the brink of death but it prevents the death of her husband, although he is willing to join her in an eighteenth-century version of *liebestod*. Their marriage serves as both a ritual death and a resurrection, destroying any remaining traces of old selves and restoring their new selves through the strength of their united passions. This same function of marriage occurs in both *The Magic Flute* and *Fidelio*, though Mozart's opera emphasizes the courtship and initiation process leading to the reward and salvation of marriage, while Beethoven's (even more than Gluck's) intensifies the sacrificial power and saving grace of marriage. All three operas show how "the struggling will completes itself . . . through the harmony of an idealized marriage."[20] One certain motif stands out to distinguish the themes of these operas from similar themes in the plays of Shakespeare and even of Dryden: there is in these operas little conflict between duty and desire for either of the partners in the marriages or courtships.

In *Alceste, The Magic Flute*, and *Fidelio* desire proves to be duty when brought within the institution of marriage, and marriage not only secures identity for the individuals but for the entire social order within which they move. In the versions of both Shakespeare and Dryden, Antony is brought to his tragic end because he is torn between public obligation and private desire; both Antony and Adam learn, as C. S. Lewis has said, that "without Grace, our wishes and our necessities are in conflict."[21] There may be an underlying assumption of security in the married state of the cosmos (that is, God's grace upholding the order of things), but as portrayed in seventeenth-century literature, individuals cannot safely assume such security in their separate lives; individuals secure themselves by finding their places in the cosmic marriage. However, in works such as these three operas, it is the cosmos itself which is saved by the virtue of marriages. Jacques Chailley, in his analysis of *The Magic Flute*, might also be describing *Alceste* and *Fidelio* when he says that the "fundamental dualism of the esoteric cosmogony" is resolved by the union of the hero and heroine.[22] (Chailley's book examines in detail the "hermetic cosmogony" represented by the characters of the opera, in which the Sun and the Moon, Day and Night, Fire and Water, etc. all are put in their proper balance once Tamino marries Pamina.)

In the high comic opera of *The Magic Flute*, then, not only is paradise regained, but the proper order of the universe is ensured by the marriage of Tamino and Pamina. Joseph Kerman says that "the magic marriage is *The Magic Flute*."²³ The "magic" of the marriage makes possible a proper subordination of dark passion to enlightened reason, creating (paradoxically) what Singer calls "a rationalized marriage."²⁴ In the action of the opera, passion is hidden at first by the sympathetic plight of Pamina's mother, the Queen of Night, who desires the return of her daughter. Tamino is moved by the mother's plea as well as by his own desire for the daughter; therefore, passion initiates honorable action by the hero. (By contrast, Papageno's mere appetite has no real initiative; Monostatos is another example of mere appetite, but his cannot be controlled even under the command of reason itself, in the person of Sarastro.) Tamino goes forward to serve his desire and at the same time puts his desire in the service of a higher passion, a mother's love. The magic flute (obviously a symbol—it may be art itself or, more crudely, the phallus controlled by reason) is Tamino's only weapon of defense, significantly a defense against passion: "When'er this power is asserted, / All human passions are converted."²⁵

When Pamina learns that her redeemer is coming, she sings a duet with Papageno on the virtuous power of love: "Let joyous love for grief atone; / We live by love, by love alone" (pp. 388, 389). Together they honor the highest good which they are capable of imagining:

> Its noble aim shows clear in life:
> No greater good than man and wife.
> Wife and man, and man and wife,
> Reach the height of godly life.   [p. 388]

Natural love (passion, desire) is consummated in marriage, "the height of godly life." But not without more instruction and experience than Papageno and Pamina realize. For Tamino must first pass a series of tests to determine whether he is worthy of the "godly life" marriage promises. In other words, he must learn to discipline his passion, to subordinate his desire.

Though the husband as hero is moved by his passion, he must learn to recognize a higher authority, the power of enlightened reason. Thus Tamino undergoes a reversal in the recognition scene at the end of act 1, when he sees that the Queen of Night has become his enemy whose powers must be repressed before he can be united with Pamina, the object of his desire. In act 3 he accepts the new terms of his mission delivered by Sarastro: to submit to the tests of his manhood and learn "what duty to humanity is" (p. 399). Sarastro tells Pamina that his mission is to teach "all erring mortals, / Their way [*Pflicht*, duty] by love is shown." When Tamino passes through his ordeals of interrogation and instruction, he and Pamina join their strengths together in a mystic marriage that survives fire and water; they pass *into* paradise through fire. In the end, night and darkness are overcome, and the kingdom of daylight is assured. In their concluding adventure, Tamino and Pamina dare even death; because their marriage is so strong, they are able successfully to pass through the portals of death. (Ironically, this anticipates the less happy view of the Victorians that, as Steven Marcus describes it, "the rites of the marriage bed, though sacred, are perilous.")[26] Like Alceste, then, Pamina risks death for her husband, and both heroines prove the great efficacy of marriage for binding together not only the forces of human passion and intellect but also all contradictory forces of the universe.

The wife as heroine risking her life to save her husband is the central action of Beethoven's opera *Fidelio*, which is significantly subtitled *The Triumph of Married Love*. This masterpiece of musical drama indicates, as do *Alceste* and *The Magic Flute*, the insistent trend of European culture during the eighteenth and early nineteenth centuries: an increasing reliance upon the conventions of marriage for preserving or even establishing an order of security between individuals, on behalf of society and as a guard against cosmic chaos. As Joseph Mazzini said, less than half a century after Beethoven's opera was written, "We must aim at making the whole of Humanity one Family, each member of which shall represent in himself the moral law for the benefit of the others."[27] This is something Beethoven, Mozart, and Gluck would have understood all too well, for Hymen was becoming the new god of the Victorian age, keeping in balance the sometimes contradictory, but now lesser, forces of eros and agape.

Like many other commentators on *Fidelio*, Edward J. Dent in the introduction of his translation of the libretto compares Beethoven's opera with Mozart's *Magic Flute*, observing that *Fidelio* is the "natural sequel" in which "Florestan and Leonora are Tamino and Pamina born again as real human beings, facing as realities what they had previously seen only as symbols."[28] And Beethoven's opera does indeed seem to be "the natural sequel" to Mozart's, in the special way that most art since the seventeenth century (and, for English literature, particularly since Shakespeare and Milton) has followed a pattern of becoming more domesticated as the "supernatural" becomes "naturalized." *The Magic Flute* is ostentatiously symbolic, or artificial, in its freight of spiritual meaning, but *Fidelio* is directly the opposite, almost a "slice of life." (This is especially so in the opening scene, the "bourgeois domesticity of which," it has been argued, "would have been more in place in a drama less tense and lofty" than Beethoven's.)[29] Both operas are formed by actions and themes of

8

marital bliss and harmony, although the earlier one journeys toward marriage as the end of the characters' lives while *Fidelio* makes marriage a foundation for greater action.

The bourgeois ideal of quiet domesticity is represented in the pleasant adolescent dreams of Marcellina. She sings of what it would be like if she were wed to Fidelio:

> In the quiet of domesticity
> I will awake each morning;
> We will greet each other tenderly,
> With no mortal care in the world.[30]

Marcellina's father, Rocco, represents the notion of married happiness as a matter of sufficient money: "If you don't have money near at hand / You can't be really happy . . . Gold will bring you power and love" (p. 11). But the action of the drama belies the ideals of both Rocco and Marcellina, for the basis of marriage is not gold nor is the goal of life domestic security, as Fidelio shows when "he" becomes Leonore, the heroic wife.

While Marcellina dreams of escaping from the mortal cares of the world into domestic quiet and while Rocco asserts that gold brings power and love, the common soldiers see their lives as rounds of duty: "Let's move on to our duties! . . . Keep sharp watch on your rounds!" (p. 12). The lives of such people as Rocco, the soldiers, and Marcellina are tied to rounds of physical restraint, and Pizarro represents the tyranny of such a world. This is the kind of world from which Leonore rescues her husband, Florestan, for her life is determined neither by escapist dreams of comfort nor by desires for wealth and power. She follows her "inner desire" as her only certain duty:

> I follow my inner desire,
> And waver not;
> I am strengthened by the duty
> Of true married love.   [p. 13]

The main theme of the opera is concentrated in this aria, communicating the heroine's (and the artists') faith in marriage as a harmony of desire with duty. (In English literature at about the same time, Shelley represents a similar faith and a similar action in his *Prometheus Unbound* when Asia follows her inner desire, especially in act 2, to rescue her "husband" Prometheus from the tyranny of Jupiter.) The aria by which Florestan is introduced emphasizes the process of love and desire becoming a power of redemption when united with duty. Florestan undergoes a wondrous transformation of spirit from utter dejection to intense ex-

pectation; from dark despair he has a startling vision as his wife appears
to lead him from his prison:

> Do I not sense a mild, murmuring breeze?
> And is not my grave lightened?
> I see, like an angel in golden mists
> Coming to my side to console me,
> An angel so like Leonora, my wife,
> Leading me to freedom in heavenly realms.   [p. 14]

Beethoven, like Wordsworth at the same time, is naturalizing the
supernatural to suggest the spiritual value of imagination as a means of
natural, or psychological, grace. The drama of this libretto represents a
triumph of faith in the power of marriage to bring meaning to mankind,
to rescue souls held captive to the bonds of both materialism and escapist
idealism. By the time of Beethoven, Wordsworth, and Coleridge, this
faith in marriage was no longer merely an underlying assumption as it
had been for generations of Europeans; it had become the symbolic form
of spiritual or psychological power evident in *Fidelio* or in the following
lines from Wordsworth's "Home at Grasmere":

> Paradise, and groves
> Elysian, Fortunate Fields—like those of old
> Sought in the Atlantic Main—why should they be
> A history only of departed things,
> Or a mere fiction of what never was?
> For the discerning intellect of Man,
> When wedded to this goodly universe
> In love and holy passion, shall find these
> A simple produce of the common day.
> —I, long before the blissful hour arrives,
> Would chant, in lonely peace, the spousal verse
> Of this great consummation.   [ll. 800–811]

Such a "marriage" did not succeed for Wordsworth, at least not in
the ambitious poem *The Recluse* for which "Home at Grasmere" is the
first book. *The Excursion* wrestles with the problems of uniting individual desires and public duties, but it falls far short of its goals. Wordsworth and the Solitary, his chief character in *The Excursion*, would perhaps have agreed with Freud's somber conclusion that "we must make
up our minds to the idea that altogether it is not possible for the claims
of the sexual [i.e., creative] instinct to be reconciled with the demands of
culture."[31]

The poem by which Wordsworth might best be known as a Victorian
is his "Ode to Duty"; it should be considered in the light of his own

10

failure to maintain his initial joy in the wedding of his mind to nature. His use of the marriage metaphor to suggest the union of such apparently opposite values as "intellect" and "this goodly universe" became less frequent as his faith in the union declined. He tended to identify the values of "this goodly universe" with his desire to recover childhood joy and spontaneity, while he increasingly identified "the discerning intellect of Man" with his growing duty to prepare for death and with the loss of all desire; the strain on the wedding of these values proved too great to maintain. The "Ode to Duty" calls for "a repose that ever is the same," a relief from "the weight of chance-desires."

When Coleridge chose to express his own version of the separation between mind and nature, it was on the occasion of his separation from the woman he loved, Sara Hutchinson. It is no surprise that one of his great poems is "Dejection: An Ode," for his art generally expressed the larger cultural dislocation which marked the nineteenth century. Coleridge was a student of the soul, and he was an artist of apathy—that symptom of psychic disease which Rollo May has described as the main attitude toward life in our century. Apathy occurs, May says, when love and will are blocked or separated.[32] The threat of this separation is a preoccupation of Coleridge's. His personal unhappiness in marriage, his yearning for Sara Hutchinson, and his increasing sense of failure as a poet to keep alive his "shaping spirit of imagination" all conspired in him to give expression to a dejection echoed in the works of several other Victorian writers. The binding power of marriage, or whatever marriage represented, was breaking apart—not only for Coleridge personally but for European culture in general, however much artists might still resort to its social, rhetorical, or even metaphorical use.

One of the significant features of Coleridge's poem on dejection is its representation of the failure of the marriage between "our life" and "Nature": "Joy, Lady! is the spirit and the power, / Which wedding Nature to us gives in dower / A new Earth and new Heaven" (5.67–69). Coleridge's duty to his wife and family (from whom he was increasingly estranged in 1802) became so separate from his desire for Sara Hutchinson that his imagination became first apathetic or anaesthetized, then despairing, and finally diabolical. His life became a wreck of divided values, and his imagination sought constantly and variously for appropriate metaphors that would unify the disparate strands of both his own life and the life of his culture. He is an eloquent spokesman for the need to prevent the divorce of "will" and "wish."[33]

In February 1810 Coleridge transcribed into his notebook a passage from Jean Paul's *Geist* anthology on the subject of birthday celebrations.

11

Coleridge significantly adapted Jean Paul's passage,[34] making it a comment on a wedding anniversary:

> On some delightful day in early spring or June, on this day some of my Countrymen hallow the anniversary of their Marriage, & with Love and Fear go over the reckoning of the past and the unknown future—the Wife tells with half renewed modesty all the sweet feelings that she disguised and cherished in the Courting time—the Man looks with a Tear full in his eyes and blesses the Hour when for the first time—and O let it be the last—! he spake deep & solemn to a beloved Being— Thou art mine and I am thine—& henceforward I shield and shelter against the world, and thy Sorrows shall be my sorrows, and tho' abandoned by all men we two will abide together in Love & Duty![35]

Coleridge had for some time realized that his own marriage had failed to keep "Love & Duty" together. He yearned, with bitterness, for someone who might have brought to him such total love that all his desires would be satisfied. Later in 1810 Coleridge again confided to his notebook his regret that he did not find a wife:

> One human Being, *entirely* loving me (this, of course, must have been a Woman) would not only have satisfied all my Hopes, but would have rendered me happy and grateful, even tho' I had had no Friend on earth, herself excepted.
>
> In short, a WIFE, in the purest, holiest sense of the word.[36]

Even had such a woman been his without benefit of "outward and sensible Sacrament," he would have enjoyed in her a "Blessing." No woman, however, had "satisfied all [his] Hopes," and so in December 1815 when Coleridge again made a note on his wrecked marriage, he despairingly yearned for what Wordsworth celebrated—that "essential nineteenth-century idea," that "pre-eminently sanctified thing"[37]—a life of duty:

> That which I have to strive for now in the discipline of my own mind is independence of female *Society*—Month after month the conviction strengthens in me, that it is my penance and my Duty to devote my future Life to *Work*, exclusive of all other views but the compensation to my Children & Friends for the indolence and ravage of intellect, which the dire self-punishing Vice of Opium has effected![38]

Quite apart from the massive problem Coleridge had with opium addiction, his more radical spiritual dislocation illustrates the cultural dilemma at the dawn of the Victorian era for all who relied upon marriage to reconcile conflicting values or to resolve increasing tensions. "We may observe that the state of being a husband was already well on its way to becoming the condition of permanent crisis that it is today" is the way Steven Marcus delineated "the other Victorians," among whom we might

12

number Coleridge (though not in the particular elite company Marcus had in mind).[39]

Victorian artists used the subject matter and imagery of marriage not only because it was the most important institution available to them for communication with their audience, but also because they needed a viable source of figurative language. The best writers, however, not only used this material but also showed its symbolic importance as a vehicle for expressing a cultural crisis—that is, as an expression of the accumulating tension which led eventually, in De Rougemont's words, to "the present breakdown of marriage" in European life.[40] Marriage had become a secular institution, a development reflected in European literature throughout the seventeenth and eighteenth centuries; but in the nineteenth century (along with medieval gothicism), marriage evoked a nostalgic regard for the religious and spiritual values it once embodied. Therefore when poets like Tennyson and Browning began their careers, marriage was a secular, social fact, much in need of some spiritual rationale to prevent its crumbling beneath the weight of an increasing demand being made upon it—a demand illustrated by the works of Mazzini and Ellis.

Victorian writers attempted to recover the religious and spiritual values which once were easily and uncritically attached to marriage as a means of grace. For the great artists, this attempt often resulted in failure, but it was a failure which produced special tensions. These tensions are the energies of marriage (or its forms as a myth) under the stress of attempting to reconcile all the differences between men and women, but especially the differences between "duty" and "desire." These terms encompass a range of values which have been differently described by many different people: Joseph Bernhart describes marriage as "the symbolic case of the ego-world tension, like the duality of the entire universe";[41] Denis De Rougemont, as "the fundamental antagonism of Eros and Agapé";[42] and Father D'Arcy, as "a metaphysical principle . . . [which may] reconcile the necessary movement of human desire which ends in the self with the duty of loving God more than the self."[43]

RICHARD WAGNER's *Tristan und Isolde* is a triumph of European art in the nineteenth century, an achievement whose importance and value is again being realized after several decades of distorted commentary in the wake of World War II. Despite the rise of the Nazis, Thomas Mann was able to recognize in Wagner a suffering and greatness which made him the "complete expression" of the nineteenth century—"his face scored through and through with all the century's impulsive force: so I see that face."[44] *Tristan und Isolde* is a stupendous gathering of emotion

13

into an art form of simplicity and profundity that is seductively terrifying; it can draw its audience into an abyss of nothingness, exercising a power over audiences "again and again in every capital of Europe and America."[45] What makes *Tristan und Isolde* terrifying also makes it seductive: it elaborates the power of passion as a yearning for death.

Tennyson, Arnold, and Swinburne recognized this power latent in the story of Tristan and Isolda, and each attempted to deal with it. Tennyson and Arnold, in quite ambivalent ways, kept the power of the story at bay while Swinburne celebrated it with something like naiveté when compared to what Wagner did with it. No other work of the Victorian era captures the artistic expression of desire and its conquest over duty with more clarity and beauty than does *Tristan und Isolde*. The great artists of the century who were attracted to the importance of the story knew, as though by instinct, that here was the essence of their cultural experience in all its splendid failure. For Eric Bentley, *Tristan und Isolde* "is great . . . as an expression of European nihilism, one of the deepest trends in nineteenth-century thought and sensibility."[46] The art which now seems most important from that era is the art which celebrates not merely failure, such as that of Arthur in Tennyson's *Idylls* or of Empedocles in Arnold's poem, but failure of great proportions—large idealisms and mammoth hopes. Darkness came to the imagination with the triumph of materialism and what William Blake called "urizenic" reason. The great artists tapped below the bright surface and, like the Pope in *The Ring and the Book*, sought to reveal a new-born power for life in the unconscious, if not in the enlightened, imagination.

Wagner's *Gotterdamerung* sensibility was most fully realized in *Tristan* rather than in *The Ring* cycle, although the Tristan-Isolda relationship is comparable to that of Sigmund-Siglinde and that of Sigfried-Brunnhilde. In all of these couples, the force of passion drives through the lovers to destroy old orders and make way for new ones. The old order is the world of daylight, reason, and duty, while the new is by its very nature obscure, not yet realized, but still potential—as the moment of climax in the sexual experience, the expression for which nearly all commentators have noticed in *Tristan*. While its structure may approximate sexual consummation, the drama's surging action of passion breaks through the barriers that normally define human life. Nietzsche thought he could hear in Wagner's music "the earthquake by means of which a primeval life-force . . . was seeking at last to burst its bonds, quite indifferent to how much of that which nowadays calls itself culture, would thereby be shaken to ruins."[47]

Francis Fergusson has compared *Tristan* with Leni Riefenstahl's film *Triumph of the Will* with predictable results that deplore such a use of

14

the Wagnerian spirit.[48] But Fergusson has done both *Tristan* and *Triumph of the Will* a disservice (however admirable his analysis of *Tristan* may be); these two works of art can better be appreciated if they are contrasted, rather than compared. Wagner's opera denies almost everything that Riefenstahl's film affirms. The film celebrates light and the bringer of light—Adolf Hitler as the redeemer come out of the sky like a god bringing sunshine and health to his adoring worshippers. The film is nearly all a grand festival of light, with only one night of passion—though not a night of darkness. This is in contrast, of course, to the deepening darkness of *Tristan*, slowly gathering out of Tristan's and Isolda's intensifying commitment to passion. In addition, the film basks in the glow of family happiness, with numerous shots of adoring children, mothers and fathers, all of whom gleefully salute their glorious leader. Wagner's opera is a firm denial of the happy family, which is left to fall into ruin when its greatest champion, Tristan, turns from it to his private desire. And finally, *Triumph of the Will* is a worship of authority and a lesson in duty. *Tristan* is a worship of nothing, not even "womanhood," though one might mistakenly think so if only the opening scenes are recalled. When Tristan is conveying Isolda from Ireland to Cornwall to become King Mark's bride, Tristan is in the service of society, doing his public duty, and inspired not only by his allegiance to the king, but also by his devotion to "the pearl of womanhood." Thus he sings when he resists answering Isolda's ironic command:

> In any station
> where I stand
> I truly serve but her,
> the pearl of womanhood.
>   If I unheeding
>   left the helm;
> how might I pilot her ship
> in surety to King Mark?[49]

But the rest of the opera is an intensifying denial of that service. When Mark arrives at the end of the action to find Tristan dead and Isolda dying, he delivers a bitterly ironic blessing over the couple whom he had come prepared to give to one another in a "true" marriage at last.

In this opera, Wagner had the audacity to declare that reality lay in the darkness rather than in the light, in the force of passion rather than in the suasion of reason and duty. The many deaths at the end of the drama represent not only the end of social order but also, paradoxically, the triumph of individual passion, as the ecstatic *liebestods* of Tristan and Isolda testify. In all of European art there is hardly anything else like this opera for expressing the emphatic action of passion and desire. Other artists developed the same theme, but without Wagner's energy and force. His large scope and sweep of vision that narrows to the single point of enormous energy compressed in an individual is typical of the Romantic spirit, and his triumphant gesture of commitment to desire is equally Romantic; but his denial of culture, of light and duty, complicates an otherwise Romantic optimism. He is a Victorian who rejects Victorianism.

The same could be said of another great artist of the time, Henrik Ibsen, with whom both Thomas Mann and Eric Bentley have compared Wagner. Of the two, however, Ibsen is the lesser artist: he loves the light too much to be the best artist of Victorian Europe, and that is the case even when his dramas represent so well the gathering gloom of mist and darkness (as in *Ghosts*). Ibsen's works are much better than Wagner's as tragedies because his characters (unlike Wagner's) lose too much when they lose life and light. Even when Ibsen's people do not die or suffer terrible losses, they cannot quite achieve the redemption that Wagner's people do. *A Doll's House*, one of the best examples of the fate of marriage as a unifying device in Victorian literature, shows how marriage must be sacrificed to free the individual from duty and to develop his (or her) own character. However, when Nora at last awakens to her predicament, she leaves her husband with all his preaching about duty, but she cannot define her own new life except as a "duty" to herself. After she tells Helmer in act 3 that she is leaving him, he responds:

> HELMER: This is outrageous! You are betraying your most sacred duty.
> NORA: And what do you consider to be my most sacred duty?
> HELMER: Does it take me to tell you that? Isn't it your duty to your husband and your children?
> NORA: I have another duty equally sacred.
> HELMER: You have not. What duty might *that* be?
> NORA: My duty to myself.[50]

This is the only way Nora can conceive of her new identity, and it is a way which Wagner, Swinburne, and Wilde reject. Others though, like the two Brownings and Hopkins, do choose to define passion, desire, and individuality in terms of the prevailing conventions, i.e., duty and self-sacrifice. "But," as George Bernard Shaw observed, "Her duty to herself is no duty at all . . . Woman has to repudiate duty altogether."[51] Nora, however, cannot see herself without the help of such conventions, a fact made clear by her concluding remarks to her husband, who pleads to know if there is anything he can do:

> HELMER: Nora, can I never be anything more to you than a stranger?

16

NORA: Ah, Torvald, only by a miracle of miracles . . .
HELMER: Name it, this miracle of miracles!
NORA: Both you and I would have to change to the point where . . .
    Oh, Torvald, I don't believe in miracles any more.
HELMER: But I will believe. Name it! Change to the point where . . . ?
NORA: Where we could make a real marriage of our lives together.
    Goodbye!   [p. 286]

She does not reject marriage and family, as do Wagner's and Swinburne's protagonists, but more like Browning's, she rejects "false" marriages and measures them against an ideal that redeems the marriage partners. Nora expresses the same hope we hear in Bertrand Russell's wistful credo published in 1929: "I believe marriage to be the best and most important relation that can exist between two human beings. If it has not often been realized hitherto, that is chiefly because husbands and wives have regarded themselves as each other's policemen." Russell looks back over the Victorian era as one in which "the role of the father [was] being increasingly taken over by the State" after "the subjection of women . . . had reached its height." Marriage, as a last "hope" for Russell, was a way to "free" the wife and rescue the father from the impositions of the state.[52]

    A Doll's House is, admittedly, not Ibsen's final word on the subject of marriage, but the drama serves to show how difficult it must have been for a Victorian artist to break through such a strong convention, without yielding much to it, and to communicate with his audience. When Nora has her opportunity to become an Isolda, to accept the love of the dying Mr. Rank, she reacts with embarrassment and rejection. And when Mrs. Linde offers to help Nora out of her predicament, Mrs. Linde certainly makes her "sacrifice" with little loss; indeed, she gains for herself all that Nora will decide to give up, the happiness of a husband and family. After Krogstad and Mrs. Linde agree to "come together" for a new life, Mrs. Linde reacts instinctively as the compulsive housewife: She "tidies the room a little and gets her hat and coat ready," saying, "How things change! How things change! Somebody to work for . . . to live for. A home to bring happiness into" (p. 266). For her, things may "change," but for the world, nothing changes. Ibsen wants us to recognize the irony of this phrase and of the exchange of roles between Mrs. Linde and Nora, but we can also see beyond the play to recognize how little things change even in Nora's experience, for she still clings to an idea of marriage that would reconcile her desire with her husband's notions of duty.

    At the end of act 3 in Shaw's *Man and Superman*, the Devil tells the Statue that the loss of Don Juan to hell "is a political defeat," the "greatest loss" since Rembrandt decided also to leave hell for heaven.[53] Heaven, we have been told, "is the home of the masters of reality" (3:616), and so that is where "these Life Worshippers" (all of whom fancy themselves "masters of reality") end up, including the inventor of "the latest fashion" among the "Life Force fanatics," Nietzsche. The Devil says that after Nietzsche died he went first to hell, where he met and quarreled with Wagner, who "once drifted into Life Force worship, and invented a Superman called Siegfried. But he came to his senses afterwards" (3:649). If we put aside the ironies, the reversals, and the dramatic functions generally of act 3, we may see clearly how Shaw suggests that among the very few "masters of reality" who choose to reside in "heaven," the most qualified are the "Life Force fanatics"—including Nietzsche. But Wagner failed the final test, became an "idealist" when he composed *Parsifal*, and so found his eternal place in "hell" which "is the home of the unreal" (3:616).

Shaw might also have put Ibsen and Shelley in heaven as "masters of reality" who waged aesthetic wars against the multitude of idealists who surrounded them in the nineteenth century. One of the most pernicious "ideals" with which artist-realists had to contend, in Shaw's opinion, was marriage. In *Man and Superman* this ideal is debunked, exposed, derided, and unfrocked; but still it prevails because it turns out to be useful for the "great central purpose of breeding the race . . . to heights now deemed superhuman" (3:637), toward which the Life Force is eternally driving. Shaw, like his own master, Ibsen, cannot renounce marriage as the great reconciler; he can only expose its abuse (as an obscuring "mephitic cloud of love and romance and prudery") and thus free its real function, its "real purpose"—breeding the Superman. In Shaw's drama, the real purpose of marriage is to unite the drive and desire of Ann Whitefield with the self-conscious intellect of John Tanner, who as a Life Force worshipper discovers himself truly in its grip by the end of the play. He is the play's greatest idealist even while he is championing reality.

Tanner's dream of himself as Don Juan leaving hell for heaven is a revealing feature of the drama, for it suggests that Tanner's greatest ideal is "realism," and that makes him the most attractive victim of the Life Force—Ann herself. This play is a Shavian "midsummer night's dream" and, as in Shakespeare's play, this version affirms the order of the universe at the end of the action by celebrating a true marriage of duty (ironically, in John Tanner) and desire (in Ann Whitefield). But Shaw's drama, while holding to the conventional notion of marriage, knocks it around a bit first; and rather than aspire to the harmony of marriage (as do the characters in Shakespeare's comedy), Shaw's people must learn to respect marriage "only because marriage is a contrivance [of the Life Force] to secure the greatest number of children and the closest care of them" (3:633). There is no great mystery of the spirit, no sacramental function, and no personal salvation in a true marriage, only a yielding of the flesh to the grand purpose of evolutionary self-consciousness.

Shaw's play is a satire of the playwright's own rather desperate groping for something to hang his imagination upon. The notion of a Life Force is not very different than Isolda's *höchste Lust* ("holiest bliss"), though indeed Ann Whitefield (being a "dutiful" daughter) is not much like Isolda. What saves Shaw's play from the fault of *A Doll's House* is that through his humor, Shaw allows us to see around and through the motives of his chief characters, letting us supply the world of his characters through our imaginative assent. His Don Juan-in-hell scene steals the show because it is Shaw's exposure of the nothingness which surrounds not only his plays but also his audience—all are, like Don Juan, moping in the mist, only waiting in the void, or, like the newly dead Donna Anna, wandering in a "slow hopeless way" until she "blunders against the thing she seeks: companionship" (3:601). Because "nothing is real" in the dream world of act 3, the characters may become what they will—figments of imagination in the dream of John Tanner, in the play of George Bernard Shaw, in the minds of whatever audience reads or watches their actions. Shaw, then, is closer to the apostate Wagner than to the arch-realist Ibsen, who at least believes in an ideal something from which his world has fallen into sordid disgrace.

All of Shaw's worlds are modifications of the hell he presents in act 3 of *Man and Superman*. As a state of mind, it is a region through which Shaw wishes to guide his audience into a higher degree of self-consciousness than could be acquired without such a tour. Like Donna Anna, Shaw's characters come into hell looking for a confirmation of all their common prejudices; but like Don Juan, there is George Bernard Shaw waiting in a pallor of the void to set them straight. Don Juan tells Donna Anna that "family ties are rarely kept up" in hell (3:607), an early signal that nothing will ever again be the same for the "slaves of reality" (3:616) who have been freed by "death" (the playwright) from their bondage to earthly compromises. In hell they may idealize without restraint, or in heaven they may "face things as they are," but there will be no middle ground any longer. As Mrs. Whitefield says in act 4, "It's a very queer world. It used to be so straight-forward and simple; and now nobody seems to think and feel as they ought." Tanner agrees, "Life is more complicated than we used to think" (3:675).

A decade later Shaw presents a new solution to the complications of life in the new age. In *Heartbreak House* he probes the marital structure of British society, exposes its essential brittleness, and suggests that the only meaning left in the world is to be found in resignation—waiting for the end of everything. The plot turns upon the efforts of Hesione

Hushabye to prevent "Boss" Mangan from marrying the young, "innocent" Ellie Dunn, who at first seems willing to sacrifice herself as her duty to save her father. Then Ellie discovers that the Othello-like hero of her dreams is a liar and the husband of Hesione; Ellie reacts with embittered determination to capture Mangan, not so much out of duty as out of a will to power, for she has decided that it is "a woman's business" to marry (1:535). In this household, desire and passion either have dissipated—deteriorated into rum (for Captain Shotover) and memories (for Hesione and Hector Hushabye)—or never existed (for Lady Utterwood).

The only characters who seem to have any claim to passion are Randall (who is sent off like a child to pout in his sentimentality), Mazzini Dunn (whose domestic happiness has been undermined by his economic blunderings), and Dunn's daughter, Ellie. But Ellie is here in this house to learn these important lessons: that romance must be stripped away, that business does not mix with romance, and that reality is the heartbreak of waiting for the end to come. After Ellie leaves behind her hopes for Hector and after she sees Mangan stripped of his only apparent strength as a man of practical affairs, she is left with Old Captain Shotover:

> ELLIE: Only half an hour ago I became Captain Shotover's white wife.
> MRS. HUSHABYE: Ellie! What nonsense! Where?
> ELLIE: In heaven, where all true marriages are made.
> . . . .
> ELLIE: Yes: I, Ellie Dunn, give my broken heart and my strong sound soul to its natural captain, my spiritual husband and second father.   [1:586]

In effect, Ellie is the future giving itself to the past, yielding up all desire to wait out the end through darkness: "In the night there is peace for the old and hope for the young" (1:577).

Mazzini, as a disappointed revolutionist, explains how anticlimactic his life has been while waiting every year for "some frightful smash-up. . . . But nothing happened, except, of course, the usual poverty and crime and drink that we are used to. Nothing ever does happen" (1:592). Ellie, the voice of the young, will not accept her father's conclusion that "life doesn't end: it goes on"; she wants there to be some grand event, some point. "I don't know what it is; but life must come to a point sometime" (1:592). She is told that her point is to have a baby—something which might have satisfied Ann Whitefield but will not satisfy Ellie Dunn, who is more a Brunnhilde than an earth mother. The captain is Ellie's true natural husband because he impresses her with the futility of all things except one; he tells her that "nothing happens, except something not worth mentioning" (1:593). Unlike Mazzini, then, the captain offers Ellie an interesting alternative to the prospect of pointless continuity, of unchanging life. Ellie mockingly asks "What is that, O Captain, my captain?" and she hears the sweet music of doom: "Nothing but the smash of the drunken skipper's ship on the rock," he tells her (1:593).

When the bombs come and the dynamite explodes, Ellie exclaims that the sounds of destruction do not merely sound like the music of Beethoven, they are the music of Beethoven. The end of nothingness lies in the promise of the great destruction at the end of the play. Sweet and innocent Ellie, dutiful daughter of her disillusioned revolutionist father, has become a hardened siren of doom. Earlier, toward the end of act 2, Hesione had taken the much weakened Boss Mangan out into the night to calm him (after the episode of the burglar), telling him that "it's like the night in Tristan and Isolde" (1:561). *Heartbreak House* is a worthy successor to *Tristan*, though the lovers have been much diminished by the passage of time. In their ship, Shaw's characters are going nowhere except into darkness and destruction, without desire. Whether Mangan or Shotover is the new Tristan (or, rather, Tristan grown old), and Hesione or Ellie the new Isolda, they are the pathetic remains of the splendid, though futile, glory of the Victorian past.

The "great central purpose" of marriage, as it was declared in *Man and Superman*, to breed the "superman," gives way in *Heartbreak House* to life without purpose, where both desire and duty await nothing but the big smash at the end. The family is a region of ghosts haunting "this house without foundations" (1:589). But at about the same time that Shaw was working on this comic-ironic tragedy, T. S. Eliot was beginning his career with a vision inspired by the very smash which so thrilled Ellie Dunn.

For Eliot, the Europe that ended with the First World War represented a wrongheaded culture, one sent off in the wrong direction, into the darkness, by the likes of such artists as Richard Wagner. Out of that waste land Eliot sought signs of a foundation that seemed to have disappeared. In two of his dramas, framing the years of the Second World War, he represented his vision of the ways out of the cosmic wreck. In *The Family Reunion*, Eliot brings back the basic mythic unit of modern literature—the family—to show how it has gone wrong and how it may be set right. Then, in *The Cocktail Party*, he subjects love and marriage to the scrutiny of a spiritual analyst and shows how marriage may still function as a path to salvation, but at a price far greater than Mozart or Beethoven knew.

In *The Family Reunion*, Harry, Lord Monchensey, returns to his

21

family home upon the occasion of his mother's birthday.[54] His mother wants to install him at last as lord and master of the estate. He returns to save his soul after a disastrous marriage that ended in his wife's accidental death, a death for which Harry holds himself responsible. His decision not to remain at home, at Wishwood, is in effect three decisions: to destroy his mother, to purge his soul, and to sacrifice himself to a life of duty. Harry's marriage, his mother's marriage with his father, and the marriage to Mary that his mother has planned for him are all ineffective ways to save his soul. Harry must become, as his Aunt Agatha tells him, "the consciousness of [his] unhappy family, / Its bird sent flying through the purgatorial flame" (p. 275). Because Agatha tells Harry (her spiritual son as well as blood nephew) to leave the family—leave the birthday party—Amy, his mother, is naturally upset and accuses Agatha of persuading Harry "to abandon his duty, his family and his happiness" (p. 283). But Harry must begin "earning [his] spiritual income" (p. 276); he must undergo the purgatorial experience, learn his true duty to God, and escape the "formal obligation" of duty to family and subordination to the power of his mother. The cleansing has begun with the family reunion —examining his past, rejecting the offer of love from Mary (which might have been another way to salvation), and finally rejecting his mother and the role she hoped he would play in keeping up the family.

Eliot does not rule out marriage as a way to salvation, although it was not possible for any of the characters in *The Family Reunion*. He was just as hopeful as his contemporary, Bertrand Russell, who—though certainly no Christian like Eliot—deplored the prospect of witnessing "the break-up of the family";[55] but Eliot had an alternative, denied to Russell. This is a crucial point of *The Cocktail Party*, in which the predominant spiritual sickness is the absence of passion, of desire. Eliot probably shared the opinion of De Rougemont that "our literatures, impotent to create the myth of ideal marriage, have lived on its diseases."[56] In Eliot's drama, Sir Henry Harcourt-Reilly helps three people find their ways to desire, and so to their salvations. He serves as a marriage counsellor to Edward and Lavinia Chamberlayne, whose marriage is on the edge of destruction when the play begins. Sir Henry helps them out of what has become a trap for them both: the Chamberlaynes have become mere objects to one another, unable to love or be loved. They have "lost / The desire for all that was most desirable," wishing that they "could desire / What desire has left behind" (p. 325), as Edward explains to Celia. The Chamberlaynes' relationship shows what has "gone wrong in our day: eros has lost passion, and become insipid, childish, banal."[57] In their emptiness, both Edward and Lavinia know hell, which is for them exactly what it was for Shaw's characters in *Man and Superman*;

thus Edward describes it, "Hell is oneself, / Hell is alone, the other figures in it / Merely projections" (p. 342). When Edward tells Lavinia, after her return, that she is "the angel of destruction," he marks her distance from the heroines of *Fidelio* and of Patmore's *Angel in the House*.

Like Shaw in *Man and Superman* (if not in *Heartbreak House*), Eliot proposes a "real" function for marriage so that it need not be a trap of emptiness or a hell of loneliness. Desire has disappeared from the lives of *The Cocktail Party*'s characters, withered into nothingness for Edward and Lavinia. For them, life has become "the shadow of desires of desires" (p. 356). Sir Henry's task is to set the Chamberlaynes back on the right track of marriage so that they might, as he later tells Celia, "avoid the final desolation / of solitude in the phantasmal world / of imagination, shuffling memories and desire." To do that, they must learn to "maintain themselves by the common route, / Learn to avoid excessive expectation, / Become tolerant of themselves and others, / Giving and taking" (pp. 363–64). Marriage thus understood can be a form of reconciliation to the human condition, and so a means of salvation. But for Celia there is another, more terrifying though less common route than marriage—the way of the saint. She must sacrifice the mediating lover for the sake of God, the ultimate lover; her "disease" has been an ecstasy of such absolute desire that she needs "to be cured / Of a craving for something [she] cannot find" (p. 363).

Celia goes to her martyrdom and the Chamberlaynes return to their marriage to work out their salvation. All three discover that duty to another is duty to God; and through their duties they may realize their desires. One way is a slow process of "give and take" in a compromise with time, maintaining the precarious balance of marriage; the other way is the dramatic choice, the sudden delivery from time in a martyrdom of self-sacrifice. Thus, Eliot has suggested that the cause for the failure of marriage to reconcile duty and desire in Victorian literature is that it sought to make a martyrdom of marriage when in fact the two states are separate ways to salvation. Martyrdom is a leap out of time and marriage is a submission to time; and both require great desire as well as great obligation. Tennyson's Arthur knew this, though Guinevere learned it too late and most of the knights never understood. Most of Browning's characters make a martyrdom of marriage, as do Rossetti's and Meredith's. Matthew Arnold and Arthur Clough may differently emphasize the balanced values of marriage in its give and take, but they choose it over martyrdom. At the last, Swinburne, choosing desire, and Hopkins, choosing duty, abandon marriage for martyrdom. Framing the Victorian range is Elizabeth Barrett's choice of the saintly marriage and Oscar Wilde's choice of the martyr's way.

W. S. GILBERT'S LIBRETTOS for the "Savoy" operas shimmer with images reflecting current interests—from "long-haired aesthetics" to "that annual blister, / Marriage with deceased wife's sister"[58]—and so the operettas of Gilbert and Sullivan deserve to be included in the list of eminently Victorian achievements. Gilbert and Sullivan productions continue to be almost as popular today as they were for Victorian audiences whose habits and beliefs the works so delightfully mock. Their popularity and endurance suggest that beneath the surface of their contemporary satire is an art deserving serious attention. There is in Gilbert's librettos the familiar Victorian structure of duty in conflict with desire, resolved through the accommodations of marriage: one of his constant themes is that there should be "a liberal interpretation of our duties" (1:383). His problem is to achieve this liberal interpretation in such a way that it will provoke, but not offend, the sensibilities of those who (like Daphne in *Thespis*) get their myths of love from "the Family Edition" (1:385).

It hardly ever seems to be in doubt that Gilbert's heroes and heroines must marry, though whether they always do is uncertain (as in the plights of Reginald Bunthorne and Jack Point). Their problems involve finding the mate who can satisfy both their yearnings of love and their obligations. The absurdities of trying to resolve these conflicts are beautifully revealed in *Patience* and *The Mikado*; but to appreciate the increasing intensity of Gilbert's satire, one should examine closely the predicaments of the major characters in *The Pirates of Penzance* (1879), *Iolanthe* (1882), and *The Yeomen of the Guard* (1888). Gilbert flirts with the tragic muse in the later two, though of course his essentially comic spirit insists on victory in the end.

In *The Sorcerer* (1877), Gilbert plays with the notion that "in marriage alone is to be found the panacea for every ill" (1:40). In *The Pirates* he tests that belief as a means of delivering this pathetic slave of duty. As a dutiful young man, Frederick hates the collective body of pirates because piracy is contrary to duty (as the guarantee of universal order); but he loves his pirate friends as individuals. Therefore, when Frederick turns twenty one and is free of his indentures, he will be in a terrible fix: he will have to exterminate his friends. They understand that he must obey his "conscience" and destroy them, because they too respect the obligations of duty. (They have their own code; but as we learn later, they are, after all, "noblemen who have gone wrong.") When Frederick realizes that there are beautiful women in the world, his sense of duty is severely tested, and in the typical Gilbertian way, Frederick preserves his integrity and at the same time satisfies his desire when he discovers the plain maiden who is willing to sacrifice herself and her worldly ambitions to rescue him from his plight. The hero must find a heroine who will sacrifice her hope of something better to lift him from his bog of desire for beautiful women. Mabel is plain and so it is easier for her than for her sisters to comply with Frederick's request.

Frederick's dilemma of love is quickly resolved, but he is plunged more deeply into the dilemma of duty, for he suffers a reversal of fortune: Frederick learns that because of his birthdate, he has had only five birthdays instead of the supposed twenty-one; therefore, he is still indentured to the pirates. He no longer has to destroy his friends; but now he must betray the police, whom he had been going to lead in a raid on his pirate comrades. It is an impossible, absurd moral quagmire, but in Gilbert's comic world the hero never sinks helplessly. After the pirates recover Frederick's loyalty, they learn the awful secret of General Stanley: he lied when he told them he was an orphan. That lie kept the pirates from "the felicity / Of unbounded domesticity" (1:140) which they anticipated when they seized the general's daughters. Now, the pirates may do their duty and satisfy their desire by punishing the general and recapturing his daughters, which they do after overcoming the police. Duty triumphs in the end when the pirates are identified as English peers who have gone wrong and who now may return to their "legislative duties" and marry the general's daughters (1:170). Mabel sings the finale, addressed to the ex-pirates but also to the audience, inviting all to abandon their wandering ways and return to duty by following their loves. Though there is very little logic in the resolutions of all the problems raised by the plot, the problems themselves are quite illogical; and so in Gilbert's view of the Victorian world—if not of all reality—the rigidity of duty is every bit as absurd as is the power of love. Much later, in *Utopia Limited*, Gilbert will have his king say that "it's a quaint world" and that when "properly considered, what a farce life is, to be sure!" (2:285).

When the pirates and the general's daughters are finally reunited (hoping to become "conjugally matrimonified"), it happens in a "ruined chapel by moonlight." Whether Gilbert wished his audience to recognize something symbolic or emblematic in the concluding scene, it is a difficult image to overlook. While the plot concludes with marriage triumphant over the absurd conflicts of duty, this scene is symbolically juxtaposed. The chapel, where lives and deaths are consecrated, has deteriorated into ruin, thus draining the final ritual of its sacred meaning. And besides the ruin of the chapel, the presence of the moonlight should not be ignored, for Gilbert presents his action as something that can be resolved only at night and under the influence of the moon. The contrast between the daylight of duty and reason and the moonlight of love and desire is a theme he will return to in *The Yeomen of the Guard* and, in the contrast between the fairy world and the mortal world, in *Iolanthe*.

25

The major characters of *Iolanthe* are the title character herself and the Lord Chancellor, although the audience might at first be inclined to think that Strephon and Phyllis will be central. The absurdities of that young couple's predicament—love declared, frustrated, and seemingly betrayed (when Phyllis see Strephon with his seventeen-year old mother)—are caused by the insistence of guardians of the law that they maintain strict obedience. The Fairy Queen has banished Iolanthe, her favorite fairy, because she broke the law forbidding marriage with mortals, and the Lord Chancellor will not allow Strephon to marry Phyllis, a ward of the court, because the Lord Chancellor himself has fallen in love with her. But the Lord Chancellor will not marry her because that would compromise his position as chief officer of the court. If he "could reconcile it with [his] duty, [he] should unhesitatingly award her" to himself (1:261), but he has not been able to do that when the play opens; the result is that he has lost a great deal of weight. After his colleagues persuade him to reconsider his merits, the Lord Chancellor decides that the weight of his character is too great to deny himself to the girl. His sense of duty is reconciled by the thought that in giving his sterling person to Phyllis, he will be a clear asset to her. When he announces his decision, he forces his supposedly dead (though fairy) wife, Iolanthe, to reveal her true identity to prevent him from compounding the evils by remarrying. It is, of course, no more absurd for the Lord Chancellor, with his power of office and regard for duty, as well as his advanced age, to arrange a marriage with Phyllis than it is for Strephon's mother to be younger than her own son.

The miraculous powers of the fairies, those immortal forces of magic and love, can help to rescue law and duty from the errors of rigidity, rationalization, and self-deceit, but the world of the fairies is just as culpable as the world of mortals when it comes to law and duty. Theirs might be a different world, but the fairies can also be ruthless. Iolanthe's revelation at the end of the drama exposes her to death, but the law is turned against itself (as a "measure for measure") when the Lord Chancellor applies his legal mind to a legalistic dilemma; what seems to be a fault in the mortal world—that is, rationalism as a rationalization—becomes a virtue in the realm of the fairies. It seems obvious that the two worlds should be married, so long as each brings to the other a complementary, not a contradictory, value; otherwise, the result will be a Strephon who is fairy only down to the waist. The metaphysical side of the play is never resolved, at least to the point of answering what will happen when Strephon's mortal part dies; but the ethical side is more clearly shaped by the mass marriages at the end. When the Fairy Queen has to choose between executing all of her fairies or revising the law to allow everyone except herself to live, she does the unselfish thing (as did Iolanthe) and revises the law. However, she immediately satisfies a suppressed desire for Private Willis (of the Grenadier Guards) as a way to fulfill her duty and obey the newly revised law: she offers herself in marriage, Willis accepts, and he becomes a fairy to share his life with her, as do many of the noble peers when they all go back to fairyland.

Thus, in *Iolanthe* Gilbert suggests that marriage may not, after all, be a matter of compromise between two worlds. Because Strephon's metaphysical problem of being divided between his human and his fairy heritages remains unresolved at the play's end, the play's frame of reference must be relocated. Mortals are transported by their love into the world of the fairies; and we may hope that after they have sprouted their wings, they will all be the happier for their exchange of the "House of Peers for House of Peris" (1:285, 286). Marriage becomes, then, not an accommodation between two worlds but rather a vehicle for transportation from one into another.

A similar conclusion marks the poignant drama, *The Yeomen of the Guard*, where Jack Point all but steals the show from the rest of the company. Jack Point's loss when Elsie's husband survives to claim his bride is not only an ironic, but also a grim, commentary upon the state of a world where such things can happen. Of course, by using the somber setting of the prison for the entire action of the play, Gilbert has given us a gloomier view than usual of this quaint world with its life of farce. Wilfred's "professional duties" as "assistant tormenter," Dame Carruther's lifetime of care for the order of the prison, and Lieutenant Cholmondeley's willingness to execute his friend out of his own regard for duty all join to create a bizarre atmosphere. Into this brightly colored world of the tower guards burst Jack Point and Elsie Maynard who set up a vital carnival that contrasts with the strictly ordered world of the tower.

The Yeomen of the Guard opens with a situation faintly like that at the opening of Beethoven's *Fidelio*: Phoebe Meryll yearns in song for the condemned prisoner, Colonel Fairfax. Like Leonore, she will become the means of rescuing Fairfax from his unjust imprisonment and death; but unlike Leonore, Phoebe will not be rewarded with the love of the man she saves. Instead, when he thinks he will soon be dead, Fairfax arranges to marry the traveling gypsy girl, Elsie, who agrees only because she needs money to care for her ailing mother. The reasons for the marriage are admirable, though the marriage itself is a mockery of all that the institution should be when partners are free to choose. Elsie's glorious discovery that her husband turns out to be the man she has fallen in love with is a triumphant occasion—even for Gilbert's usual triumphant comic spirit. There is also an aesthetic tension that is rare in his work:

27

out of the sad clown whose life of wit and spontaneity has been so little regarded, Gilbert has created a counter movement, a somber tone. Consistent with the conclusion of *Iolanthe*, he shows how the resolution of life's problems by marriage is available only to those who are willing to give up much of the delightful peculiarity of life.

Early in *The Yeomen of the Guard*, Dame Carruthers sings of a legend written on the old tower:

> There's a legend on its brow
>   That is eloquent to me,
>   And it tells of duty done and duty doing.
>
> . . . .
>
> And the wicked flames may hiss
>   Round the heroes who have fought
>   For conscience and for home in all its beauty,
> But the grim old fortalice
>   Takes little heed of aught
>   That comes not in the measure of its duty.   [2:142]

Dame Carruthers is the voice of this tower-like duty, successful in the end in making Sergeant Meryll her husband; and since the assistant-tormenter, Wilfred Shadbolt, has also succeeded in his courtship of Phoebe Meryll, the tower has been fed with new life despite giving up its prized prisoner, Colonel Fairfax. The continuity of order, as represented by the solid old tower with its sinister guardians, can be secured but at a high price, exemplified by the less-than-blissful matches of Sergeant Meryll and of his daughter, on the one hand, and by the desolation of the sad clown, Jack Point, on the other. In its own way this operetta teaches what Swinburne's *Atalanta in Calydon*, Browning's *The Ring and the Book*, and Tennyson's *Idylls of the King* had so painfully shown, "that the human mind, in the course of instituting civilization, has so contrived its own nature that it directs against itself an unremitting and largely gratuitous harshness."[59]

2

Tennyson

Tennyson had many personal reasons to be interested in the theme of love conflicting with duty and to make use of the family as a symbolic image. Wendell Stacy Johnson suggests in a note to his discussion of "Marriage and Divorce in Tennyson" that "it is tempting to associate these concerns [i.e., sexuality and marriage] with events in the poet's life." But Tennyson's use of the symbol and his explorations of the theme are motives of art quite as much as they are analyses of personal or social problems. His symbolic uses of marriage and of the family are very often the technical means whereby he gives form to his poetry. But rather than signaling a clear perspective, Tennyson's use of the family as a symbol, and of love and duty as themes, is often ambiguous, a technique important to express the obscure complexity of modern life, in which goals are not clear and identities are not secure.

Frequently Tennyson's poetry turns upon a dialectic of values in conflict with one another. In various ways, this dialectic aims for the freedom and identity of someone seeking to reconcile love with duty. When desire impels a person in one direction and duty in another direction, integrity and identity are threatened, leaving that person anxious and inactive with frustration. To follow desire without regard to the claims of duty may degenerate into acts of self-destructive, bestial, chaotic instinct without direction—into selfishness and alienation. On the other hand, to follow duty without passionate commitment is to surrender utterly to another person, becoming merely an instrument of someone else's ends and denying one's self. To act in either direction while excluding the other is moral slavery and spiritual chaos; to find that one's desire is also one's duty is to experience freedom and spiritual release. Such an analysis of marriage was undertaken from the ethical point of view by Kierkegaard's persona Judge William in *Either/Or*. Judge

William argues that marriage is the means whereby the aesthete may reconcile his love in duty.[1] Kierkegaard later emphasizes the limits of the "validity of marriage" to achieve this reconciliation, pointing out the need for yet another "stage" of life—the religious stage. Although Tennyson does not come as close to the Kierkegaardian insights as does Browning, Tennyson nevertheless explores the same subject in his poetry, and he also discovers that marriage ultimately fails as a symbol to maintain its fusion of opposing values.

For Tennyson, then, the dialectic of love and duty is more than a personal or ethical matter. It is an epistemological and metaphysical concern. To know one's duty is hard. And even if it is known (that is, if what *ought* to be done is known), it is still hard to do one's duty (because of the potential conflict with desire). From a question of knowing what ought to be the right action, one must move on to the problem of how or whether to do it; thus the question of epistemology becomes a problem of psychology, of will. To resolve the knowledge of duty with the desire of action is to synthesize the opposing terms in the dialectic of duty and love. The problem of knowledge is a matter of separating illusion from reality. And the engagement of self with reality in a fulfilling way is a crucial event in the spiritual history of any man.

Tennyson's poetry often agonizes over the problem of knowing what is real, what one's duty is, and how one can reconcile that duty with conflicting desires. The answer sometimes is found in the symbolic and institutional ideal of marriage and family, although the poet does not readily yield to conventional notions about either. "The Two Voices" concludes with a reference to the family as an expression of rescue from despair, and *In Memoriam* concludes with an epithalamion, or marriage song, which climaxes the motif of married love that runs throughout the poem. *The Princess* concludes with the happy consummation of a courtship endangered for a while by threats of feminine independence. However, other poems, such as "Ulysses," "The Lotos-Eaters," "Tithonus," "Enoch Arden," "Lucretius," *Maud, Idylls of the King, Becket,* and "Demeter and Persephone," express in various and often beautiful ways the difficulties, dangers, and failures of marriage and the family as institutions to integrate the often conflicting motives of love and duty.[2]

TENNYSON'S EARLIEST POEMS are urges to avoid, withdraw from, or escape through death a world of "stormy darkness"; and to give all for the love of a woman is one way to accomplish such urges. Later he designs poetic strategies to suggest that the women of his dreams who might save him from a world of troubles are not so much real women as symbols of his attraction to a particular kind of art—an art of sensuous, emotional fulfillment at the expense of duty to the world at large.[3]

The "Supposed Confessions of a Second Rate Sensitive Mind Not in Unity with Itself" outlines the failure of religious faith to survive a close attachment to the mother, who typifies it in emotionally fulfilling ways. In the absence of a warm and loving source of religious authority, such as the mother, whom one can trust, love, and learn to obey, the "second rate sensitive mind" is lost in a whirlwind of the spirit and "moved from beneath with doubt and fear." He is caught between his memory of infant security, with maternal affection as a personal symbol of faith in a loving God, and his present adult condition of doubt and disbelief because of an absence of experiential or visible signs of that loving God. And so he ends his confessions with an exclamation of perplexity. Torn between the memory of desire fulfilled and the present state of desire frustrated, between the duty to submit to the God of his mother and his present intellectual incertitude about whether there is such a duty, this soul is caught up in a "damned vacillating state."

This is an all-too-common resolution of desires in conflict with duties inherited from the past. But Tennyson's title for this poem suggests an ambiguity concerning his own attitude toward the confessor of these lines. In the original title, Tennyson calls him a "second-rate" sensitive mind "not in unity with itself." Are first-rate minds those which are essentially in unity with themselves? It is possible for people living in the 1830s to be in unity with themselves? Are unity and first-rate minds ideals of attainment, or is Tennyson making a little fun of all those priggish and stupid people who have unquestioningly accepted as their duty the superstitious faiths of their ancestors and who then accuse all doubters and tormented souls of being second rate? Whether there is a single answer to any such questions, Tennyson's poem does set up the problem with which his later poetry grapples: that is, the "damned vacillating state" of a "mind not in unity with itself," torn between conflicting values.

The confessor held on to the memory of his mother as the vessel of fulfilling faith; the poem on "Isabel," which Hallam Tennyson said was based on his father's mother, describes the perfect wife as a "type" of God in her "great charity" of loving tenderness. It is perhaps too easy to say that Tennyson's ideal love-object in these poems is a wife-as-mother, but certainly that is the suggestion in some of the poems of this early period. If a man could find in his wife all those qualities he remembers as emotionally and even physically fulfilling in his mother, he will have resolved to a large degree the psychological "vacillation" between two objects of desire: sexless passion and passionless sex. Tennyson complicates his women further by suggesting that their attraction may or may

31

not coincide with religious duty, again, as typified by the charitable and loving mother.

To escape from these vacillations, the young poet found imaginative excitement in private visions of the kind nourished by the "Arabian Nights." He joined his escapist urge with his desire for sensuous delight in the fascinating poem "Recollections of the Arabian Nights." Much of this poem's attraction depends on rendering the experience of desire rather than simply stating what the desire is. But the congregation of images—such as voyaging into the past, into the remote, through gardens of sensuous luxury, into a palace of wonderful loveliness where an epiphany occurs, seeing sweetness in a woman and merriment in a man—all suggest a happy resolution of the "vacillation" that is usually present in Tennyson's early poetry. To go a step further, this poem reveals a discovery of satisfying beauty and authority, though the discovery is made at the expense of escape from a troublesome world, where time always moves forward.

In the 1832 *Poems*, Tennyson's epiphany of authorized loveliness takes on more of the dangers than were admitted in the "Recollections of the Arabian Nights." In many of the poems published in 1832, the difficulty of resolving conflicting values is central to the poems' meanings. "The Palace of Art" seems to take up where the "Recollections of the Arabian Nights" leaves off—elaborating the attractions of withdrawal into the imagination for private happiness, but the palace proves to be a haunted house out of which the Soul must move if it is to survive. "The Palace of Art," however, only seems to take up where "Recollections" leaves off, because in the earlier poem the self had not withdrawn into a world where there were no other souls; in that earlier poem, the poet included an image of a central authority (Haroun Alraschid) who ruled over and approved the sensuous beauty of the garden and palace. In "The Palace of Art," the Soul attempts to usurp that authority for herself, denying the existence of any law higher than her own sensuous indulgence; there is nothing for her to love but things, and so they are not ends in themselves—only means whereby her own desires are fulfilled and her own ego extended.

Art as an extension of the self is no substitute for art in the service of some higher authority; this is the general conclusion reached in much of Tennyson's 1832 poetry. On the other hand, such poems as "The Lady of Shalott" and "The Hesperides" show that the sources of art must be protected against the invasion of forces from the everyday world of work and time: both of these poems turn upon a stationary point of inspired art (the picture-making of the Lady and the music-making of the three daughters of Hesperus), surrounded by a field of energy and motion (the laborers, lovers, and knights in Shalott, and the sailor-adventurers in Hesperides). Separating the motionless point from the field of energy seems to be an impassable barrier. When the Lady attempts to leave Shalott, she dies and her artwork fragments. And it is the duty of the three Hesperides to keep the guardians of the golden fruit awake so that it will not be stolen. The values embodied in works of art are so alien to the "real" world of workaday life that any attempt to make a direct translation of one into the other has disastrous results. The artist cannot live totally immersed in art without danger to his humanity and spiritual health, but neither can he live totally in the world of everyday social action without endangering his sources of imaginative vision. The problem Tennyson must face over and over again—the problem of the modern tradition—is this: how may the beauty and fulfillment of art be reconciled with the energy and process of daily life? This question is related to the broader theme of duty in conflict with desire, love in conflict with service. The artist desires to fulfill himself in his vision, and it is his duty to share it with others. But how is he to do this in a world which seems to deny any need for his services and often fears his vision?

Like John Keats in his unfinished *Fall of Hyperion*, Tennyson in 1832 is eager to find his proper duty as an artist without betraying his private vision. In Keats's poem, the poet seeks to know what value there is in poetry when the world is filled with wrongs and sufferings crying out for relief. What can poetry do to help? Keats did not know the answer, although he was working his way toward a conception of the poet as mythmaker, value-giver—one who orders human experience so that pain, though it cannot be eliminated, may be subordinated and the nobility and dignity of man increased, rather than diminished, by suffering. This world-view had been the burden of Christianity and before that of the Greek religions; in both instances the world views had been communicated by artists as prophets, by Isaiah or St. John, by Homer or Aeschylus. Keats was beginning to see that this must be the role of the artist in the nineteenth century as well: to bring a vision of the beautiful and moral order to bear upon a fragmented and spiritually dislocated culture. That vision might be an "illusion" by standards of scientific measurement, but unlike the lower animals, man cannot live without such illusions of meaning.

Tennyson also was coming to the same conviction, and his "Hesperides" is an indication of this. If he could "steal" away the golden apple, as did Hercules in one of his many heroic exploits of service to love and humanity, then he might help to heal the world of its old "wound" and unseal for it a life of glory. The imagery of this poem is religious: the wound may be sin; the healer, Christ; the dragon, Satan;

and the glory, lost innocence or lost paradise. The Grail stories of medieval romances are the source of such symbols, and in Tennyson's own time, they would be put to similar uses by Richard Wagner in *Parsifal*. For Tennyson, the important thing is that in his role as an artist he must somehow find a way to serve those purposes formerly served by religion, without usurping the authority of God.

To make himself or his art the source of moral authority would be exceedingly dangerous, as the soul in "The Palace of Art" discovered. To yield to the seductive attractions of sensuous beauty without regard for moral responsibilities would also be exceedingly dangerous, as the poem "The Sea-Fairies" (1830) suggests: the call of the sea fairies to the mariners is a temptation to abandon their quest on a dangerous sea. The Hesperides are like the sirens whose song is, from their point of view, a responsibility to guard a treasure from discovery and theft; but from the mariners' point of view, the song is a temptation to abandon a life of search and action for a life of withdrawal and alienation. The song of the Hesperides may keep the dragon awake, but it also lulls its human listeners into dreams and so distracts them from their workaday duties.

"Oenone" shows how common duties to others can be sacrified for private desire because of a failure of perception. Paris was eager to judge divine beauty, but he was not astute enough to foresee the moral and aesthetic difficulties that must arise. To choose one divine beauty from among three is to deny two others: Paris cannot win. The best he could do is to change the terms of the judgment altogether and to restrict himself to what he really knows best—human beauty. This is exactly what Oenone thinks Paris should have done, to have chosen her and thereby to have satisfied his duty to choose and his love for her—both at the same time. But he presumed too much, yielded to his least human instinct, and chose Aphrodite, the beautiful goddess of sexual love. Even Oenone's prejudiced view of Aphrodite cannot conceal the strength of such a temptation for mortal man. Aphrodite is but one of three; Oenone is the one. In Oenone those dialectical virtues of desire and duty would have been united. When they are divided, as the judgment of Paris causes them to be, life is fragmented and the consequence of it all is chaos in the form of the Trojan War.

His own sensitivity to the strong appeal of the beauty represented by Aphrodite frequently led Tennyson in his early career into a "dream of fair women." In his poem by that title, he gives us a reformulation of Chaucer's "Legend of Good Women," a palinode or recantation of heresies against the law of love and women. For Tennyson, the dream of fair women is a deepening investigation into his own psychic landscape, across which moves the dialectic of his attraction to women of the kind represented first by Helen and then by Helen's opposite, Iphigenia. Helen was, from Iphigenia's point of view, the cause of Iphigenia's death, just as Aphrodite and Helen were the causes of Oenone's death, from her point of view. Helen is the sensuous object of possession who blinds men to moral obligation, and Iphigenia is the victim of religious superstition (another form of blindness). They are the two sides of the same coin: choose Helen and destroy Iphigenia. Early in the poem we are made to observe how closely these two fair women are bound to one another within the soul of the dreamer. Iphigenia was no willing sacrifice to the political, religious, and lustful ends of the Greek kings, but she does not blame them as much as Helen, the ultimate object of their desire.

Within the finely chiseled verse of this poem is a moving struggle of strong wills and of opposing values, as portrayed by Cleopatra and Jephtha's daughter (whom the dreamer meets later in his journey through this forest of his soul). Jephtha sacrificed his daughter because he had vowed that if God allowed him victory in Ammon, he would sacrifice the first person to meet him when he returned. Jephtha's daughter, un-like Iphigenia, is proud to have been murdered in the name of God; but the dreamer is appalled at the religious sacrifice of this woman, exclaim-ing that "Heaven heads the count of crimes / With that wild oath" of Jephtha. The dreamer is much more attracted to Cleopatra, who is the heroine of the poem because in her are combined the virtues of desire and duty. Cleopatra arouses such love that a man will gladly lose all the world and its powers for her, but she will not be used merely as an instrument either of human or of divine will: she reciprocates the love of Antony by choosing to die with him. She sacrifices herself instead of allowing others to sacrifice her, as do Iphigenia and Jephtha's daughter. Cleopatra comes into a central point in the dream: on each side of the dreamer's meeting with Cleopatra are two others. This focus on Cleo-patra as an epitome of his "dream of fair women" is a sharpening of Tennyson's earlier interest in her in his lyric of 1827, "Antony to Cleo-patra." The difference between that earlier poem and this later one is a product of the larger perspective Tennyson has gained on both himself and his obligation to moral as well as to aesthetic values, to duty as well as to desire.

IN THE POEMS Tennyson published in 1842, his speakers are usually involved in searching self-examinations. Tennyson makes poetry out of the soul's confrontation with death and its implications of futility and nothingness. Rescue from despair over the apparent meaninglessness of life requires an act of individual will, an affirmation (in the absence of any firm and external supports) of the conviction that life is little more than a moment of sensation. One private experience substantiates the hope that even in the face of annihilation, life is meaningful; that one experience is love, denoting different kinds of emotional and ethical values. These may be selfish and sensual, a fulfillment of desire without regard for anything outside the self; or they may be selfless and sensuous, a mutual fulfillment of desire without regard for anything outside the beloved object. They may be, in another mode, a mutual fulfillment of desire coupled with regard for a higher authority than either the lover or his beloved.

The differences between various kinds of love were elaborated by Milton in *Paradise Lost*: first, Adam and Eve loving one another in obedience to God's laws, with Eve loving God *in* Adam, and Adam loving God in service to God's will; second, Adam loving Eve without regard to God's law, loving her for herself, imperfect though she was, and so failing in his duty to God through devotion to one of God's creatures; and third (ultimately under the circumstances of withdrawal from duty to God as an ideal of constancy and perfection), Adam's selfish and sensual love for Eve, her selfish love of herself as an instrument to bend Adam's will, and their mutual disgust for one another. There is still another denotation of love, not touched upon in Milton's story of Adam and Eve. This love is selfless and senseless; it denies desires and seeks identity only in union with God, sacrificing the self totally. This is a difficult love for anyone at any time, but it is impossible during a time when God, as the object of desire, has disappeared and made Himself inaccessible to His creatures. But if God is love, as generations of Christians have affirmed, is it also true that love is God? Many have wanted to believe so, including the Victorians, but first they must find love, hoping that love will lead to God. Finding love is difficult enough, even when He is incarnate as God Himself, but to find love in lesser and sometimes illusory forms is one of the greatest challenges there is. Alfred Tennyson was coming to know truth in bitter and demanding terms.

"St. Simeon Stylites" aspires to love God by hating the flesh, lifting himself as high above common mortality as possible. He is filled with anxiety in expectation of deliverance from his mortal condition; he really thought he would have died long before these thirty years had gone by. Now rotten with disease, he sets himself as an "example" for all to follow. And he ends his monologue with a stunning prophecy: "I shall die to-night, / A quarter before twelve." From his advantage then, Simeon Stylites tests what is most immediate to his experience, his flesh, to find its limits of endurance as an obstruction between his soul and God. But his God has not manifested Himself to Simeon Stylites, at least not in the terms Simeon Stylites chooses. Whatever is absurd about this martyr of the flesh is not necessarily a consequence of Simeon's faith, which is somewhat admirable as evidence of our great potential for spiritual strength; rather the absurdity is a consequence of God's failure to acknowledge the heroic sacrifice made by this pitiful creature. The agony of Simeon Stylites is less in his physical suffering, which he glories in, than in the waiting for something spiritually momentous to happen, preferably as a descent from heaven. His pathetic cry at the end of what he hopes is the epiphany he has been waiting for suggests something of his very real pain. His is an agonizingly problematic epiphany that "crowns" thirty years of self-sacrifice; but unfortunately for modern man, it is the nature of spiritual reality that it is only problematic, just as problematic as the rest of reality. Conviction of spiritual assurance for right action is difficult to come by; it may be a function of the will alone, since there are so few, if any, external signs that provide spiritual guidance. And so, although St. Simeon Stylites may appear absurd, he is a suffering saint in his desire for some sign that his life has not been lived in vain.

In "Northern Farmer, Old Style" there is again a potentially humorous situation in which a stubborn old man refuses to give up his pint of ale, as recommended by his doctor. It is comparable to "St. Simeon Stylites" in these respects: both speakers are old, near death, and justifying the ways of their lives—more to themselves than to their audiences (who seem not to be very responsive in either instance). An important difference between the two poems is that whereas Simeon Stylites sought the certainty of union with God through negation and denial of fleshly needs, the old Northern Farmer has sought no such certainty, has not even understood what the preachers talk about, and has so indulged in the desires of flesh that he has made their regular satisfaction into the most meaningful and unifying events of his life. He says, "Git ma my aäle, fur I beänt a-gawin' to breäk my rule."

His "rule" is to have a pint of ale every night and a quart every market-night, which he has done for forty years. It is the ritual of natural rhythm—the ordering of life by some standard of activity and the working of the land (the "waäst")—that has given meaning to his life, and it has served him well: his desires have been identical with his duty as he saw it. In his ignorance of the ways of God and of the necessity for his death, he wonders if there is any sense in it at all. For a moment, then, he asks the same question posed by Simeon Stylites: whether this is the way he is to be repaid for all his years of devoted service. But the Northern Farmer has found fulfillment in the service itself, not requiring that it be justified by any authority higher than the Squire. He knows that he has "done [his] duty boy 'em, as [he has] done boy the lond." His terms have been less demanding than Simeon Stylites's were; consequently, the Northern Farmer's disappointment over the lack of spiritual answers is less acute and certainly shorter lived. His will, his personal integrity, is as strong as that of Simeon Stylites, and perhaps it is stronger, for whatever the "ultimate" truth of the Northern Farmer's way of action, it has been a fulfilling way: "I wëant breäk rules for Doctur, a knows na moor not a floy; / Git ma my aäle I tell tha, an' if I mun doy I mun doy!"

The "old style" of the "Northern Farmer" is an ethic of duty that is not divorced from desire; it is a code of honor, honesty, and dignity of independence. Marriage is a public acknowledgment of duty that sometimes costs the old-style farmer some discomfort: "An' I hallus commed to's chooch afoor moy Sally wur deäd, / An' eärd 'um a bummin' awaäy loike a buzzard-clock ower my 'eäd." This man of duty lived by rules, but sometimes they were private as well as public. He did not sacrifice his independent desires in life any more than he is going to in death. After all, he did "cast oop, that a did, 'bout Messy Marris's barne," and so "done moy duty boy 'um, as I 'a done boy the lond." His life has been, as he vows his death will be, a linking of his duty with his desire, something his marriage seems to have symbolized as at least an ideal model. But the *"new* style" of "Northern Farmer" has so divided duty from desire that he can see no connection between them in marriage. Like Rocco in *Fidelio*, the new-style father advises his son to marry for gold: "Luvv? what's luvv? thou can luvv thy lass an' 'er munny too." Marriage is merely a contract for "proputty, proputty, proputty," not a sacrament of love.

The power of marriage as a religious force is not manifest in either of the poems spoken by Northern Farmers. In the old style, marriage is an ethical power that preserves the integrity of duty without diminishing the value of desire, while in the new style, marriage has deteriorated to become little more than a weapon of law and parental tyranny. This tendency toward tyranny, at least in its emphasis on bondage and restraint, is a major feature of marriage as it appears in "Ulysses" and as it is suggested by the predicament of "Tithonus." Ulysses leaves his "aged wife" and their "still hearth" behind, when he abandons the hoarding, feeding savages of his kingdom to be ruled by his more prudent son. His desire for adventure and self-fulfillment has been reduced by marriage, home, and government. Because he acts on his desires at the cost of domestic security, Ulysses has posed for the poem's readers quite as many hostile responses as Browning's Don Juan in "Fifine at the Fair." Neither hero quite fits the conventional mold of Victorian husband. But Ulysses is hungry for more life; he is discontented with the materialistic standards of those he is called upon to govern. By choosing to leave Ithaca, Ulysses affirms, with even more courage than the old-style Northern Farmer, the value of his private desire as a better measure of his identity than the public duties that have been imposed upon him by his subjects' expectations.

"Tithonus" reverses somewhat the predicament of the hero as husband. In this poem, the lover yearns for release from the immortal beauty who has outlasted his capacity to enjoy her. Like Ulysses, Tithonus has had enough of this "marriage," but for Tithonus it is a bondage to desire rather than to duty. He had wished to distinguish himself from other men, to live forever, as it were, in the land of the lotus, but having achieved his distinction, he is dismayed by the price he has paid for it. "Let me go," he cries, "take back thy gift: / Why should a man desire in any way / To vary from the kindly race of men?" In his own way, Tithonus suffers from the same fault as the new-style Northern Farmer: each has separated duty from desire. At least Tithonus knows what his fault is, and he knows what a true marriage should be as well. Desire as a capacity (or motive) for self-assertion carries with it a heightened consciousness of talent that needs to find an object to serve. Tithonus represents the agony of a talent, or a vision, without an object; and thus, he is self-consuming desire. Ulysses represents the atrophy of desire under the deadening restraint of duty as merely service. As spokesman for these poles (between which Tennyson himself vacillated), Tithonus speaks for the artist cursed by his vision of beauty unmarried to any conviction of purpose, and Ulysses speaks for the artist disheartened by the world of routine and dreary materialism, where marriage binds one to an "aged wife" and a "still hearth."

Indeed, the poet behind Ulysses, Tithonus, and all the others, knows that he must not betray his gift. He cannot risk destroying his identity, for what else is a man's identity if it is not knowing himself, knowing what he can be and do? His duty then is to fulfill himself, to translate himself to others in the symbolic terms of action. If he denies his talent, whether for poetry or for carpentry, he will have failed to be himself and will wither and fracture his identity. The same consequence may occur if anything or anyone else obstructs the fulfillment of that potential (which is part of the complaint of the speaker in "Locksley Hall"). To preserve his chance for identity, the artist must risk alienation. Perhaps he will be fortunate enough to find an audience yearning for the same kind of vision he is capable of offering, and he will not be so alienated. He may become a prophet then, but even that has its liabilities, as Tennyson soon discovers—he then regrets having lost the privacy of alienation. The truly rewarding thing for the artist may be, however, that he can pour whatever happens in his life into his work, and not only will

39

that allow him the same satisfactions of labor enjoyed by the old Northern Farmer plowing his fields, but the artist's work will bring joy, pleasure, and emotional satisfaction to generations after him. The great secret of spiritual survival that Tennyson learns to apply in his poems is concentrated in the concept of *will*, a force produced by the true marriage of duty with desire.

The speaker who battles with himself in "The Two Voices" is rewarded for his victory over despair with a vision of a true marriage. A "secret voice" seeks to exploit what two other voices call a "sickness" of the self caught up in a division against itself. The effect of the argument by Despair is to raise a spectre of doubt to drive the mind further against itself, for one part wants certitude and another part insists on the impossibility of certitude. Like Ulysses, the speaker wishes for "some good cause, not in [his] own," and when he dies, to be "like a warrior overthrown"; the "secret voice" exploits this desire, mocking it with the same view that dismayed Ulysses: " 'This is more vile,' he made reply, / 'To breathe and loathe, to live and sigh.' " Truly, life so divided may not be worth the dreariness. Heroic duty seems impossible, and private passion is appalling: "Pain rises up, old pleasures pall." Doubt is the product of such a divided life, and the speaker is tempted to end it with suicide, the one heroic action still left to a man with no certain call to duty.

But doubt is a double-edged weapon. Even if the arguments of despair have no answers in naturalistic or materialistic terms and leave the mind hovering over the abyss of nothingness, those same arguments awaken the consciousness to a new awareness of its own strength. The speaker possesses the weapon of doubt, which can be used to doubt Doubt itself. It can be used to turn the questioning of reality back upon the doubter of spiritual integrity to prove that hope for a united will is not something given from without, from science or society, but rather something generated from within: it is the "dawn" within the doubter, not the darkness surrounding the self, that counts. The conclusion of the poem objectifies this discovery when a beautiful Sabbath morning breaks through the long night to confirm the speaker's new-found health of mind. Heading the procession of faith which ties together the human community is the family, "sweet" symbol of "three made unity":

> One walked between his wife and child,
> With measured footfall firm and mild,
> And now and then he gravely smiled.
>
> The prudent partner of his blood
> Leaned on him, faithful, gentle, good,
> Wearing the rose of womanhood.   [ll. 412–17]

The speaker of "The Two Voices," like Tennyson, is not himself walking "between his wife and child." Both the poet and his poem's speaker are satisfied with the vision of such unity as a sign of the living imagination within themselves and within society at large. Love united with duty is the sign of human strength, in the artist as much as in the man. Tennyson betrays how important it is to him as a man in his poem called "Love and Duty," where the union is prevented by a strange alliance:

> For Love himself took part against himself
> To warn us off, and Duty loved of Love—
> O this world's curse, —beloved but hated—came
> Like Death betwixt thy dear embrace and mine,
> And dying, 'Who is this? behold thy bride,'
> And pushed me from thee.   [ll. 45–49]

This poem, published in 1842, expresses a private dilemma of self-doubt which marriage might resolve for the poet just as it had confirmed the unified will of the speaker in "The Two Voices." Tennyson's most ambitious long poem of the 1840s, *The Princess*, aims for yet another way to realize the self through marriage. It proves to be difficult, problematic, and, for the artist at any rate, still conditioned by much self-doubt.

TENNYSON EXTENDS THE RANGE of his concerns in *The Princess* (1847), embracing the social and topical matter with which he would increasingly occupy his art. This poem has many affinities with Tennyson's other, more succesful poetry of the same era, including *In Memoriam* and *Idylls of the King*. Princess Ida's dream of a high ideal for all women is comparable to Arthur's dream for his kingdom; the princess's vision of a future ideal woman, "the woman [of] the fuller day" (to which Ida's work is directed), is comparable to the future man who will be "a closer link / Betwixt us and the crowning race" in the vision that concludes *In Memoriam*. In addition, marriage is a central preoccupation of all three poems—literally, metaphorically, and symbolically.

Clearly Tennyson has some sympathy for Princess Ida's cause, just as he does for Arthur's dream and even as he does for someone as unrealistic as Becket. All idealists, like Ida, Arthur, and Becket, risk personal and social dangers; this is emphasized in Tennyson's poetry which shows how abstracted ideals are dreams that become nightmares, illusions that become delusions. Princess Ida was concerned with a topic of such current interest that Tennyson had some trouble getting a proper distance from it. Its medley of tones has caused much difficulty in reading (something

41

Gilbert and Sullivan have not done much to solve in their version, *Princess Ida*). How, then, to rescue for romance this matter of tragicomedy is the poet's first challenge.

The story's framework allows a background of realism for what is otherwise a tale of fantasy, a form of medieval romance. Tennyson's decision to set the tale in such a way suggests at the start a kind of ambivalence, an affirmation of the value of imagination conditioned by social reality. Within the tale itself, however, Tennyson works out a thematic relationship between his main characters that results in a compromise—if not a reconciliation—between duty and desire, engineered by marriage. In simple terms, Princess Ida represents an ideal of duty; the prince's father, an "ideal" of desire; and the prince himself, a principle of harmony, or the ideal of marriage that unites duty with desire.

Princess Ida has declared to her father that she would "live alone / Among her women; certain, would not wed" (1.48–49).* This vow she repeats to the three young men in disguise: "We dream not of him: when we set our hand / To this great work, we purposed with our self / Never to wed" (2.45–47). Her "great work" is a task of education among womankind, mainly teaching them all that men know—and more. That additional knowledge turns out mainly to be a history of women's intellectual contributions to the progress of the race. She admits that women must first catch up with men in their knowledge and powers, but as Lady Psyche explains in a lecture to novitiates, "woman ripened earlier, and her life / Was longer" (2.138–39). How women are to come into existence without their mothers having some kind of attachment with men is a problem that Ida does not confront directly (thinking perhaps that there is plenty of time to work out women's equality so that true marriages may one day be possible—in the remote future). She admits to the disguised prince that babies are of value to her, but she wishes "they grew / Like fieldflowers everywhere!" (3.234–36). Until that far-distant time, however, all marriages are mockeries, and her hope is that "this same mock-love, and this / Mock-Hymen were laid up like winter bats, / Till all men grew to rate us at our worth" (4.125–27).

Her ideal of the free woman is a "high desire" (3.263) to which she wishes all women, now "dwarfs of the gynaeceum," might be raised by her own example. One of the most obvious points about Ida's scheme is that it was already weakening internally at several places even before the three young men arrived. Their appearance does not cause the faults that will destroy Ida's ideal, but merely brings them into focus. Her women are not happy with their situation—neither the ones who are overheard to wish they might marry, who are fearful that "men hated learned

---

* References are to part and lines.

42

women," and who are willing to settle for "rule" of a household (2.441–42) nor her main administrators and teachers, Lady Blanche and Lady Psyche (both of whom have been married already), who are torn by internal allegiances and competition. When anyone poses a threat to their ideal of feminine freedom, the women react defensively, readily interpreting it as a challenge to do their duty by their ideal. In other words, Ida's "high desire" has already become a matter of duty (albeit sometimes unthinking duty) both for her followers and equally so for herself. "High desire" has become synonymous with self-denial, intellect, and loyalty to a leader.

When Psyche learns the identity of the men, she experiences a conflict whose terms starkly identify the theme of the poem: "O hard, when love and duty clash!" (2.273). After she relents from her threat to expose the men, she exclaims to her brother that "it was duty spoke, not I" (2.288). Afterwards, when Blanche listens to the appeal by Cyril that she help them in their plight, "she replied, her duty was to speak, / And duty duty, clear of consequences"—even if those consequences meant the men's death and destruction (3.135–36). When the noble edifice of her ideal begins to crumble, turning into "a new-world Babel, woman-built, / And worse-confounded" (4.466–67), Princess Ida vows to be rid of her disloyal followers, all those "that love their voices more than duty." She determines to teach them a lesson in authority and discipline: they will "learn / With whom they deal," for she will dismiss them "in shame to live / No wiser than their mothers, household stuff" (4.490–93). But her "iron will" has itself two major weaknesses: her comfort from "the little child" (5.420) and her sympathy for the mother of the prince (5.396–98). These two weaknesses will combine to bring down totally her ideal of female independence, for she will give herself as a nursing mother to care for the seriously wounded prince.

If we think of Ida as the goal of the prince's quest (and behind her, the image of his mother as an ideal of womanhood), then on the other side of the prince is his father's arrogant demand that women shall be little more than the chattel of masculine authority. The prince's father is an "ideal" of man as a power dealing always in power, even in the exercise of his intellect:

> "but this is fixt
> As are the roots of earth and base of all;
> Man for the field and woman for the hearth:
> Man for the sword and for the needle she:
> Man with the head and woman with the heart:
> Man to command and woman to obey;
> All else confusion."   [5.435–41]

A woman's duty is to serve the man's desire—that is the vision of the prince's father; the only "wisdom" he will allow to women is in "the bearing and the training of a child." It is, of course, a major irony of the poem that Princess Ida's "high desire" should become little more than this same duty to obey. Neither the princess nor the father of the prince can be totally correct. The prince must find a way to marry these extreme positions, to reconcile his desire for Ida with his duty to his father.

When their disguise falls away from the prince and his companions, he hears Ida's departure as "a knell of [his] desires" (4.156). In his appeal for her to honor the contract of marriage (a matter of legal duty), he tells her that she has become such a passion for him that he "cannot cease to follow" her even if it should mean his death. He "desire[s her] more / Than growing boys their manhood" (4.429–37)—although in his case, to have her will mean the achievement of his "manhood." He is ejected from the palace and tries to negotiate through King Gama; wanting Ida's love more than revenge, he tells Gama that "this knot" is "more soluble" by "gentleness than war" (5.129–30). Unlike Ida or his father, he ultimately prefers a compromise to the loss of life:

> much that Ida claims as right
> Had ne'er been mooted, but as frankly theirs
> As due of Nature. To our point: not war:
> Less I lose all.   [5.194–97]

All nature prompts his love; there is "a song on every spray / Of birds that piped their Valentines, and woke / Desire in [him] to infuse [his] tale of love" (5.228–30). This passion of desire will be tempered by a will to battle, to become a champion of duty, when he confronts Ida's brother, Arac. And so the prince will experience both ideals within himself, his father's and Princess Ida's.

Ida falls into despair when her college breaks up to become a hospital for the wounded knights. Sorrow, self-hatred, and shame fall on her soul; she feels useless, and "so blackened all her world in secret, blank / And waste it seemed and vain" until she found a new use for her life (7.14–28). Her new work is to nurse the wounded, especially the wounded prince. Therefore, although at first all was confusion, "by and by / Sweet order lived again with other laws" (7.3–4). The new law is the law of love: "Love in the sacred halls / Held carnival at will," and Lady Psyche is engaged to Cyril. In the midst of this, Ida's sorrow is transformed through service into a new passion, for she who had so devoted herself to an intellectual cause now sets herself with equal dedication to a cause of passion: this more than ever is a "high desire." She bends to the prince, and when "from [his] arms she rose / Glowing all over noble shame; . . . / Her falser self slipt from her like a robe, / And left her woman," Venus Aphrodite herself (7.144–47). This transformation allows the prince to claim her as his bride, "like perfect music unto noble words" (7.270).

Dreaming of "the world's great bridals," the prince proposes that together they might set an example of "true marriage" in which there is no question of equal and unequal, but rather one in which "each fulfils / Defect in each":

> and always thought in thought,
> Purpose in purpose, will in will, they grow,
> The single pure and perfect animal   [7.285–88]

His idea of a "true marriage" is a dynamic one, a developmental one that unites thought, purpose, and will in animal being. Ida is doubtful that she can satisfy his high ideal of marriage, and in this doubt Tennyson has brought his comic poem to an ironic conclusion. For Ida's ideal of intellectual independence and the king's ideal of passionate mastery have yielded to the prince's ideal of a marriage that unites both in one animate being. The model for this is motherhood, for it was the prince's mother who taught him such a dream. Through the ideal of motherhood, then, the royal couple can reach for the harmony that their minds and hearts require; both Ida and the prince can be true to themselves by being true to their mothers from whom they both discovered the meaning of duty and of desire.

The balance of opposing values in this manner, through the medium of marriage, is forecast by the poem's opening scene, when the poet observes how Sir Walter Vivian's lawn was occupied by happy families, "His tenants, wife and child" (Prologue, 3–4):

> babies rolled about
> Like tumbled fruit in grass; and men and maids,
> Arranged a country dance, and flew through light
> And shadow.   [ll. 82–85]

The poet narrator and his friends look out upon this happy scene of "sport" and "Science" through the arch of a "Gothic ruin." The family is as much a symbolic image as is any other grouping in the poem—"A Gothic ruin and a Grecian house" or "sport [that] went hand in hand with Science." These images of apparently conflicting values are brought together into a harmony, a marriage, by the action of narrative imagination. Collegiate boys on holiday, tenants sporting on aristocratic lawns, a Grecian house leading to Gothic ruin, and sport and science—they all picture the ideal life that the prince hopes to accomplish by his marriage:

45

order and reckless abandon with a single purpose in being. Because Tennyson, like Princess Ida herself, recognizes this as an ideal, he can picture the union as but temporary (a holiday) and as a compromise ("a strange diagonal") in the method of the narrative itself.

THE COMPLEXITY AND SUBTLETY of a spiritual dialectic between despair and hope, between darkness and light, could be represented only in a sophisticated work such as *In Memoriam*. Tennyson learned an especially important lesson in working out the lyrics of this poem: the lesson was, and is, that for the modern poet, *style* may be the only orderly and reliable form of activity available to him. The order of art may provide a sense of order and pattern for the artist who pours his life into it; and for the audience that yields to it, the art employs readily accessible imagery and symbols, including marriage and the family.

Tennyson interweaves his meditations on death and on the meaning of life with his examination of the function and meaning of his art. His hope for meaning is a function of his aesthetic urge for the balance, harmony, and unity of art. In lyric 34 he compares the lack of meaning and purpose in his life with the lack of meaning and purpose in art, "such as lurks / In some wild Poet, when he works / Without a conscience or an aim." The speaker has himself been somewhat of a "wild poet" without "conscience or aim" in the early stages of this poem. But near the end, he has discovered the purpose and meaning of his life within the terms of his art as a unity. In lyric 127 the terms of the problem are stated explicitly: "And all is well, though faith and form / Be sundered in the night of fear." Again, the solution of the problem is compared in lyric 128 to the successfully unified piece of art:

> I see in part
> That all, as in some piece of art,
> Is toil cooperant to an end.

Life with meaning is like art unified by a dominant, organizing principle of purpose. *In Memoriam* is a search through art for a resolution of faith and form. And one of the more fascinating things about it is its exploitation of style and literary form to serve the ends of a religious quest. J. C. Mays has summed up this point by noting that "one of the themes of the poem is winning through to confidence in form, and to an ability to sustain it in faith."[4]

After the encounter with nothingness, forced by death upon the speaker, his fragmented and sickened spirit embarks upon a search for integrity, for wholeness, and health. This quest is the burden of the poem's spiritual narrative, but its most affecting presence comes through the poem's extranarrative style—its imagery and literary allusions. Its patterns of style embody a quest for formal unity, a way of fragmentation, at the same time that they body forth the narrator's quest for religious faith. One pattern builds upon the speaker's nostalgic hope for feeling once again the hand of his dead friend, another searches for light through darkness, and a third compares the loss of a friend to the loss of a wife or a husband, using what Alan Sinfield has called "Tennyson's images of domestic situations."[5] These are very noticeable images that recur often enough to create highly emotive symbols of fulfilling love.

The widowhood motif begins in lyric 8. Here the speaker's sense of loss and disappointed loneliness is mildly represented by a young lover coming to court his beloved, only to find that she is gone. Like the lonely lover, the poet-speaker will memorialize his love through the "flower of poesy" which had so pleased his beloved. This temporary disappointment of a lover becomes profound bereavement in the widow whose beloved is dead, the first allusion to which is made in lyric 9. There remains, however, a strong hope of reunion in death even during the periods of darkest unhappiness. Nevertheless, the trial of an existence laboring under the burden of loneliness is not underemphasized; T. S. Eliot observed that the poem's "concern is for the loss of man rather than for the gain of God," and that it "is a poem of despair, but a despair of a religious kind."[6] The heart-wringing sense of loss felt by the poet is again captured in his picture of a widowed soul (this time, the widower) in lyric 13. At this point the poet's consciousness is absorbed by emptiness, loss, and silence.

The strength of his hope is, of course, weakened by his loss of someone who had been a support. But agonizingly, the poet slowly discovers that there is some value in the suffering he is experiencing. The discovery of love sharpened by loss is found to be fundamental in the growth of his moral being, in the growth of an individual soul, setting him above the beast with no conscience. In lyric 27 the image of the heart that stagnates when it has "never plighted troth" becomes part of the widowhood motif; the main force of this lyric contributes largely to the theme of real value coming from the void of loss. Untested security is no guarantee of worth, and the ultimate test of a "plighted troth" comes when the rewards it brings are removed. Faith and loyalty, like freedom, are not *given* as essences of being at birth; they are the products of the experience of life, of suffering, of testing the potential to become fulfilled when all one's props are removed.

The steps of the poet toward that discovery of faith and freedom are indicated in the poem by the renewal of the married state after widowhood. In lyric 59 the poet accepts his sorrow as a "wife," to fill the void of his love. His existence is made up of sorrow, but it becomes a sorrow he can accept and even cherish when he learns to control it. Later, in lyric 85, he again alludes to his widowhood, but his sorrow is now so fully under control that he can think again of his responsibilities to others. The values of love, faith, and freedom, learned through the experience of loss, are not left to languish unexercised, for the poet now seeks to affirm their worth in a new union of heart with heart. The *form* of love as an eternal ideal, or value, has been learned through experience and here finds a new incarnation, a new substance. The viability of this eternal value of love is emphasized in lyric 97 where the soul is no longer a widow, but a wife faithful to a husband whose wisdom is so beyond her own that she is lonely for lack of equal companionship. This lyric unfortunately attempts too much, for in it the poet tries to make us appreciate the point that his soul is both widowed and not widowed at the same time, through the example of a marriage in which the wife is intellectually incompatible with the husband. Still, his point is clear enough: the soul may not understand the workings of death and eternity, just as the wife in lyric 97 does not understand the mind of her brilliant husband. But the soul as wife nevertheless retains her identity through love for the soul as husband, whose intelligence is beyond her comprehension.

In the bright light of renewed love, of a new marriage celebrated in the epithalamion, the darkness and vacancy of widowhood seem less substantial than they had appeared. The paradox is that the brighter light which makes the darkness seem insubstantial, the larger love that makes the loss acceptable, and the new marriage that makes the widowhood fade—none of these could be were it not for that darkness, loss, and widowhood. By the end, then, the broken relationship has been restored. And not only is the widowed soul made stronger by its widowhood, but it feels itself remarried in the greater love that overcomes time, uniting the past with the future, just as the marriage at the end of the poem looks back and forward at the same time.

The poet has moved from not being able to say all that he felt to being conscious of saying something more than he knew: from a "mechanic exercise" to a song infused by the spirit of love. He has heard the voice he yearns for, he has found the light he had lost, and he has been rewarded for his widowhood. These are all discoveries of the dark night of grief and sorrow, when the self confronts the vacancy and nothingness of death and must fill it with the meaning that comes from deep within, not relying upon the evidences of a very limited and very changing world without. The shape of that inner meaning is a function of the total form which a unified art attains, and that is what the whole of *In*

Memoriam aims for. What had seemed mechanical, fragmented, and unsuccessful as full communication, is now seen as having had a purpose from the beginning: love has been the guiding spirit, so much in control that it could play with the "gracious lies" of darkness and despair, confident of its ultimate mastery. Because the artist has learned to wed his aesthetic duty with his spiritual desire, his poem affirms the triumph of his faith in love as a function of submission to form.

WHETHER FOCUSING ON ITS SUBJECT MATTER, imagery, or themes, the reader of *Maud* (1855) is likely to recognize that this is an important poem in Tennyson's canon. *Maud* is important in its own right, but it is also important as a transitional, even pivotal, poem in the development of Tennyson's art. The many sources that have been suggested, from the *Bride of Lammermoor* to *Alton Locke*,[7] add to the argument that *Maud* is a rich and sophisticated poem. Tennyson told his son that it "is a little Hamlet," and if any single source should be emphasized in a reading of the poem, then it should probably be this one. If *Hamlet* can be read so that one is sympathetic with Hamlet's vows and acts of bloody vengeance, then the concluding part of *Maud* might also be read with a comparably sympathetic imagination.

Some acts of aggression may be just and honorable if the motives are. This is a key to understanding Hamlet, to understanding how he can do God's justice against a foul corruption of the public weal without, at the same time, tainting his own soul by his deeds. (This is the single most important qualification made by the Ghost in his message to Hamlet.) The same point is a key to understanding the hero of *Maud*, to understanding that he is, in fact, guilty of private vengeance, has tainted his soul, and has suffered the death of his beloved. Both heroes must suffer to be wise and to purge themselves of their guilt by becoming servants of the public good, not avenging private wrongs. This is to learn the terribly difficult lesson of transforming a private desire into a public duty so that nothing of value is lost from either. The madness of both Hamlet and the hero of *Maud* is a kind of wisdom in which each discovers the humility of common humanity, that one must suffer the indignity of death before deserving the honor of life.

Tennyson's poem is a sophisticated piece of art, capable of provoking serious disagreement among its critics, but its very power is affirmed by the strength of the critical reactions, especially those that decry its conclusion. How one could be surprised or, as some have been, appalled by the literalism of the hero's commitment to a war of such sordid dimensions as the Crimean War is strange to consider. For this same poet had

49

concluded *The Princess* with a war *in petto*, and he would spend most of his long career working out in *Idylls of the King* the details of an epic warfare. It seems that critics will have to be as far distant in time from the Crimean War as Tennyson was from medieval jousts before *Maud* can be read with as much aesthetic detachment as *Idylls of the King*.

The hero of *Maud* undergoes a major spiritual conversion that changes his nature in terms familiar to the most casual reader of Tennyson's poetry. Part 1 shows a soul in retreat—"I will bury myself in myself" (1.75)*—where he fashions a luxury of desire when he contemplates the figure of Maud that grows and grows in his imagination, until she and her garden of rich fragrances and colors become one in his vision. This scene echoes "The Palace of Art" and "The Lotos-Eaters," both of which emphasize the power of sensuous loveliness to tempt one into imaginative retreat. Part 2 of *Maud*, with its famous mad scenes, elaborates in psychological and moral terms the very similar mad scenes of "The Palace of Art" and the mood of hallucination in "The Lotos-Eaters." In part 3, the hero of *Maud* makes a commitment to public endeavor, to a life of action, that bears striking resemblance to similar conclusions of not only "The Palace of Art," and "The Lotos-Eaters," but also even "Ulysses."

In short, in part 1 the hero is fearful of becoming a Telemachus ("centered in the sphere / Of common duties"), or worse, one of those who need the rule of a Telemachus ("a savage race, / That hoard, and sleep, and feed"). Like Ulysses, the hero of *Maud* scorns the life of the "still hearth" where one must suffer from "unequal laws":

> Sooner or later I too may passively take the print
> Of the golden age—why not? I have neither hope nor trust;
> May make my heart as a millstone, set my face as a flint,
> Cheat and be cheated, and die: who knows? we are ashes and dust.
>
> [1.29–32]

He has, also like Ulysses, a "gray spirit yearning in desire." He needs to turn that yearning outwards, again like Ulysses, to undertake "some work of noble note" ("Ulysses," 1. 52). The aesthetically troublesome quality of *Maud*, then, is not that it concludes in an uncharacteristically Tennysonian manner, but that it makes more explicit than it should what that "work of noble note" is to be.

Setting *Maud* in the context of Tennyson's other works or comparing it with analogues or sources such as *Hamlet* ought not to be necessary, but to do so can mitigate the force of some hostile readings as well as emphasize the literary wealth of the poem. One can demonstrate this

---

* References are to part and lines.

further by showing how the mad scenes of part 2 echo lines and recreate images from *The Rime of the Ancient Mariner,* and how they anticipate (if they do not, in fact, supply) situations and images that appear in T. S. Eliot's "Prufrock" and *The Waste Land. Maud* can thereby be seen as an important poem not only in the development of Tennyson's art, but in modern English poetry at large.

Maud shows that as a source of literary values for modern poetry, marriage is an ambivalent institution. This poem is one of Tennyson's earliest that shows how marriage fails to hold desire and duty together. It is a transitional poem for Tennyson's changing uses of the marriage motif; there is not the celebration of ideal marriage that concludes *The Princess* nor the triumphant epithalamion that concludes *In Memoriam,* but neither is there a darkness unto despair that marks the last of the *Idylls* nor an ironic bitterness that marks the marriage of "Lucretius." Instead, in *Maud* marriage is not only represented as a compromise but as something that is compromised. The focus for understanding the function of marriage in this poem is on Maud herself, as she is seen and valued by the speaker. In part 1, Maud is increasingly an object, if not a force, of sensuously all-possessing desire, perhaps Eros itself; in part 3, she has become the voice of conscience, or more exactly, the voice of public duty. Insofar as she is both the personal choice of the hero as well as the bride of the arranged union promised years earlier by their fathers, marriage with Maud "marries" the values of desire and duty that divided the soul of the speaker in the beginning of the poem. Part 2 is crucial for achieving the identification of these two values in the single person of Maud, to whom the hero is married in imagination if not in fact.

Our appreciation of Maud's importance as a symbolic force in the poem turns upon the following passage, from near the end of part 1:

> But the true blood spilt had in it a heat
> To dissolve the precious seal on a bond,
> That, if left uncancelled, had been so sweet;
> And none of us thought of a something beyond,
> A desire that awoke in the heart of the child,
> As it were a duty done to the tomb,
> To be friends for her sake, to be reconciled;
> And I was cursing them and my doom,
> And letting a dangerous thought run wild
> While often abroad in the fragrant gloom
> Of foreign churches—I see her there,
> Bright English lily, breathing a prayer
> To be friends, to be reconciled!   [1.727–39]

To this point, the hero has slowly discovered the "desire that awoke in the heart of the child / As it were a duty done to the tomb" (1.731–32). Maud has changed from an image of "dead perfection" that broke in upon his "slumber," awakening him from his delusion that life without desire is preferable to "a garden of spice":

> For not to desire or admire, if a man could learn it, were more
> Than to walk all day like the sultan of old in a garden of spice.
> . . . .
> And most of all would I flee from the cruel madness of love.
> [1.142–43, 156]

Gradually, as she grows upon him, breaking down his preconceptions, Maud becomes his "bride to be, [his] evermore delight, / [His] own heart's heart" (1.671–72). He hoped once while standing in her garden that she might come forth, like Juliet to Romeo:

> And I thought as I stood, if a hand, as white
> As ocean-foam in the moon, were laid
> On the hasp of the window, and my Delight
> Had a sudden desire, like a glorious ghost, to glide,
> Like a beam of the seventh heaven, down to my side,
> There were but a step to be made.   [1.505–10]

After the hero killed her brother in a duel, Maud became a ghost indeed, though not "a glorious ghost." She was first "the ghastly Wraith of one that [he] knew, . . . a shadow there at [his] feet" (2.36,39); then, after her death, Maud became "a hard mechanic ghost" singing "an old song [that] vexes [his] ear." She moves through his mind, disturbing him with her shadow and with her song. As a ghost whose shadow lifted "high over the shadowy land" and whose song rang out "like a trumpet's call" to battle, Maud is taking on the identity of England itself in the imagination of the speaker. She had been "but a cold and clear-cut face" (1.78) and then became "luminous, gemlike, ghostlike, deathlike, . . . growing and fading and growing, till [he] could bear it no more" (1.95); but after he hears her singing her "passionate ballad" of "men . . . in battle array" (1.165,169), she becomes, finally his own "bright English lily" (1.738).

She wanted through her friendship with the hero to honor the pledge of their fathers, to honor the desire of her dying mother, and so as his wife she could fulfill the hero's desire "as it were a duty" (1.731–32). The hero has from the beginning of his monodrama thought in metaphors of marriage, first with nature and his native land: "ah, wherefore cannot I be / Like things of the season gay . . . half-lost in . . . the silent sapphire-spangled marriage ring of the land?" (1.103–107). Maud in her garden recovers for him a paradise of harmony and identification with nature; and in her duty to her family's honor, Maud restores, or rather creates, for him a faith in his native land, his "bright English lily." He may not marry Maud, but he can "marry" England, and that he does when he, "a dead man," is linked in part 2 with "a spectral bride" (318). At this point Maud, or her spectre, becomes his conscience, his sense of duty, the force that restores reality for him. As "the shadow" that "will not let [him] be" (2.230, 231), Maud awakens the hero to a distinction between "the public foe," "a public merit," and "a private blow" (2.327, 329, 331). When he realizes that "lawful and lawless war / Are scarcely even akin," he also realizes that "maybe still [he is] but half dead" (2.332, 333, 337). Even though he might wish still to be completely dead, the simple realization that he is but "half-dead" is enough for him to turn the corner from madness to sanity.

In part 3, after he has committed himself to "defence of the right," the hero sees "the dreary phantom arise and fly / Far into the north" (36–37). Henceforth, he can feel that he is "one with [his] kind" because he has been awakened from delusions of private desire; he can join with other people in a single heart that can "beat with one desire" (49). The enemy is not the Russian czar, but rather all deceit, betrayal, hyprocrisy, and abuse of language, the most precious of all civilizing tools. When trust breaks down, when men betray the function of language and become liars, then they are the enemies of all public order, private order, and human sanity. Whether it is Maud's father who was a liar (1.56) or her brother (1.761) or the common tradesman (1.26) or the czar of Russia (1.110), "a giant liar" (3.45), the enemy is exposed by his abuse of language and trust. To the extent that Tennyson as poet agrees with his hero that the main enemy of civilization is the lie, then he is the poet's hero, and to battle against such an enemy is the sacred cause: "we have hearts in a cause, we are noble still" (3.55).

SINCE TENNYSON HAD FOUND the evolution of the soul analogous to the evolution of a poetic style and form, he next considered the possibility that the benefits of order and integrity available to the individual self might also be available to the community of mankind at large. This is a link between what Tennyson learned through the two decades of experience—embodied in *In Memoriam*—and the motive and scheme for *The Princess, Maud,* and finally *Idylls of the King.* As Walter Bagehot observed in commenting on the *Idylls,* in this poem "Mr. Tennyson has sided with the world."[8] Tennyson was tempted, as were many artists and thinkers of his time, to hope that the private vision of the artist could be communicated to all men as a basis of social and moral order in the absence of any other viable cultural mythology. The dream of King Arthur, that through himself could come new inspiration to revive men when the old schemes have begun to die, is also Tennyson's dream: that his personal affirmation could be translated in a way to serve the community at large.

His grandson reports in his biography that Tennyson said in 1886, "I tried in my 'Idylls' to teach men the need of an ideal, but I feel sometimes as if my life had been a very useless life."[9] There are very real affinities between this disappointed sense of uselessness expressed in 1886 and the pattern of futility traced in the evolving scheme of the *Idylls of the King*. Although this work is much less an expression of Tennyson's private, subjective experience than is most of his earlier poetry, it contains a growing sense of frustration at his failure to maintain an illusion of order and meaning in life; this is especially discernible in the history of the poem's composition. The poem grows more melancholy as much because of the poet's own deepening disillusionment as because the story he chose to tell leads him, necessarily, to a sad conclusion.

The additions Tennyson made to the "Morte d'Arthur" for the *Idylls* in 1869 reveal some of his self-doubt, some of his sense of failure both to maintain the illusion of hope he had generated in *In Memoriam* and to make his private vision of meaning available to all. Arthur found God in the "shining of the stars" and in "the flowering of His fields," whereas the poet of *In Memoriam* could find no evidence of divinity in such places (as he remarked in lyric 124). Rather, the foundation for faith in *In Memoriam* was discovered in the poet's personal experience of love for another human being. In the *Idylls*, however, Arthur says, "But in His ways with men I find Him not." And in the end, even that vision of God in His creation has been lost to Arthur, who, blaming himself, cannot quite understand why.

The region of Arthur's last battle is desolate, wintry, dark, and broken. The battle itself is one of confusion, mistakes, and hopeless cries, as well as of futile memories of happier times. This is an unendurable conclusion to a lifetime of selfless dedication to order, civilization, and enlarged human consciousness. John Rosenberg is quite accurate in saying that "modern literature offers no more chilling prospect than the closing books of the *Idylls*."[10] At the end, then, there is little more certitude about meaning than there was at the beginning. This is more an ironic than a tragic view of life, because the hero seems not to know for sure what he has lived and died for, though he hopes it has been for something. It may remind us of Matthew Arnold's "ignorant armies of the night." But if so, Arnold's poem is more comforting than Tennyson's; at least Arnold's speaker has his loved one present to secure him from the pains of spiritual alienation. Tennyson's hero is left alone with a single retainer, Bedevere.

And so are we, the readers, left alone with Bedevere, the old and lonely man who remembers how it felt to watch the disappearance of Arthur's funeral barge. He remembers how he climbed to watch the ship disappear "into light," while the "new sun rose bringing the new year." It was no definite promise of anything better, but within the scheme of a seasonal motif in the *Idylls*, a new year would bring light and new life to a land of darkness and sterility. Hope, however, is caught up in the eternal round of the seasons, as the old order gives way to the new, and that in turn decaying to give way to another. Beneath the illusion of order imposed as though "from above," there is the fact of nature, resisting human and spiritual order, obedient only to the principle of change. And so Bedevere, the old survivor of a glorious dream, stands alone to remind us of the ultimate, and perhaps inevitable, failure of such dreams as Arthur brought into the world.

But Tennyson had said that he wanted to "teach men the *need* of an ideal," not that ideals are eternally viable and permanently true. What is true is that men need ideals; they need a shape for their desires and a direction for their duties, if they are not to be slaves of passion and fall back into the brute creation without a struggle. Even though the ideal must yield to natural fact in the process of time and change, it sustains the spirit of those men who choose to follow it and fight the good fight. It is the fight that counts; the style, the manners, the grace, and the submission to a principle beyond self that contain whatever meaning there is in an existence where darkness and confusion seem to be the only manifest certainties. Did Tennyson then mean that he had failed to be useful in teaching "men the *need* of an ideal"? This is very possible, considering Tennyson's late views of naturalism, thinking that the likes of Swinburne and Zola had yielded the fortress of art to the forces of brutality. Such is partly the theme of "Lucretius," and we can see in Tennyson's composition of the various *Idylls* that his disappointment and sense of defeat deepened with experience.

From the beginning of his scheme for the Arthurian stories, Tennyson was concerned with courtship and marriage as symbols for the dialectic between certainty and uncertainty, between loyalty and treachery, between the realism of agape (in Enid) and the naturalism of eros (in Nimue, or Vivien). His insight into the truth of the dialectic sharpens with the continued additions to the stories gathered around King Arthur. He continued his early interest in the types of women whose attractions to, and for, men may either unite duty and desire or separate them. Enid encourages fulfillment, Vivien frustrates it, and Lancelot is caught between Elaine and Guinevere.

In 1869 he added not only "The Coming of Arthur" and "The Passing of Arthur," but also "The Holy Grail" and "Pelleas and Ettarre," with their own forms of the same visionary dreariness that permeates "The Passing of Arthur." Tennyson's idealism not only is lost in the darkness of the last great battle, but it is found to contain within itself the very seeds of its own destruction. "The Holy Grail" narrates the madness of a quest for private religious certainty when life cries out for selfless social action; and "Pelleas and Ettarre" bitterly narrates how exclusive devotion to an ideal may blind one to the very real evils in life, leading to a disillusionment so shattering (as in the example of Pelleas) that there is no possibility of rescue from despair by any ideal.

In 1872 he added two more idylls, "Gareth and Lynette" and "The Last Tournament," again suggesting the dialectic that is still going on in his mind. The experiences of the young, even naive, and optimistic Gareth prove the practical value of pursuing an ideal in the service of a higher authority, while "The Last Tournament" is one of Tennyson's most cynical and depressing pictures of life without any ideals, of life measured by "the laws of nature," "red in tooth and claw." Finally, as though to resolve the dialectic between naturalistic desires and idealistic duties into some dramatic confrontation, Tennyson composed the last of the idylls, "Balin and Balan," between 1872 and 1874 and published it in 1885. In this idyll, the idealism of Balin not only yields to the bestial naturalism within his character, but that idealism (figured as his duty to the Queen) even leads Balin to his destruction and the destruction of his brother, all in an atmosphere that suggests a battle raging within a single soul. In this surrealistic battle, brother kills brother out of ignorance and out of deception by misguidance from those who, like Vivien, distort the ideals of duty and desire or, like Pellam, withdraw religious idealism from any active engagement with a brutal creation or, like Mark, slink in the dark, like a beast of prey, and slay without challenge.

It is no wonder that Tennyson's city of art and ideal social order is disintegrating. It comes as something of a shock to realize that this disintegration may be the result of the Grail quest itself. But the knights en masse desert Camelot for something less substantial; the city had inspired action for the fulfillment of self rather than for the negation of self and the world along with it, as the Grail quest does. Percivale tells how, when he returned to Camelot, he found it in ruins. The ornaments of illusion and mystery fell away from the once enchanted city. The paradox that Camelot demonstrates is that when an ideal fails to hold the loyalty of its believers, it cannot become real, and its illusion becomes a delusion.

The city is surrounded by dark forests in which the knights do battle with the beasts and brutes of nature, and insofar as the city of Camelot is built to music, and never completely built, it is the imaginative effort of man that civilizes the brutality, clears the forest of darkness, but the effort requires continuous application. The artist's work is never done. There is much singing in the poem, from the first *Idyll* where Arthur's men sing in celebration of his marriage, to the last *Idyll* where the sounds made by the passing of Arthur's funeral ship are compared with the death song of a swan. In the idyll of "The Last Tournament" that music becomes a mockery of the order and idealism of Camelot; here Tristram sings of "free love" and the fool, Dagonet, refuses to dance to Tristram's "broken music." Tristram does not move in harmony with the Round Table as Arthur had founded it, upon the ideals of service to others, of loyalty and duty in love. Tristram's music is broken, an index to the failure of the art that has shaped the kingdom of Camelot. While Arthur's had been the music of the imagination, guiding as well as harmonizing, Tristram's broken music is selfish, sensual, and delusive even in the possession. He cannot imagine the reality of anything not immediate to his senses. Dagonet said Tristram never would see the star which constitutes "the harp of Arthur," making "a silent music up in heaven" for some like Dagonet and Arthur to hear. Tristram admits, in his song to Isolt of Ireland, that he has chosen the star that is "near," though it is only a reflection of the one in heaven, and though it is water to that heavenly one of fire. He chooses the near, the transient, and willfully chooses the delusion. Arthur's is a steady, guiding, distant star, the goal always to strive for, while Tristram's is transient, changed by every wind of passion and every change of circumstances: it is as immediate as a goal which, when gained, is empty of content.

Arthur stands opposite to Tristram in his attitude toward the ideal. Arthur's relationship with Guinevere seems hard and inhuman in their last encounter, but this is because he is true to his duty as neither Tristram nor Guinevere has been. Like music, marriage has become a mockery, but Arthur will not surrender his faith in its symbolic efficacy. Guinevere lies repentant at the feet of the man whom she has betrayed and whose judgment she now receives. Anticipating Bedevere's own narrative of his parting with Arthur, Guinevere narrates her experience of Arthur's departure, his declaration of love for her and his offer to protect her. She tells how Arthur disappeared forever from her, in whom he had placed such a great trust, such as perhaps no mortal woman can bear:

> she did not see the face,
> Which then was an angel's, but she saw,
> Wet with the mists and smitten by the lights,
> The Dragon of the great Pendragonship
> Blaze, making all the night a stream of fire.
> And even then he turned; and more and more
> The moony vapour rolling round the King,
> Who seemed the phantom of a Giant in it,
> Enwound him fold by fold, and made him gray
> And grayer, till himself became as mist
> Before her, moving ghostlike to his doom.   [ll. 591–601]

This would have made a good ending for the *Idylls*, as Tennyson realized; he let it stand as the conclusion until 1869 when he added "The Passing of Arthur." Guinevere watches here the man—whose worth she has come to know too late—as he disappears into the mist. As Arthur disappears, so too does the dream he sought to realize; his value as an effective ideal disappears into the misty nothingness from which he seemed to have emerged in the beginning. The scene of Arthur's departure from Guinevere demonstrates how well Tennyson has retained his ability to assume the mask of the deserted woman, which he had done so well in his earliest poetry. But here the woman is the culpable one, and she has abandoned herself, making the pain of the separation even more acute for her. We are haunted, as is Guinevere, by the sounds of those "armed steps" moving away into the mist; the next time we shall hear such sounds, they will be the steps of Bedevere, carrying Arthur's mortally wounded body over the rocky coast in the mountains "by the winter sea."

Ward Hellstrom is wrong to emphasize in his recent study of Tennyson the failure of the poet's solution to what Hellstrom calls "the woman problem."[11] What should be emphasized, instead, is Tennyson's poignantly successful presentation of the failure of myth—of imagination in the form of marriage—to sustain the human spirit in its effort to unite its desires with its duties. Tennyson's poem is more depressing for its suggestion that always the particular ideal will crumble because the corporate imagination cannot successfully maintain for long the requisite intense effort. The "problem" is not "woman" nor marriage in itself, but a flagging imagination. The "problem" is that the human condition is problematic.

The poem's theme of the dialectic between the poles of "Sense and Soul" is embodied in the run of the stories from the marriage of Arthur and Guinevere as a synthesis of duty and desire, through stories showing the testing of the synthesis, until in the story of Merlin and Vivien, duty is paralyzed by desire. Then, in "Guinevere," duty is shown divorced from desire. Interwoven through the texture of these narratives is a metaphor of great importance to the theme of a search for the synthesis of desire and duty; the metaphor works as a pun on the concept of "the word made flesh." A man's word is extremely important to the order and security of any community, and Arthur insists that it is the very thing in a man that makes him significant. He establishes this point early, in "The Coming of Arthur": "And Arthur said, 'Man's word is God in man: / Let chance what will, I trust thee to the death'" (ll. 132–33). The king himself speaks "simple words of great authority," and he speaks "with large, divine, and comfortable words." This is in contrast with the "savage yells" of the kingdom of darkness which Arthur has come to tame. Mutual trust, depending primarily upon honesty of word and deed, is the only viable communion among men. Tennyson exploits the central fact of civilization, that the community is stable only so long as communication is trustworthy. Thus the poet may feel a special responsibility, for his is a medium of words, the primary means of communication. Through the poet, society may establish its communion, with the poet as its guardian of the divine in a community of the word becoming flesh.

Hence, as the various protagonists weaken in their words, in their vows, the divine begins to die within them and, by extension, within the community. Arthur repeats the importance of this ideal in the beginning of a key idyll, "Balin and Balan": "Man's word is God in man." It is profoundly significant that in the woods Balin and Balan should pursue the particular demon they do, for it is the force of what Hallam Tennyson identified as "slander" or "evil tongues." Balin is driven into the woods by "evil tongues," by the disillusionment of discovering the infidelity of Guinevere, and he is finally betrayed into becoming the fiend itself by the evil tongue of Vivien. She taunts him with what is, as far as she knows, nothing more than rumors about Guinevere, and Balin responds as a fiend. He let out a "weird yell, / Unearthlier than all shriek of bird or beast" that "Thrilled through the woods." Balan became the fiend he had been seeking.

Ironically, the next time the concept of the word as God in man is invoked, it is by Lancelot:

> Then answered Lancelot, the chief of knights:
> "And with what fact, after my pretext made,
> Shall I appear, O Queen, at Camelot, I
> Before a King who honours his own word,
> As if it were his God's?"   [ll. 140–44]

And Lancelot, "the chief of knights," has just lied to the king about not being able to attend the tournament for the diamonds, putting into words the deceit he has practiced towards the king in action. When Lancelot cannot honor the God that is in man, there is little hope for maintaining the integrity of the community for very long. In the very end, the final test of Bedevere is a measure of his honesty, his word, which is twice betrayed. Finally, however, Bedevere's word survives the test and confirms Arthur's divine authority.

The heroic leader, for whom Carlyle had been calling over a period of several years, may find within himself the imaginative and moral resources to envision a significant order of meaning for personal fulfillment, and so he may, through his own word and act, seek to realize his vision. But he must secure the trust of others to extend it beyond his own experience; that requires a living tradition of symbolic action and linguistic excellence. When the symbols of act (as ritual) and word (as myth) are inert, when they do not command the respect of those who use them, their effectiveness for communion and communication breaks down. And perhaps Tennyson is as concerned for the broken word and the gap between the present and the past as is, say, T. S. Eliot, for both would agree with King Arthur that the strongest force available to civilized man for protecting himself from the chaos of an irrational world is the cultural weapon of the incarnate word, creating and preserving and transmitting the ideal of order—or, at least, keeping the imagination alive and alert to its need for such an ideal.

IN THE IDYLLS we see how an ideal of civilized social order works for a while to make men better than beasts. But then it weakens from the strain of a dialectic between delusion (as in the "Holy Grail") and cynicism (as in "Pelleas" and "The Last Tournament"); the result is darkness, chaos, and uncertainty once again. We have in the *Idylls* a panoramic view of existence as a cyclical round of change, within which the forces of darkness and naturalistic desire battle the forces of light and idealistic duty. In *Becket* (1884), probably the most successful of his efforts in drama, Tennyson chooses a moment from that round of history, dealing again with the conflict between light and dark; but here the middle area of shadows and uncertainty make this play more ambiguous than most of the *Idylls*. The ambiguity may be, as some have argued, the result of Tennyson's failure to realize coherent dramatic form. Terry Otten recognizes the "psychological implications" of "Becket's willing martyrdom," but Otten focuses his study on the "inchoate movement of the external action." The play's inherited form of historical realism and Tennyson's effort to "expose Becket's inner conflicts" are not unified, in

Otten's opinion; therefore, the drama is marked, in his words, by a "structural impasse imposed by Tennyson's divided interest in plot and character."[12]

However much these divided interests might bring the drama to a structural impasse, there is a unity of concern between Becket as a character and the plots in which he plays out his roles: absolutists are dangerous for the commonwealth of modern culture. What happens to Becket, what happens in his psychological development, is what happens to the kingdom and to its political and spiritual structure.

The reign of Henry II follows many years of political anarchy during which Stephen and Mathilda jockeyed for control over England. Henry has come onto the scene, like King Arthur in the *Idylls*, to restore order and some measure of civilization based on justice. There is much wisdom in Henry's decision to appoint his chancellor as archbishop and thereby to unite secular and religious authority; that is the logical culmination of the process of civilizing a state of chaos and anarchy. One thematic point made by the chess game which opens the drama is that the kingdom needs a powerful man to assume the leadership of a church which has lost its sense of justice, ironically at the same time it has "climb'd the throne and almost clutch'd the crown."[13] Henry attempts to provide, through Becket, a man of justice to lead the Church out of "the pell-mell of Stephen's time" into the order of Henry's own reign.

The result is disaster, for not even Thomas Becket can reconcile secular and religious authority in the modern world. Becket does—and does not—subscribe to the "customs" which Henry has written down for describing the orderly relationship of the state to the church. First, Becket resists the appointment and then questions whether he is indeed the right man. He is answered in a dream by God, who tells him he is the right man, but He strikes Becket down at the same time. When Becket yields and accepts the appointment, he immediately thinks of himself as estranged from the king; he transfers all the energy he once had as chancellor into his new office as archbishop. He finds himself very much alone, as he refuses to accept the king's legal authority, and finds little or no support from the other churchmen, including the pope, who is himself a virtual prisoner of European politics. Becket is his own authority, claiming a primacy of judgment that makes him the inevitable antagonist of the state. Eventually he and Henry reach a very uneasy peace wherein Becket anathematizes anyone who has usurped upon his own spiritual authority in favor of the king's. Then, in the last act, when Henry has reached the point where he wishes Becket were dead, Eleanor twists the truth of Becket's rescue of Rosamund into a lie, saying that Becket has taken Rosamund for his own pleasure; that lie unleashes Henry's wrath and seems to sanction Becket's murder. Becket chooses to die rather than compromise his spiritual duty with a secular duty.

Becket may seem heroic for opposing the state and king, even though he takes his stand in the name of a church that does not support him and in opposition to a plan by the king for achieving greater social justice than the church has been willing to allow. What further diminishes the value of Becket's stand is the atmosphere of doubt in which he makes his choice. Has he chosen the right course of action? This is the question with which T. S. Eliot's Becket is concerned and, to a large extent, so is Tennyson's. We are made to consider whether—and how much—Becket doubts his own spiritual authority, and this is somewhat hard to judge. Though he feels that God has withdrawn Himself (1.3), the archbishop nevertheless commands others to yield to the authority of God in himself. This command over others becomes less and less effective, until at the end, the murderers mock Becket's spiritual authority altogether: "How the good priest gods himself! / He is not yet ascended to the Father." Even though we certainly do not admire DeBrito, he has a point.

Others in the drama question Becket's course of action. Walter Map, the cynical critic of the church, considered friendly to Becket, advises Becket to "diagonalize" (a proper move for a bishop in a game of chess):

> WALTER MAP: My lord, the fire, when first kindled, said to the smoke, "Go up, my son, straight to heaven." And the smoke said, "I go;" but anon the Northeast took and turned him Southwest, then the Southwest turned him Northeast, and so of the other winds; but it was in him to go up straight if the time had been quieter. Your lordship affects the unwavering perpendicular; but His Holiness, pushed one way by the Empire and another by England, if he move at all—Heaven stay him!—is fain to diagonalize.
> HERBERT: Diagonalize! thou art a wordmonger.
> Our Thomas never will diagonalize.
> Thou are a jester and a verse-maker.
> Diagonalize!   [2.2.182–98]

We may hear the voice of Tennyson himself in these lines of Walter Map, the wordmonger. Map's advice points back to something Tennyson included in *The Princess*. In the "Conclusion" to that poem, the narrator describes the strategy he has pursued to bring order, harmony, and unity out of variety (or what Tennyson called a "medley" of differing viewpoints); the strategy is one that is echoed in the advice given by Walter Map to Becket. In *The Princess*, the narrator describes how

> Then rose a little feud betwixt the two,
> Betwixt the mockers and the realists:

And I, betwixt them both, to please them both,
And yet to give the story as it rose,
I moved as in a strange diagonal,
And maybe neither pleased myself nor them.   [ll. 23–28]

When truth is relative, when all views of reality have claims upon the imagination, when the primary responsibility of the poet is to secure an *order* within which truth may be found, then perhaps the best strategy is to "move as in a strange diagonal," even if it cannot altogether please either the artist or his audience. Thus Walter Map's advice to Becket: to diagonalize in unquiet times—move upwards, yes, but as smoke must when there are contrary winds.

John of Salisbury also admonishes Becket on the difficulty of knowing what is the truth: "We are self-uncertain creatures, and we may, / Yea, even when we know not, mix our spites / And private hates with our defence of Heaven" (5.2). Later in the same scene, Becket describes John of Salisbury as his "other self, / Who like [his] conscience never lets [him] be." Yet Becket moves on to his death which he hopes is martyrdom and which he hopes may be the fulfillment of his dream when God struck him down.

In such an atmosphere of doubt about the certainty of judgment, we cannot feel deeply moved by Becket's choice to die when he could have escaped to live with honor. In *Becket* we see an example of what we see in Tennyson's other poetry: Becket is another man who finds it enormously difficult to know what is good or how to act upon what little knowledge there is. What Tennyson was trying to show in *Becket* is the suicidal death of religious authority when it cannot "diagonalize" in times of disquiet and general doubt. Becket's refusal or inability to unite spiritual and secular authority is a fact of modern life; and it may be the tragedy of an era of spiritual fragmentation. It is the gloomy conclusion of the *Idylls* that when spiritual ideals insist upon independent authority, upon *essential* truth, as in the careers of the knights on the quest for the Holy Grail, then *existential* truth, and social justice, will suffer terrible consequences. When ideals of duty and authority of spirit withdraw from natural reality, man is left at the mercy of elementary passions tending toward chaos and destruction. Becket does not diagonalize, choosing instead to withdraw from the union of spiritual authority with secular authority, from the identification of essential and existential values; the result is his own destruction. And in Becket's destruction is the loss of the king's last hope for a spiritual and physical power.

Through the subplot involving Rosamund and Eleanor along with Henry and Becket, Tennyson returns again to his concern for the public symbol of marriage as a reconciliation of dialectical opposites. And here again marriage is found to fail. Rosamund is the immediate victim of the split between Henry and Becket, for her safety depends upon their cooperation; she is torn between her love for Henry and her faith in Becket. Rosamund is more than the mistress of the king; she becomes an expression of the soul torn between opposed values (the soul as "rose of the world"). But just as she is caught between opposing forces, so does she represent one pole of attraction that strains Henry's life: he is caught up between love and desire for Rosamund and his responsibility and duty to Eleanor. In the end we see a helpless and pathetic Rosamund bent over the dying Becket; at the same time, an equally pathetic Henry has yielded to the pressures of fear and jealousy, driven by the deceit and ambition of Eleanor and her followers. The world is in shambles at the end of the play, having sunk back into the social and moral chaos out of which it had risen with the combined leadership of Henry and Becket. Tennyson's drama attempts in another mode to show the concerns expressed in the *Idylls*: to show the necessity for an ideal, but to show how difficult it is to secure public order out of a devotion to a private and personal ideal.

This is also a theme of "Lucretius" (1868), which is not so much "an indictment of the naturalism which [*De Rerum Natura*] so memorably expounded"[14] as it is an indictment of a marriage that fails to work because it does not satisfy the conflicting demands of flesh and spirit, sensation and mind, desire and duty. The philosophy of Lucretius is not "wrong," but it is inadequate as a substitute for living. It is the man, not the philosopher or the poet, who is here indicted. Lucretius can no more live in his poetry and his philosophy than could the Soul live alone in her "Palace of Art" or Princess Ida in her women's college. On the other hand, Lucretius cannot harmonize his divided being, and just as Paris failed Oenone, so does Lucretius fail Lucilia. In denying his lust, Lucretius denies his wife; the result is madness and chaos. He does not affirm his will when he kills himself, he denies his body, much as Simeon Stylites did and as Pelleas does in the *Idylls*; all three abuse the flesh to deny its claims. "Lucretius" is bitterly ironic, perhaps even darkly comic, for it turns upon the paradox of a naturalistic philosopher-poet who denies his own nature.

Like all such Tennysonian heroes, Lucretius expires from a failure to balance his idealism and his sensuality, or his duty and his desire. His wife does not kill him with her aphrodisiac, unless a man can die from too much love; but certainly, she acts from an honest motive (comically so) to rescue her husband from his madness of idealism. Her error is to act too late and perhaps with too much passion, for his imagination is powerful, whether in dealing with philosophy or with passion. Thus, starved as his imagination has been from a life of feeling and sensation, it bursts with an uncontrollable frenzy of sensuality. Most of the poem is devoted to an elaboration of this frenzy, but Tennyson's art is in the scene he establishes with the opening and closing passages.

In the framing passages lies the drama of the poem, and there also lies the comic irony. Lucilia is "wedded to Lucretius," but she is not married to him. Lucretius is a master of poetry and philosophy, but he is no master of his passion, any more than he is a master of his wife— though, "wedded" as she is to him, Lucilia must consider him her "master." "Passion and the first embrace had died / Between them," but clearly as the poem will show, passion has not died out of the wife and only waits to be aroused in the husband. Tennyson deftly tells us that Lucretius "loved her none the less," in a stock phrase of those who defend exhausted passion on behalf of high ideals. Lucretius does not notice, or rather takes "small notice" of, his wife's presence; instead, austere as he is, his mind is "half buried" in argument or lost in fancy, intent "upon the rise / And long roll of the Hexameter" (ll. 9–12). It is possible to read this opening passage as grand mockery, and were it not for the grave consequences that come in the end, the poem would be a Roman comedy.

But the poem is extremely serious by the end of Lucretius's mono- logue. After he has "wedded" himself to the "passionless bride" of death, thus divorcing himself from his passionate bride, Lucilia, Lucretius de- nies all meaning to all life in his last words: " 'Care not thou! / Thy duty? What is duty? Fare thee well!' " These words express a sentiment that will become the dominant note of Tennyson's later poetry, and so, in retrospect, we may rightly think they are approved by the poet him- self. However, in the setting of the poem, Lucretius's final words are consonant with the prevailing tone of mockery throughout. He has de- nied the value of desire, and in the end he denies the value of duty. The marriage that has failed is, figuratively, the harmony of the philosopher- poet's own being. In the context of the poem, Lucilia may appear to be a silly woman, not deserving such a grand man as this austere poet, but she at least had the right idea. Indeed, exactly what her "duty" to her husband is or should have been is something Lucretius does not know. We should take Tennyson's poem seriously, but we cannot take seriously the postures of his Roman hero.

There was something ominously true about the prophetic main theme of the "Ode on the Death of the Duke of Wellington" (1852), that "the last great Englishman is low." This is a motif of modern literature, and in Tennyson's stirring tribute to Wellington, the new poet laureate artfully lamented the passing of an ideal as well as the passing of a man. The ideal of heroism which the poem celebrated was the same ideal that

Wordsworth addressed in his "Ode to Duty." It had been a real possibility for Wordsworth, but for Tennyson, the ideal is merely an echo, like Wellington, receding into the past: "The path of duty was the way to glory." With this line repeated as a refrain throughout the mournful eighth stanza, Tennyson pays tribute to the power of duty as a motive of heroism—but only as a thing of the past: "The path of duty *was* the way to glory." For the present age, duty is an obscure and often meaningless word, unless somehow it can be kept alive in memory as exemplified by selfless persons like Wellington: "let his great example stand . . . till . . . the path of duty be the way to glory." It is, thus, a future as well as a past possibility; but for the present, there are only dreams of heroic duty.

The theme of the ode is ominous because it aptly describes the temperament of the time, a temperament which Tennyson most dramatically conveyed in his greater poem of *In Memoriam* (1850) but failed to rouse by his later poem of *Maud* (1855). All three poems are alike in their concluding commitments to an ideal of duty, but there is a pall over their commitments, for duty in all three poems is a function of death. The later poems are increasingly dominated by this elegiac tone of lament for the lost leader, and many of them are formed by the metaphors of marriage in a process of breaking apart. The tales of the *Idylls* as well as "Lucretius" increasingly emphasize this process, until finally, in some of his last poems, Tennyson suggests a permanent divorce of duty from desire in this life and for this time. Even the mythic understructure of "Demeter and Persephone" cannot save that poem from its intense bitterness, spoken as it is by a "desolate Mother" who "envied human wives" when her child Persephone disappeared. In her desolation, Demeter expresses her dismay that Hymen has given place to Hades, for her daughter has become "the Bride of Darkness." Divided as they are by Hades, Demeter and Persephone know the meaning of the phrase "the living-dead," which "The Leper's Bride" uses to describe her husband in the gruesomely ironic poem "Happy." Finally, with continuing irony, Tennyson brings the matter to rest with "The Death of Oenone" (1892), in which Oenone is told that it is her husband whose body is being consumed by the funeral fire she sees:

> and all at once
> The morning light of happy marriage broke
> Through all the clouded years of widowhood,
> And muffling up her comely head, and crying
> 'Husband!' she leapt upon the funeral pile,
> And mixt herself with *him* and past in fire.   [ll. 101–106]

3

Browning

Browning in his poetry, like Kierkegaard in his philosophical meditations, set himself "the task of determining whether Christianity can still be lived or whether a civilization still nominally Christian must finally confess spiritual bankruptcy." Browning's central subject is "the unique experience of the single one, the individual, who chooses to place himself on trial before the gravest question of his civilization. . . . Christianity."[1] In *Christmas-Eve and Easter-Day*, the speaker is made to ponder this "gravest question" in explicit terms:

> How hard it is to be
> A Christian! Hard for you and me
> . . . To realize it, more or less,
> With even the moderate success
> Which commonly repays our strife
> To carry out the aims of life.
> ["Easter-Day," ll. 1–12][2]

Browning often takes his subject matter from periods of history when the essence of Christianity is challenged by new conditions of human existence; the period of crisis most dramatic for his purposes is the Renaissance. During the Renaissance, the Christian essence of faith had become an inert fact demanding an unquestioning obedience to its authority in all matters that count, including politics and art, as well as ethics and theology. But the spirit of pre-Christian art and thought, particularly from the classics of Greece, challenged the authority of medieval Christianity. Out of the clash of cultures came a reexamination of assumptions long held sacrosanct, and many sought a reconciliation between the forms of Christian duty and the passions of desire celebrated by classical Greece, between what Matthew Arnold called "strictness of conscience" and "spontaneity of consciousness." In such major poems as *The Ring and the Book* and "Fifine at the Fair," Browning examines this clash with its attempts at reconciliation in the various trials of marriage; in other poems, such as "Fra Lippo Lippi," he proposes the reconciliation as a function of art at its best. That there be a marriage of art and life is as important for Browning as that there be an art of marriage.

For Browning, as for Arnold and Pater, his own time required a renaissance and reformation: a renaissance of the spirit and a reformation of the substance. His poetry reveals such a renaissance and reformation— or, better yet, a birth and a formation—in the souls of his characters. Browning's poetry shows us that the examined life is worth living, even for his "evil" characters. This purpose is a process of enlarging consciousness, either for the character in the poem or for the reader observing that character. The process is an exercise of imagination, a power that generates value, whether aesthetic, moral, or religious. When the reader submits to the design of the poem, he yields to Browning's strategy for bringing him into an identification with the character and with the poet. What we all have in common, as the neutral ground of our being and communion, is that strangely human power of imagination. Being is thus becoming, an energy of participation; and communication is thus an act of creation. The more alien the consciousness of the character in the design, the greater is the power of imagination required of the reader. Suddenly, the reader sees himself in the design, caught there in strange fashion as though he were looking at himself in the crazy mirror of a carnival.

Browning's strategy is to educe the imagination to rescue the soul from shapelessness to shape, from its essential nothingness into an existential something. This process of renaissance and reformation, or birth and formation, follows a design of ascent through enlarging spheres of values: aesthetic, ethical, and religious. Both Kierkegaard and Browning focus on the importance of the living moment, of experience and existence, rather than of reason or essence.[3] The self becomes and grows, develops to find its unique and individual route to the truth. That path, however different it may appear for different people, takes the soul through stages of consciousness in which the previous stage no longer seems adequate as a goal of life, encouraging a belief that the present stage may also be inadequate when measured against a larger possibility. "The real way seem[s] made up of all the ways," as Sordello puts it (6.36).

The birth of a soul begins with an act of choosing. Sordello hesitates to take any step toward political or aesthetic accomplishment, overwhelmed by the difficulties in his way, when "a low voice wound into his heart" telling him to "wake":

"God has conceded two sights to a man—
One, of men's whole work, time's completed plan,
The other, of the minute's work, man's first
Step to the plan's completeness."   [5.84–87]

Sordello is frustrated by his anxiety over the last step from taking even the first step. In *Christmas-Eve and Easter-Day* the speaker in each of the two parts is driven by the emergency of his vision to make what the Pope in *The Ring and the Book* calls "the terrible choice":

Meantime, in the still recurring fear
    Lest myself, at unawares, be found,
    While attacking the choice of my neighbours round,
With none of my own made—I choose here!
                        ["Christmas-Eve," ll. 1338–41]

The intuition burned away
All darkness from my spirit too:
There, stood I, found and fixed, I knew,
Choosing the world. The choice was made;
And naked and disguiseless stayed,
And unevadable, the fact.   ["Easter-Day," ll. 550–55]

As each person encounters alternative ways of acting, feeling, and thinking, he is plunged into a crisis of profound significance on all levels —psychological, ethical, social, political, and religious. When the claims on truth, on attention, on desire, and on duty are multiplied, choice increasingly becomes the responsibility of the individual, who cannot trust anyone except himself to make his choice. Even then he knows that he may not understand his motives well enough to make the best choice possible. But Browning's world was not yet one in which you are damned if you do and damned if you don't. As a recent commentator on Browning's religion has observed, Browning "did not choose to view the world as absurd or meaningless or without order—but he did share the belief that he must choose for himself how he would view it."[4] In Browning's world, you may choose wrong, even evil, but the choice itself rescues you from annihilation, from the wasteland of Eliot's hollow men; you enter instead into the first stage of growth—selfhood. It proves inescapable for a maturing human being to choose, for even not to choose is a choice of a kind. Never to feel the necessity of choice is never to be human, never to be anything more than a rock. A key term, then, to determine the design of a Browning poem is *choice*.

To plunge into the pathos of choice initiates the action of the soul and imagination in which the self must consider possibilities not yet actualized; to choose is to actualize, to create something that was not.

69

The most important thing actualized is the self that makes the choice. At this point the terms "aesthetic" and "ethical" become useful analytical tools. The root meaning of *aesthetic*, "to perceive" at the level of "sensation," justifies its use as a term to describe that primary choice to live in the moment, for the gratification of the senses, as the purpose of existence. This definition is the foundation for the so-called "aesthetic movement" of the late decades of the nineteenth century, and it is just this temptation that the young Tennyson constantly had to resist. Browning's poetry deals with the same temptation—though to call it a temptation in Browning is misleading, since it may be the necessary first stage of growth; the temptation lies in the power of aesthetics to prevent any further growth. It is a necessary stage, perhaps a crucial one, as even the great medieval poet of Christianity, Dante, realized when he found himself in the dark woods of spiritual despair, apparently lost to all means of grace save poetry—represented to him by the appearance of Virgil.

Like Dante's hero of the *Divine Comedy*, Browning's characters should not be contented with the aesthetic alone; some are, and they become examples of arrested development. The aesthetic consciousness ultimately must discover its own ethical inadequacy, for its existence becomes a flight from boredom, from the self that tries to escape into outside objects. When the escape proves impossible, and when the effort has exhausted all energy, the self "comes home" to itself. In the experience of choosing the self, rather than fleeing into the objects that surround it, is the second stage of growth: the ethical as duty and obligation. But Browning's aesthetes do not make the choice of self which summons into existence the potentials of good and evil.

Often the aesthete discovers the insufficiency of his way only when forced to confront death. When death as an inevitable fact of his personal existence looms up amid the objects of his aesthetic search, he may realize the futility of the search. This forces him to consider his self, naked of its aesthetic props. It is the self alone that matters and that cannot be escaped. The choice of self over objects is not selfishness or egotism, for the ethical stage of development brings with it a sense of responsibility not present in the aesthetic stage. For the aesthete, art may be an end in itself, existing for itself alone; for the ethical man, art exists for man. He may use it to diminish or enlarge his existence, to control others for his own sake (as in propaganda), or to share with others as a means of communion (as in ritual, myth, or poetry). The ethical man may also use art to flee from the self which acknowledges death, and so regresses into a deluded egotism of desire for the world of objects; or he may use it to encounter the self acknowledging death as the great question which forces one to ask the meaning of life. The outstanding characteristic of the ethical stage of growth which helps to distinguish it from the religious stage is the emphasis on duty—choosing between right and wrong, good and evil, as potentials for relationships among men. The ethical self subordinates its aesthetic desires to its duty, serving the interests of community, and thereby it enlarges its ethical consciousness. One dramatic way to affirm this subordination of self is to marry. Indeed, Kierkegaard's character Judge William advocates marriage as the *telos*, or end, of the ethical way of life.[5] Browning's own telling insights into what Kierkegaard calls "the aesthetic validity of marriage" contribute to the power of *The Ring and the Book* and to such later poems as "Fifine at the Fair."

The problem of knowing what is the proper relationship, what is the right or good choice in a relationship with others is a difficult matter. Indeed, spiritual growth may be indicated by this intensifying difficulty in making choices; responsibility increases as the self matures, realizing that what really matters must be measured against the timelessness of death. One way out of the ethical dilemma, a way of facilitating the individual's ethical decisions, is to utilize a system—to appeal to an institution or to a code of generalized principles of behavior which will work in most cases to ensure the greatest probability of right and good among men. Few individuals who have reached the ethical stage of existence can do without such a system or code of duties. But the code may not, probably cannot, cover every situation. When the code or the institution becomes identical with what is right or good, when the code becomes a substitute for the experienced truth, when the means become the end and doing one's duty above all else matters most to a person, then the code's—and perhaps the person's—rationale for existence has ceased. To challenge the code and institutions of ethical guidance, whether in marriage or in politics, is the awful responsibility of the religious experience, and that process is accompanied by fear and trembling. To perform the challenge in awe of the ethical risk is to penetrate the religious sphere, and Browning's poetry aims for this penetration.

Religion in his poetry means to be religious, to be in a state of consciousness that transcends the ethical without losing a sense of the ethical, to be in a state of marriage (which Pompilia discovers only in death and Don Juan asserts as a matter of will and imagination). Everything is risked on the decision that institutional ethics obstruct rather than facilitate the growth and fulfillment of the individual soul. If the choice is in error, perhaps the soul has merely made an ethical judgment, choosing what is indeed diminishment (and so evil) and taking whatever consequences time and place will determine. But if the choice proves to have been correct, it is a religious act, and it brings the soul closer to God,

71

closer to the fulfillment which is the quest of life. Browning's characters strive for fulfillment in the belief that "there is a right to be chosen; there is a God above," even if He is "a homemade God," as LeRoy Lawson quaintly puts it.[6]

PUBLICLY VERIFIABLE FACTS are used as vehicles for the artist's fancies in such dramas as Tennyson's *Becket* and Browning's *Strafford*. Unfortunately, for the historical dramatist and his posterity, even the facts of history become suspect under the close scrutiny of critical and sometimes cynical students, so that a compromise between public "facts" of history and the private values of the imagination may result in a weakening of the appeal which either might present alone. As Terry Otten has put it in his study of nineteenth-century English dramatic form, "The problem then is structure—the conflict between subjective matter and objective form."[7] Relentlessly, the intellectual forces of the nineteenth century drove the search for truth, for certainty, away from the external and historical verities and toward a greater concentration upon the internal, psychological processes of the self, lost in a maze of facts that contradict one's past beliefs and seem to have little to contribute to the enrichment of the emotional, spiritual, or imaginative life. Drama, being an especially public form of art, was bound to suffer in its attempt to render the private, subjective experience. In Otten's words, looking to the past for models and materials in drama was "too much like grafting an alien myth onto a new vision. The modern concern with the individual and the internal 'dialogue of the mind with itself' worked at odds with a communal drama directed to a homogeneous body of believers."[8]

The career of Tennyson moved from the private interiors of his early lyrics to the public mode of his dramas, from a poetry of personal experience to a poetry of community history. Browning's career moved the other way, in a direction more harmonious with intellectual developments: from the more public to the more private, from the realm of verifiable action to the realm of psychological interiors. It would not be true to say that Browning does not deal in public materials, in the facts of history and sociology, for indeed he does. But it is true to say that when compared with Tennyson, Browning's interests tended toward the obscure in history, toward the unfamiliar details, as in *Sordello* or even (though less so) *Paracelsus*. Browning's poetry is obscure for many readers because both his techniques and his subject matter make his world of the imagination unlike the conventional, popular notion of the "real" and the "true" world of familiar experience.

Browning's career as a dramatist helped the young poet find himself by failing to find a theatre. Still, his search for a theatre took him in directions which sometimes anticipated the important developments of drama in the nineteenth and twentieth centuries: toward the intellectual drama of Ibsen and Shaw, the psychological drama of Strindberg and O'Neill, and even the violently intimate drama of Albee. Browning's drama should not be rated alongside these, but his short dramatic career headed him in the directions which later dramatists have explored. He was, as Otten says, "consciously aware of the problem of dramatic form . . . more than any of the other poets" of his time.[9] Had Browning come late to drama, as did Tennyson, rather than in the 1830s and '40s, his experience of writing dramatic monologues and the more exciting conditions of the theatre in the '70s and '80s might have encouraged him to become one of the great English dramatists of modern times. However idle that speculation might seem to some, there is a woeful amount of evidence that suggests how unlikely it was that Browning could succeed as a dramatist during the early years of the Victorian era.

One of Browning's first opportunities to test his dramatic skills came when he met the actor William Macready in 1835. That year, Browning published *Paracelsus*. This poem in five parts was written as an experiment in the form of drama, each part representing stages of consciousness (or moods of mind) achieved during the quest by the Renaissaance scientist, Paracelsus, for knowledge and God. Each part is a sustained dialogue in which Paracelsus talks with friends about the present stage of his quest; the whole dramatic poem is about 4200 lines long. There is no action, no bodily movement, to provide the spectacle which the eye requires in drama. It is obvious from a mere sampling of *Paracelsus* that Browning's interest is in the action of imagination, of thought, of the spoken word, not in spectacle and bodily movement. Still, when Macready looked into *Paracelsus*, he predicted in his diary that Browning "can scarcely fail to be a leading spirit of his time."[10] Macready encouraged Browning to write for the stage. In 1841 he and Browning reached agreement for producing *A Blot in the 'Scutcheon*, although the play did not reach the stage until 1843.

THE EVOLUTION OF THE SOUL is a predominant theme and an important strategy of dramatic structure in both *A Blot in the 'Scutcheon* and *Pippa Passes*. The drama is especially capable of concentrating on the moment of transition for a character as it realizes a change. Most of the drama of the soul is communicated through the spoken word, with nuances of tone and connotation achieved through rhythm and imagery. When Browning adapts to the requirements of theatre to produce a drama based on spectacle, however, the violence and suddenness of transition in a character may be crude and shoddy—as in the bloodshed and sudden deaths of *A Blot in the 'Scutcheon.*

This drama presents a society in which souls are trapped like flies in a tangled web of conventions and institutional habits of behavior and belief. Donald Hair has suggested that all "tragedy, for Browning, usually involves some character who is caught in a web of circumstances from which he cannot escape."[11] Although Hair does not focus on the importance of the web imagery of *A Blot,* he has correctly identified a controlling metaphor of Browning's design. Another critic, William E. Harrold, has analyzed the imagery of entrapment in *The Ring and the Book* to show how death is a summons into "the final trap" as the last test of human potential;[12] the imagery of webs functions similarly in *A Blot* to trap characters in a last testing of their potential to grow.

Mildred and Mertoun suffer from pangs of guilt because they cannot rise above the conventions of honor that bind their lives to the rest of society. They have violated the codes that condemn their premarital love as sinful. Roma King notes the guilt of both Mildred and Mertoun, but he interprets their tragedy as not so much their fault as Tresham's.[13] All three main characters are caught up in the web of conventions, and each is as guilty or as helpless as the others. Many critics, including Hair, believe that Tresham is the one who has the most potential for growth, since he is forced to consider the limitations of his conventional scheme of values to discover that the machinery of morality has displaced the spirit it was designed to advance. It is true that Tresham's failure to realize his moral limitations early enough results in the destruction of three lives which had been bound together in a communion of love; but it is equally true that Mildred and Mertoun fail to act boldly in defiance of those moral limits to which they meekly submit until death draws them into its final trap.

The plot of the drama is developed and brought to its tragic climax by the action of Gerard, the keeper of Tresham's game preserve. He is loyal to the Tresham family name, but he is treacherous concerning the welfare of Mildred. He first saw a man coming from Mildred's apartment while he had been tracking "the stranger stag / That broke the pale" of the game preserve, but instead of a "stranger stag," Gerard found the human stranger. The motif of hunting had been introduced earlier in the dialogue of the drama by Mertoun himself when he told Tresham he had "come upon [Mildred's] wondrous beauty unawares" while wandering "carelessly / after [his] stricken game." *His* "stricken game" will be himself and his beloved. These souls are victims of the hunt, a kind

74

of institution long the prerogative of the aristocracy in a social scheme that valued sport over the human lives which suffered because of it.

When Gerard came to inform Tresham of Mildred's dishonorable behavior, he felt torn between his love for her and his duty to the family. He describes the agony of his conflict between love and duty as a result of his being caught in "a fiery net" plucking him "this way and that" (2.50–54). After Tresham has heard of Mildred's dishonor, he speaks of time as a spider that spins a shroud-like web over human lives. He vows to "rend this web, tear up, break down / The sweet and palpitating mystery" (2.201–202). When Mildred refuses to disclose the name of her lover and yet desires to accept Mertoun's hand, she does so with an overwhelming sense of guilt, which she describes as a stain needing the purgation of fire (2.221–27). Tresham is astonished, thinking Mildred is now so corrupt that she will marry Mertoun and also corrupt him. Either way Tresham turns, he is bound to make a choice between the honor of his family and the love for his sister. For if she were to reveal the name of her lover, nothing could avert the sense of dishonor Tresham would have attached to both Mertoun and Mildred, but at least there might have been some hope, as we know from the responses of Guendolen and Austin when they learn the truth. However, both Mildred and Mertoun have accepted the ethical mores of their time and place, both feel guilty for their liaison, and both hope to redeem themselves from that guilt by means of the conventional cover of marriage. But the threads of those conventions have spun a terrible and ironic web in which honor has motivated love to betray its beloved until in the end all are dead: Gerard betrays his love of Mildred; Mildred betrays her love of Mertoun by not revealing his name for the sake of his honor; and Tresham betrays Mildred for the sake of their family honor.

Dying, Mertoun confesses to Tresham that Mertoun has "entangled other lives with" his own (3.104). When he looks up to see the lamp of his love, Mertoun exclaims to Tresham that Mildred's "life is bound up in the life / That's bleeding fast away." In the bitterness of his disappointment, the dying Mertoun cries out to Mildred, asking her to join him in death. Mertoun's encounter with death has done what his commitment to love could not; it causes him to scorn the "honourable world" and all of its values as insignificant.

Mildred does indeed die, of a broken heart. She collapses without the love or the honor that had given her identity. However, she also transcends the conventions which had made up her world until now:

> As I dare approach that Heaven
> Which has not bade a living thing despair,
> Which needs no code to keep its grace from stain,

> But bids the vilest worm that turns on it
> Desist and be forgiven,—I—forgive not,
> But bless you, Thorold, from my soul of souls!   [3.331–36]

Browning will create a more persuasive character of grace in Pompilia Comparini, but here Mildred serves as the grace which takes the evolution of soul a stage further than does Mertoun, who dies with bitterness in his heart.

Tresham's spiritual growth is more intense, more dramatic, but also more ambiguous than the evolution of soul in Mildred and in Mertoun. Tresham has chosen to defend the ethical world as he understands it: he has stood for the norms of society, and he has destroyed those he cared most for. He acknowledges that "earth would be no longer earth" for him and that the "life out of all life was gone" for him. He further acknowledges that the neat little conventions of traditional life must give way to the "blind ways" to allow the birth of a new order out of the one that has led to the destruction of the human spirit. As Donald Hair has noted, "Tresham thus seems to intuit a more comprehensive moral order" than the one he has known until now, but his hope for a new order makes unlikely Hair's conclusion that "the world has become for Tresham . . . only an illusory pageant."[14] Unfortunately for his vision of a new moral order, Tresham reverts to the same concepts of social honor that formed the strands from which the spider-time spins the tangled web, trapping all the souls of this drama. The ambiguities of Tresham's character result from a confusion of judgment and responsibility which are better sorted out when Browning assigns judgment to the Pope and responsibility to Guido in *The Ring and the Book*. ·

The ambiguities and confusions present in *A Blot in the 'Scutcheon* disappear into a structure of ironies in *Pippa Passes*. The naive and innocent Pippa affects many lives and skirts many dangers of which she is ironically unaware. Pippa's is a dream of pathos, of frustrated imagination that fails to raise her own soul to new levels of consciousness. She seizes the one day when she can make her escape from her usually sorrowful, dreary existence; she makes her escape by means of what she calls her "fancy." But her fancy is uninformed; she mistakes her characters as the happiest persons in her town. Though it may be true, as Roma King suggests, that there is a progression in the kinds of love—"physical, maternal, and divine"[15]—represented by the groups of characters whom Pippa passes, Pippa herself does not go through these stages. This is clear from the last scene, where Pippa reflects upon the "drear, dark close to [her] poor day!" If Pippa is Browning's way of dramatizing the operation of the imagination, his character portrays it as a naïve and uninformed power. Pippa would be imagination made narrow by the conditions of her time and society which exploit her in such a way that she is unable to grow, only to escape for a while. One of the few critics to emphasize this point about Pippa is Roy E. Gridley, who reminds us that she "is a child-labourer: she works three hundred and sixty-four days a year in a Po Valley silk-mill."[16]

As the imagination, Pippa exists only on an aesthetic level. She strives to reach the ethical, but she is never really put in a position to make the kind of choice that will enlarge her consciousness to become ethical, much less religious. She is in the state of being which William Blake called "unorganized innocence" (in contrast to the "organized innocence" of Pompilia). Pippa exists only at a primary level of being, where the self chooses to act simply for the senses. Her life is determined by the physical world of light and dark, songs and fragrances.

We notice this feature of her character from the opening lines of the drama, in the rich sensuousness of Pippa's song to the first day of the new year. Her song is a glory of color and energy, alert to the beauties and pleasures of her world. This is an important first step in the growth of imagination. But Pippa does not have any ethical or religious sense of the place and function of this natural beauty. As Roy Gridley has noted, "the poem ends by Pippa's misreading the little she has seen of the day's events," and "the world has been revealed as much darker and more sinister than Pippa's opening paean to the dawn would imply."[17] It is true, however, that she hopes at the end of her journey that she has "touched" the people to whom she has sung: even to "do good or evil to them some slight way." To "do good *or evil* to them" makes hers a morally ambivalent, if not an amoral, position, and it lets her approach, without reaching, an ethical awareness.

Because Pippa does not grow, she seems inhuman. To appreciate her significance, we must explain her as a symbol, a metaphor, a structuring principle. She is a character in search of the drama that forms itself around her. She is a tool of vision, the art itself as practiced by Robert Browning and as defined by Sordello: to produce "deeds but not by deeds,"

> Swaying, in others, frames itself exceeds,
> Assigning them the simpler tasks it used
> To perform till Song produced
> Acts, by thoughts, only for the mind.   [5.570–75]

She is the art that "may tell a truth / Obliquely, do the thing shall breed the thought, / Nor wrong the thought, missing the mediate word" (*The Ring and the Book*, 12.859–61). Pippa is meaningful only as a medium of focus, for when we consider her as a character she suffers from arrested development.

77

The drama which forms around Pippa's aesthetic activity is designed according to a strategy of spiritual evolution from the aesthetic to the ethical sphere of existence. The artist uses Pippa to call into existence several questions of right and wrong, good and evil, in the lives of people "touched" by her passage. Sebald is called home to himself, brought face to face with what he is or has become through his life of devotion to sensual indulgence; and what he finds in himself is an abyss of chaotic blackness. He transcends the aesthetic level of desire to conceive of a realm of ethical obligation within which he has done wrong—specifically, to the sanctity of marriage; his act of self-renunciation evokes an act of charity from Ottima. Next, Jules, the sculptor, is obviously awakened in soul by Pippa's song, as he makes the ethical judgment that raises him above the aesthetic. In fact, Jules has so far transcended his previous stage of being that he can no longer accept a vocation of imitative art. He chooses to give himself to a new art as well as to his new bride, signaling the birth of an individual spirit in his life. Jules makes what comes close to a religious decision, because it is of such momentous importance to the young man, who will be abandoning the socially safe for the individually treacherous (a fact made clear by the letter which the Monsignor later receives from Jules). Browning thus balances the first scene of self-awareness achieved through the negation of marriage and duty (in Sebald) with the second one of self-awareness achieved through the affirmation of marriage and desire (in Jules).

Browning also balances the next two scenes: Luigi chooses to take a life, while the Monsignor chooses to save a life. Luigi risks the possibility of error in choosing to commit political assassination, interpreting Pippa's song as a sanction for his decision. He renounces his life of selfish indulgence and chooses to act in the name of patriotism; this is an ethical decision since it is based on his hope for a better society. He decides to act for the sake of a code, an institution (the state), not for the enlargement of his soul nor for the domestic comforts of a wife and family for himself. He is forced by his mother, who wishes he would "settle down," to weigh the ethical implications of his choice. When he makes his decision, he does so with the conviction that it is right, feeling none of the "fear and trembling" or possessing none of the hesitancy that a religious soul might. The Monsignor may come closer than any of the other characters to making a religious decision, for he is acting contrary to the way his society might expect, given an opportunity to rise above both self interest and class interest. But even he is motivated primarily by his sense of duty to his family's honor, which has been tarnished now for "century after century." The Monsignor saves Pippa for the sake of his family, while Luigi will take a life despite his family.

Most of the poems in *Men and Women* were composed between 1850 and 1854, a time when Browning's religious doubts were being tested by his wife's more fundamental Christian faith. It is not at all surprising, then, that so many of the poems, such as "Karshish," "Blougram," and "Cleon," are concerned with the "truth" of religious faith and the meaning of a life without such faith. Browning's uncertain state of mind at the time may be reflected by his different versions of *Men and Women*, the original collection for which was never reprinted in Browning's lifetime. The poems under this title were shuffled about several times until the final design was achieved in 1868.[18] *Men and Women* includes:

"Transcendentalism: A Poem in Twelve Books"
"How It Strikes a Contemporary"
"Artemis Prologizes"
"An Epistle Containing the Strange Medical Experience of Karshish, the Arab Physician"
"Johannes Agricola in Meditation"
"Pictor Ignotus"
"Fra Lippo Lippi"
"Andrea del Sarto (called 'The Faultless Painter')"
"The Bishop Orders His Tomb at Saint Praxed's Church"
"Bishop Blougram's Apology"
"Cleon"
"Rudel to the Lady of Tripoli"
"One Word More"

The strategy behind this design is to move the reader from a poem in which the poet speaks in his own voice concerning the proper mode of his art, through the eleven intervening dramatic monologues spoken by other characters, and to conclude in the poet's own voice once again with "One Word More," addressed to his wife as the fulfillment of his soul's quest throughout these thirteen poems. Within this framework are eleven characters, each reflecting various ways to pursue the goals of life. The reader is gradually led to a deepening insight into the heart of the matter, as he moves from the present time and away from the voice of the poet into the past; he moves obliquely away from the man as poet, existing for his art, to Fra Lippo Lippi as the whole man whose life is art and whose art is life; he moves from Lippi back into the present, where he hears the voice of the poet as man.

The second poem, "How It Strikes a Contemporary," provides a transition in perspective, as does "Rudel to the Lady of Tripoli," the twelfth poem. The second poem is a step beyond the first, taking us from the subjective view of the poet to an objective view of his life, as a contemporary sees it; the twelfth poem moves in the opposite direction, from the objective back into the subjective, from the medieval Troubadour Rudel's desire for a sight of the beautiful lady of Tripoli into the last poem, where Robert Browning's desires are satisfied by his love for Elizabeth Barrett. Once the first two and the last two poems are seen as structural balances, the other poems appear clearly as parts of a larger pattern within the frame.

"Artemis Prologizes" is the poem of an ancient Greek goddess, and it balances "Cleon," the poem of a humanist Greek artist whose culture gave birth to Artemis. "Karshish" is the skeptical empiricist whose encounter with spiritual mystery has left him astonished, and his poem is balanced in a dialectic of opposing truths by "Bishop Blougram's Apology," in which the skeptical empiricism of Gigadibs is met on Gigadibs's own grounds and defeated by Blougram's empirical faith. "Johannes Agricola in Meditation" is spoken by a man with such absolute faith in the grace of God to save mankind that not even works of evil may hinder salvation; this poem is balanced by "The Bishop Orders His Tomb at Saint Praxed's Church," in which a man speaks of the vanity of life while vainly acting as though the sensuous life is all that really matters. Johannes Agricola is a heretic of too much faith and the Bishop is an orthodox churchman of too little faith.

Then there is "Pictor Ignotus," the artist who retires from active encounters with the world of experience, balanced by "Andrea del Sarto," the artist who submits to the mercenary terms of a world that limits experience to selfish acquisition. Finally, at the heart of the collection is "Fra Lippo Lippi," the man who contains within himself the artistic talent of the "Pictor Ignotus" and Andrea del Sarto, who appreciates the pleasures and loveliness of this world as much as the Bishop of St. Praxed's and Cleon and who also possesses the spiritual insights of Johannes Agricola and Bishop Blougram. "Fra Lippo Lippi" is the poem Browning chose to read on 27 September 1855 to his friends—among them Tennyson, D. G. and W. M. Rossetti. It is Browning's showpiece, and it is conspicuously central to the design of the 1868 *Men and Women*, deserving extended attention.

Fra Lippo Lippi moves through various levels of spiritual existence in his argument with the night guards. His very freedom, if not his life, is at stake. He must successfully persuade the guards not to betray him to the authorities or his freedom to escape occasionally into the streets and satiate his desire for life will be lost. Lippi's situation is more critical than Park Honan assumes when he concedes that "it might even be argued that though Fra Lippo Lippi is shown in a jam—it is still not a very bad jam, at least not an unusual one for Lippo to be involved in, considering his nightly habits."[19]   The tone and direction of Lippo's monologue grow out of his sense of urgency to return to his room before his absence is discovered.   Lippo does not indicate that he has been caught before, even if nighttime adventures are his habit; the occasion is more special than Honan implies, for it is carnival season, a point much in favor of Lippo's chances for escape.

He has been trapped ever since he was born.   He was trapped by poverty into dependence upon an institution that has discouraged the fulfillment of his talent, of his soul, while putting that talent to a use which denies the very foundation of what he has experienced as reality. If the truth of the self cannot be had in a life torn between obedience to opposing authorities, opposing poles of reality, and conflicting duties, then some means of reconciliation must be found.   One way might be to escape into Pictor Ignotus's comfortable retreat and never exercise his talent of giving shape to the world of experience; or Fra Lippo Lippi might submit his talent to the uses of a world whose purposes are only aesthetic—sensuous pleasure and selfish gain—as Andrea del Sarto does. But Browning's Lippo and Blougram do what Tennyson's Becket should have done: they "diagonalize." They refuse neither the flesh with its desires nor the spirit with its duties, rejecting neither the disbelief nor the belief. For Lippo, art is the means whereby the aesthetic, the ethical, and the religious facets of life may be reconciled into an organic unity. Art is not merely aesthetic and not merely religious; it is both, while serving the ethical end of communication and communion among men.

Lippo takes his listeners toward this concept of art:

> Can't I take breath and try to add life's flash,
> And then add soul and heighten them threefold?
> Or say there's beauty with no soul at all—
> (I never saw it—put the case the same—)
> If you get simple beauty and nought else,
> You get about the best thing God invents:
> That's somewhat: and you'll find the soul you have missed,
> Within yourself, when you return him thanks.   [ll. 213–20]

Real art calls forth soul when it captures the aesthetic experience of beauty for the imagination. Lippo's argument rises toward the religious, to a vision of God in the garden of His world, creating the primal scene of ideal marriage:

> I always see the garden and God there
> A-making man's wife: and, my lesson learned,
> The value and significance of flesh
> I can't unlearn ten minutes afterwards.   [ll. 266–69]

He continues, elaborating the duty of the artist to reveal God through the beauty of experience in the world. Art, Lippo says, was given for the ethical purpose of helping one another and the religious purpose of interpreting God to all, as well as for the aesthetic purpose of giving pleasure. And so Lippo unites in himself the experience of the flesh and the vision of God.

He ends his apology, which has become a confession as well as a defense of his whole way of life, with the promise of a painting that will serve as payment for the error he has committed this night. He will paint "God in the midst, Madonna and her babe, / Ringed by a bowery, flowery angel-brood," with all the ornaments the Church wants in a religious picture, but he will also slip into the corner of his heavenly scene a picture of himself, with all his fleshly, earthly humility. Then he will be hailed by the heavenly congregation as the very means whereby they have been realized for the imagination: *"Iste perfecit opus"*—he is the one who has made the work. His promise may be taken by the watchmen as a voluntary act of penance after confession of contrition, and so they let him go. The whole force of Lippo's argument, from his appeal to the aesthetic, sensual appetites of the watchmen, through his appeal to their ethical sympathy for his lifelong plight of suffering, to his last appeal to their religious love of God, all has resulted in their allowing Lippo to escape arrest.

Lippo has, from the existential point of view, dared to commit a religious act when he slipped into the street at carnival time. He has done so because he is a creature with fleshly desires and because that is the foundation of experience for his art, but he has done so in defiance of the ethical codes of the society in which he finds himself. He does what his spirit and flesh require for fulfillment despite the ethical expectations of his time and place. And, when he successfully persuades the guards to release him, he makes them accomplices to his action. In effect, then, he has brought them also into the religious sphere of action for a purpose that transcends conventional ethics. Lippo has been forced to discover something about himself in the process of his apologia; his talk began as a rationalization and ends as a justification. His rhetoric has effected the religious experience of charity transcending justice in those very men charged with the responsibility for securing the order of society. That is a spiritual value which Browning creates from a very mundane physical fact of ethical ambiguity.

AT THE OPENING OF THE LAST BOOK of *Sordello*, a "sudden blaze" reveals to Sordello that his life has lacked direction and commitment, that it has collapsed into a series of moods without decisive action. His life has been a glittering "display" of diffuse energy, lacking the objective that gives direction—and so, form. His life is compared to the "foam-showers spilt" as ocean waves rise to their height and then collapse. Instead, he might have concentrated that energy on some formative purpose, gathered it up and hurled it "right from [his] heart, encompassing the world." His life has been "without a function." In this last book of the poem, Sordello decides that he has reached the "stage . . . to stop at." Unable through the stages of his past life to adapt his means of accomplishment to some worthwhile end, Sordello dies without having brought the value of form into his world, either through art or through government. He refused to "take that step . . . for the world's sake" which later would be taken by Dante.

The narrator of *Sordello* deplores the protagonist's failure but realizes what would have saved the Italian poet-politician:

> Ah my Sordello, I this once befriend
> And speak for you. Of a Power above you still
> Which, utterly incomprehensible,
> Is out of rivalry, which thus you can
> Love, tho' unloving all conceived by man—
> What need! And of—none the minutest duct
> To that out-nature, nought that would instruct
> And so let rivalry begin to live—
> But of a Power its representative
> Who, being for authority the same,
> Communication different, should claim
> A course, the first chose but this last revealed—
> This Human clear, as that Divine concealed—
> What utter need! [6.590–603]

Roma King finds in the speaker's "act of objective detachment" for Sordello and in Sordello's condition "an advance in his spiritual development."[20] Indeed, the speaker has accomplished, in his "act of objective detachment," precisely what Sordello should have done to save himself. To find a "Power" so "utterly incomprehensible" that it "is out of rivalry" is to reach an important stage of growth. To find in the "Human clear" a representative of that power, of "that Divine concealed" is the way to reach that stage. This is to achieve what Kierkegaard calls the life of religion.[21]

In Browning's masterpiece, *The Ring and the Book*, his major characters come to this "utter need" and find different ways to satisfy it. Pompilia achieves it through her child, Caponsacchi through Pompilia, and the Pope through Caponsacchi and Pompilia. Count Guido Franceschini mistakes the representative for the power itself; but as Guido undisguised, he approaches—if he does not actually cross—the threshold of religious insight through his despair of help from anyone except Pompilia's dead self.

In book 5 Count Guido performs magnificently behind the mask of the ethical man. Here we have a man apparently at ease with his conscience, sure in the lucidity of his self-knowledge, and oblivious to any mysteries or darknesses at work in his life. He assumes a standard of moral perfection and universal order against which he measures the lives and institutions around him; when they are found inferior to that standard, he presumes to correct and chastise them. The marriage into which he so disastrously entered promised to fulfill his life as the *telos*, or goal, of the ethical way: the marriage vow should be a sign of duty to subordinate one's self to law. The Count is the champion of the law and the order of society; duty and law become ends in themselves and their enforcement assumes the highest priorities. He shows how marriage is crucial to the support of law and order, how Pomilia betrayed her duty and Guido's honor, how the Roman court failed in its duty, how the church has degenerated, and how his own courageous action may be the beginning of a new order of things, when "the wholesome household rule" may be "in force again."

Marriage is the salvation of the aesthete since it rescues him from the despair into which he must inevitably fall; marriage saves the aesthete from himself. Guido looked to marriage when he failed in other ways of life; but marriage does not rescue Guido. He sought to use marriage to serve his own purposes, though he speaks in book 5 as though he sought to serve God and the law. In discussing the meaning of marriage, his favorite word is *duty*:

> The obligation I incurred was just
> To practise mastery, prove my mastership:—
> Pompilia's duty was—submit herself,
> Afford me pleasure, perhaps cure my bile.　　[ll. 716–19]

In his view, Guido acted properly when he intimidated Pompilia, intercepted her flight, and finally murdered her, since she had failed in her duty to him.

The Count ends his argument in book 5 with a grand prophecy of a renewed social order made possible by his lifelong defense of the law. Picturing himself as the very God whose will and law he has given his life to enforce, the Count reveals the limitations of the ethical position that gives too much authority to an absolute law or to social order both as a means and as an end in itself. In this book he is the modern man who identifies his welfare with social welfare and that, in turn, with universal order, which is his God. He is the rational man blind to the limits of reason. When the Count is forced to confront the irrational, he rationalizes and exposes the desperation of his condition, as he does in book 11.

Guido begins his second monologue with an attempt to maintain his pose as the ethical-social man. However, when his ethical posture ceases to be useful, he assumes one closer to his own image of himself, the aesthete. His reason for abandoning his ethical mask grows out of his belief that the two churchmen to whom he is speaking have been sent to elicit his confession of sin. If that is so, he reasons, then he will not only refuse to confess (and thus confirm the Pope's judgment), but he will attack the Pope and the church—even to the extent of denying religious belief of any kind. Guido's strategy is to rescue his life by losing his soul, believing that the church will not permit him to die as long as he does not confess. But his strategy backfires, for he discovers in himself an abysmal capacity for self-deception: as he argues more and more desperately for his life as the only thing worthwhile, he realizes more and more certainly the nothingness and lack of value in the life which will soon be taken from him. This monologue is a drama of an aesthetic soul discovering the inadequacies of his assumptions and plunging into a crisis of profound religious importance. Guido's strategy to save his life by refusing to confess leads him into making the confession that will save his soul.

He undertakes to show the churchmen how bestial he is, how unrepentant he is. He has sought to use all means to satisfy his lust for life's pleasures: his family name, the church, the law, and Pompilia. He calls himself "a primitive religionist" made to "stand on solid earth," desiring to glut his appetites on the goods of the earth but continuously finding the way to "life's feast" blocked or too difficult (11.1903–2010). He betrays puzzlement and bewilderment in the face of limits of his individuality. He gradually admits to discovering that "the luck that lies beyond a man" (l. 1567) becomes "the spite of fortune" (l. 1674) and that that leads to "God's hand between" himself and Pompilia (l. 1686). He has been forced to recognize what Pompilia knew, that "all human plans and projects come to nought." Because his plans collapsed, Guido blames "irrational Rome." The mystery of Pompilia's survival despite his scientific murder haunts him, driving him to exclaim that his knowledge of anatomy was "learning all in vain" and that her dying testimony turned his "plausibility to nothingness!" He is perplexed at the way the law failed to serve him: he blames loaded dice and stacked cards as tricks that have cost him his life. Even this mission of the two churchmen to his cell seems to Guido to be "just a well-intentioned trick." In his strategy to trick the tricksters, however, he falls into the existential trap.

At first he pretends to derive strength from his encounter with mystery. But then he becomes frightened when he recognizes that his posturing for evil has apparently not moved the two priests to stay his execution. He gropes for "a foothold in the sea" now that his confidence is crumbling and collapsing. At the same time, he has "gone inside [his] soul," just as the Pope thought he might.

When Guido realizes that his play-acting has not succeeded in saving his life, he exclaims:

> Sirs, have I spoken one word all this while
> Out of the world of words I had to say?
> Not one word! All was folly—I laughed and mocked!
> Sirs, my first true word, all truth and no lie,
> Is—save me notwithstanding!   [11.2417–21]

He has confessed even as he pretended not to confess, justifying the Pope's assessment. And in the end, Guido saves his soul, even as he is about to lose his life, when he admits that his life has been "all . . . folly" and all a lie. This indeed turns out to be his "first true word," and the confession will cleanse his mind, allowing him finally to perceive the means of grace that has always been available: Pompilia is the "Human clear" communicating the "Divine concealed."

Giuseppe Caponsacchi became a priest "I' the way of the world." He performed the rituals of his calling in a mechanical way ("punctual" to his "place"), and he indulged the tastes of high society ("diligent" at his "post"). He lived a divided, fragmented life, held together only by the same concept of duty which was so important to Guido. Caponsacchi tried living the life that Guido so wanted for himself and others: a life of duty, of "prescription." Pompilia learned to her sorrow that there were priests who put their duty to the church, to "prescriptions," before the welfare of individuals; when she turned to Caponsacchi, she turned less to a priest than to a "fribble and coxcomb," used to pleasing the ladies for his church and Bishop. Pompilia's appeal inspired in him an image of himself as a courtly lover, a romantic hero, who could carry her out of danger for the sake of an unselfish love. And, of course, Guido would never have begun the series of false love-letters, pretending they were written by his wife, had Caponsacchi not had the reputation for being a "fribble and coxcomb." Thus develops the glorious irony: Caponsacchi's compromising life in the church becomes the means of Pompilia's salvation.

On another level, Pompilia's role in Caponsacchi's life becomes his own salvation. She appeals to the capacity for idealistic action beneath Caponsacchi's appearance of a worldly coxcomb; she finds that same quality of awful humility which had caused him to question his rightful place in the priesthood. The church had failed to cultivate that quality in Caponsacchi; but Pompilia challenges him to betray his duty to the church for the sake of an individual soul, to risk his worldly station for nothing more than her gratitude. The church allowed Caponsacchi to compromise his conscience, but Pompilia will allow no compromise. The priest must finally choose, and his choice will be as decisive and fraught with dangers as his earlier compromise was indecisive and comfortable. Caponsacchi, quite naturally, hesitates.

Far from being the "athlete on the instant" who rushes into the arena in a "great undisguised leap" to save "the martyr-maid"—as the Pope believes him to be (10.1138–43)—Caponsacchi delays, rationalizes, even equivocates, before returning to Pompilia (and even then, he returns to prove to her that he is not afraid of the dangers, though he intends to dissuade her from her flight). In the interval of time that passes between his two meetings with Pompilia, Caponsacchi learns the true meaning of duty, the prime virtue of the ethical man. He learns his lesson from passion and devotion, and he learns the true meaning of marriage. After his night of wandering through the city, he finds himself in front of his church, which "seemed to say for the first time":

> "But am not I the Bride, the mystic love
> O' the Lamb, who took thy plighted troth, my priest,
> To fold thy warm heart on my heart of stone
> And freeze thee nor unfasten any more?
> This is a fleshly woman,—let the free
> Bestow their life-blood, thou are pulseless now!"   [6.977–82]

His church called upon him to " 'leave that live passion, come be dead with me!' " (l. 1001). But he has learned a lesson that cannot be unlearned, a living truth: "that life and death / Are means to an end, that passion uses both, / Indisputably mistress of the man / Whose form of worship is self-sacrifice" (ll. 996–99).

Caponsacchi has found his way to the true ethical stage, where he acts selflessly for another, where duty comes from the "inner necessity" which he calls "passion."[22] The ethical level is not governed by a set of abstract principles, but rather is radically concrete and immediate. Thus Caponsacchi realizes, as he tells his story, how important it was for him to learn his duty to God by doing his duty to Pompilia; the particular human crisis becomes the "Human clear" through whom Caponsacchi finds the "Divine concealed." In his passionate action for Pompilia, Caponsacchi divorces himself from the frigid abstractions of the church, and he frees himself for an honest marriage of soul to soul, the fulfillment of the ethical stage of growth.

He achieves religious insight only during the act of delivering his speech to the court. His insight has come from suffering, building toward a beautiful conclusion in his exclamation, "O great, just, good God! Miserable me!" We realize from the very beginning of his monologue that Caponsacchi is indignant, impatient, overcome, and even confused by the force of his passion. His speech is punctuated by outcries of helpless sorrow: "I left Pompilia to your watch and ward, / And now you point me—there and thus she lies!"; "Sirs, / Only seventeen!"; "Oh, they've killed her, Sirs! / Can I be calm?"

The rhythm of his monologue is determined by his rising passion, building toward the awful realization that Pompilia is dead; he stops himself short at that point and tries again to speak calmly and rationally. Caponsacchi is groping "in this sudden smoke from hell" for some truth, some reality, some value which will justify both his expense of passion and Pompilia's sacrifice of life. The ethical stage has to be transcended if Caponsacchi is to find any meaning in her death and in his love for her. The urgency of his need, the confusion of his understanding, and the power of his passion drive him toward a faith without understanding, "faith as absolute trust."[23] He draws gracefully toward the end of his speech, quietly attempting to discipline his grief, accept the worst, and prepare to cope with a world that goes on in its little ways.

The world that had meant everything to the aesthetic, coxcombic priest—the world whose ways the "warrior priest" had opposed to rescue Pompilia (whose authority the ethical man challenged to find a true motive for duty)—no longer seems to hold much meaning for Caponsacchi. He wavers for a moment, his sense of duty rises to command him for a moment, and he thinks he may have to leave the dream of life which Pompilia has inspired in him. But suddenly he realizes that to relinquish that dream would be to abandon himself to "the old solitary nothingness" which he now realizes was his life before meeting her. His encounter with that "nothingness" arouses the last passionate outcry of Giuseppe Caponsacchi: "O great, just, good God! Miserable me!" In this poignant cry, he affirms at once his absolute trust in God and his "acceptance of the worst, all the time holding to a good purpose as the end of its trial."[24] This is the religious stage of his life.

Like Count Guido in his first monologue and like Caponsacchi, Pompilia ends her monologue on the theme of marriage. Her short life has taught her a truth which Guido could not admit in his first monologue and which Caponsacchi found so painful to accept: there can be no perfection in this earthly life. The means of her discovery is marriage. The Ideal of marriage she knew very well: " 'T is duty, law, pleasure, religion" (7.154). She yielded to the requirements of her parents, her government, her church, and finally, as far as she could, she yielded to the demands of her husband. But her marriage of four years has been a "blank" and a "nothingness" at best; at worst it has been a "terrific dream." Pompilia tries thus to forget those four years of terror by interpreting all their evil as blank and nothing. In this extremity of her life, she shares with Caponsacchi a vision of life as a "nothingness" insofar as it cannot be religious. She discovered the religious possibility only after she had exhausted the resources of society to help her in her battle against evil. In her misery and despair of finding help where she had been taught to expect it, Pompilia found only herself and God (7.854–59).

At first she was passive in her helplessness. In her despair she did not desire to live, until "one vivid daybreak" in the last year of her marriage, she awoke with new resolution. During the night, she had put together the fact of a temptation to call out to Caponsacchi for help and the fact of her pregnancy. The result was hope for escape and the energy of determination: "Up I sprang alive, / Light in me, light without me, everywhere / Change!" (7.1223–25). This marked the beginning of her active rebellion against the law, the church, and her husband. Caponsacchi and her child were two lights in the darkness, "two truths" she held to amid the nothingness.

Pompilia's marriage to Guido marked the end of her first and aesthetic stage of life; the four years of marriage drove her "to choose despair," when "everything has lost its value" except death. In her despair, Pompilia learned that "the ethical is not something outside personality standing in an external relationship to it," as Guido has insisted in his first monologue, but rather the ethical life is centered on a sense of duty, "an obligation arising from an inner necessity,"[25] as Caponsacchi learned from his response to Pompilia's call. Pompilia entered into the ethical life when she discerned the "requirement," the "obligation" to save her own life from Guido; that obligation was signaled by the conception of her child. She chose as the mode of ethical action not the way of marriage (which is no longer viable for her), but the way of friendship: she found in Caponsacchi the friend who would satisfy her own ethical requirements.

Eventually, however, Pompilia witnessed the breakup of her ethical achievement by the "ambiguities of existence." The "two truths"—hope in Caponsacchi and promise in the child—were the only clear facts in her recent life, and when they were realized, she was cast into a confusion of duties that conflicted with one another. She seized upon one strong hope as the only anchor amid her confusion: she found fulfillment in an absolute trust in God. Her religious fulfillment is marked by her faith as "an act of will without any interior grasp or intuition of reality."[26] Her ability to believe in something good despite the evils of her life, to trust without certain knowledge, is in marked contrast to her husband's inability to believe.

Pompilia gropes toward an "understanding" of her past: "I see how needful now, / Of understanding somewhat of my past,— / Know life a little, I should leave so soon" (7.1664–66). What she begins to understand is that "plans and projects come to nought," and from this new understanding she is forced to consider the meaning and value of life's mysteries, of the unforeseen and unplanned conclusions of life's ways. What she knows and what she cannot explain is the mystery of love and the paradox that a good may come of an evil, that a "truth" may be found in lies and nothingness.

During her period of calm, just after she bore the child, Pompilia came to know love. She discovered, "realized," the mystery of the incarnation as the birth of love in her life, the sign of her fulfillment in God (7.1676–95). Life with its absurdities and strangeness gives way to her individual certainty in the reality of "God's birth" for her. As she prepares to "withdraw from earth and man / To [her] own soul, compose [her]self for God," Pompilia suddenly discovers another dimension in her relationship with Caponsacchi: "Here, here, I have him in his rightful place! 'T is now, when I am most upon the move, / I feel for what I verily find" (7.1774–76). Her new insight takes her toward an identification of the priest's passionate devotion for her with Christ's sacrificial Passion:

> He is a priest;
> He cannot marry therefore, which is right:
> I think he would not marry if he could.
> Marriage on earth seems such a counterfeit,
> Mere imitation of the inimitable:
> In heaven we have the real and true and sure.
> 'T is there they neither marry nor are given
> In marriage, but are as the angels: right,
> Oh how right that is, how like Jesus Christ
> To say that!   [7.1821–30]

Pompilia thus finds fulfillment through a religious identification of her experience of love, as an incarnation of God's love, with both her infant and her "one friend"; they are human manifestations of a divine grace. The mockery that men have made of marriage through "their plans and projects" has been fully revealed to, and through, Pompilia's sad and strange life. The aesthete despairingly pursues love as the erotic, the ethicist futilely pursues it as marriage, but the religious soul finds it in the paradox of self-assertion and self-sacrifice, as Pompilia found it in defiance of the law and the church as well as in her despair of any meaning in life for its own sake.

The Pope is on trial along with Guido: "As if reprieve were possible for both / Prisoner and Pope" (10.201–202). His monologue is an examination of himself and of his motives for condemning Guido. His condemnation of Guido is also a condemnation of his own church, which requires a daring of immense danger not only to the souls of "both Prisoner and Pope," but also to generations of men to come. Knowing that God will judge motives more than the consequences of judgments and actions, the Pope hesitates just long enough to "review / Intent the little seeds of act" which he will "give the world / At chink of bell and push of arrased door."

The review of Guido's marriage and eventual murder of Pompilia takes up a relatively small portion of the Pope's monologue (10.532–868). The tone of the review is confident, certain, and firm: "plain in act and life, as painted plain"; "I see"; "These letters false beyond all forgery"; "absurdly plain i' the path!"; "Such I find Guido." But when he examines and judges Guido's claim to clerical privileges, the Pope's language and tone changes. Although it is perfectly clear to him that Guido has failed in his obligation to the church, it is perfectly astonishing to him that the church has thus far failed in its religious obligation to Guido, not to speak of how it has failed Pompilia. It is in the Pope's consideration of the failure of the church, that he is most concerned: to what extent is the Pope implicated in the failure of his church, and to what extent can he act to correct those failures? These are the questions he attempts to answer in the course of discovering that "to the very end is trial in life." (10.1304).

The church allowed itself to be used for immoral purposes; certain of its members have even conspired to encourage immoral behavior. For truth and good to assert themselves, the church boundaries had to be breached. Is the church really serving God or only the world and therefore "the arch-tempter"? There was a time when men like Euripides could live ethically courageous lives without benefit of the church's armor (10.1670–1790); and in this time, men like Count Guido Franceschini can live beastly, cowardly lives behind the protective cover of the church. What is the value of the church, of Christianity even, if these facts are true? "How should I answer this Euripides?" who questions the presumption of Christianity to judge pagans like himself, the Pope asks (l. 1791).

The Pope's answer is a religious one; in presenting it, the Pope achieves the religious stage of his own soul's growth. The simplest answer is that one can make the kinds of judgments made by Christianity of such virtuous pagans as Euripides because theirs was not a religious devotion, only an ethical determination. But the Pope does not offer a simple, abstract answer, giving instead an existential answer. He makes a religious decision when he decides to condemn a man claiming clerical privilege in order to save that man's soul—at the cost of his earthly life. The Pope also makes a religious decision when he dares to chastise his church which has allowed such a man thus to use it. And the motive that the Pope discovers behind his own decisions is what makes this action religious: the motive is absolute faith in God—"I have light nor fear of the dark at all" (10.1660).

If Guido's soul can be saved, it must be through "surprise and fear" (10.1180) or, as Kierkegaard put it, "with fear and trembling." And it is with a special kind of fear and trembling that the Pope approaches his discovery of faith as the motive for his judgment. We may first notice hints of that fear and trembling early in the monologue: "Have I to dare?" (l. 13); "my uncertain hand," (l. 165); "dare perchance / Put fancies for a comfort" (ll. 198–99). And, in the middle, when he speaks of Caponsacchi's "chastisement," he defines his own duty this way: "The penalty I nowise dare relax." But the most revealing language for understanding the Pope's state of mind as he draws toward his conclusion is the language of fear. Early on the Pope asserts that he can make his judgment of Guido with no hesitation and no doubt that it is the right one: "Therefore I stand on my integrity, / Nor fear at all" (ll. 276–77). Yet later, he shows signs of fear:

> Whence, then, this quite new quick cold thrill,—cloud-like,
> This keen dread creeping from a quarter scarce
> Suspected in the skies I nightly scan?
> What slacks the tense nerve, saps the wound-up spring
> Of the act that should and shall be, sends the mount
> And the mass o' the whole man's-strength,—conglobed so late—
> Shudderingly into dust, a moment's work?   [10.1253–59]

The Pope feels this way as an existential manifestation of his fear, the natural consequence of his decision to act as he thinks he must "whatever prove the peril of mistake." He asks himself, "shall I too lack courage?— leave / I, too, the post of me, like those I blame?" And then, dramatically, he exclaims, "But this does overwhelm me with surprise, / Touch me to terror" (10.1440–41).

The fear has grown as he has methodically analyzed the church's role in this sordid affair. If even the men of the church choose, and choose with zest, the things of the flesh over the things of the spirit, then what is left to prevent the Guidos from always having their way? The answer is the one that the Pope gives, with the fear that makes his decision an act of courage and daring: execute Guido, pull away the prop of the church, and therefore chastise the church for allowing itself to be a cover for evil. The action may stir doubts about the church in the minds of the people, and that increase in doubt may usher in a new age of spiritual darkness.[27] But the Pope dares to think that the darkness is what is needed. His fear is that he may help to initiate a darkness that plunges men back into despair. But the risk is necessary to save the church from confusing spiritual light with natural light. He hopes to contribute to a dimming of the kind of unquestioning faith that misleads the Guidos into thinking that whatever is done in the name of the church is also right and good.

The answer to Euripides, then, is to return to the sunrise of Christianity, when men acted, as the Pope here acts, out of a passionate conviction of faith, not out of blind restraint or enlightened self-interest. It is necessary to learn again to distinguish the ethical from the religious, so that means are not mistaken for ends. If the Pope's decision to condemn Guido can plunge Guido into the spiritual crisis of darkness illuminated by God's grace, perhaps the Pope can shake away the religious parasites of his time (clinging to a church which no longer aids but obstructs spiritual grace) and plunge the whole era into a consciousness of the darkness against which the light must shine. Here would be his own contribution to the "gloriously-decisive change" which he has sought in the seemingly insignificant events of this Roman murder case.

He imagines the spokesman of "culture" and "civilization" interrupting him as he raises his arm to strike Guido down; he hears a warning of the chaos to come unless Guido is let live. The plea for culture and civilization as dependent on Guido's acquittal climaxes the Pope's determination to do what he can to "break up" this "faith in the report" (belief in the letter of the Bible), to reshape this society held together by the "report" rather than the "thing" itself (the spirit of the Bible). Challenged thus to risk the welfare of a society propped up by the likes of Guido Franceschini and the Aretine Archbishop, the Pope feels his spirit quicken as he writes out his command for Guido's execution. In this last stage in "the trial of [his] soul," he has dared to choose for God over society and the church. And he has answered, by his action, these questions:

> At this stage is the trial of my soul
> Danger to face, or danger to refuse?
> Shall I dare try the doubt now, or not dare?
> [10.1305–1307]

The four principal figures in Browning's Roman murder story reveal by their lives, or rather by their new understandings of their lives, that

"Life's business [is] just the terrible choice" which comes somewhere during the trial of the soul (10.1233). The Count chose to murder Pompilia for the sake of social order, to restore "the wholesome household rule in force again." The priest Caponsacchi chose to divorce himself from his lifeless church to save Pompilia and learn the lesson that "priests should study passion." Pompilia chose to save her life and therefore died; her experiential knowledge that "marriage on earth seems such a counterfeit" allowed her the vision of a true marriage only in religious fulfillment. The Pope is appalled at his church's inadequacy in the modern world, and so he condemns Guido, hoping to bring back some of the darkness of doubt to a man and to an age when it is so difficult to discern "the gloriously-decisive change" that manifests religious growth. Finally, Guido uncovers the darkness in himself, exclaims as he approaches death that "Morality and religion conquer [him]," and learns the spiritual value of that conquest. Behind the strategy of rhetoric devised by each speaker is the strategy of the poet: Browning shows how his characters resolve their conflicts of sense and soul, of desire and duty, through submission to the forces which make them parts of a larger pattern, the design of the artist who imitates the design of the human universe.

"Fifine at the Fair" is a disturbingly beautiful, complex poem. It is a convenient poem to conclude with because it deals so frankly with the aesthetic limits of marriage as a means for reconciling duty with desire, ethical obligation with aesthetic yearning. It is a disturbing poem because it exposes the nothingness which underlies aesthetic, sensuous existence, because it shows the fundamental instability of human relationships, and because it lays bare the utter need of something permanent for human belief. The means which Browning employs to render these disturbances result in a design of experience which has baffled many of his readers, even some who were predisposed to charity.

J. Hillis Miller says that Browning's poems are based upon "profound organic rhythms of selfhood," "the pulsation of passion," the "rhythmic alternation," and "a struggle of irreconcilable forces."[28] His notion of rhythm as struggle is appropriate for describing the structure of "Fifine at the Fair." Don Juan is the man caught between opposing poles of value. As different readers have recognized, Don Juan is a mask for many meanings: the sensual casuist; the guilt-ridden Robert Browning; the anonymous monologuist; the evolving soul of any man. Whatever category he most easily fits, Don Juan is a force demanding attention, like the red pennon which compels his own attention. That pennon so "frenetic to be free" is not only a significant image for the heart of Don Juan, it is also an admirable image for the structure of the poem itself: driven by the wind toward something outside its reach, yet held fast to the pole which gives it a central hold upon a circle of form always in danger of collapsing with every drop of the breeze.

As Don Juan says many times, Elvire is his spiritual center and Fifine is but one of many fleshly forms toward which he is constantly fluttering. Restless as the pennon, Don Juan is constantly on the move throughout the poem. He walks with Elvire along the beach late in the afternoon after they have been to visit the fair, and while they walk he explains to her why he is attracted to the Fifines of the world. After we have heard him out, we realize that the poem has begun *in medias res*, and what began as a rationalization for his behavior has quickly become a confession and a justification for all human life. We learn that Don Juan had been out walking late enough the evening before to see the arrival of the gypsy caravan, that he was up early enough to see their tents raised in the morning, that he went swimming in the bay later in the morning, that he played Schumann's "Carnival" after his swim, that he fell asleep while playing the piano and dreamed of carnivals and other things, and then he took Elvire to the fair. But the poem is not constructed along this simple chronology; it is about Don Juan's *fear*—not about his amorous adventures.

Still trying to explain to Elvire why Fifine is important to him as a means of proving to himself that he is a truth amid so much falsity, Don Juan suddenly notices the fog and darkness of evening:

> How quickly night comes! Lo, already 't is the land
> Turns sea-like; overcrept by grey, the plains expand,
> Assume significance; while ocean dwindles, shrinks
> Into a pettier bound: its plash and plaint, methinks,
> Six steps away, how both retire, as if their part
> Were played, another force were free to prove her art,
> Protagonist in turn! Are you unterrified?
> All false, all fleeting too! And nowhere things abide,
> And everywhere we strain that things should stay,—the one
> Truth, that ourselves are true!   [ll. 1462–71]

No wonder Don Juan is terrified, for his surroundings are collapsing again, just as they had in his dream. He is baring his soul, with all its fears and hopes. He is alone in a mist of shapelessness, and to survive with dignity he must forever practice swimming, become skillful at it, master his environment by mastering himself: like the swimmer who pretends the liquid medium is "solid-seeming" in order to move through it at will. The man who expects to find truth in a world of foam and seeming must be an amphibian: capable of swimming out and back to his island of

95

security. Nothing is possible, however, if a person does not master himself, believe in his own self, practice his own skills of perception, and define himself in an otherwise indefinite existence.

There is a terror at the heart of Don Juan's insight: that all of reality is like the ocean in which he alone is swimming, that he exists only as a thin layer of consciousness floating upon the surface of a profound nothingness. It is no wonder that he needs Elvire to return to. But can Elvire understand why he must swim out in search of the Fifines, or why he must swim out at all? She is his static center, his axis of repose, his island of security—the wife, the home, the defense of civilization. What Don Juan tries to tell her is that she is only one end of his being. He would cease to exist if he locked himself inside her comfortable house and stayed away from the sea.

Browning makes us realize that such a retreat for Don Juan is death to the imagination, just as swimming forever is not only terrifying but a surrender through exhaustion to elemental formlessness. As Don Juan moves along the beach, he moves between the town and fair, between Elvire and Fifine, and between the land and the sea—between, in essence, his duty and his desire. Browning has placed this man within the same boundaries as Fra Lippo Lippi, who also had to move between the carnival and the domestic prison and who also had to learn to become an amphibian to maintain his identity with dignity. These two characters are Browning's versions of successful "diagonalizing" during an era of conflicting claims and collapsing truths. And there is, or should be, no shame in this strategy, for it keeps afloat the possibility of a new flight into meaning, a fresh thrust into fulfillment.

Don Juan chooses the fair and Fifine at the end of his monologue, though the epilogue shows us that he will die a householder, exhausted, "savage," and almost in "despair." He welcomes death as an end of his weariness, although his Spirit-Wife seems to promise a new beginning: "Love is all and Death is nought!" The line, however, does hint at the possibility that only in life where there is love can there be any reality, because in death there is only nothingness. But the epilogue is puzzling ultimately because the end of life is puzzling to the living.

"Fifine at the Fair" is Browning's boast of intellectual and imaginative energy; it is his boast of a creative desire choosing to swim in passion rather than to dry out in dutiful old age. He has given us in this character of Don Juan a wonderful poem of pure desire, the poem which Kierkegaard's aesthete could not find when he analyzed Mozart's *Don Giovanni*. Browning's Don Juan is, in Kierkegaard's terms, the "intensive," the "reflective" Don Juan who contemplates his experience rather than enjoying it in its immediacy, as does Don Giovanni. Kierkegaard's aesthete is well qualified to analyze this greatest of the world's aesthetes, and what Kiekergaard's persona can tell us about Don Juan is that he is "desire, the energy of sensuous desire," that he "does not have stable existence at all, but he hurries in a perpetual vanishing." What the aesthete hears in the "musical Don Juan" is "the whole infinitude of passion, . . . its infinite power which nothing can withstand."[29] Browning takes us into the mind of that energy and passion of desire to know it as it knows itself—restless with hunger and nervous with fear of the indefinite.

Browning thrusts upon his reader the mask of life, made to order for a self-reflective age. Behind this mask we may act out our desires, flaunt our flesh, and affirm the utility of our passions. Don Juan is Browning's dare, and to wear his mask is to risk religious failure just as much as religious affirmation, however strange that might ring in Victorian ears. Browning catches up in this poem all the motifs of his grand career: rhetoric of indirection, careful self-scrutiny, and masks to mirror social concerns while concealing personal convictions. But here he concentrates in the single character of Don Juan all the brilliance of his other monologuists, the evil with the good, the complex with the simple, and the cynical with the credible. Don Juan rises to a consciousness of himself which transcends the limits of the flesh without betraying the claims of the flesh: he is, as Kierkegaard says of Mozart's character, *desire as desiring*,[30]—that is, desire conscious of itself as desire.

This dimension of a human being is frightening for others to behold as well as for a person to discover in himself. Browning may be showing us something of his own capacious imagination in this character, but he is also showing us a potential in ourselves which has been bridled and disciplined and domesticated into a tame enough creature. It is no wonder that this poem unsettled and disturbed its Victorian readers, and so it disturbs its readers still today. That is its virtue, that it can continue to disturb. When a woman, like Pompilia, finds that marriage (which is supposed to rescue desire from despair and lift it into the refined discipline of duty to another) is, after all, a cheat and only "a counterfeit," then we are properly sympathetic. But when a man, Don Juan, finds the social bonds upon his aesthetic desires unacceptable because those bonds imprison his imagination, stultify his intelligence, and diminish his identity, he evokes our hostility. He wants and needs both the freedom of desire and the security of duty, but we want him to choose one or the other, to define himself more clearly for us, because he is a threat to order and comfort in our world of accommodation with time and nature: he would show us what lies outside the pale of the household.

Browning's Don Juan is as much a threat to civilization as is Mozart's Don Giovanni, but Browning's character is a peculiarly modern version of the intellectual, rather than the sensuous, threat. Both are threats of disorder and pure desire, which if left completely free would devour all peace and stability and collapse all structures into the dark chaos of ego as pure desire. Don Juan must be caged, tamed, and housebroken or all civilization will collapse into nothingness. He pays (we pay) a price of limited freedom for a structure of temporary civilization, and he incurs (we incur) a debt of conscience, of desire turned inwards to gnaw at its own incompleteness. Such is the "discontent" of civilization, as Freud explained it,[31] and no wonder Browning's Don Juan disturbs.

Discontents, then, must be tamed, like Don Juan; they must be translated, like Pompilia; arrested, like Caponsacchi; purchased, like Fra Lippo Lippi; destroyed, like Guido Franceschini; or they may bring primitive darkness to pall our civilized enlightenment, as described in the Pope's monologue. Browning's people of energy are like Freud's characterizations of the libido; not only expression but also discipline is needed for the sake of life. Dis-ease is a consequence, but also a condition, of the social order. Duty to another is uneasily balanced with desire turned in upon itself.

4
Arnold and Clough

The careers of Matthew Arnold and Arthur Clough have a certain completeness, even a logic, although each would probably smile with incredulity to hear it said. Their lives are deserving of one of Arnold's favorite epithets, "adequate," and their poetry shows us that each "created a style equal to his need."[1] Each spoke with a voice of moderation, urbane humor, and cultivated good sense in a time filled with shouting and vulgarity. Their lives were adequate for their time, for their society, and for themselves, because they evolved a wholeness out of early personal experiences of intellectual and spiritual fragmentation. In the life and work of Arnold and of Clough are to be found "a resiliency and toughness and an integrity"[2] which allowed both to make "intellectual activity dramatic" in their art.[3] Their poetry testifies to the need for an ease of spirit, but they employed different strategies for supplying that ease of tension between the poles of public duty and private desires, "between [the] innate sense of vocation as a poet, on the one hand, and, on the other hand, [the] ethical sense of duty as a Victorian citizen."[4]

Arnold discovered that he could not write the poetry that he thought was necessary for his time, and so he tried to create conditions which would make possible the kind of poetry he desired—the kind he found exemplified in the age of Pericles: a poetry of restrained joy, when poetry and religion were identical. In his inaugural lecture from the Poetry Chair at Oxford, Arnold said that "an intellectual deliverance is the peculiar demand of those ages which are called modern . . . [and] the literature of ancient Greece is, even for modern times, a mighty agent of intellectual deliverance." He observed that "in the age of Pericles we have . . . a highly-developed, a modern, a deeply interesting epoch. . . . Now, the peculiar characteristic of the highest literature—the poetry—of the fifth century in Greece before the Christian era, is its adequacy." The

99

highest literature ought to be "adequate" to the needs of its time; it should represent "human nature developed in a number of directions, politically, socially, religiously, morally."[5]

Arnold recognized that the modern artist particularly needed a myth, what he called "an Idea of the World," so that the "multitudinousness" of the world would not overwhelm him.[6] One may submit to the complexities of modern life and risk the fragmentation of his energies in contradictory activities (and risk as well a paralysis of imagination—as Arnold felt Clough was in danger of doing), or one may withdraw into an isolation of self away from the world of ideas and actions (as he believed Wordsworth did). The challenge to poetry is therefore something larger than aesthetic—it is psychological, spiritual, and metaphysical. Poetry was for Arnold a strategy, an idea, for confronting the multitudinousness of life. During the 1840s and '50s, he discovered the difficulty of that task: he had to confront certain fears and desires within himself before he could meet the world as a poet. During those two decades he was shoring up the fragments of his life by writing poems, making designs in language which would adequately represent his own and others' human nature "in a number of directions." J. Hillis Miller, who states the case for Arnold's despair at trying to find himself through poetry, has described Arnold's career as a struggle "to rescue himself and his readers from 'the bewildering confusion of our times' by writing poetry which would be like the poetry of Homer or those other lucky bards who lived near the sources of time."[7]

IN THE POEMS which he published in 1849 under the title *The Strayed Reveller* Arnold pursues a main theme of "quiet work" as a means of reconciling the opposing values of duty and desire. In the sonnet "Quiet Work," he suggests that Nature can teach "one lesson of two duties": the duty of "toil" and the duty of "tranquillity." The making of these into "one" is the task of Arnold's poems, as he believes it should be the ethos of his era. He is often uncertain of himself, of his ability to learn well this lesson of Nature. He knows his duties, but he also feels the power of "two desires": "One drives him to the world without / And one to solitude" ("Stanzas in Memory of the Author of 'Obermann,'" ll. 95–96). In "Quiet Work" the speaker hopes to learn the lesson of unity, but in the later work of "Stanzas in Memory of the Author of 'Obermann,'" the speaker resigns himself to a fractured being, a divided consciousness. Underlying these poems we may hear the same "groundtone / Of human agony" which Arnold heard "through the hum of torrent lone" in the pages of *Obermann*. Arnold's "feverish blood" tosses him about between "two duties" and "two desires."

His usual resolution of his protagonists' feverish divisiveness is to stop their movement, withdraw them from life's activities, quiet their excitement, and teach them the lesson of "resignation," of "quiet work." These lessons are taught in such seriously sober ways that usually we cannot take them ironically, as perhaps they should be. If there were not the note of "agony" and anxiety humming through nearly all the lines of these poems, the postures of repose and listless withdrawal would be tolerable only as ironic commentaries on the silly business of Victorian self-importance. "The Strayed Reveller" is a perplexing poem because it seems to celebrate the withdrawal of the reveller from his revels, but it also acknowledges that the reveller has, after, all, "strayed." The poem shows the situation of a young protagonist lured from his pleasant, unselfconscious existence amid natural and human activity into a languorous, dreamy, inhuman artificiality. It reminds us of Tennyson's "Palace of Art" and "The Lotos-Eaters," but "The Strayed Reveller" does not strike out for the Tennysonian resolution; Arnold's poem leaves its protagonist drooping in the palace of art, situated between the man of action (Ulysses) and the woman of sensual dreams (Circe). The "young, languid eyed" boy with the "white, delicate neck" contrasts strongly with the "spare, dark-featured, / Quick-eyed" Ulysses. Arnold chooses to make his languid boy the center of our focus, suggesting through the presence of both Ulysses and Circe that the virtues of toil and tranquillity are harmonized here.

Across his entire poetic landscape move several couples who suggest these twin values of work and quiet, as Ulysses and Circe seem to do in "The Strayed Reveller." Along with Ulysses, Arnold thinks of Hercules, Haemon, Fausta, Margaret, Goethe, Marguerite, Iseult of Brittany, and Clough as persons of "action," persons with commitments to life and labor; paired with them, he thinks of Circe, the new Sirens, Antigone, the Merman, Wordsworth, Iseult of Ireland, and the "poet" Arnold as persons resigned to or desiring lives of quiet, though determined, detachment. Arnold's poems, as distinguished from the poet or speaker in them, are usually expressions of sympathetic regard for the claims of both values in any pair. Unfortunately, the total effect of these poems is one of indecisiveness, uncertainty, and listlessness. Arnold cannot make up his mind or he cannot apply the lesson of nature to the practice of his art. However much he desires to unify the twin duties or to reconcile the twin desires, he can only hold them in suspended animation while he attends to their respective claims. His speakers or his protagonists are like the strayed reveller, passive beneath the spell of visions, drained of energy,

101

but questioning and even pleading at times. These are poems of obvious anxiety, and they are devices for preserving the self from hopelessness and despair.

"The Forsaken Merman" is one of the most satisfying of Arnold's early poems because it keeps under control the various conflicting emotions common to his work. It is one of the few poems in this early collection which suggests that marriage may reconcile the opposing claims of duty and desire. In an earlier poem called "The New Sirens" there is a scene of "divorce" when "scores of true love knots are breaking," when "heart quits heart and hand quits hand" (ll. 261–64) during an "unlovely dawning" of cold truth; in a "Fragment of an 'Antigone,'" Haemon is bitter that Antigone has chosen cold death rather than passionate life with him; and in "A Modern Sappho," the speaker resigns herself to a patient wait for truth and for the time to bring her lover finally into marriage with her.

In "The Forsaken Merman," Arnold has positioned his usually tranquil speaker on the margins of his habitual world of comfortable retreat, drawn by the desire to find his wife who has left him for a life of action. Margaret's action seems trivial, but its importance is suggested by her work of spinning—she is involved in the "whizzing wheel" and she "sings her fill." When the wheel stops, she looks longingly out to the sea where her children live, but she remains at her task, fixed in her resolve to work and pray. The Merman has utterly no desire to join her on land, though *she* obviously feels the strong lure of the ocean depths to rejoin her strangely beautiful family. This is one of the attractive features of the poem, that its words are put into the mouth of the aesthetic visionary, forced to consider a life alien to his own temperament; he is incomplete, needing Margaret, but he will not or cannot translate himself into workaday terms.

There can be no permanent resolution of the two worlds represented by the Merman and Margaret; she may bear children, create living forms in the depths of tranquil beauty, but she cannot reside there with them forever. Their's is a sorrowful existence because their duties will keep them divided from their desires. She has twin desires, and twin duties, but the Merman does not; he has no duty to the land, to action, and he has no desire for anything but Margaret. She, on the other hand, is torn; indeed, she has a kind of courage to sacrifice one desire and duty for another. The Merman cannot see the truth in her situation, which is so much more complex than his own. But Arnold can, and so should his readers. The Merman is like Wordsworth, who could keep a "quiet home" because his "eyes avert their ken / From half of human fate." But Arnold has done a witty thing by forcing the Merman to leave his quiet home and wander along the restless beaches, longing for a renewal of his connection with human vitality. The marriage of the Merman and his Margaret has been fruitful, though it was doomed to divorce.

There is no question of marriage in "Resignation," but this poem, like "The Forsaken Merman," is one of Arnold's best and so deserves more comment than others of the 1849 volume that have similar themes. The speaker here draws from a concrete and immediate presence the lessons which nature has to teach someone like Fausta, "time's chafing prisoner." The speaker is Arnold's "poet," one who sees widely enough to know that "This world in which we draw our breath, / In some sense . . . outlasts death" (ll. 229–30). Fausta is not the speaker's wife; she may be his sister, but she is certainly his companion of many years. They have trod this path together before, at a time when they had a leader who could "make clear [their] goal" and take them to it; now they have no leader. She is alone with an aspiration to be about the world's business of progress and improvement, and he is alone with nature, cautiously lending his voice to its hills, streams, rocks, and sky.

Arnold is neither of these persons, any more than he is Wordsworth or Clough, the Merman or Margaret. He is both the speaker and the audience, both the poet and Fausta. The gypsies represent for him a life of unselfconscious freedom from spiritual anxiety, though they are prisoners of time and fleshly mutability. The lost leader, probably Arnold's own father, was a master of himself and of time, but he is dead. The speaker may counsel withdrawal and quiet observation while leaning on a rustic gate, casual and apparently without care (like the strayed reveller of this volume or like the scholar-gypsy of a later date), but at the same time this speaker will never lure Fausta away from her commitments to involvement any more than he will be able to separate himself permanently either from her or from his memory of the past, when he marched "many a mile of dusty way" to bathe his "hands with speechless glee, . . . in the wide-glimmering sea" (ll. 80, 84–85). He knows and feels that past, quite as much as Margaret does her life with the Merman; but he must play the role of the Merman and let Fausta do the part of Margaret. Imitating Wordsworth, Arnold has hit upon the perfect-imperfect marriage, brother united-with / divided-from sister: they can never be totally at one, but neither can they ever be totally divided.

To withdraw, to renounce, to resign, to sit, loll, or drift—all are postures, or strategies, of self-control in a world that seems frenzied, emphatic, acquisitive, aggressive, and busy. Clearly Arnold and his speakers who counsel such a strategy do so because they wish for more of life, not less: they desire the integrity of the self and the fulfillment of being, which seem not to be available to anyone who chooses to throw himself headlong into the stream of time and so lose himself to the divisive current of opinion. One of the 1849 poems that does a fine job of realizing this virtue of patient desire for fulfillment is "A Modern Sappho." Arnold's speaker here is a woman standing alone, leaning against a "cold balustrade," waiting for a sight of her beloved who will come soon upon the river which she sees in the scene below her. A modern Sappho will be patient in her passion, let nature work its quiet will, and submit herself to its processes. She seems to loll, to lean carelessly, to be indifferent, but she is burning with passion, controlling it with a will made strong by the hope that patience is a force of nature. She may suffer, but her suffering will be rewarded with a fulfillment of her love. Her beloved only seems to be strong, determined, and forceful in his love for someone else; but in reality he is drifting with time and will eventually be fatigued by it. Then he will break his bonds of passion and look "languidly round on a gloom-buried world" where she will join him.

The modern Sappho is, despite her wisdom of patience, a sinister figure among the characters who parade through Arnold's 1849 poems. She combines the features of the new Sirens, Circe, the Nature of "Quiet Work," and the poet-speaker of "Resignation"; but she speaks of her lover as a victim rather than a partner. In fact, with some little exaggeration of faint suggestions in the poem, we might imagine her as a spider-like character, waiting patiently for her prey. Her anxious heart is sensitive to movement; "nothing stirs on the lawn"; she will suffer while she waits, but he "will be brought" to her in a passive, dejected state, even a bloodless, "languid" state of helpless dependence upon her; she will move toward him from out of the shadowy gloom, where he will be waiting for her possession. Arnold's Nature of "quiet work" exacts a high price for tranquillity, maybe even life itself. The artist in Arnold knows this and refuses to let the "quiet" take total possession of his poems, though he must make room for it to preserve a cool dignity and grace for dusty, care-worn travelers who have lost their way to the wide-glimmering sea. Arnold's preserve of art tries to keep in balance the quiet nature and the work of man, but he must always be wary of the danger that quiet tends to deathly cold and work tends to heated frenzy.

"Stanzas in Memory of the Author of 'Obermann'" acknowledges the rupture of the worlds containing values that have been held together so tentatively by couples such as Ulysses and Circe, Margaret and the Merman, and Fausta with her poet-companion. This poem is a tribute to the memory of an artist who practiced the code of Matthew Arnold's speaker in "Resignation," but it is also a signal of the speaker's intention to follow a different course than the one represented by Obermann. What precisely that course is we may not know, but we do know what it is not. This poem is a form of "hail and farewell" in which Arnold releases himself from a bondage quite as strong as any made by time, the bondage of listlessness. The speaker is active, though he acknowledges the importance of the life chosen by Obermann. Whereas the divided aims of life were called "two duties" in "Quiet Work," they are here called "two desires"; the emphasis on desire rather than duty helps to create conviction and affirmation in this poem. Whereas most of the poems in *The Strayed Reveller* imply or state clearly the preference for stoical withdrawal at the price of a certain passivity, "Stanzas in Memory of the Author of 'Obermann'" and others like it in the 1852 volume, entitled *Empedocles on Etna*, introduce more emphatic choices, more vigorous commitments, and more decisive confrontations. Desire and duty may remain divided, but the issues are clearer and action is just as possible in the realm of desire as it is in the realm of duty.

When the speaker ends his lines on Obermann, he bids farewell not only to Obermann and the life Obermann represented, but also to the "unstrung will," "the broken heart." Kenneth Allott writes in his note on this concluding stanza that "it is his own 'unstrung will' and 'broken heart' as much as Obermann's that A[rnold] is dismissing. . . . The lines are A.'s farewell to youth, insouciance and Marguerite—and also, in the long run, to the writing of poetry."[8] Critics all too often hasten Arnold's demise as a poet, finding (as Allott does here) earlier and earlier signs of Arnold's farewell to poetry. But from the beginning of his career, Arnold's poems are often about the lack of inspiration for poetry both in his life and in the life of his era. There is evidence in this poem as in several others of the 1852 volume that Arnold's speaker is dismissing the mode of life that heightens the consciousness of divided wills and broken hearts. Like Tennyson's speaker in *Maud*, Arnold's speaker tries in poems like these "Stanzas in Memory of the Author of 'Obermann'" to give himself to his own deepest nature, to lose himself in an action that will free his buried self, bringing it into harmony with fate, history, even nature. By choosing to "leave / Half of [his] life with" Obermann, the protagonist makes a commitment to *be*, even if his choice narrows the scope of his life. Whatever of his life is left to him will at least be genuine and less fractured. The "fate" that "drives" him is no less than the real or buried self, establishing its authority over his consciousness.

Arnold's Marguerite poems continue his experiment with choosing. These poems show how the self begins its journey in search of identity when it is plunged into a crisis of self-examination by a disappointed love affair. Marguerite and Obermann represent ways of life which the speaker must consider for himself and finally reject to be free for other more fulfilling possibilities. When he meets Marguerite on the strand separating a lake from a town, he springs to embrace her, and he is checked by a voice of mysterious origin. This scene and action of the poem called "Meeting" captures in cameo the experience of the Switzerland poems, and it employs symbolic imagery common to Arnold's poetry: the man caught on an isthmus, on a beach, on a line of division between the attraction of the town and society (i.e., culture and civilization) and the lure of the lake, representing the profound quiet work of nature. Caught between these two attractions, the tension is broken by the experience of human love, acting as the catalyst to force a decision upon the man. He chooses, and that act awakens the forces which have until then been held in a balance of opposition. If he chooses the love of the girl, a commitment to a life of passion and fleshly entanglement, he is reminded of the life of calm retirement he will give up. Or, if he chooses the town, he will give up the lake; he would, in choosing the town, be choosing society with its manners over nature with its depth of feeling. The experience of love awakens his awareness of the necessity to choose, and that stirs depths of feeling.

Arnold's Switzerland poems, like the stanzas on Obermann, announce a freedom of the spirit. Freedom from the entanglements of a passion is as important as freedom from the prejudices of a mountain hermit, though both are desires of the heart. Most important in these poems is the speaker's discovery of what he comes to call a "buried self," which the speaker cannot know until he is forced to choose between his duty and his desire. In "Meeting," the "tremendous voice" of "a God" and the "guiding Powers who join and part" are manifestations of this insight that he has suddenly discovered in his own unconscious, or buried, self; it restrains him from making a choice that would be fatal to the fullest development of his life. The "tremendous voice" and "guiding Powers" may also be ways of naming what Arnold in the 1840s was calling by the sometimes disparaging name of "Zeit Geist," or "Time-Spirit," a force he feared might be hostile to his buried self. In this poem, the ambiguous identity of the "guiding Powers," like the "fate" in the stanzas on Obermann, constitutes a problem for Arnold's speakers who are trying to determine if the Time-Spirit helps or hinders the discovery of the true self.

About the time he composed "Meeting," Arnold wrote to Clough expressing his refusal to allow himself to be "sucked for an hour even into the Time Stream in which [so many Englishmen] plunge and bellow," preferring to withdraw into a refuge of the imagination and nature against the "Zeit Geist."[9] Arnold feared that the *Zeitgeist* ("the spirit of the time") inhibits an honest expression of the self, and much of his poetry admonished retreat from contact with the *Zeitgeist* of the modern world. However, by 1873, in *Literature and Dogma*, he refers to the *Zeitgeist* as the power which led him to a correct "notion" of the "history of the human mind"; indeed, by 1873, the *Zeitgeist* in Arnold's poetry is equivalent to the unconscious power in the self, to the complex of institutional forces making up history, and to the "Eternal not-our-selves" which is God.[10] In the context of the 1860s and '70s, Arnold congratulates himself (with some irony) for having reached correct notions by having been tossed about in the winds of time, rather than having developed a systematic dogma of any kind.

In other words, the *Zeitgeist* is a term Arnold uses to describe the essence of things, whether it be the psyche or God, the imagination or reason, which works to fulfill the potential of all being. Learning to submit to its authority is quite as painful for Arnold's seekers as it was for Milton's Adam to learn the lessons of obedience to God or, in an even more appropriate comparison, for Virgil's Aeneas to learn to do the will of Jupiter. When Nautes consoles Aeneas for the loss of some of his ships, he tells him that "we master fortune by fully accepting it" (5.710), but Aeneas typically is disturbed and anxious.[11] Aeneas must give up his past before he can become a servant of providence, and that is no easy task. Arnold's speakers are not so grand as Aeneas or Adam, but they must suffer the same trials without the advantages of a Nautes or a Raphael to explain things and guide them. They have only nature to instruct them, and she is silent in her working.

Arnold's psychological myth of the "buried life" is most fully worked out in the poem by that title, and it is done so in the imagery of cavern-like "deep recesses of our breast" through which flows "the unregarded river of our life." This "unregarded river," it turns out, is really in control of our life's direction even when we seem most at the mercy of chance. The poet is thankful that this is so, and his discovery is an important step along the way to some accommodation with the *Zeitgeist*. Usually the self lies buried beneath manners and appearances, drowned out by the "din of strife"; but sometimes there is a revelation of the true self, evoked especially by the experience of love. Such a revelation acts as a summons. However brief or even problematic, it lays the basis for believing that one can give himself to his time—to his culture, to his *Zeitgeist*—and still not lose himself. Or, perhaps more accurately, one may be unable to resist the call or the tendency of his time and still be himself and not what others choose to make of him.

"The Buried Life" elaborates what "A Farewell" hoped for: a fulfillment of the self regardless of the choice which seems to deny a particular mode of life. The joy of discovering the buried self, with its calm and harmony beneath the surface appearance of frenzy and fragmentation, is the object of Arnold's quest, and he will search for ways to release that self more easily, with less pain, and with more constancy. One possible way to accomplish that kind of release is through the harmonizing power of art, and specifically of poetry. Another way is through a reshaping of the "Time-Spirit" itself, so that the buried self is more frequenty evoked than covered or concealed. To those tasks Arnold turns, first in his own poetry, then in an examination of the value and limits of poetry, and finally in the society which embodies the "Time-Spirit."

As JOHN P. FARRELL HAS SAID of Empedocles, "we hear him rail at both sophistry and superstition."[12] Empedocles tries to teach Pausanias not to be a slave to superstition, not to be bound by fanciful conceptions of the metaphysical and supernatural shape of the world. One should not look to heaven or to hell for help or to lay blame for the way things are; one must look within himself and temper his desires and his will to fit the conditions of nature and history, over which he has little control. Within those limitations, if they are accepted and not resisted, man may find joy—but it is a joy which comes only through restraint of will and desire. In the second act of the poetic drama, Empedocles cannot practice all that he teaches Pausanias: Empedocles is near despair because he cannot accommodate his life to the conditions of his time. He considers the great difference between the present time and the time when he was young. Just before he leaps to his death, he remembers the days of his youth as a time when "outward things were [not] closed and dead" to him, when thoughts flowed freely in a "delightful commerce of the world." But now, when (as Pausanias had remarked to Callicles in act 1) "broils tear us in twain"—that is, when broils between superstitious fools and cynical aesthetes are the order of the day—it is not possible to receive "the shock of mighty thoughts / On simple minds with a pure natural joy." And so, in his intellectual loneliness, Empedocles destroys himself while he still has some remnant of the poised consciousness which once was his.

Here then is the plight of a man who attempts to live a life of the mind in the nineteenth century. Such a person cannot feel a part of the community of men, who are torn in their squabbles over dogma and beliefs, either religious or scientific: such men cannot live loosely in feeling and thought; they cannot be disinterested, taking life as it is, knowing it as it is in itself rather than as they wish or fear it to be. Men of the present era cannot feel a "pure natural joy" in discovering "the shock of mighty thoughts" because they have preconceived notions of the way things should be; and when conditions do not conform, such men recoil in fright, anger, and bitterness. This is, of course, what Empedocles had taught Pausanias earlier, but Empedocles has not been able to adjust to the new, "sophisticated" way of things. The difference, Walter Houghton suggests, between the Empedocles of act 1 and the Empedocles of act 2 is the difference between "thought" and "feeling," thus dramatizing not only a split in sensibility but also a division between duty and desire which can be resolved only in death.[13] Empedocles represents not only one who tries to live a life of the mind: in his life's conclusion, he represents the doom of the intellectual life as it once was known, when thought and feeling were unified in simplicity and "natural joy," when there was an identity of public duty with private desire.

Callicles hopes to "cure," to "tend," to "soothe" Empedocles, and Pausanias encourages Callicles to use his art to help Empedocles through his time of distress. But Callicles's singing does not cure Empedocles, not even with the help of the "sweet night." Neither art nor nature is able to rescue the ideal of the past from fragmentation. When Callicles is first heard singing, he is telling the story of Chiron teaching the young Achilles "of the Gods, the stars, / The tides," telling him of the heroes and of Elysium, their resting place. Empedocles corrects the myth of Callicles while he instructs Pausanias: to believe in Gods and Elysium leads not to heroic action, as Callicles's song implies, but rather to further discontent with the way things are and so contributes to suffering rather than alleviating it. Callicles next sings of the beautiful country of Greece, far away and long ago, when Cadmus, the founder of Thebes, and his wife Harmonia were transformed into serpents and thereby "wholly for[got] their first sad life, and home, / And all that Theban woe" (2.2.458–59). As a complement to Callicles's earlier song about Chiron teaching Achilles, this one implies that the only relief from heroic suffering is through a descent from consciousness, from the very condition which defines humanity, to become not heroes, lolling with reward in Elysium, but serpents that "stray / For ever through the glens, placid and dumb."

In his third song, Callicles recites a story concerning the very mountain they are climbing. Etna lies atop the groaning Typho, a rebel against Zeus, and now Typho is being punished for his rebellion. Callicles presents the groans as nearly drowning the "sweet notes whose lulling spell / Gods and the race of mortals love so well." Empedocles comments that Callicles "fables, yet speaks truth." To Empedocles the groans of Typho represent his own "plainness oppressed by cunning," his own greatness weighed down by the "littleness" of life "united" to "become invincible." Again, the poetry of Callicles does little to relieve Emped-

109

ocles of his sorrow. Instead, the song aggravates his sorrow and leads Empedocles a little closer to his suicide. He throws aside the emblems of his kingly office in protest against the inadequacy of mortal authority to deal with justice in a world where "great qualities are trodden down" by "littleness united."

The final song of Callicles recounts the tragic music contest between Marsyas and the young Apollo. After the defeat of Marsyas, Apollo orders Marsyas to be flayed alive for his presumptuous challenge. It is a song of the defeat of one kind of music by another, the defeat of the pastoral simplicity of Marsyas with his flute by the sophisticated Apollo with his lyre. It is also a story of the moral limits of poetry, when Apollo can haughtily watch "in proud repose" while Marsyas is flayed and while Marsyas's friend, the young Olympos, stands "weeping at his master's end." For Empedocles this is another example of the defeat of simplicity and the victory of sophistication, the destruction of lovely, humane desires and the triumph of cold, dutiful abstractions. Alan Roper has concluded that "a Calliclean poetry, charming though it may be in its descriptions, inspiriting though it may be in its accounts of heroic life, is now irrelevant to the life of all those small men in towns, troubled by fear and contentiousness."[14] "Calliclean poetry" is "now irrelevant," but Empedocles does not seem to be even charmed, much less inspirited, by Callicles's poetry. Arnold's poem (along with his withdrawal of it) shows there is no modern poetry that is "relevant." Empedocles throws aside his sign of poetry: "And lie thou there, / My laurel bough! / Scornful Apollo's ensign, lie thou there!" (2.191–93). He laments the difficulty of retaining the power of the poet and, at the same time, participating in the community of men. One cannot keep "delightful commerce [with] the world" and be a poet too.

For the man of mind and heart, poetry deepens the pain of life rather than relieving it. Poetry does not seem to unite the self with society, but rather it drives the two further apart. And so in 1853, Arnold makes a gesture as symbolic as *Empedocles* itself. He removes the poem from his new edition, explaining his reasons for doing so in his Preface. *Empedocles on Etna* does not provide joy; it only pictures the loss of the capacity to feel joy. Empedocles in the poem expresses his hope that by giving himself back to the elements, he may purge his spirit and recover his capacity to feel joy again or annihilate the consciousness which has enslaved his feelings throughout this life. He is under no illusion that he has found the ultimate solution, but he knows that life is intolerable under the present conditions, when words and conflicts obscure the true self that lies hidden deep within. His plunge into Etna is a daring risk, undertaken in the hope that he is plunging into the recesses of his own

110

being. He thinks that the mind, which may survive death, may be forced to return to "go through the sad probation all again":

> To see if we will poise our life at last,
> To see if we will now at last be true
> To our own only true, deep-buried selves,
> Being one with which we are one with the whole world.
> [2.368–72]

TRISTRAM, LIKE EMPEDOCLES, withdraws from the world of broils and frenzied activity, but he is dying when we hear him speaking at the opening of Arnold's poem. The death of Tristram, joined with the death of Iseult of Ireland, are symbolic equivalents of Empedocles's leap into Etna: all are making an absolute resignation from the turmoils and emptiness of modern life. But *Tristram and Iseult* is a poem of magic, dreams, visions, longing, and anxiety. As a poem of magic, it suggests that desire is like a magic potion, binding two people together in "fatal bands / Of a love they dare not name." Tristram is bound to Iseult of Ireland; and in the story of Merlin and Vivian, a magic spell forever fixes Merlin (with all his wisdom) in his passion of unfulfilled desire for Vivian, who is "passing weary of his love." Dreams are strategies for escaping the "gradual furnace of the world" and for finding careless happiness: Tristram dreams of former happiness, of his green world of freedom in love with Iseult of Ireland; and his children by Iseult of Brittany dream of worlds more fair and more innocent than any imaginable to the narrator. Visions possess Tristram as he lies dying, but they did so no less while he was living. He sought to escape his aching desire for Iseult of Ireland by his marriage with Iseult of Brittany, and when that failed to bring him relief, he rushed into battles with Arthur and the Knights of the Round Table—but in the midst of battle, he could see only his beloved Iseult of Ireland, "her form glid[ing] through the crossing spears."

The magic of desire may enslave the soul, but the sacrifices to duty cannot bring freedom; they may only relieve the anguish, in battles for higher causes or in marriage for higher loves. There is no final release for the soul distressed by its passionate desires—except in death or in art. Arnold's poem presents itself as a variously shaped drama becoming a narrative, in which the chief actors become the subjects of stories well told. Tristram's two desires—love for the dark-haired Iseult of Ireland and love for the timid, innocent Iseult of Brittany—are not only irreconcilable *in* marriage but are impossible *because* of marriage. One of his desires is consummated in death, as he and Iseult of Ireland are transformed by death into marble-like forms of beauty. The other desire is consummated in the lives of his children by Iseult of Brittany; but also

111

that desire is transformed after his death into the stories she tells her children, specifically the story of Merlin and Vivian. Tristram's desires are therefore productive in several directions at once: frozen in graceful beauty by death; continued in innocent life by his children; and continued in graceful beauty by the narrative art. The sad drama of his divided life becomes a mysterious tale of enchantment, a tale capable of entertaining both Iseult and her children, of lifting them from their ordinary selves—the carelessness of childhood and the care-fullness of adulthood.

Arnold's strategy here is to transport the reader from the dramatic moment of Tristram's langorous death, through his reunion with Iseult of Ireland, beyond their funereal climax, and into the magic world of Merlin and Vivian. The action of Arnold's own imagination takes the reader from the fleshly entanglements of life with its heated visions of unfulfilled desire to cool worlds of moonlit dreams and children's innocent sleep, from the dreams of part 1 to the art of part 2 and finally to the myth of part 3. Implied in the structure of the poem is a metaphorical ladder of ascent from the world of fleshly turmoil that is resolved only in dreams of frustrated men and inexperienced children. Out of that mire of experience and inexperience, life climbs dialectically to a resolution in death, captured in climax at the expense of passion lost; this is witnessed by the passive hunter in the tapestry moved by cold winter winds. But that cold art of passivity is elevated to the active narration of part 3, in which Vivian's pale hand is scratched by the brambles of an artificial tree and Merlin is kept alive by his passion, forever in a trance. Arnold shows how art is a narrative of forms, from dreams and visions to painting and poetry; he shows how life is a formless matter that begins to take on form in dreams and visions, threatens to freeze into the form of art, but is rescued by the power of myth. Art is the action which makes a unity of divided desires, though art does so through a question mark—what is most real is what is fictive. The boldness of such a suggestion is the very element that makes *Tristram and Iseult* "one of Arnold's most adventurous and original poems," as Stange has described it.[15]

The questions raised about the relationship between art and reality in such poems as *Empedocles on Etna* and *Tristram and Iseult* are continued in many of Arnold's other poems, including "The Youth of Nature" and "The Youth of Man." Taken together, these two poems raise the question of reality in terms of the relationship of man and nature, a theme common to the poetry of Wordsworth. Mourning Wordsworth's death, the speaker of "The Youth of Nature" wonders if it is nature or the poet who fills us with joy in its beauty, grace, charm, and romance. Noting the silence of a moonlit evening, he hears a murmur of Nature, reproving him for thinking that a singer may be greater than his themes, that a poet may be greater than the nature of which he sings. Nature mockingly inquires if an artist can recapture "the figure, the bloom of thy love, / As she was in her morning of spring?" Men may not even know one another, themselves, or their mates; how can they know Nature, know its secret of being, know its utter loneliness? In describing itself as "the mateless, the one" which no man can know, however much he may "scan" or "read," Nature is asserting its uttermost inhumanity of being; Arnold is implying that the capacity for uniting with a mate, for marrying and fulfilling oneself in another through love, that this capacity is what distinguishes a human being, raising it above a creature of nature. Nature, whose enduring unity is a triumph over the mortality of humanity, is so alien to human consciousness that its unity should not be envied, or else those who do seek to identify with it will doom themselves to loneliness and perhaps even to eccentric inhumanity.

In "The Youth of Man," Arnold juxtaposes in an ironic setting an aged couple looking out over a scene of natural youth (a scene with associations from their own youth and a landscape over which move their children); they are contrasted in their present mundanity with their youthful enthusiasm. Their lives have been worn away by the eroding power of time, leaving them languid and weary. They may not have been able to retain their youthful halo, but they have acquired in age what they could not appreciate in youth: the calm of Nature. Ironically, youths, proud of their energy and activity, are further from Nature than this aged couple with its tranquillity of resignation. The price of learning that Nature is, after all, *something* is to believe that existence is *nothing*: this revelation comes from a couple who had asserted when young that "Nature is nothing." When they look into their past lives together, the narrator imagines them looking "for a moment" upon "their faded, ignoble lives" as though they had lived in a "desert / In its weary, unprofitable length." But no man can believe that human existence is nothing and that Nature is the only true something. The speaker of this poem is a fool to believe that youth should "yearn to the greatness of Nature," for it can only mock man with its silent loneliness. The passage most alive with feeling and warmth is the one beginning, "Here they stand to-night" (l. 61), which describes the aged couple looking out over the human landscape of the present, with its perfumed evening, children playing on the lawns, and "far off, a glory of day" that "still plays on the city spires." If the speaker ignores the virtues of this human couple and rejects their moderated happiness as faded ignobility, he does so at the risk of freezing himself into an unfeeling quietist.

113

"The Scholar-Gipsy" also practices the art of juxtaposition, holding out a hope of poise which Arnold, with good reason, did not think was evident in *Empedocles*. The poise is in the balance achieved by the narrator, who looks back to the example of the Scholar-Gipsy (sometimes glimpsing him moving through the countryside of a simple life) and yet remains part of this present life, not fully sharing in the spontaneity and joy of the past. This poem embodies both the restraint and the joy which Arnold yearned to find in art: a restraint of duty accepting the conditions of his own time, and a joy of desire envisioning the more simple conditions of the past. For the speaker, the value of the Scholar-Gipsy is not so much learning a secret of gypsies or even finding heavenly inspiration as it is his ability to live with such simplicity, relaxation, and easy accommodation to his environment *while* waiting for "the spark from heaven." The Scholar-Gipsy had what his title represents: a balance between the distinterested curiosity of the scholar and the spontaneity of the gypsy. Such a balance is missing in the modern sensibility, though perhaps not entirely absent in the speaker of this poem; he unites in himself the world of the countryside and the world of thought—something of the pastoral and the urbane, the work and the quiet.

The poet-speaker preserves the past in the present, the ideal of harmony in the conditions of disharmony, even as he advises the Scholar-Gipsy to flee from contact with the poet's own age. There is, then, a delicate balance in this poem. The balance is genuine because the speaker is relaxed in expectation, uniting within himself a vision of harmony with an awareness of disharmony, but the balance is also tenuous because the poem's conclusion suggests a fading of the vision, a breakdown of the trust in adequate communication between self and society, between ideal and actual or between the past and the present. Breakdowns of trust and inadequate communication are thematic concerns which Arnold takes up again in *Balder Dead* and, later, in *Merope*, where they are synonymous with the breakup of families.

LIONEL TRILLING DOES NOT EXPLAIN why he thinks *Balder Dead* is "more poignant" than "Mycerinus," even though he goes on to say that *Balder Dead* "laments the passing of spring and of the gods with a more immediate and personal emotion."[16] It is perhaps the "helpless plaint" of the poem, a tone it shares with *Sohrab and Rustum*, that Trilling admires. Austere resignation in the face of doom is an estimable quality of Arnold's poetry, and this seems to be the quality Trilling most admires. Surely, however, it is not the dreary business of Odin and his bloody crew, with their silly games and monotonous fighting, that evokes the "immediate and personal emotion" of *Balder Dead*; nor is it the tedious affair of Hermod's journey across strange terrains to enter the land of the dead. The aspect of this poem we most admire is that which is the least Nordic, that which is at least Homeric or Virgilian and, more to the point, that which is the most Victorian—namely, the relationship of Balder with his wife, Nanna.

Clyde de L. Ryals has probably explained as well as can be the reason for the dreariness of "heaven" in this poem, for Valhalla is a picture of mid nineteenth-century culture "at the point of decay."[17] But Ryals does not bring into focus the particular reason why Balder can be content, if not happy, in "hell." As Ryals says, "We note the change in Balder's speeches" between his first and second meetings with Hermod; and again, Ryals says later that "he now has Nanna with him," but Ryals does not make enough of this fact. It would not quite fit Ryals's argument to acknowledge the importance of the domestic virtue in marriage, for that is a particularly *Victorian* quality as we popularly imagine it. If Valhalla is "the decadent society" that Arnold criticized in his England, it is so only insofar as its divine heroes do not more fully incorporate the virtues of their women, their wives, into their own working lives. What two of Balder's mourners most lament is his power to console them for the loss of their spouses. Balder himself will not rest in hell until his wife joins him there. If—again, as Ryals suggests—Balder is the poet who "sought to revivify the decadent society of Valhalla" (p. 76), it is particularly in this single respect that he kept alive Freya's hope of recovering her husband, Oder, and that he filled Regner with "yearning joy" for his wife and children.

Balder, as poet, sang of domestic happiness, and Balder, dead, is happy in his domesticity. Odin, in a touch of unintentional irony, says that "what the dead desire" is "to burn" (1.45), and so he directs preparations for the funeral that will send the burning ship out to sea, carrying the corpses of Balder, Nanna, and Hoder; what the dead desire (as Odin says at another place) is something more than annihilation or even the sympathy of grief (3.51–52). When Odin throws "his golden ring" upon the corpses of Balder and Nanna, he is marrying them in death. This is not, as Kenneth Allott has said in his note, a "pointless" detail (p. 371). When Balder gives Hermod his ring as a "memorial," he is not particularly asking Odin to remember him (2.275); rather, he is summoning Nanna to join him in death; sending the ring back to Odin is a gesture of divorce and remarriage.

As a divine hero, we know Balder not at all; as a poet, only slightly (and to that extent he reminds us of Empedocles); but as a husband, we know him very well (and as a dying, or dead, husband, he reminds us of

Arnold's Tristram). He is, as a ghost appearing in his wife's "dream" most solicitous for her comfort, anxious that Nanna might join him in a death as painless as his own has probably been (1.268–342). This episode is a long invention by Arnold in imitation not only of Patroklos's ghost appearing to Achilles, but also of Creusa appearing to Aeneas. Both Nanna and Balder desire to be reunited and not to "prolong" the wife's existence beyond her husband's death. It is not only Nanna's "desire" that she die, but it is "right" (1.312–13). In other words, it is her "duty" (a thing that is "right") to join her husband in death. Balder's ghost warns Nanna that "Hela's mouldering realm" is a "dim world" over which Hela presides "with austere control." This may not seem very inviting to us, but for Arnold the idea of "austere control" is a positive virtue, especially when contrasted with the absence of control in Valhalla, where things are running amuck. In addition to the virtue of control, Hela's realm will offer Balder and Nanna the solace of one another's company without interference from the competitive frenzy of Valhalla's senseless games.

Arnold emphasizes the attractiveness of Hela's realm in at least two more passages, both at the end of the poem. After the success of Lok's trick to prevent Balder's return from the dead (something that doesn't much bother Balder), Hermod again journeys into Hela's kingdom, where he encounters the spirit of Hoder, who tells Hermod that Balder has left his place next to Hela in order to be with Nanna:

> Nanna came
> Lately below, and joined him; and the pair
> Frequent the still recesses of the realm
> Of Hela, and hold converse undisturbed.   [3.433–36]

Balder greets Hermod in a much different tone than he had earlier:

> 'mourn not for me, Hermod, when thou sitt'st
> In Heaven, nor let the other Gods lament,
> As wholly to be pitied, quite forlorn.
> For Nanna hath rejoined me, who, of old,
> In Heaven, was seldom parted from my side;
> And still the acceptance follows me, which crowned
> My former life, and cheers me even here.'   [3.456–62]

Balder much prefers this situation to the one he has left behind in Heaven: " 'I am long since weary of your storm / Of carnage, and find, Hermod, in your life / Something too much of war and broils" (3.503–505). Hermod yearns for the disappearing trio of Balder, Nanna, and Hoder:

Fain had he followed their receding steps,
Though they to death were bound, and he to Heaven,

. . . .

So Hermod gazed, and yearned to join his kin.
At last he sighed, and set forth back to Heaven.
[3.556–57, 565–66]

This is Arnoldian irony with a vengeance, with a touch of Virgilian melancholy. For Hermod returns to the world of us all, bearing with him a vision, an image, of a happy—or at least contented—pair. Balder and Nanna are better off in their realm of the dead than are Dido and her husband, whose departing ghosts Aeneas observes with pain. Hermod returns to do his duty, divided from his desire to "join his kin." If Matthew Arnold is to be found in his poem, like Hermod, he is divided from the austere gloom of domestic felicity as an ideal of harmony forever behind him, but resigned to "set forth back to Heaven" to join the world of his life, even if he does so with a sigh.

The notion of domestic felicity as a lost ideal in the world of the living is the central concern of Arnold's second completed poetic drama, *Merope*. The main characters of this play stumble their ways through a classical scene of broken families and of a mother torn between her loyalty to the past and her hope for the future. When Polyphontes repeats his desire to marry Merope, he is establishing a main point of the drama: that marriage in this situation will establish a harmony of opposing forces, a harmony which has not prevailed since the assassination of Cresphontes. He hopes for a "union cemented for this nation's weal" (1. 103), a "union . . . based on pure public welfare" (ll. 1717–18). Polyphontes advances a notion which makes marriage a metaphor of the rational imagination, uniting his own stern action with Merope's affectionate contemplation. But, typically for Arnold, this proposal of marriage is doomed to an ironic, if not a tragic, frustration and failure. Polyphontes hopes to forget himself in union with Merope, inviting her to sacrifice with him "the bent / of personal feeling to the public weal" (ll. 1711–12). But Merope cannot do that because she does not know what the public weal is. She is sympathetic to his argument for peace and unity, but she is unable to reconcile his means with his ends, and she certainly is unable to reconcile her desire for revenge with his offer of marriage as a public duty.

Her son Aepytus has no problems of this sort, being self-confident and filled with self-righteousness. Merope makes one dramatic effort, and the action turns out to be so ironic that we feel astonishment at the twists of fate. In hoping for Aepytus's return from his exile, Merope hopes for the return of a son, not an avenger; she yearns for the fulfillment of her heart, not for the satisfaction of her anger. To Polyphontes, she has appeared cold and distant, but this has been her defense against his patient appeal; she tells Aepytus later that she has learned to respect Polyphontes for his self-control and civility. When she first hears the hint that her son may have been murdered, she gives way to terror and confusion (ll. 932–33). If Aepytus, her last connection with the happy past, is dead, then she will be doomed to utter loneliness; and just as terrifying to her is the realization that she alone would have to avenge the murders of her family. She feels she must do it, but she thinks she cannot. And she is not certain if she would be right to do so. Giving herself to her anger and disappointment when she thinks Aepytus is dead, she resists the temptation to "fade away," to die without doing a foul deed—an act that would provoke the rebuke of the dishonored dead and would ignore her duty to the past. She feels herself lost in a "rushing, thundering, mad, / Cloud-enveloped, obscure, / Unapplauded, unsung / Race of calamity" (ll. 1104–1108). When she moves through this obscure moral haze, she decides to strike a blow that will unite her duty to her family and her desire for vengeance; but she would have killed the very son whose supposed death has prompted this decisive action.

The act is too terrible, too mockingly absurd. Arnold's choice of action and character betrays his own ironic view of life. Merope echoes Empedocles in her imaginative capacity to sympathize with others, and like Empedocles, Merope is more often paralyzed than liberated by her sympathetic imagination. It is fortunate that she does not resolve to act upon her carefully examined motives more often. The character of Polyphontes is like that of Pausanias, committed to prudent action of a pragmatic kind. And Aepytus is single-minded: he is passionate for action without regard to the consequences. Merope finds herself surrounded by men of action—she is sister to one, mother to another, and courted for marriage by a third. She sympathizes with all and imagines the best and worst motives for all, but she can hardly reconcile them within herself and she certainly cannot bring harmony among them. She cannot triumph over the death of Polyphontes because she finds "worth" as well as "badness" in him (l. 1990), and she cannot triumph in the victory of her son because his way was the "slippery way of blood" (l. 1464). She hopes that in his rule, Aepytus will unite the virtue of his "father's passion for this people's ease" (l. 2000) with the virtue of Polyphontes's sternness of authority, and so be loved as well as obeyed by his people (ll. 2005–2009). She imagines for Aepytus a reign of "twofold color" (l. 1994), echoing Arnold's imaginings of two desires and two duties in his previous poems. Merope herself, however, like so many of Arnold's characters, is caught between her two desires—her past, now dead, and her future, born in this chaos. The world of this play remains a bleakly ironic one, however much Arnold aimed for a mutually acceptable compromise and reconciliation.

BY 1861, WHEN HIS FRIEND CLOUGH DIED, undistinguished and worn out in spirit as well as in body, Arnold had established himself as a critic of society and a leader in education. During the five years between the death of Clough and the composition of the elegy, Arnold was working in both his roles as inspector of schools and professor of poetry. The course he chose to follow when he gave up Marguerite and when he rejected *Empedocles on Etna* proved to be the correct one for releasing his buried self. On the other hand, the course his friend Clough chose to follow—railing against his time and abandoning the ideal of the past to plunge directly into the eddying stream of the *Zeitgeist*—proved to be the death of him and of his efforts.[18] Consequently when Arnold lamented the death of his friend, he used the occasion to examine the two ways of life. He examined his own life in the context of deploring his friend's untimely death.

"Thyrsis" opens with an observation of the changes which have occurred since the speaker last visited the Oxford countryside. Impressed by the many changes in the man-made world, the speaker anxiously hopes that nature has left something stable and unchanged for him to cling to. He interposes a note of personal appeal for some acknowledgment of his identity, for some sign that the past yet remains to recognize and be recognized by him. The loss of his old companion has aroused and sharpened his sense of mutability and change. The death of that companion has become the occasion for examining himself and his own past to find evidence of something that endures.

Arnold laments the fact that his friend submitted his art to the harsh world; instead, he should have waited out the storms as Arnold himself has done. Now his friend is dead, and the times are not as encouraging for poetry as they once were, when the Greek poet Moschus moved the Underworld with his music of lamentation and when Proserpine herself "loved the Dorian pipe, the Dorian strain." But the present time, so deaf and so discouraging, does not hear the artist at all: "Well! wind-dispersed and vain the words will be." This line marks a turning-point in the poem (l. 101), for here the poet decides to create his art even if the words be "wind-dispersed and vain." And he will continue his quest even though everything seems to have changed. This resolution to endure change and indifference paradoxically generates the discovery of the ideal, symbolized in the signal-elm. The refusal to yield to obstacles, to give way to the demands of the time, is the very principle that has supported Matthew Arnold as well as the pastoral poet of this poem.

In Arnold's view, Clough was swept away by the hurry of modern life, his art disintegrated along with his spirit, and he could be heard again speaking only in whispers from the peace of the grave. Either the *Zeitgeist* will wear away the spirit of those who oppose it (as with Clough), or the *Zeitgeist* must be met on different terms. Arnold chose to meet it on new terms, not to harangue it, but sweetly to modify it, to make it conscious of its limitations and thereby soften it, to quiet it to hear the harmonizing voice of poetry. Through his message of criticism and culture, Arnold hoped to redirect the *Zeitgeist* to encourage creativity and fulfillment of a kind which he believed had escaped Arthur Clough.

Clough was someone with whom Arnold had always to struggle, whom Arnold had to wrestle to overcome and put at a distance from himself. Several years after Clough's death, Arnold still felt he "was somewhat too near." The "right distance" was at some further remove than Arnold was able to achieve, though he tried all his life to get that distance. Clough was probably always a reminder of Arnold's own father, the man whose "apostrophes to duty" kept the young Arnold anxious about his own worthiness. Both Clough and Thomas Arnold were men who presented Matthew Arnold with the "spectacle of a writer striving evidently to get breast with reality." Such a spectacle posed a profound threat of insecurity to the young and uncertain observer, for in such a spectacle could be seen a Jacob wrestling with the angel of God, a Samson resisting the will of Jehovah, or an Aeneas agonizing over the providence of Jupiter.[19]

Arnold could not wear, nor had the desire to wear, the costumes of Jacob, Samson, or Aeneas. He declared that "we deteriorate in spite of our struggles," that he could not give himself to the dark and inscrutable ways of God, that he must find a "distinct seeing of [his] way as far as his own nature is concerned." Clough was his inscrutable adversary, and no wonder Clough remained "one of the few people who ever made a deep impression upon" Matthew Arnold. When Arnold entered the arena to wrestle with Clough, or with the spirit of Clough, Arnold knew he was up against a powerful adversary—a friend misled by the contrary winds of mere opinion. To strive with Clough was to wrestle with reality itself—and Arnold never shirked an encounter with reality.[20]

Writing to or about Clough kept Arnold in touch with reality—a reality he otherwise might have rejected. Clough represented the world of hurry, of passionate activity, and of idealistic endeavor which Arnold suspected of meaninglessness. But Clough was a creation of Arnold's imagination as much as was Ulysses in "The Strayed Reveller" or Pausanias in *Empedocles on Etna* or even Thyrsis as Clough "himself." Whoever or whatever Arthur Clough really was, to Matthew Arnold he was a force of truth and duty to whom Arnold had to cling in order to keep a hold upon "genuineness" and so keep himself from the "languor of spirit, and fickleness and insincerity" that he otherwise would have fallen into. Clough retained for Arnold "the duty of doing all [he could] to keep alive [his] courage and activity."[21]

The "courage and activity" Arnold needed were important in an "Uninvigorating atmosphere of the decline of the Empire"; for in such a period of time, he felt himself "three parts iced over" and tempted to withdraw into an "intellectual seclusion" from which Clough's spirit rescued him with a "salutary effect." Certainly there was much insecurity in Arnold's spiritual challenge to Clough—from 1847, when Clough's "precision and force" seemed to "put [Arnold] quite wrong," making him feel that he did "not really know that [he thought] so," to 1848, when Arnold felt he had to retreat into himself against the *Zeitgeist* of Clough and the "confused multitudinousness" of Browning and Keats, to 1849, when Arnold felt driven "so strongly into [him]self," a "not altogether comfortable state." But 1849 was a crucial year for this contest between Arnold and Clough: in that year, Arnold found himself. Driven "strongly" into himself, he refused to be either a fanatic or "chaff blown in the wind" as he suspected Clough might be.[22]

In 1849 Arnold set himself against these "damned times" when "everything is against one"; he dealt in his art with "the spread of luxury" in such poems as "The Strayed Reveller," later with "our physical enervation" in *Tristram and Iseult*, with "our own selves" in the Switzerland poems, and with the "sickening consciousness of our difficulties" in *Empedocles on Etna*. To Arnold, Clough represented the voice of these "damned times." Whoever the real Clough was, for Arnold he was, without doubt, a crucial and important force. Arnold "clung" to him, felt "attracted" to him, was "linked" with him, and retained memory of him as "one of the few people who ever made a deep impression upon" him. But from that close attachment there arose the strength of a separate identity for Arnold, so much so that he could condescend to teach his friend the important lesson of "conformity" (since it "frees us from the unnatural and unhealthy attitude of contradiction and opposition") and pragmatic accommodation (since it frees one from "the mental harass of an uncertain life," which "must be far more irksome than the ennui of the most monotonous employment").[23]

While it is important to remember that Arthur Clough was a character of Matthew Arnold's imagination (whether in Arnold's letters or in his poetry), it is equally important to remember that Arnold is one of the best critics of Arthur Clough's poetry. For even if Arnold was "somewhat too near" the person of Clough, he had probably "just the right distance" from the poetry—with sympathetic good taste. And so Arnold reminds us that Clough's poetry has "precision and force," that it is "powerful" and "invigorating." He pays Clough the high tribute of comparison with Homer: "That in him of which I think oftenest is the Homeric simplicity of his literary life." Clough deserved such comparison because "he possessed these two invaluable literary qualities,—a true sense for his object of study, and a single-hearted care for it."[24]

On his side of the relationship, Arthur Clough was sometimes relieved not to have to set the pace for the younger Matthew Arnold. Clough once wrote of his relief to be free for a while from Arnold's company, because when "Mat is here, I am painfully coerced to my work by the assurance that should I relax in the least my yoke fellow would at once come to a dead stop."[25] Clough often worried over the apparent frittering of Arnold's talents, while Arnold was impatient with Clough's sober idealism for social and moral reforms. It is ironic that Arnold became the spokesman for culture and criticism, the more "successful" man of letters, of literary and educational reform, while his older "yoke fellow" appeared to be a "failure" in poetry and in life. Both assessments have undergone considerable modification by critics in this century, but especially the appraisal of Clough. He can now be examined in his own right—perhaps even more clearly than Arnold, whose authority has become something of a weight and burden for some critics.

Clough's decision to give up his post as tutor at Oxford, his difficulty in finding gainful employment, his domestication, and his early death were all taken at the time as evidence that he had fallen victim to the relentless Time-Spirit with its power of cumulative trivialities. But we can now see that Clough was a fine artist, recording with delicacy and tactful humor the tragic pettiness of modern life and the occasional triumphs of modesty still possible for the spirit bent on keeping its balance. Clough the artist no longer needs any defense, but his reputation still lags behind his talent. He kept a quiet tone while going about his spirit's business in a world trying unsuccessfully to grind him down. He learned better even than Matthew Arnold what true virtue lay in compromise, although, as Michael Timko says, Clough "refused to advocate easy solutions or timid compromises."[26] Clough believed that Arnold too easily became "sadly synical,"[27] too easily gave up the struggle and lapsed into languorous indifference, like his own "strayed reveller." But Clough knew that in Matthew Arnold there was something powerfully appealing to his own spirit.

He wrote to Blanche Smith that Arnold's "Strayed Reveller" once "had a great effect on" him; he hastened to add that not only the poem but the author had had that effect, something which he hoped was over and which he meant not to allow any more.[28] That poem and its author represented for Clough in 1852 those features of Horace's weak and hopeless people not daring to dream or to aspire. When Clough told Blanche that his feelings about "The Strayed Reveller" could be described by Horace's "mollis et exspes" (in *Epode* XVI), he was revealing the depth of his disappointment with Arnold's poetry; for if Clough meant to put Arnold's poem (if not Arnold himself) in the fuller context of Horace's theme, he meant to say that Arnold was one of those feckless Romans who cling to ignoble beds while civilization crumbles around them.[29] This is overstating it, of course, but Clough was putting some distance between himself and his younger colleague, a distance necessary for his own aesthetic integrity, not to speak of its necessity for marriage with Blanche.

Arnold's poetry and ideas of poetry drove Clough "into opposition," into "a spirit of contradiction,"[30] primarily because Arnold held too firmly to the virtues of detachment and resignation during a time that could ill afford such luxuries. Clough knew the importance of meditation and retirement from frenzied action, but he also knew that both are possible in a spiritual, or metaphorical, sense that does not require literal resignation or literal withdrawal. He probably knew that Arnold did not intend literal resignation either, but Clough's metaphorical terms had to be his own, not derived from or identical with his friend's. Therefore, Clough's poetry elaborates strategies of dealing with the need to preserve personal integrity in a time of impersonal fragmentation; and his poetry, even more obviously than Arnold's, deals with that need in terms of duties conflicting with desires.

The poems of *Ambarvalia* may be read as Clough's counter to Arnold's *Strayed Reveller* volume and, later, to the Switzerland poems. Clough's lyrical works explore the meanings of lives passed in dreams, in ignorance, in strife and work, in love and in duty; as Wendell V. Harris observes, his "questioning in *Ambarvalia* extends not only to the nature of duty and religious truth, but also to that of true love."[31] Whereas Arnold's poems look for the balancing powers of nature, with its lesson of "quiet work" summoning the human spirit away from involvement in petty strife, Clough's poems in 1849 show how there can be no richness, no joy, no meaning in lives that avoid strife, however petty it may be or seem to be. His speakers realize how narrow the pass is between the emptiness of mere duty, mere conformity, and the emptiness of personal arrogance, mere eccentricity, but the poet confronts his speakers with the necessity to make that passage. A successful passage through such narrow confines requires a delicate balance between the opposing claims from without and from within, and some of Clough's most lovely poems are strategies of defense by the proud man against the presumptuous world. We overhear a clear voice humbled by its mask of compromise, but not at the price of its integrity.

First of all, the spirit must learn to distinguish between a true and a false duty. The false duty is mere compliance, unquestioning obedience to patterns of behavior set by "the world," as in the poem "Duty—that's to say complying."[32] A life submitted to such formalities as going to church, attending balls, and marrying because "the world require you" is a life finally drained of all meaning, and the poem registers the narrowing process of duty becoming "atrophy, exinanition" until finally such duty stands exposed as "pure nonentity." This kind of duty is false to life because it is death itself, a "moral blank, and moral void." This poem mockingly exposes the falsity of such a tyrannous notion, showing us that Clough feared the emptiness of mere compliance just as keenly as did Arnold—although ironically, Clough could recognize in the atrophy of false duty the same blank void of languor he feared in Arnold's strayed reveller. The common element is atrophy, an enemy of life and imagination.

One image Clough employs to illustrate mere compliance is dancing, which in "Duty—that's to say complying" is equivalent with walking, sitting down, rising, never opening one's eyes; one's individuality is lost not in the group action (whatever pattern it takes), but rather in the surrender of will and judgment. The loss of self-consciousness while participating in mass activity is a frightening spectre. Whereas Arnold advocated an aesthetic ideal of beautiful objects arranged in meaningful patterns, Clough insisted upon an art of subjective consciousness, to keep the object in human perspective. The self must not become a mere object filling a space in a pattern of objects. Only a consciousness of one's own worth, sustained by the artist, can keep alive the pattern in which one participates. And a person must remain a part of a larger pattern, or he will merely obstruct and threaten chaos. If false duty is mere compliance, then true duty is deliberated participation. This is a point of the poem "Why should I say I see the things I see not."

A person says he sees things he does not see for the same reason that he dances to music he does not hear: because the dance, the ritual, the report, and the myth are all fictions shared by many people to protect what might otherwise be lost to nature—individuality. Someone who

124

stands still during a dance will "be shoved and be twisted by all he shall meet," and more importantly he will be abandoning his "partner" in the dance. If he cannot hear the music which governs the pattern of the dance, he must pretend to hear it—and perhaps he actually will discover the music he pretends to hear. Submitting to the pattern, pretending to hear the music, making contact with people through rituals may all be necessary prerequisites for hearing the music which keeps the soul alive: "are there not, then, two musics unto men?" One of them is loud and crude, a false music to which false duty must subscribe, while the other is "soft and low," a true music to which true duty conducts the soul. Clough's poem seems at first to be suggesting a submission to divided consciousness; but on reconsideration, it hints that the true music cannot be heard unless one pretends to hear the false, and that is a process of enlargement, not division. The ideal may be reached only through participation in the material world: true duty is found through false duty just as true music is heard through false music. There is a music and a duty for the masses—a popular myth—and there is a music and a duty for the individual—a private myth; the harmony or balance of the two is the ideal of the artist for Clough.

True duty is, after all, a self-defense against false duty. In the poem "Come back again, my olden heart," the speaker summons the return of his youthful heart which he had cast aside when he thought courage was the same as certainty; but the pride of certainty has led him to doubt himself even more than he doubted the many conflicting claims of the "jostling throng." True courage is faith in the self, not reliance upon the truths of others. Therefore, in this poem, the public man who has assumed the posture of certainty is giving way, in a confession and act of contrition, to his own uncertainty, and in that giving way he discovers the freedom and courage to be himself. Clough's speakers cannot come easily to this freedom and courage, however. They must learn to deal with the world on its own terms, to move through "the mazy dance" as it is called in the poem "With graceful seat and skilful hand." The courage of a doubting heart may serve as a guide through this maze, but the emphasis ought to be on the heart as desire rather than on its duty of doubt. The heart keeps the pettiness of daily ferment in proper perspective, converting "trifling play" into "strange realities" by dancing in unison with "love's music sweet."

Desire prompts both the heart and the body; and in the poem "When panting sighs the bosom fill" Clough makes clear his point that there must be a harmonious unity of desire in both the heart and the body. This poem answers Arnold's Switzerland poems with their drama of choice by rejecting "high Prudence" which rises to plead "the bitter,

125

bitter sting" of an "irrevocable choice" made too soon and too emotionally. Clough's lover casts off the counsel of Prudence, who explains love
as a rational matter, better removed from the entanglements of flesh and
feeling; the speaker humbly backs away from Prudence, accepting his
ignorance about such lofty matters as prudent Love and finally affirming
the self-sufficiency of his heart's delight. If it is not Reason, it is nevertheless sufficient unto itself, as the speaker echoes in mocking tones the
language of abstract philosophy:

> Itself was Reason, or, if not,
> Such substitute as is, I wot,
> Of seraph-kind the loftier lot;—
> Itself was of itself attested;—
> To processes that, hard and dry,
> Elaborate truth from fallacy,
> With modes intuitive succeeding,
> Including those and superseding;
> Reason sublimed and Love most high
> It was, a life that cannot die,
> A dream of glory most exceeding.   [ll. 80–90]

Left alone, Clough's lover would never rise to such heights of linguistic
ecstasy, but he is prodded into such language by the fatuous presump-
tuousness of "high Prudence." Certainly one who experiences the fleshly
signs of love may mistake a fleshly desire for a spiritual confirmation (a
zestful pleasure denied to lower animals), but he should not for that
reason deny its satisfaction. It may be "prelusive to the strain of love /
Which angels sing," or it may be merely a "zest" of the more "subtly
organized" creature, man; but it is a value not to be lightly denied. The
greater error would be to find that behind one's choice of love is lurking
a duty, making love a mere compliance. In the poem "Thought may well
be ever ranging," Clough establishes his warning that desire cannot be
"an idle duty-play," a form of "duty-fancies." Love is answerable only
to the self, an authority to which disobedience would be disastrous.

In the loveliest of Clough's love poems, "*Natura Naturans*," his
speaker recalls a wonderful encounter he had with a girl on a city bus.
They were simply passengers passing one another in time and place, but
between them there passed a force of nature that has survived the ravages
of time and change. It is a "witty and serious poem" about a serious
subject; it is "one of Clough's most remarkable evocations of sexuality."[33]
What the speaker retains from his encounter is a memory of discovering
"young Desire" before it learned "the mystic name of Love." There was
between them a working of quiet nature, uniting them in a cosmic blos-
soming of comic proportions. Who she was did not, and does not, matter,

any more than whether she had gold or black hair; she was nature naturing itself through the speaker's presence. He is proud of his privilege of having been her mate for even so brief a time; for through her, he learned the meaning of Eden, and he learned that he exists as a part of the flow of life through all its forms. To stray from that revelry is to stray from bliss, and Clough's characters will not willingly do that as long as the artist can give them direction.

When he tried to explain in a letter to his friend Shairp that he loved his "Mother Earth," Clough elaborated an analogy for the human condition which helps to explain his uncomplicated but profound philosophy of compromise.[34] Shairp was apparently concerned that Clough might become victimized by the attractions of philosophical idealism, and so Clough sought to explain that he loved his mother earth too much ever to float off into the air. In the meantime, he must always keep one leg on the ground, but he must also keep moving, unlike the "stationary gentleman" so solid in his position. He must therefore also always keep one leg off the ground, and if he cannot march as stately as "the sublimest mammalian type," he can at least move with the leaping "locomotion of the kangaroo." That explanation is essential, if not quintessential, Clough. And his bantering self-description properly keeps him from the deadly influence of languorous types as well as stately, sublime mammalian types. His poetry may move like the kangaroo, but it *moves*; and it moves with all the grace of nature (albeit kangaroo nature). This hopping motion is a way of dealing with opposing forces which may lead to the catastrophe of falling on his face, but there is little danger of his disappearing into the "intense inane." Clough's own awareness of the dangers of his grace of form comes in his second analogy in that same letter to Shairp: "The spirit truly is centrifugal, but the flesh centripetal. Wherefore Man, being a compound, revolveth in a Sphere." Arnold's Empedocles uses the spinning mirror as a metaphor to criticize self-deluded men, but Clough finds in the spinning, a ground for stability—a form which man has in common with the earth itself and which the earth has in common with all heavenly bodies. Clough thinks in images because he keeps always one foot on the ground, which is his desire; he can also do his duty, lift the other foot into the air, and move forward—even at the risk of spinning.

THE STORY OF JACOB'S TOIL for Rachel and Leah was important for Clough. He narrated it in a dialogue between Rachel and Leah, called "Jacob's Wives," giving to each a claim on Jacob that satisfies her particular need. In this poem, Rachel voices the claim of desire and Leah that of duty; Rachel has the heart of Jacob and Leah, his body. The poem is a version of the debate between body and soul in which marriage is the union of both claims. Clough's version gives Leah the last words:

> And Leah ended, Father of my sons,
> Come, thou shalt dream of Rachel if thou wilt,
> So Leah fold thee in a wife's embrace.   [ll. 119–21]

Leah has the most immediate and most fruitful claim on Jacob, while Rachel endures in the hope that she will bear, though late, "the Child of Love" and make all her suffering worthwhile. The reader knows that Rachel's hope will be fulfilled and that the redeemer of Israel will come from her womb. But Jacob can only wait and listen to these wives, listen in patience and endure, loving them both in duty and in desire.

"Jacob's Wives" is a pastoral rendition of a tale which Clough made into an allegory of marriage. It is gently ironic because we know that Rachel will prevail in the end, after Jacob has done his duty by Leah. This same pastoral irony pervades the major work of Clough's early career, *The Bothie of Tober-na-Vuolich*, in which one of the characters, Hobbes, celebrates the marriage of the hero in words of eloquent "wit" and "wisdom" (9.164). The wit comes in a letter and the wisdom in a postscript. Hobbes bids the bridegroom go unto his bride as "both Rachel and Leah unto" him (this being the "wit" of the speech), "which things are an allegory" (this being the "wisdom"):

> For this Rachel-and-Leah is marriage; which, I have seen it,
> Lo, and have known it, is always, and must be, bigamy only,
> Even in noblest kind a duality, compound, and complex,
> One part heavenly-ideal, the other vulgar and earthy:
> For this Rachel-and-Leah is marriage, and Laban their father
> Circumstance, chance, the world, our uncle and hard taskmaster.
> [9.167–72]

Philip Hewson is the poet-hero becoming educated in the right way of the world, learning from the example of Jacob. Hobbes tells him that "Rachel we dream of at night: in the morning, behold, it is Leah," but Hobbes also tells him that such truth is not to be deplored.

Hobbes gave the newlyweds "a Bible and iron bedstead" (9.147). His gift is also "an allegory" of the two modes of sanctification for marriage. But to discover those sanctifications has not been so easy for Philip. He retreats from the abstractions of university life and from "the whole great wicked artificial civilised fabric" of the city; away in the peaceful mountains, he tests his theories of politics and love. In this pleasant pastoral setting, Philip reenacts the labors of Jacob to earn his Rachel, but given the new day and new place, the customs of Laban (of "circumstance") are different, and so he first labors for Katie, then for Lady Maria, and finally for Elspie Mackaye. Throughout he has been counseled by his tutor, Adam, his voice of prudence who keeps him from extravagant ideas, though Adam has little to do with Philip's "real" education in women.

Clough takes his hero through several episodes of speech-making and love-making before letting him find the truth for himself. It would be a mistake to identify Clough with his hero, whose idealism and pastoral resolution are perhaps more appropriate for a strayed reveller than for a Thyrsis. Clough likes Philip Hewson, but he keeps him at a distance through the mock-heroic form of the poem. The characters are heroic in a pastoral, not an epic, setting. Clough can rescue the ideal marriage of Philip and Elspie only by developing the courtship in mountain retreats and by settling the marriage in faraway New Zealand. The poem shimmers with the colors of nature at its loveliest, and it contains a vibrancy of life which is several times captured in scenes of water and swimming. All these features of life in its most harmonious accommodation with nature are emphasized as Philip becomes a force of nature, like the ocean tides, sweeping into the brooks and mountain streams to which Elspie compares herself in her dream (7.120–36). She later realizes that she also has force, deriving from mountain heights, to meet his, and in that meeting of feminine strength from the mountains with masculine power from the oceans, the marriage of Elspie and Philip is indeed "an allegory." Their marriage is not only sanctified by God (through Hobbes's Bible or Elspie's architect positioning the keystone), but more importantly it is sanctified by nature (Hobbes's bedstead and Elspie's "one big tree" to which she belongs as a "leaf" [8.89–94]). Philip's odyssey to marriage is a process of becoming a nature hero, a bearer of the life force, conscious of its creative mission.

Philip Hewson is Clough's challenge to poetry, for by means of this hero, Clough declares his love for "the plain present, / Scorning historic abridgement and artifice anti-poetic" (6.99–100). Just as Philip undergoes a "true education" (8.43) of the imagination, so Clough experiments in a natural poetic. But he does so in one of the most artificial of styles—the heroic. Still he keeps one foot on the earth and one in the air, for that is his nature as a poet and as a man. Through the artificial form, Clough finds the meaning in his matter, just as Philip finds his heart's desire by submitting to the various forms of circumstance. When Philip writes to Adam, agreeing that the person who defies Providence is like the soldier who wilfully chooses to move in the wrong direction when the battle begins, Philip nevertheless complains that he is puzzled by Providence, not knowing where it begins and Circumstance ends. Philip does not lack will to do the duty of Providence or Circumstance, but he does lack understanding, not even knowing who the enemy is:

> What are we to resist, and what are we to be friends with?
> If there is battle, 'tis battle by night: I stand in the darkness,
> Here in the melee of men, Ionian and Dorian on both sides,
> Signal and password known; which is friend and which is foeman?
>
> [9.50–53]

Anticipating the perplexity of Matthew Arnold's speaker in "Dover Beach," Clough's hero resigns himself to his duty: "Though I mistrust the Field-Marshall, I bow to the duty of order. / Yet is my feeling rather to ask, where *is* the battle?" He finds the only significant battle to be within himself, and to win that battle he must labor for Circumstance, figured forth by his Laban, David Mackaye, and nature. Clough's hero is diminished by his perplexity, not knowing the will of Providence as did Achilles, Odysseus, Aeneas, or Milton's Adam; but Clough has found for his hero a place of significance by putting him in the frame of art inherited from the epic poets. Natural man is the hero in the modern epic, which may be pastoral or ironic or both, but not sublime or tragic. Circumstance shades off into Providence, discovered in the right education of the mind and body, leading to a new Eden through a marriage of work and love.

Amours de Voyage is an ironic epic which complements the comic epic of the *Bothie*. When Philip submits to the order of Circumstance, he finds a place for himself in the order of nature and fulfills himself in marriage with Elspie; but when Claude delays, resists, and flees from submission to Circumstance, he finds himself drifting, alone, dissatisfied, and bored. For Claude, Circumstance (or Juxtaposition) is a trap when it begins to form itself into personal bonds, particularly into commitments which lead to marriage. The *Amours* is a poem not only with an anti-hero, but it is also a poem with a theme against marriage. The hero must hang loose and keep his identity separate from the claims of other human beings, particularly from the possessive claims of a woman. Whereas the *Bothie* is a comic celebration of natural courtship and the marriage ritual, the *Amours* is an ironic celebration of individual freedom and cultural dislocation. Claude's refusal to marry is his refusal to compromise, and "his refusal to compromise results in his defeat," as Michael Timko has described it.[35] The hero wanders among the decaying artifacts of imperial Rome during the warfare between the Italian republics and the French tyrants; this background of decaying culture and warfare functions as an objective correlative for the sensibility of the hero, a proud, sensitive, and inwardly uncertain young man who cannot cope with the entanglements of the heart. After it becomes clear that he and Mary will not be reunited, he writes off his experience as "moping" "for the loss of a single small chit of a girl" (5.116); he has lost her because he stood "fiddle-faddling" when the tide of his love affair swept by him (4.38).

Claude is lost in this ancient city because he is lost in the world. He is a late version of Childe Harold, who, in Byron's poem, had found in Roman antiquity a means of resolving his spiritual dilemma. But Clough's Childe is too empty of spirit and too uncertain of direction to find meaning in the art of Rome. When he first arrives in the city, he is disappointed; it is "rubbishy," but it is "better than London, because it is other than London." We realize from the very beginning of his letters that Claude is fleeing human contacts. Gradually we realize that he is spiritually an empty person, that he is only a shadow of a self (1.83–86). He lives in a spiritual desert after the modern flood of theology, the protestant rebellion of Martin Luther, has ruined European culture. Modern religions have covered over the shadow with "pseudo-learning and lies," with "metallic beliefs and regimental devotions" (1.110, 111). Against this, Claude is self-consciously defensive.

His strategy for defending himself from lies and metallic beliefs is to adopt the posture of a clever aesthete. This exposes him for what Timko has called "a serio-comic analysis of a Victorian dilettante,"[36] but Claude's self-conscious posturing makes him as much his own satiric victim as he becomes for the reader. It is this strategy in his character which causes Walter E. Houghton to declare that "self-mockery is Claude's most modern characteristic and the principal link with his later counterpart, Eliot's Prufrock."[37] Claude, like Prufrock, does move through bourgeois circles of people who misunderstand him much more than he misunderstands himself. Some of the Trevellyan entourage interpret his posturing as a sign that he is about to convert to Roman Catholicism, but Mary considers it all to be absurd and even stupid. Beneath his posturing she sees in him a hardness, a dryness of spirit to which she could be attracted only as an ivy might cling to a stone wall:

> She that should love him must look for small love in return—like the ivy
> On the stone wall, must expect but a rigid and niggard support, and
> E'en to get that must go searching all round with her humble embraces.
> [3.37–39]

Claude realizes to himself that "all the natural heat" has escaped him (2.70), that he lacks a genuine cultivation of the spirit because he cannot find his roots, cannot be comfortable with mother earth. Life is like the ocean for Claude, a medium in which one holds fast only as a limpet might, clinging to rocks and hanging his mouth or mind open to take whatever sweeps his way (2.44–47); or one merely floats along the top of it, a passive victim of its ebbs and tides (3.51–55). He knows that he lacks "individual culture" (2.34), but he cannot do what a "grain" must do if it is to live and reproduce, i.e., accept the earth, embrace the flesh, and lose one's self in the union:

> Tell me, my friend, do you think that the grain would sprout in the furrow,
> Did it not truly accept as its *summum* and *ultimum bonum*
> That mere common and may-be indifferent soil it is set in?
> Would it have force to develop and open its young cotyledons,
> Could it compare, and reflect, and examine one thing with another?
> [3.40–44]

The grain could not sprout, and neither can Claude grow as long as he makes mental abstracts of his experience rather than embracing the flesh as a confirmation of identity.

His intellectualizing, abstracting of reality, is what Mary interprets as his stony hardness. Because he thinks his identity is his intellect, Claude himself is removed from the richer reality that is represented by Mary Trevellyan. Because he fears a compromise of his intellectual integrity, Claude fears the compromise of marriage between heart and flesh. As one of the "contemplative creatures" (2.309), he decides to "aspire" only for the "Absolute" when he realizes he will not rejoin the absent Mary; he can deal with his failure in the flesh and in the concrete particular by losing himself in contemplation of the grand Absolute (5.51–62). When that fails to sustain him, as it must, he is shattered—in "fragments"—and left to drift about the world, "languidly" slinking from the field of battle, a moral coward (5.71, 81–85).

There is no happy ending for this rootless man, this "cold intellectual being" who cannot cleave to reality, cannot reconcile mind with flesh. He can only wander about the earth, fleeing first one thing and then another. He began by fleeing London with its press of people; he was quickly bored by the artifacts of Rome; and in the end, he will flee even the winter. All the things that remind him of his fleshly being are a torment to him. He can deal with Mary as an abstract from his unreal past, and that will allow him to continue to live out his dreamy life to its hopeless conclusion. He is an absurdist character of a sort we are thoroughly familiar with in twentieth-century literature, but he may have been born into the world of English literature several decades before audiences could appreciate him. Certainly through Claude, Clough knew that intellectual heroes are more absurd than comic: they are absurd because they lack any spiritual framework within which to orient their thoughts and they lack any spiritual authority to which they can subordinate their desires. Claude is an Odysseus who cannot find his Penelope.

IN THE LYRIC beginning "O Land of Empire, art and love!," the speaker sounds something like Claude when he first came to Rome, for both are deeply disappointed not to find the purity of beauty which they expected from the grand art and architecture of the Imperial City. The speaker of the lyric is at first distressed to find such a disparity between the beautiful artifacts from the past and the ugly habits of people living in the present. This disparity is like the difference between the pure sky above, where gods dwell, and the corrupt earth below, where pigs wallow. The speaker details the various corruptions and dirty habits of the present while he lingers amid the beauties of the Pantheon. But unlike Claude, the speaker here can adjust to the juxtaposition of earth and sky, past and present, beauty and ugliness, for he discerns a necessary connection between these seeming opposites:

> The stem that bears the ethereal flower
> Derives that emanative power;
> From mixtures fetid foul and sour
> Draws juices that those petals fill.   [ll. 47–50]

The imagination of man is the stalk of the flower, drawing life from the earth to support the flower in the air; man stands between the earth and the sky, the past and the present, the ugliness and the beauty. Clough's speaker advocates a resignation to necessity, but unlike Arnold's, his resignation is not a withdrawal from the dusty ways of life:

> With resignation fair and meet
> The dirt and refuse of thy street
> My philosophic foot shall greet,
> So leave but perfect to my eye
> Thy columns set against thy sky!   [ll. 84–88]

The speaker in this lyric makes an accommodation between the real and the ideal which Claude cannot in the *Amours*; here the speaker marries—in imagination—the heavens with the earth, keeping in balance what Claude loses in fragments. This same balancing of life's opposites is the process at work in Clough's last completed major poem, *Dipsychus*. For this poem, Clough has shifted the scene from Rome to Venice, a setting more appropriate for his theme because this beautiful city of art is bathed by the waters of the ocean and so is less harshly imposing than Rome. The scene of the poem changes from the piazza, to a garden, to the quays, to a gondola, and back finally to the piazza; in structure, the poem is a night passage by water from the solid piazza of scene 1, wandering among the canals of scene 4, and back to the solid piazza of scene 10. Reality is rendered as a blending of the hard and soft, the solid and the liquid, the permanent and the changing. Dipsychus journeys from passive doubt to active doubt, always the self-conscious hero of the comic adventure but learning to live with his self-consciousness as some of Clough's other protagonists could not.

The character Dipsychus is a blending of Philip and Claude, and so he "represents," as Timko well observes, "the compromise that Clough saw so necessary to make."[38] Dipsychus possesses the resolution of Philip to make a commitment to action (though most of the poem deals with the dynamics of his making that resolution), and Dipsychus also possesses the skepticism of Claude. Dipsychus is Clough's way of affirming the negative or, less paradoxically, educating those whom the Uncle in the Epilogue calls the "Hobbabi-hoy cherub[s]" to better understand "the laws of the life they will have to enter" (ll. 46, 50). Value is not to be found in a resignation from the turmoils of life nor is it to be found in a sacrifice of the self to those turmoils; Philip believed the former, while Claude believed the latter. Dipsychus represents an ironist's balancing of the two through a dialogue of the mind with itself and with the world. While Arnold was deploring the tendency of modern art to enter into such a dialogue with itself, Clough was transforming that tendency into an outrageously successful poem.

When Dipsychus tries to steady himself from drifting into fleshly temptation, he thinks of "sweet domestic bonds, / The matrimonial sanctities" (2A.79–80), and the Spirit mocks him with the offer to help Dipsychus "go home and marry—and be damned." If Dipsychus were to marry in order to keep from burning, he would indeed be damned. Therefore, as the hero of this poem, he will have to go through the burning first; then he will be better prepared to marry because he will know that marriage is not a retreat from reality but a constuction of reality, made from all the contradictions of life. When Dipsychus can say, toward the end of the poem, "The ordinance says, 'and cleave unto his wife.' / O man, behold thy wife, th' hard naked world" (12.67–68), he has learned a more adequate way to approach marriage. Throughout this process of his education, Dipsychus needs the attention of the Spirit to help bring into balance the conflicting forces within himself. If Dipsychus thinks of marriage as a retreat, the Spirit mockingly corrects that notion to make Dipsychus see it, therefore, as damnation; if Dipsychus thinks of love as a dreamy private knowledge, best kept alive "within the closest veil of [his] own inmost heart," the Spirit mocks him as a victim of illusions, since the world must be taken for what it is, not for what one would rather have from it:

> This world is very odd, we see;
> We do not comprehend it;
> But in one fact can all agree
> God won't, and we can't mend it.   [4.113–16]

When Dipsychus narrates his dream of "joy and terror," when the bells tell him there is no God and so swing him from the extreme feeling of liberation to the other extreme of spiritual despair, the Spirit soothes him by explaining that the duty of complying with the forms of life will help keep away such nightmares, which are no more certainly true than are the forms of compliance (5.7–185). The cure for such despair is to plunge into the ocean of life, which is exactly what Dipsychus does (5.201–27), finding in the billows of the Adriatic a healthy corrective to his nightmarish visions. Even in this action, however, the Spirit is a corrective, because he will not join Dipsychus so fully in his sport—he reminds Dipsychus that he will need "some towels and a sheet," that "these thistles" hurt the bare feet, and that "animal spirits are not common sense," though "they're good enough as an assistance" (5.213, 217, 227, 230).

Without the assistance of the Spirit, Dipsychus would be a tormented victim of his own divided nature, tossed about by his passion and his mind. Without the steadying influence of mockery (and of "common sense"), Dipsychus would be a hopeless, hollow man, swaying in the winds of opinion, doubt, belief, passion, and ideals. As long as he can keep in touch with the Spirit, Dipsychus should be able to make his way through the world with some integrity. Of course, Clough wants us to see how ironic all this is, because for many readers the Spirit is a devil, leading this poor innocent into his damnation; but the point is that without this Spirit, Dipsychus would be damned by his own nature to the most horrible of hells, rootless drifting forever. The Spirit forces Dipsychus to be human, neither a whining angel nor a snuffling human; Dipsychus is forced to recognize the beauty of simplicity and the ethics of "common plain good deeds close by one" (6.140–81). The strategy of the Spirit is to puncture Dipsychus's pomposity wherever it appears, sometimes as idealism and sometimes as cynicism. The Spirit is Clough's comic spirit, akin to Byron's narrator in *Don Juan* and to George Meredith's comic spirit in such novels as *The Egoist*. The presence of the Spirit helps to keep in perspective the proper dimensions of human possibilities, and that is the most important need of modern man, so vacillating or so arrogantly absolutist in whatever he does. The Spirit is not Arthur Clough, but he is often present in the voice of Arthur Clough, just as Dipsychus is. This poem might well be seen as Clough's answer to *Empedocles on Etna,* with Dipsychus choosing to embrace the world in a gesture of life rather than of death.

Readers, including the Uncle in the Epilogue, have thought the poem's last scenes (from about scene 9 to the end) somewhat tedious, for they lack the spark of dialogue between Dipsychus and the Spirit. These last scenes echo the soliloquies of Hamlet, particularly Hamlet's sentiments as he learns to resign himself to the designs of providence (act 4 on); Dipsychus, like Hamlet, has been brought to the point where he can properly discipline his nervous ego and can properly subordinate it to a larger will than his own. His problem, like Hamlet's is one of action:

> Action is what one must get, it is clear,
> And one could dream it better than one finds,
> In its kind of personal, in its motive not;
> Not selfish as it now is, nor as now
> Maiming the individual. If we had that,
> It would cure all indeed. . . .
> Yes, if we could have that; but I suppose
> We shall not have it, and therefore I submit.
> [9.147–53, 158–59]

These lines echo Hamlet's decision to submit to the same providence that takes note of the fall of a sparrow, to make readiness his all. Dipsychus has no such grand mission, and so his problem is greater insofar as it is a problem of motivation. He has no large kingdom to rescue from an evil king; he has no conviction of sin which can define acts of murder, incest, suicide, etc.; and he has no princely height from which to fall if he should err. He is but a common mortal, one bit of what Hamlet styled quintessential dust. Dipsychus can find nobility only in submission to the way of the world in all its compromises, expressed in the comic spirit of both the Spirit and the Uncle. When Dipsychus is alone, thinking and debating with himself, he is pathetic, but when he is set in dialogue with the Spirit, he rises to a vigor and assertiveness that make him an appealing character. After his decision in scene 9 to submit, he is at peace, and even though he submits with the thought that he is thereby abandoning heroic action, he is ironically finding himself in the very act of submission.

After he has abandoned the idea of great Action, Dipsychus feels first tranquillity, then void indifference, and finally happiness (10.1–9, 11.1–16, 37–39). But the Comic Spirit will not let him rest so self-satisfied, for he enters at the moment when Dipsychus feels happiest about his decision to renounce Action, and the Spirit proceeds to raise questions about his own identity. He makes Dipsychus wonder if the Spirit is an "ill spirit" or not. The point is not whether the Spirit is a devil—he can take any name we apply; the point is that Dipsychus must be kept vigorous, alert both intellectually and imaginatively, for that is the sign of his life and his meaning. The Spirit is a gadfly for the human condition, goading it into questioning and flexibility. To realize that his humanity is conditioned by the Necessity of physical fact proves to be a cleansing act for Dipsychus; when he thinks he can endure without the company of the Spirit, he is punished by dreams of mortal corruption (11.72–86), from which he is awakened by the Spirit's call to "take life as she has ordered it." Hearing this, Dipsychus is baptized into a new life, where he learns "the Second Reverence, for things around" (11.104–19). Earlier, he had been at peace with himself for having resigned ambition for noble Action; now he must rouse himself from the lethargic self-satisfaction of that resignation, go among the "things around," and mingle with "the large world, / The thronged life" which awaits him and his Spirit.

That he has learned his lesson well is made clear by Dipsychus's speech in scene 12, where he declares that "how much soe'er / [he] might submit, it must be to rebel. / Submit then sullenly, that's no dishonour" (ll. 50–52). Likening himself to Samson made a slave among the Philistines, Dipsychus resigns himself to his honorable labor. He later tells the Spirit that his submission has been with "reservations," but this is exactly what he ought to say if he is still alive and not merely a tool of the Spirit. Dipsychus will marry, make a living for himself and his family, and live the unheroic life, but as long as he does it with "reservations," he will keep alive the Comic Spirit within himself and in his society. Walter Houghton admits the comic element of the poem, especially when he notes that "Clough insisted that people must 'settle the question of reconciling the world and the Spirit' by serving God *in* the world"; but Houghton still insists that Dipsychus's submission must be viewed "as a tragic necessity."[39] Houghton seems to know that he is drawing an erroneous conclusion in the face of contrary evidence, but he is committed to explicating a pattern in Clough's career which requires a despairing conclusion in *Dipsychus*:

> Claude's soliloquies in Rome point forward to those of Dipsychus in Venice a year later, and the three poems [i.e., *Bothie, Amours,* and *Dipsychus*] may be viewed as a progressive movement from objective to subjective art—or, in temper of mind, from gaiety, to ennui, to something like despair. That would parallel Clough's own history from 1848 to 1850.[40]

But, as Houghton admits, one ought to stress the satire of the poem. To do so will reveal that Dipsychus is educated in the "need for flexibility and growth of the human spirit," as Timko has argued; "he comes to know that to face the truth is to have change," and so "his compromise is one that is both ennobling and fruitful."[41] Dipsychus bids farewell to dreams and welcomes the world (13.21). To some this may seem a farewell to idealism; to others, an embrace of the reality principle; but to the Spirit, it is pure comedy, something to celebrate because Dipsychus has landed on his philosophic feet:

> O goodness; won't you find it pleasant
> To own the positive and present;
> To see yourself like people round,
> And feel your feet upon the ground!
> Little Bo Peep, she lost her sheep!   [13.81–85]

The Spirit is the wolf of the world, but Dipsychus is well out of the care of a Little Bo Peep, at any rate.

When putting Clough's career into focus, it is well to remember that although his final work, *Mari Magno*, may be an unsatisfying and often pedestrian poem, it is a final effort by Clough to put the common themes of Victorian literature—duty and desire—into a framework of the greatest comic spirit of English poetry, Geoffrey Chaucer. Clough moves shoulder to shoulder with the earthy characters of Chaucer, but he cannot find the audience and the medium to release his genius for the fullest appreciation by his contemporaries, but especially by his friend Matthew Arnold. Arnold might finally have been correct in saying that Victorians were not expansive enough, did not know enough to be disinterested critics and so ideal readers; but Arnold was not right to dismiss his friend as a victim of the *Zeitgeist*. Clough's answer came often and in various forms, but it came most vigorously in the dialogues of Dipsychus with the Spirit. Arnold is Dipsychus to Clough's Spirit, and between the two poets there was a healthy combat of taste and imagination. Each man was tired out by the "mental conflicts of the day" ("The Lawyer's Second Tale," 1. 70), but each was renewed by "home's happy breath" ("The Clergyman's Second Tale," 1. 323); that is, each found in his domestic tranquillity a stimulant, not a depressant. The stimulus was a challenge to overcome the banal, the common, as well as the extremism of their age and place. They had to reconcile their imaginative needs with their intellectual skepticism, and they had before them the models of Goethe, Wordsworth, and Carlyle—models which did both men good service.

5

Rossetti and Meredith

Dante Gabriel Rossetti and George Meredith were, for a brief season, housemates in London. Their relationship did not become a strong personal friendship, but it does establish a basis for considering their works together. Rossetti saw in Meredith's fiction a "very great merit of a wonderfully queer kind," and that is about the limit of his recorded estimation of Meredith as an artist.[1] Perhaps it is true that for Rossetti this new acquaintance was merely useful in helping to advance his own career, as at least one critic has suggested.[2] Whether Meredith was useful seems debatable, and whether Rossetti saw in him nothing more than usefulness seems even more questionable. The fact remains, however, that they could not inhabit the same house together for very long, and they did not maintain a long or strong personal friendship with one another (though not for Meredith's lack of trying). When Rossetti wrote in 1863 that "Meredith has evaporated for good,"[3] he meant more than that the household had broken up—George Meredith did "evaporate," in most significant ways, from Rossetti's life. As William Michael Rossetti remembered it, "It pretty soon became apparent that Mr. Meredith's subtenancy was not likely to stand much wear and tear, or to outlast the temporary convenience which had prompted it. . . . Friendly intercourse between the two men continued for some years, and gradually wore out without any cause or feeling of dissension."[4]

The two men shared a common enthusiasm for poetry, and they seem to have suffered from a common personal ailment: egoism. It is hardly surprising that they could not live together for very long, and it is less surprising that each had to go his own way if he ever hoped to conquer the monster in himself. Their poetry is comparable on this single point: that it deals with, and devises strategies for, containing an ego that threatens to consume the self utterly. For Rossetti, the special strategy is to identify the ego with passionate desire, learning how to yield its claim upon the objects of this life and this world. For Meredith, the major poetic effort is to find ways of losing the ego in an embrace of desire for nature. Both men frequently rely upon conventions of marriage from which they draw imagery and metaphors to express themes of egoistic desire and social duty.

Rossetti frequently alludes to his various duties to satisfy the many claims on his talent. He felt a duty to perform up to the expectations of his family, perhaps even to compete with his talented sisters and brother. He felt a duty to satisfy the claims of friendship from many people who were emotionally dependent upon him. And he felt a duty to himself to realize his talents as an artist in designs of language and painting. Hoxie Neale Fairchild, who does not care much for Rossetti otherwise, has nevertheless recognized this quality in the poet, for whom "heaven's peace . . . is to be attained through *work*—the application of a 'regenerate' will to the performance of duty."[5] Surrounding Rossetti's life and career is a vast silence on the subject of duty to God and country, however; Rossetti was an exile like his father, but in the more distant country of the spirit. The strategies of his poetry are ways to fulfill these various duties, making them at one with his constant desire to escape from the prison of his own self-consciousness.

Given the circumstances of his birth and domestic arrangements, it is no wonder that Rossetti had to struggle all his life to overcome egoism, even egotism. As his brother wrote, "The very core of his character was self-will, which easily shelved into wilfulness."[6] Almost everybody who knew Rossetti expected great things from him. Doughty's biography is the story of a man who was greater than his biographer wants to admit; it is also the story of a man who exhausted himself for his friends and for his art. Doughty does not take his reader into Rossetti's heart; to get there, one must often read between Doughty's lines or, better yet, read Rossetti himself. One of several appealing features of Rossetti's character is his occasional realization that he must curtail the growth of his ego. In a letter to William Bell Scott in 1853, Rossetti exclaims with irony that heroes of such works as Alexander Smith's *Life Drama* (which he had just finished reading), Goethe's *Wilhelm Meister*, and St. Augustine's *Confessions* all put "self-culture" before "self-sacrifice" in "a great process, amusing and amazing" to Rossetti; this advancement of self-culture at the expense of others amazes and amuses Rossetti because of its sanctimonious tone of self-righteousness. He calls it a "noble theory" "that scoundrelism is a sacred probation of the soul."[7]

Rossetti realized that he might suffer from the same "scoundrelism" if he is not careful to distinguish self-culture from selfishness. Writing to

John Everett Millais in 1855, he concludes a paragraph by saying, "On running over what I have written above I find it is full of Is and stinks altogether of identity."[8] Rossetti's notion of himself as a selfish ego "stinking" of identity lies behind his playful drawing of himself "with a great rent in the back of his waistcoat and trowsers: he is tearing his hair."[9] He included this drawing in a letter to Ford Madox Brown in 1866 with this description:

> The burden of conscious fat and hypocrisy, the stings of remorse, the haunting dread of exposure as every motion wafted the outer garment to this side or that, the senses quickened to catch the fatal sound of further rents,—all this and more—but let us draw once more over the scene that veil which Fate respected.[10]

Such graphic and verbal undressing of his soul may be done in a humorous mood, but it suggests Rossetti's sense of a self hidden behind the appearance of "elegant languor and easy grace." It is a self threatening to break out in total possession of his character, and it is a self which Rossetti consciously tries to keep under control. He described himself in 1870 as a "Sancho" accompanying the Don Quixote of his friend Stillman on a country adventure which they took in the spring of that year;[11] Rossetti as Sancho is not the usual view of him by his friends or, unfortunately, by Rossetti himself. But by such occasional representations he does show his awareness of the need to subordinate his ego to something outside itself, to keep it in proportion. Sancho as the earthy realist would be an important role for Rossetti to play if he hoped to find any peace in his life; otherwise he would suffer all the spiritual knocks of a Quixote trying to make vulgar women into a heavenly Dulcinea. Rossetti's problem of ego, of divided self, of consumming desire, was something he knew required constant vigilance. He remarked in a letter at the end of his life that "self-scrutiny and self-repression will be a very large part in the poetic 'Survival of the fittest.' " Later in this same letter, he "pray[s] pardon" for his "several pages of self."[12]

Rossetti's Dante at Verona is a poet in exile, discovering the means of delivering his gift of song for a lovely ideal beyond his earthly possession.[13] Dante is a man suffering loneliness and alienation, he is a poet suffering envy and stupid misunderstanding, and he is a patriot suffering rejection and expatriation. His relationship with Beatrice and Florence is a tense and complicated one in which the character of the woman and the features of the city try to merge in his imagination; but the union fails, just as the body fails to become spirit. Dante is a man doomed to unhappiness because he tries to be both "a servant and singer"

141

of two beautiful ideals, Florence and Beatrice, neither of which may be realized in an earthly form. Beatrice must die to be rescued and Florence becomes a "shameful and shameless prostitute."

Dante's soul is identified with the dead Beatrice, and that inspires his singing; his body is identified with the prostituted Florence, and that causes his suffering. He is torn between his desire to return to his earthly home and his duty to sacrifice his comfort for the sake of rebuking its crass tyranny; his way of balancing these opposed values is to sing of his spiritual marriage with the dead Beatrice, a reunion which retains childhood innocence and mature longing. Rossetti typically ignores the place of God in Dante's scheme of reunion, instead replacing God with Beatrice as his single object of desire. Fleshly desire for satisfaction is represented by the relationship with Florence, a desire not to be indulged because the object is sordid. But it is a desire safely removed from temptation by the distance of the exile.

The narrator invites us to follow Dante into the darkness of his exile, to speculate on the nature and quality of his life during that time. We may hope for some significant glimpses of his "twofold life" of "chainless thought and fettered will." Time as a coiling darkness is a heavy chain which implicates the narrator as well as his protagonist, binding them together, implicating all men in spiritual exile and existential perplexity. The past is haunted with all the dead souls who denied their one "undying soul" (Dante, or any man like him) his due recognition, which must wait for the loosening of time's hold through patient suffering. The song which Dante made out of his anguish is the controlling force which the present exerts on the past and the future, just as the *Commedia* held together the three spiritual realms of Dante's cosmos. Each singer adds to the increasing power of the timeless realm of art, struggling through darkness and against heavy time. The narrator's consciousness of time as a burden and a weight is revealed by his frequent references connecting time with images of darkness or heaviness, such as "the Sacred Song . . . [that] toiled to ope that heavier door" and, in the final image of the poem, "those stairs" which grew steeper with the passage of the years in exile.

These stairs, as an image, take on symbolic meaning of an ambivalent kind, the sign of duty becoming more laborious as desire is worn away, of spirit becoming firmer as flesh begins to fail, and perhaps even of endless pain in a spiritual ascent which can never be finally completed. D. G. Rossetti knew the stairs, knew the pain of trying to climb them, but he did not find "those stairs" which Dante found in Verona, leading to the stars of heaven. David Sonstroem puts it well when he concludes that "at the last [Rossetti] was not the Dante that he desired to be—the visionary poet who comprehended the universe and spoke of it coherently and

142

clearly. He was rather a retrograde Dante of darkness, who had glimpsed a vision, and then had lost it in his pursuit."[14] Sonstroem, however, does not give Rossetti the credit he deserves for realizing all of this himself and for making such a realization into his own special form of poetry; but Sonstroem is surely right to observe that Rossetti did not have the religious faith to make a darkening life bear spiritual significance.

For the man of duty, "the task is long, / The time wears short to compass it." Time is like desire, wearing away at last, yielding up the singleness of purpose which commands the artist. Time is of the body, and the timeless is of the Spirit; the body is prostituted by the claims of time, just as Florence is by its thieving tyrants, and so the artist must sternly live out his exile away from the claims of the flesh, devoting himself to the timeless, even bodiless spirit. Death severs the links of time that enslave the spirit, but art constructs its own means of deliverance from time. The tensity of the singer serving two mistresses produces his song at the cost of his comfort and even of his happiness. The singer must be a servant, desiring always but never wavering from his duty. The reward of endurance is aesthetic freedom, in which there is no consciousness of time or its burden.

Even though the narrator is obviously championing the austerity of the exiled artist, he cannot refrain from celebrating the beauties of the flesh, particularly as he envisions the festivities of Can Grande della Scala. The fleshly forms of beauty are rendered in the exquisitely sensitive detail that we recognize in the painter's work. Dante dreams of Florence as a lady holding court beneath a tent covered with golden lilies; we glimpse the work of women in a courtyard in Verona where conduits "sing / And meet in scoops of milk-white stone," where damsels "hold / Their hands in the wet spurt of gold"; we hear the laughter, merriment, and joking in Can Grande's banquet halls—all of which Dante either ignores or puts a halt to by his scornful remonstrance. It is no wonder that Can Grande learns to "hate" Dante. Dante is a man on the outside, always the exile, never finding home, never realizing the values of the flesh; he is forever fixed in the narrator's memory as the man who leaned his forehead against the window, weeping for the past (p. 7).

Dante lived only for his dreams, dreams of the dead Beatrice and the prostituted city of Florence. It is the narrator, not Dante, who notices the festival of life through which Dante moves and which he sets in such stern, austere order; it is the narrator, not Dante, who notices that the pane against which he leans his haggard visage is painted. Dante is a victim of monomania, translating all experience into the terms of his own vision. If D. G. Rossetti could identify with Dante as an artist caught between opposing dreams, the poet could more easily see in the figure of the exiled politician something of his own father, whose life in exile increasingly became one of monomania. D. G. Rossetti is not the Dante at Verona he describes in his poem: on the one hand, he is not so blessed; but on the other hand, he is not so narrow. There is in the art of D. G. Rossetti a place for Can Grande with his banqueting, just as there is a place for Dante Alighieri with his visions of innocent damsels guiding him through the hell of this earth; there is a place for the visionary ideal of innocent beauty in Beatrice, and there is a place for the fleshly, sometimes prostituted reality of corrupt beauty in Florence. Try as he might, the man in the artist cannot abandon hope of returning home in the flesh, even while he is learning to climb the ever-steepening stairs of spiritual obligation.

When one tries to love a woman in her innocence, as Dante did Beatrice, he must love her as a child. And to do that is to arrest her development, halt one's own spiritual growth, and prevent the marriage of souls which should consummate the love relationship. Unlike the narrator of "A Last Confession," Dante could successfully love Beatrice because she was always as a child to him—both of them were children in the care of God, whose love Dante was ultimately desiring even when he thought he desired the love only of Beatrice. Beatrice's childhood, distance, and then death all conspired to maintain in her the ideal of heavenly love for the poetic vision of Dante Alighieri. Those who try to sustain such love through time and in the flesh are likely to find a sympathetic voice in the character of "A Last Confession" (pp. 18–34). Like Dante, this speaker is a patriot who identifies his love for a girl with his love for a place, a homeland, and like Dante this speaker is surprised by his love of innocence. But this patriot does not find his salvation in the girl; rather, he finds her to be his hell, and that is the consequence of his attempt to love the woman as if she were the child, a mistake not allowed the poet Dante.

The speaker of "A Last Confession" tells how he came to kill this girl of his love, how he found himself becoming her lover after being her father. He is a man who has become possessed by Eros, driven into such a passion of desire for total possession of the object of his love that he has brought annihilation to them both. She is dead and he is dying, which is a state much to be desired by such hunger of possession. In an ironic way, his confession to the priest is but an occasion for his wedding vow, marrying in death the girl he could not have in life. The fleshly reality cannot be accommodated with the spiritual ideal in any other way.

He has given the girl two significant gifts, a dagger (most recently) and a glass cupid. Rossetti could hardly have chosen more obvious images for symbols of sexual desire. But obvious as they might be, both gifts

144

are complex in their values. The dagger was purchased to be a final gift, one which would serve to protect the girl from "a German lover" or aid her in the eternal struggle with other women for a man. It seems an odd gift unless we realize both the political setting and the psychological condition of the patriot speaker, for whom the dagger will be an extension of his own protective, patronizing power and for whom, less consciously, it will be his phallic claim on the girl's identity. When he kills her, confessing that he lost consciousness of his deed when he identified her laugh with that of a harlot, he does what he most wants to do, what he has wanted to do throughout their association: possess her utterly and free her from flesh and time.

She came into his life when he had been hiding from political foes, and in his strained, tense condition at the time, she was like "that heavenly child which in the latter days / Shall walk between the lion and the lamb," her voice was "like the talking of the trees," and with her he "seemed there so alone" that he "thought the world / Must be all over or had never been." From the beginning, it seems, he wanted her to end for him the world of political chaos and personal dissatisfaction. When he kills her in the end, he brings about the apocalypse for which he had hoped when he found her:

> The sea and sky were blood and fire, and all
> The day was one red blindness; till it seemed,
> Within the whirling brain's eclipse, that she
> Or I or all things bled or burned to death. [p. 33]

He has hoped to find in her love a bond that could unite "the lion and the lamb" in his life, but time, which never stands still for him, required changes in himself and in his relationship with her that he could not make. He tried to fix their relationship, and he found that it would break just as his first gift to her—the glass Cupid—did.

In that image Rossetti gathered the meanings of a life which tries to fix time into a static form and, more particularly, tries to idealize beauty out of the erotic love of innocence. Such beauty must be broken if there is to be any growth of spirit. The speaker does not want time to exist; he wants to arrest its flow and capture it in some form such as the glass Cupid. The spirit in the girl knows it must escape the crystal cabinet of such an illusory prison, and so she breaks it while trying, ironically, to "fix" it onto the wall "fronting her little bed."

"THE BRIDE'S PRELUDE," "Sister Helen," and "Rose Mary" are all poems of betrayal and mockery—betrayal of desire and mockery of duty. Each poem centers on the consequences of erotic treachery for the female victim, and each investigates the use of marriage as a means of reconciling disparate values. In each poem there is a main speaker, the betrayed maiden, and an innocent listener—although in "Rose Mary" the mother's innocence is of a different kind than that of Amelotte in "The Bride's Prelude" and that of the "little brother" in "Sister Helen." In "Rose Mary," Rossetti associates physical health and medicine with erotic desire, and in the other two he associates it with magic and witchcraft. In none of these three poems is love redemptive, and in all three, love is destructive in one form or another.

The oppressiveness of time, the weary burden of it, is a major theme in "The Bride's Prelude" (pp. 35–65), as it is in so much of Rossetti's poetry. The protagonists of many of his poems, including "The Bride's Prelude," are alienated from the ordinary human community not only by their consciousness of time as a burden but also by their mania of unsatisfied desire. Dante and the speaker of "A Last Confession" are driven by their desire, and for them, time is like an endless stream, sometimes swift and sometimes slow. But for Aloyse, time is like a dead weight, stifling and oppressive. She is set apart from the stream of activity in which her "busy" sister participates; Aloyse is "listless," sits "within the shade," where "the stir / Of thought made noonday heavier." Aloyse is strikingly like Dante at Verona in her withdrawal from the stir and festival of life, and her situation is paradoxical like his, for both are the probable centers of attention by a fascinated audience, but both scorn to notice the values of the world around them. Aloyse, like Dante at Verona, withdraws into a private vision—hearing only "the inward voice," but hers is not much like Dante's vision or Dante's voice. Aloyse's story is part of the story of "The Bride's Prelude," but it is not the whole story of the poem, which is more complex than her tale alone.

Like Coleridge's Ancient Mariner, Aloyse is telling a tale of guilt to implicate her captive listener in a world of misery and unhappiness against a background of wedding festivity. We are interested in her story of sexual initiation, social friction, family honor, personal tragedy, and political chaos, but we are more interested, through Rossetti's artful presentation, in her own state of mind, in her present circumstances, and in her presently evolving relationship with her sister as Aloyse tells her this story just before Aloyse is about to be married to the man who was a cause of her misery. Her present state of mind is "listless"; then, after she begins telling her story, her voice grows strong, and "her thought,"

> long stagnant, stirred by speech,
> Gave her a sick recoil;
> As, dip thy fingers through the green

That masks a pool,—where they have been
The naked depth is black between.   [p. 44]

She becomes an agency of a power that is beyond her conscious will to
control:

Aloyse did not hear at all
   The sounds without. She heard
The inward voice (past help obey'd)
Which might not slacken nor be stay'd,
But urged her till the whole were said.   [p. 45]

While she delivers her tale of guilt, she trembles "between shame and
pride," speaks "strongly" with a "fierce effort," grows faint and wan, but
continues with her story to its sordid conclusion.

Not only are we made to realize that this is a story Aloyse must tell,
as a last confession before her wedding, but that it reveals depths of
despair in her character; she becomes an agent of that despair, spreading
it out into the bright and innocent world of her sister's existence. For
Aloyse, her marriage will offer little opportunity for reconciling her natural desires with her spiritual duties; instead, it will realize in visible
form the psychological hell into which her recent experiences have
plunged her. Her marriage with Urscelyn will be a marriage with the
devil who seduced and betrayed her. Instead of anticipating fulfillment
through love and marriage, Aloyse experiences emptiness, a progressive
emptying of her life until she is left with what Coleridge once called
"positive negation." Her sickness in life began long before she fell from
the horse which her brothers insisted she ride; she was ill with fatigue of
the spirit even while she was a girl receiving her "proper" education in the
convent, where she had little "to spend [her] heart on," and where she
felt there had been a "lifelong theft / Of [her] life." Aloyse was spiritually starved when she rejoined her family, a family busy about the affairs
of living and playing, but into which she could not enter. When she fell
from the horse, Aloyse became conscious of her strange, lingering sickness—she made of her body an expression of her spiritual disease, and it
was unto that particular disease that Urscelyn ministered his special
remedy:

" 'Cousin, I grieve
Your sickness stays by you.'
'I would,' said I, 'that you did err
So grieving. I am wearier
Than death, of the sickening dying year.' "
"He answered: 'If your weariness
   Accepts a remedy,

147

> I hold one and can give it you.'
> I gazed: 'What ministers thereto,
> Be sure,' I said, 'that I will do.' "   [pp. 46–47]

The "cure" Urscelyn prescribes for Aloyse is, of course, sexual satisfaction. When he tells her that it must be kept secret because their "kin" would frown upon it as "wizardry or magic," he is telling a truth he does not intend, for Eros is a magician working through natural passion. And Aloyse liked his cure, welcoming it as often as possible. Both young lovers courted their destruction while satisfying their desires: neither had the sanction of authority, and certainly Aloyse had been trained to subordinate her private desire to her public duty. Without the sanction of authority, her desire could manifest itself in dangerous ways, as indeed her subsequent experience testifies. When the full dimensions of her needs had been revealed through this affair, Aloyse discovered something new in her identity and was close to spiritual health and independence; then her child was taken from her and she was again brutally betrayed by both family and lover. As she tells this tale to her sister, her power of desire (expressed as a power of capacious darkness) possesses her, and through her story, it begins to possess her sister as well.

The weariness of Aloyse, a condition of her existence as well as a consequence of her environment, is Rossetti's metaphor of spiritual sickness when psychic needs are disoriented, unsatisfied, and unreconciled with public forms of expression. Sexual satisfaction proves not to be a deliverance, but it does initiate a process of discovery for Aloyse, a process which could culminate in full imaginative freedom. Without the sanction of public authority, this freedom might seem diabolical, but it will nevertheless be vigorous, energetic, and—on its own terms—creative. For Aloyse to be able to tell her story is to realize a little of that creative energy, to express herself more fully than she has been accustomed to. Carol Christ is wrong in maintaining that Aloyse is reluctant to recite her past;[15] Aloyse's reluctance is increasingly a strategy of suspense, drawing her listener more deeply into the horror of her story. She is transforming the power of desire into a power of vision, of imagination. Through this character, Rossetti has taken a conventional exploration of premarital anxiety and made it into an analysis of a human soul so possessed by despair that it cannot reconcile its private experience of hell with the public display of heavenly happiness. Aloyse is not only a nervous bride, and she is not only Rossetti's ironic exposé of the nervous bride, she is, more importantly, a type of the human soul drained of spiritual satisfaction, yearning for some adequate form through which to express itself. Whether the marriage with Urscelyn can prove to be adequate to that need may, after all, be a matter only of speculation, for the poem was left unfinished. Like Coleridge's unfinished *Christabel*, this poem plunges one into a nightmare darkness and leaves us there, waiting for the conclusion with its hope of rescue that never comes.

"Sister Helen" (pp. 66–74) narrates the efforts of a family to rescue the soul of one of its members, Keith of Ewern, from the hate of Sister Helen, whom he jilted for another woman. His brothers, father, and wife all beg Sister Helen to forgive Keith of Ewern so that he may die in peace. Rossetti has made a haunting poem of intensifying horror as each member of the family rides out in the night to beg for Keith's salvation, only to be scorned by Sister Helen through the mediation of her "little brother." Helen makes the wedding celebration into a funeral rite by way of her destructive magic, slowly melting a waxen image of Keith of Ewern. While the family embassy makes its appeal, Helen brings her magic to its conclusion, destroying the wax form of her former lover. Ironically her little brother is playing while she is about her "work," setting up between them a strange tension of evil and innocence, of work and play, of a female will exercising enormous power over an alliance of masculine authority. This poem effectively dramatizes the destructive power of "Hate, born of Love," of a single soul alienated from the normal community by its maniacal obsession with vengeance, and of a bizarre twist to the marriage ritual. Sister Helen is relentlessly condemning her lover's soul to an eternal marriage of damnation with her own soul in the hell of their mutual hate.

This poem varies a theme that very much interested Rossetti: the destructive powers of passion when it cannot be contained by the usual forms of social expression. When Sister Helen tells her little brother that "Fire shall forgive me as I forgive" (p. 71), she is expressing this theme ironically: destructive passion, erotic power, consumes the self as well as the object of its desire. Forgiveness for such a soul is synonymous with annihilation, and love is fundamentally the same as hate, for both are but different shapes for the same force of consuming destruction. Helen's relationship with the wax doll is a nice representation of the relationship between passionate desire and the object of its attention. While we may be tempted to condemn Helen for her hardened heart, we are prevented, largely because we are at such a distance from the sympathetic appeals of Keith's family and because those appeals are filtered through the innocent words of her little brother; Helen's own agony is underemphasized until the very conclusion of the poem, and so our admiration of her self-control is thereby heightened. She is a beautiful form, holding and directing a terrible force.

Sister Helen is fully conscious of her powers and of her intentions in the use of her powers, and so she is strangely heroic in her willingness to damn herself to achieve her objective. Rossetti's fascination with the destructive force of feminine desire again emerges in the poem "Rose Mary" (pp. 103–36), in which the female protagonist is less conscious of her powers than is Sister Helen. Rose Mary, like Sister Helen, is betrayed by her lover; but unlike Sister Helen, Rose Mary does not, and never will, know that fact. Whereas Sister Helen brings her former lover into hell with herself by ritually consuming his soul, Rose Mary ironically separates herself for eternity from her beloved by sacrificing herself for him. In Rose Mary, Rossetti has embodied the power of desire that characterizes Sister Helen, but he has removed the taint of evil and replaced it with innocence. The twist is that Rose Mary is sexually guilty, having known her lover in the flesh, while she is morally innocent (or, more accurately, epistemologically innocent), and so she becomes the unknowing vehicle of death for her lover, Sir James of Heronhaye.

Rose Mary is a more complex character than Sister Helen, and "Rose Mary" is a more complicated poem than "Sister Helen." To say this is not to say that "Rose Mary" is therefore a better poem, however. The earlier poem may be more effective because of its simple intensity and limited vision; but the later poem does aim at more ambitious themes that indicate Rossetti's subtle sensitivity to the many threads in reality's web of ironies, tragedies, and comedies. The most important image for giving focus to "Rose Mary" is the beryl stone, the magic of prophetic vision, which Rose Mary consults to discover how her lover may be kept safe from danger. Rose Mary's mother delivers this magic power to her but she does not fully inform Rose Mary of the beryl stone's peculiar properties, namely, that it deceives those who are not "pure." The stone is another of Rossetti's many symbols of sexual power or desire that may become destructive when it fails to find adequate means of expression. In this situation, it is working its destructive will despite the conscious intention of its mistress; and as it turns out, there is some justice in its doing so, because Sir James has been unfaithful to Rose Mary without her knowing it. The "Beryl-song" tells us how the "fire-spirits of dread desire" gain their entrance into the beryl stone by way of "secret sin," and if they are opposed, they render their opponents "sterile." They ensure sorrow for all those whose desires are secretly satisfied, and they consume by the energy of their fiery natures all souls that come into their possession.

Rossetti "rescues" the heroine of this tale from the damnation of Sister Helen, but the rescue is an ambiguous one, because it comes as a reward for ignorance and perhaps even unself-consciousness (though Rose Mary's final act of great will power brings her to the threshold of such consciousness). Rose Mary does her duty when she destroys the beryl stone, but she destroys her desire at the same time. She not only separates forever her soul from that of her dead lover, but she forgets even his name in the blessed state of her heavenly reward. After she dies, a "clear voice" tells her,

> "Already thy heart remembereth
> No more his name thou sought'st in death:
> For under all deeps, all heights above,—
> So wide the gulf in the midst thereof,—
> Are Hell of Treason and Heaven of Love."   [p. 134]

The "clear voice" is the voice of duty triumphing over the "fire-spirits of dread desire." The "Heaven of Love" is the love so difficult to define—agape or *caritas*, not eros—which is left to burn without consummation and without clear human form. For Rossetti's protagonists, "the path to salvation led into the senses, not away from them," as Sonstroem maintains; but in Rossetti's most effective poems, his characters are just as likely to discover damnation at the end of the path that lures them with the promise of "a heavenly state achievable on earth." Sonstroem, like many other critics, comments on Rossetti's effort to fuse "heaven and earth, spirit and flesh, *eros* and *agapé*," but he does not give the poet enough credit for irony and tragedy when the fusion fails.[16]

THE AMBIGUITIES OF LOVE, whether the hell of eros or the heaven of agape, are present in two of Rossetti's most famous poems, "The Blessed Damozel" and "Jenny," where the tension between these two forms of love strains, yearning for some relief or resolution. For the "Blessed Damozel" (pp. 232–36), this yearning is expressed as a leaning "out / From the gold bar of Heaven" whence she looks with desire for the arrival of her beloved; on his side, her lover expresses his desire as a discovery of her presence in various forms of natural sensation—"the autumn-fall of leaves," "that bird's song," and "those bells." For both the Damozel and her lover, the possibility of fulfillment is merely problematic. Their mutual desire is for a union of eros and agape, an identification of sensuous desire with spiritual obligation, but the poem suggests that such a union is impossible. When, as Jerome McGann says, Rossetti is "replacing Love as agapé with Love as eros," McGann must show that suffering is the consequence.[17] To say that Rossetti is "replacing" one kind of love with another is to impose the critic's own value system rather than admit that what Rossetti was actually trying to do was to unite, or identify, one with the other. In the imagination, if not in heaven, such a unity of love is possible, even though it falls victim to the remorseless burden of time. In "The Blessed Damozel," however problematic that union might be, it is still movingly imagined as a possibility. In "Jenny" (pp. 83–94), on the other hand, the speaker is unable even to imagine that identification. Indeed, he labors to separate his desire from his duty.

The Blessed Damozel leans out with hope, awaiting the arrival of her lover in "God's house," fixed as a "rampart" in Heaven. Thus Rossetti locates the destination of all human happiness in that most Victorian fortress, the family home, surrounded by a peaceful grove of trees in which heavenly maidens dutifully weave the clothing which will serve the newly born, "being dead." And like a bride, the Blessed Damozel dreams of the occasion when she and her lover will receive the blessings of their "Mother" and "Him round whom all souls kneel," the heavenly Father. But for Rossetti's lovers, such a happy home, heaven though it may be, is not a certainty. The earthly lover dreams with little hope of reunion, and the Blessed Damozel at last ends her yearning with a quiet smile that dissolves into (hopeless?) tears. The poem is framed by the "golden barriers" which separate the lovers, suggesting an absolute bar dividing the two loves, heavenly and earthly. This "bar" is interpreted by Richard L. Stein as "one of the many small ironies in the poem. . . . [The bar] suggests the protective barrier placed in front of paintings in nineteenth century galleries."[18]

Jenny has some of the features of the Blessed Damozel—eyes like "blue skies," hair which "is countless gold incomparable," and a hand like a lily. Jenny is also like the Holy Mother, "full of grace." And though she has not yet been redeemed by death, her sleeping form puts her at considerable distance from the speaker, who buys her time if not her body. Rossetti's treatment of this subject was bold, but his effort is consistent with most of his poetry that concentrates on the dual loves of sensual desire and selfless sacrifice. The speaker in "Jenny" has so abstracted his desires that he compares Jenny with his books, objects all for his study. His condescending attitude toward the girl is a posture appropriate for one who is trying to do his "duty" and to do it with feeling and compassion; he even seems to "enjoy playing the proper Victorian."[19] But this speaker does not have a moral reference outside himself and his own past. He cannot submit his will and his heart to the "otherness" of the girl, to the essential worth of her being as shared on an equal basis with his own when measured by some mutual standard. He lacks the capacity for *caritas*, for agape, and so his "duty" is an empty, even mocking, gesture of frustrated desire. Nothing is fulfilled by his self-denial. Rossetti indicates the emptiness of his speaker's life in several ways, and he emphasizes the empty center of the man's ego. The sleeping-beauty relationship of Jenny to her "prince charming" suggests something of Rossetti's mocking treatment of his speaker, and it suggests something of the "sleeping" soul in the speaker himself—"sleeping," if not indeed already dead.

Very little of what the speaker observes is untouched by his own prevailing state of mind, and what he observes reflects his sterile, void psyche. It is he who is "languid" in the more important sense of the word; Jenny only appears languid because she is tired and asleep, but the speaker is languid of spirit if not of body. He sees her as a flower against a background like a "whirlpool's shrieking face," and since he later describes his own brain as possessed by a dancing cloud "that made it turn and swim," he betrays the source of his earlier whirlpool image; his view of reality is either a projection of, or is heavily modified by, his own moral disequilibrium. That his moral confusion is a function of his intellectual confusion is shown several times by the speaker's association of his studies with his view of the prostitute and more subtly by his picture of himself as a pilgrim of the night, laboring through a darkness that is sometimes illuminated by lightning. His speech is dominated by the vision of himself spinning through darkness, even plunging into frenzy; his nightlong dancing has been merely the material for expressing his lifelong frenetic search for meaning.

The speaker refers all questions about Jenny to himself, as "the lodestar of [her] reverie," wondering if she is thinking of him even while she sleeps (pp. 84–85). Imagining himself as she might imagine him, he becomes a subject of conjecture, a potential victim drawn by the revolving lure of Jenny's "grace." Like the medieval knight drawn into the garden of sensual delight, he surveys Jenny's charms as though they were lilies and roses for his delectation. But his survey is a mockery of the Petrarchan analogy of the beloved with a beautiful garden, for Jenny's lilies are dead and her roses conceal "the naked stem of thorns." This way of thinking shows how far the speaker is from being able to reconcile his disparate impulses: the object of desire is either a faded lily or a dangerous rose. His inability to reconcile the opposing values represented by the lily and the rose comes to a climax when he cries out to know how there can be any atonement

> for the body and soul which by
> Man's pitiless doom must now comply
> With lifelong hell, what lullaby
> Of sweet forgetful second birth
> Remains? All dark. No sign on earth
> What measure of God's rest endows
> The many mansions of his house. [p. 90]

In the darkness of his soul sits a monstrous lust, like a toad trapped at the heart of a stone, sitting there "deaf, blind, alone." The speaker imagines that so sits lust at the heart of "this world," which is typically an extension of his own psychic state. He imagines that the toad of lust will "not be driven out / Till that which shuts him round about / Break at the very Master's stroke." His notion of desire is thus an entrapped lust, needing release by the "Master." The release he consciously considers is a driving forth, not a liberation. But if he could release his concentrated desire, it would liberate his spirit. When the dawn breaks, he realizes that his own incapacity to act upon his desire has kept him prisoner like the toad of his own imagination—"deaf, blind, alone." The prince charming of this poem has turned into the ugly toad, and his sleeping beauty sleeps on in the speaker's darkened consciousness. Jules Paul Seigel argues that the speaker "passes through . . . what the modern consciousness might term a 'night of anguish' [toward] the crucial point of redemption" at the end;[20] however, the speaker is not redeemed from anything significant. His realization that he is empty of spirit might be a first step toward some ultimate redemption, but the mere knowledge is not, in itself, a redemption. The emptiness remains, and the grey dawn into which he moves at the end of the poem is, at best, a mockery of his desire for fulfillment and awakening.

IN THE MAJOR WORK of his poetic career, Rossetti turns to his obsessive theme, the relationship of desire and death; this theme is the consequence of "the lover's desire for unity" of such a radical kind that it must be "expressed as if it were a desire for death."[21] But *The House of Life* is equally concerned with other qualities and experiences of life, including art itself and Rossetti's own particular notion of duty, as the poem carries the reader through the "house of life," from the birth of Love, its death, the birth of Art (as painting and poetry), and finally to Death itself, for which all of life has been a sorrowful preparation.[22]

The passion of erotic desire helps to bind together all these experiences of man as he moves through the house of his life. Because this passion is so powerful and so little under the control of conscious will or conscience or duty, its power often threatens to become destructive, to prevent the house of life from becoming a comfortable Victorian bastion of emotional security. For those who are bound to this earth, like the lover in this poem, to be alive is to be caught up in a "passionate wind" (1.10) which drives him in all directions, like the lovers in the second circle of Dante's *Inferno*. Rossetti's lover, swept by passionate winds, yearns for the gifts of life, including "Fame" (1.13), but most of all he yearns for escape from the force of these passionate winds, escape into a region of "breathless bowers" "far above / All passionate wind" (1.11, 9–10). Above the chaos of passion sits "Love Enthroned" and it is toward that god of peace, as the speaker believes this god to be, that all passionate desire is ultimately directed. It is clear from the beginning, then, that Rossetti's notion of love is a complex of eros and agape, that he views passionate desire as a means of discovering the final peace of love as god, if not of God as love.

The birth of love is a "quickening in darkness" (2.7), and one's first consciousness of this birth is a feeling of desire coming like a dawn after a long darkness (2.1). Love's maturity is like a music evoking souls, summoning them to a rebirth, a release from bodily desires (2.12–13) and so a release from the dark winds of passion into breathless bowers of bright light. In "The Kiss" (sonnet 6), this music of Love's salvation is elaborated, described as like that made by Orpheus when he rescued Eurydice from the dark underworld of death. It is a music experienced not through the power of sound but rather through the power of a kiss, a kiss such as that Orpheus "longed for when he wooed" his beloved from death's realm (unsuccessfully, we should remember). Yearning for such a kiss motivates the music of rescue, and the yearning is an experience of concentration, discovering "Fire within fire, desire in deity" (6.14). The sestet of this sonnet follows the ascending passion of the speaker, rising with desire toward the fulfillment which paradoxically rescues him from desire; he "was a child," then "a man," then "a spirit," and finally "a god" within whose deity burns an intense fire that finds release through "the kiss." Rossetti identifies passion as fire, but it may burn darkly in realms of earthly desire or in realms of heavenly peace, it may burn with light. Like Orpheus making music to rescue his beloved, so the poet of *The House of Life* makes his poetry to rescue his love: both Orpheus and the poet yearn for the kiss which consummates their lives and frees their desires from captivity.

Orpheus yearning for Eurydice, singing to rescue her from death, is a trope for releasing the "fire within fire, desire in deity" in an outflowing of passionate expression. When one yearns for an object outside and beyond the self, rather than for an expression of something within the self, his relationship is like that of Endymion yearning for Diana, the moon. In sonnet 20, "Gracious Moonlight," Rossetti explores this side of desire, changing not only the mythic trope but also the image of light from fire to moonlight. Longing for Diana is much less frenzied than longing for Eurydice, and the benefits of the hoped-for consummation are the gifts of loveliness and grace. The two ladies of these sonnets, Eurydice in the underworld and Diana in the starry heavens, are the

155

familiar pair of Rossetti's poetry—one associated with passion and death, the other with chastity and tranquil satisfaction. But for each, the lover yearns with desires of equal intensity; his are the desires of a "drear soul" beneath a darkening sky (20.5) for expression of his fire within fire and for union with the light of an "intenser radiance from afar" (20.3). Dreams are, like music, a vehicle of escape and rescue; out of the "dark growths" of life, dreams channel the energies of our dark desires and carry them toward the quiet bowers of restful music where Love sits enthroned (39.1–2, 9–11).

It comes as no surprise that the end of such a dreamer's life is full of bitterness and distraught disappointment. Neither Eurydice nor Diana can be united with the living man, and his dreams cannot, finally, release him from himself—his greatest darkness and his greatest entanglement. In sonnet 92, "The Sun's Shame," Rossetti describes the consequences of a life yearning with desire for such opposed values as Eurydice and Diana represent. In this sonnet, life is looked back upon as a series of traps that have "caught" up most values and snatched them away from the speaker, leaving him only with the "mocking pulses" of continuing desire but with no objects of desire. Such a state is soulless, and the last desire remaining, with any possibility of realization, is annihilation of the desire itself, of the "mocking pulses." The only reality left is the "longing," an insatiable force which neither the woman who is desired nor the man who is desiring can satisfy: "longed-for woman longing all in vain / For lonely man with love's desire distraught" (92.7–8). The sovereign grace and radiance of Diana in the moon and the hungering lips of Eurydice have ceased to be the promises of repose and consummation they once were; their lights have become mockeries of "the blushing morn and blushing eve" which express a cosmic embarrassment at "The shame that loads the intolerable day" (92.13–14). The increasing burden of unsatisfied desire has brought the speaker to this mocking conclusion. "The One Hope" remaining to such a person is that utter forgetfulness may be the final gift of life, and in that forgetfulness would be the end of desire. Annihilation of memory, and so of identity, would be an appropriate satisfaction for insatiable desire, whose only constant attribute is vanity (101.1–4).

The sequence of sonnets in *The House of Life* thus follows the dreary course of desire flowing through darkness and yearning for light. One of the lights that commands its attention is represented by Diana, and her attributes are most of those which Rossetti recognized as forms of duty. She is a "radiance from afar," beaming with "sovereign grace" like a "governing star" that "gathers . . . [a] silent penetrative loveliness" (20.3–8). As a distant ideal whose force of attraction imposes acts of grace and governance, she is queenly duty. Rossetti's lover knows the experience of longing for this ideal, though it is a rare experience, like glimpsing moonlight through dark fog. The need of love for this ideal, though rarely glimpsed, is still quite as strong as is the need of love for other ideals. Its music is equally effective, if passion will let it be heard: in sonnet 9, for example, Rossetti identifies eros with the "hautboy's rapturous tone" and agape with the harp's "cadence deep and clear." The speaker commands "flame-winged" Eros to make room for "white-winged" Agape, to mix his "mastering music" of the sunlight with this other "wan" music of moonlight. The lady, if not the lover, recognizes in this latter music a power of discipline and control which makes her "its voluntary" (9.9–14).

If the lover could harmonize both kinds of music, blend both kinds of light, he would not find himself in the special hell of his own making at the end of his life. We saw how his life ends with a kind of exhaustion in mocking unfulfillment of desire, and now we can recognize one reason it does: he has not been able to harmonize or blend differing, and apparently opposing, values. Pursuing each apart from the other, not finding a common ground to bind them together, his will has become divided from his desire and his soul dies before his body. As though he did not, or could not, keep the "hautboy's rapturous tone" in harmony with the harp's "cadence deep and clear," Rossetti's speaker describes himself as a divided being in sonnet 65, "Known in Vain." There his shame-divided self is compared to two lovers who scoffed at "music high and soft" when once they were privileged to hear it. But even though the speaker uses the image of two lovers to explain his theme, he is, after all, speaking of himself alone, though divided into two selves. He knows these two sides of himself, or rather one knows the other, as "Work and Will." They have become permanently divided because he, like the two lovers, "scoffed" at the "music high and soft." That same music, like the moonlight of Diana, was a necessary restraint upon passionate desire, and ironically it is the goal of all desire, known to this lover too late for his own achievement.

The harmony of two musics and the blending of two lights are ways of expressing the unity which Rossetti's lover yearns for. Separation of the self into splinters of desire, breaking off into a "sad maze" of directions (65.12), has been the consequence of the soul's failure to achieve unity within itself, to realize and satisfy its erotic longing in another, whether human or divine. And all of this has happened because marriage failed, since marriage on earth is a promise of marriage in heaven. Johnson is right when he says that Rossetti makes "true earthly marriages seem all but impossible," that "throughout Rossetti's poetry . . . true marriages, it seems, are to be realized only in death, only in heaven"[23]— and, Johnson might have added, only in hell, though that contradicts some definitions of marriage. *The House of Life* should be a type of "The Home in Heaven." The poem is a "monument" in time of "the Soul's eternity" (introductory sonnet, ll. 1–2); the sequence of sonnets are "coins" of tribute to "Life" and payments of "the toll to Death." Most importantly for the theme of love and marriage in the poem, the sonnets are also a "dower in Love's high retinue." They are gifts of love for Love, and the giver expects in return gifts from Love. The dowry of his art is what the speaker brings to his anticipated marriage, a marriage which will unite his divided soul and satisfy his yearning desires.

Those values of a united soul and satisfied passion which the poet anticipates are themselves the dowry he expects from Love. In certain of the sonnets Rossetti describes valued experiences of spiritual and fleshly union as his reception of his dowry. In "Silent Noon," the beauty of his beloved is identical with the beauty of the natural landscape, and the beauty of both is captured for one precious moment at the midpoint, a still point, of earthly mutability; this moment is a "deathless dower . . . When twofold silence was the song of love" (19.12, 14). When the speaker catalogues the gifts of his beloved in "Her Gifts," he summarizes them as a bearing of "high grace, the dower of queens" (31.1); the attributes of "high grace" are "sweet simplicity," glancing light, "thrilling pallor," "passionate forms," "all music and all silence," the "sanctuary" of "Love's shrine." Union with his beloved will fulfill his worship of "Love, the lord of all" (34.9), and a union with his beloved in the present will bring them "to-morrow's dower," a release from time itself.

Later in the sequence the speaker confesses that all these gifts of Love have been merely a dream, albeit a painful and haunting dream for one who has quickly gone "from faithful life to dream-dowered days apart; / From trust to doubt; from doubt to brink of ban" (66.3–4). In the sestet of this sonnet, "The Heart of the Night," he invokes several gods to aid him in the recovery of his dead soul: "Lord of work and peace! Lord of life!," "the awful Lord of will," and even "Lord of death," but not the lord of love. His release from the dreams of love, the only remaining gifts, is what he desires most in the second half of the poem. Since marriage has failed on earth, his last remaining hope ("The One Hope") is that death will be a great divorce from all memories of painful life.

Rossetti uses many images, metaphors, and situations of marriage to express his speaker's yearning for spiritual and fleshly fulfillment. As we might expect, most such references occur in the first part, "Youth and Change," which documents the hope for success from the ventures of life and love. Sonnet 2 is entitled, significantly, "Bridal Birth" and initiates the motif of marriage with its glorious promise of benefits not only for earthly life but for life beyond death, "when Death's nuptial change /

Leaves us for light the halo of [Love's] hair." This sonnet mixes flesh with spirit, man with woman, desire and darkness with duty and light— all as functions of a love so satisfying that it is a marriage of life and death, earth and heaven; the formal development of the sonnet is an imitation of the form of sexual climax, conception—gestation—birth— growth—death, and apocalyptic vision all at once. The Victorian burden of marriage could not be any more fully expressed in so compact a way than it is in "Bridal Birth."

The bedding of the bride occurs in both "The Kiss" (6) and "Nuptial Sleep" (6a), where the marriage of bodies is a revelation of souls. In "The Kiss," the speaker tries to imagine what awful power could rob him of the promised bliss about to be his, but Rossetti is able to express this imagination in language of erotic suggestion: what could "denude / This soul of wedding-raiment worn to-day?" In the perfect union of the kiss, the body is "honourable" and the soul is "wedded" to the body. Still, Rossetti is able to suggest the undressing of the bride by describing the difficulty of undressing the soul. "Nuptial Sleep" discovers the lovers after the climax of "The Kiss," where their bodies lie apart like the "outspread" stems of "married flower"; in the exhaustion of their bodies, their souls are revealed to them in their dreams, though the revelation occurs in the somewhat ominous terms of swimmers struggling to keep from drowning. The conclusion of this sonnet hints at the strange loss of consciousness at the climax of loving union, a hint of the mystical vision, the unself-consciousness, the nothingness which identifies love with death and which the speaker longs for at the end of *The House of Life.*

After the loss of his love and the failure of his duty, the speaker imagines the horrible possibility of consciousness after death in "Vain Virtues" (85), where life's unrealized ("vain") virtues are virgins and sin is a bride eagerly awaited by "the Torturer" yearning for "his destined wife." Rossetti's sonnet is not only a nightmarish vision of death's reward for vain virtues, but it is also an expression of repulsion for fleshly pleasures that are not married with spiritual ideals (hence, virtues not realized are still "virgins"). With marriage as a metaphor of the self fulfilled, this sonnet predicts an eternal marriage with torture as the price of failing to achieve and sustain an earthly marriage with pleasure; the torture is a consequence of disunion, the pleasure, a consequence of union, between persons or between parts of one's self, such as "work and will" or eros and agape. When this division occurs or when it returns upon the self, marriage becomes an image of haunting mockery, as in sonnet 91, "Lost on Both Sides," where the divided self is a consequence of "separate hopes" competing against one another while the object of their pursuit fades out of existence. Rossetti compares this psychological,

spiritual phenomenon with two men who "have loved a woman well, /
Each hating each" until the woman dies, leaving them to a lonely life
while she goes to be the bride of Death on "this stark marriage-sheet";
the two men are mocked by the tolling of her death-bell—a wedding-bell
that is not for them. When Rossetti compares the divided and disappointed soul with two men "in restless brotherhood," roaming together
through various backstreets and "knocking at the dusty inns," he is presenting a typical Victorian image of the incomplete life (comparable with
the restless wanderers of Tennyson and Arnold), of the desire still alive
though without hope of satisfaction. This image contrasts with a modernist version of what happens when even the desire has disappeared: in
Eliot's *Waste Land*, there is a picture of the neurasthenic woman and her
companion who are "waiting for a knock upon the door."

SOMETIME DURING 1861 Rossetti and Meredith became acquainted;
from approximately January 1863 to sometime during that summer, they
were joint tenants with Swinburne and William Michael Rossetti at
"Tudor House," 16 Cheyne Walk, Chelsea; afterwards they were in occasional contact with one another until Rossetti's death in April 1882.
When they lived together at Tudor House, both Rossetti and Meredith
were recent widowers, Elizabeth Siddal having died in February 1862 and
Mary Nicolls having died earlier in 1861. Rossetti was grief-stricken and
beginning to nurse guilt feelings for Elizabeth's death, while Meredith
had become hardened and perhaps cynical since his estrangement from
Mary in 1858. The poets' respective attitudes toward love and marriage
are expressed in *The House of Life* and *Modern Love*.

Rossetti told Meredith that *Modern Love* was the best poem he had
written,[24] and in that judgment most readers would concur today. Meredith was anxious to be thought of as a good poet; indeed, he may have
desired to be a great poet more than the great novelist he did become.
He certainly found in Rossetti a fraternal spirit of the arts, and he looked
to Rossetti for encouragement and inspiration. When Meredith first discovered Rossetti as a poet, he exclaimed that Rossetti's work "is so good
that he will rank as poet as well as artist from the hour of the publication" (of the translation from the Italian poets).[25] Meredith's high
opinion of Rossetti as poet never wavered to the end of his life, forty-
eight years later. In 1870 Meredith declared to Rossetti, "You are our
Master, of all of us. Some of the Sonnets and lines throughout the poems
[which were just published that year], hang about me like bells."[26] When
he sent Rossetti a copy of his latest novel in 1871 (*Harry Richmond*), he
apologized that it was not a poem, saying, "I wish it were poetry."[27] In

160

that same letter Meredith invited Rossetti to visit him at Box Hill, where Rossetti would "be always welcome. . . . And how delightful it would be to me to stroll and have talks with you." In 1881 he was anticipating with pleasure reading Rossetti's *Ballads* and Swinburne's *Mary Stuart*.[28] In 1904 Meredith deplored Hall Caine's narrative alluding to Rossetti's exhuming his poetry manuscripts from his wife's grave; Meredith told Theodore Watts-Dunton that he felt disgust for anyone who would so use the memory of the man he "loved."[29] He wrote to William Michael in 1906 that "anything relating to Gabriel animates me with the spirit of the past days" and thanked him for sending *A Bibliography of the Works of Dante Gabriel Rossetti*.[30]

With the passage of years after Rossetti's death, Meredith's remarks are increasingly affectionate for the man rather than for the poetry, although he says nothing negative about the latter. His admiration for Swinburne's poetry seems to have increased so much during this time that Meredith began to ignore the qualities of Rossetti's poetry—or at least occasions for making remarks about it were increasingly rare. When he remembers Rossetti in his later years, Meredith remembers a man who "was wilful though he could join in a laugh at his ways. . . . Devotion to his work in contempt of our nature killed him."[31] In his last recorded reference to Rossetti, Meredith compared him with Swinburne, "a peer among our noblest," who had just recently died:

> [poetic geniuses] are the most generous of men in dealing with their fellows whom they see to be true poets. We have the example of Rossetti writing to the editor of a penny weekly paper in praise of verses he had read by chance in his columns. Tennyson in the height of his fame could write of envy of a youngster's first effort. Swinburne was as wholehearted and as prompt.[32]

In this remark Meredith has indirectly paid tribute to the man who so many years before had praised his own verses and so given Meredith the encouragement he needed to sustain his faith in himself as a poet.

Meredith knew himself to be a very different poet from D. G. Rossetti, and he may even have known that he was a poet of lesser talents. He wrote to Frederick A. Maxse in 1861 to say that Rossetti "is a poet, without doubt. He would please you more than I do, or can, for he deals with essential poetry, and is not wild, and bluff, and coarse; but rich, refined, royal-robed!"[33] Rossetti's example was a standard by which to measure his own accomplishments, and by that measure his work fell short. As a poet, Meredith may have occasionally felt insecure, but he never abandoned his hope of becoming a good poet, whatever it might cost him: he said in 1863 that he could not "give up writing poetry, which keeps your poet poor."[34] And toward the end of his life, in 1905, he said, "I began with poetry, and I shall finish with it."[35]

Meredith was a good poet, something he knew even if the world would not say so. His style was different than Rossetti's as anyone could see, including especially Meredith. Both poets shared at least one intense concern, an anxious regard for the power of egoism to isolate and alienate, to imprison the self in its own consciousness. Both Meredith and Rossetti devised strategies in their art for combating the power of egoism which expressed itself as a strong desire sometimes for possession of a woman, for expression as art, or for public fame and success. While he often dealt with this power in his fiction by exposing it to the ridicule of comedy, Meredith rarely did so in his poetry; there he more often celebrated an ideal of harmony between desire and duty, though he frequently revealed his scepticism about its realization. At his best, Meredith dealt with his subjects in a style that was, indeed, "wild, and bluff, and coarse"—but for all that, it did not lack the finish of accomplished poetry.

EROTIC DESIRE drives Rossetti's protagonists through the "house of life," searching for the peace of fulfillment and finding at the end only a hope for self-annihilation; Rossetti's speakers are divided souls, yearning for twin desires, expressed as women of opposite personalities representing opposite values. The metaphorical situation of Rossetti's protagonist in *The House of Life* is like that of Orpheus losing Eurydice while journeying back to life from the darkness of the underworld and like that of Endymion yearning for Diana in the moon; to unite his two ideals of desire would be like harmonizing two kinds of music and blending two kinds of light. Neither happens, and the speaker falls back into darkness, mocked by his dreams of fulfillment. Something similar happens to the "husband" speaker of Meredith's *Modern Love*, a poem which invites comparison with *The House of Life* both in form and in subject.

Meredith's protagonist analyzes the failure of marriage to hold together the values of people whose desires have lost the direction of moral obligation. Such is the situation of modern love when the purpose of life disappears into doubt and perplexity. Meredith, like Rossetti in *The House of Life*, uses music in communicating his theme, but he does not attempt the pleasant harmonies of hautboys and harps; instead, he accepts the wreck of ideals, recognizes the lost harmony of "the golden harp [that] gives out a jangled strain," and strives through his own "wild, and bluff, and coarse" art to discover a new chord, one particularly appropriate for his time. *Modern Love* is an experiment to discover this new chord.

Meredith's experiment—in point of view, in the sonnet sequence, and in the medley of tones—has excited the critical interest of many skillful readers. These aspects of his experiment are important and useful, but they show us the modernist in Meredith, not especially the Victorian. We should not lose sight of Meredith's preoccupation with a very Victorian concern, the plight of the soul cut off from God and retreating to the security of social work. In his novels and in his poetry, he obviously wished for some stable order of things to secure the soul from drifting and being driven by its passions; and so he sought it, and believed he found it, in the natural rather than the supernatural. However, it was easier to recognize the presence of a driving force than it was to hear the summons of a distant ideal in the processes of nature. Most of Meredith's poetry deals with the predicament of the man who feels the continuous need to make a "vital choice" between Artemis and Aphrodite and yet who knows that he must somehow balance the claims of both, according to some principle of natural order and evolution. *Modern Love* differs from Meredith's other poetry in its concern with the unnatural institution of marriage—or, at least, marriage which no longer has any raison d'être; what Arthur L. Simpson calls "the frailty and transience of the marriage relationship" may therefore be used by Meredith to dramatize "man's extensive social isolation."[36]

For a modern person to enter into marriage as if it were sacramental, leading to ultimate and blissful union with God, would be for that person to enter a dark tomb upon whose "blank wall" the self might be seen "like [a] sculptured effig[y]" (1, p. 181).[37] Thus *Modern Love* begins in a tomblike atmosphere of dead love and ends on a darkened ocean shore at midnight after much suffering and, finally, death. Such a framework is gloomy indeed, but Meredith prevents the poem from becoming sentimental or morbid by using a complex point of view and ironic detachment. Like so much of Victorian poetry, but especially that of Browning, Arnold, and Clough, this work of Meredith's gains our approval by the strategy of self-mockery. Besides the ego, however, there is another subject exposed to ironic analysis—marriage itself, which is presented by Meredith as a vehicle for conveying otherwise lost souls across an ocean of tumultuous passion. And the poem works itself out in terms of this mental geography: marriage is a ship upon an ocean of desire, and duty is divided between the guiding star of one ideal and the bewitching moon of another.

The wife, "Madam," once was a bright star for the husband, giving direction to his soul's movement. Even after the failure of their marriage, she remains for him a star, though "with lurid beams," that shines above "the pit of infamy" into which he has fallen (2, p. 182). When the husband discovers his wife's interest in another man, he suggests that his wife's relationship to her lover is like a "rich light striking out from her on him" (3, p. 183); the lover is "nothing" until Madam "singles" him out with her "rich light." Without some light, such as comes from a star-like ideal, the poor man is a nothing, left without definition in a vast darkness. No wonder the husband rather desperately tries to recover the old feeling of inspiration in his wife's presence. Recognizing the importance of her "rich light" prompts him to confess that he is still "drawn to her even now," when she has become for him "a star whose light is overcast" (3, p. 183).

The wife as a star has associations with what the speaker calls "high Philosophy" in sonnet 4, though she is not that Philosophy itself (which is compared with a mountain); the star is a point above the mountain and so is even less accessible to "self-caged Passion" than is the mountain. The husband's renewed desire to reach beyond the mountain peak comes ironically at a time when his "fire is dying in the grate" (4, p. 184). Her ability to stir his dying fire of passion is a torment to him, but it also "awakes" him to something valuable, her beauty: "She issues radiant from her dressing-room, / Like one prepared to scale an upper sphere" (7, p. 187). When he feels like releasing the "wild beast" of his passion upon her, to destroy her in the act of possession, he is forced to relent by the influence of her "soft starry" voice and the beam of her starlike eyes (9, p. 189). His inability to overcome her influence torments him, since he feels mocked by her continuing power to counter his secret rage of passion with her "delicate" beauty.

While going through the drawers of an old desk, the husband discovers "a wanton-scented tress" hidden there from an affair out of his distant past (20, p. 200). The discovery reminds him of his need—and duty—to be charitable toward his wife in her affair. This recognition is expressed as a notice of "some aged star" gleaming "luridly" from out of his past. In this instance, the wife herself is not the star, but her starlike qualities which have previously been identified in the poem serve to unite her with a notion of the husband's duty, ironic though it may be. In the very next sonnet (21, p. 201), the wife plays the game of happy marriage while she and the husband entertain a friend who has recently fallen in love; that evening she is to her husband as a "star that thro' the cedar shakes." When she appears so to him, the wife is a reminder of their previous happiness, and her starlike qualities are mockeries of his desire for a fulfillment which is no longer possible. As an ideal, she is distant, hidden by the night and the forest, gleaming with lurid rays which at one point seem to the husband like the "corpse-light" of love (17, p. 197).

By sonnet 22 we realize that the wife's star of duty has waned and grown lurid for the husband because both he and she had set too high a standard for their love to maintain. He wonders if his might not have been "a happier star" had he set his goal somewhat lower, perhaps a level closer to the more animal one of "burly lovers on the village green." When the husband tries to compensate himself for his wife's infidelity by courting a lover for himself, he looks upon her (known as "my Lady") as the moonlight of his imagination (38, p. 218; 39, p. 219). But the strategy fails him, he cannot sustain his balance between the starlike Madam and his moonlight Lady. Tormented by jealousy, he is so frenzied that his moon becomes "a dancing spectre." Finally, his Lady wanes until she disappears into the darkness of evening, when there remains for the husband's notice the single star of ideal love; Venus now becomes Hesper (45, p. 225). The irony of sonnet 45 is that the Lady's mild beauty is a function of the evening star, just as the husband's attraction to her is a function of his lost ideal, his dying love for his wife. Much like the lost lovers of Rossetti's poetry, the husband in Meredith's poem becomes the victim of his divided aims, expressed by his tormenting predicament of being torn between these two women.

His desire for fulfillment and expression is often figured in metaphors of the ocean. The husband is not the ocean to his wife's star and his mistress's moon, but his desire for them is like the tossing waves of an ocean within. His desire for his wife and his mistress is as futile as the ocean waves' reaching for the moon and the stars. When the husband compares his attraction to his wife with "the great waves of Destiny" (5, p. 185), Meredith surely wants us to recognize the irony—though for the husband, as for some of Matthew Arnold's protagonists, the passion within is something like a life-force current through all nature and something to which even men must submit in order to find any happiness. The irony results from the mistaken belief that Destiny is a supernatural force needing the direction of a supernatural goal. The husband cannot give in to his passion of desire, nor can he eliminate it. As Norman Kelvin interprets the poem, Meredith presents through the torment of the husband a view of nature which he later modifies in more optimistic directions; Kelvin suggests that "in the guise of 'passion,' nature is hardly the beneficent mother she becomes elsewhere in Meredith's work."[38] But even here, in *Modern Love*, there is a balance between the natural force of passion and the human force of will, or wit—a norm against which the marriage of this couple is measured and found wanting. That is not a fault of nature, necessarily, and so nature is neither malevolent nor beneficent. The husband must learn to accept the passion (or "nature") for what it is and to balance it with his uniquely human gift of intellect, or "wit."

Through the first third of the sequence of sonnets, the wife as star dominates the husband's tidal waves of destiny, but midway through, we notice an increasing frequency of reference to the waves of a mysterious and dark ocean. In sonnet 24 (p. 204) the husband hears his wife's footsteps as though they came to him "from a magic shore" (he apparently is out to sea and is dying of thirst). In sonnet 29 (p. 209) he despairs of ever reaching any satisfying goal, the force of his life has ceased to be so grand as a wave of destiny; but in sonnet 34 (p. 214) he compares what he expects to be a passionate outburst from his wife with "the Deluge or else Fire." As long as he feels himself to be an agent of overwhelming forces, the husband is only a pathetic victim of his own delusions combined with the real but dangerous powers of nature. It is his Ego which tosses him about to become a "thing mocked at" (40, p. 220); and when he begins to realize this in sonnet 40, the husband is on the verge of an important spiritual breakthrough. He may feel "helplessly afloat" at this point, but he is nevertheless learning to adjust his pleasure principle to the demands of the reality principle.

When the husband finds the place for digging Love's grave in sonnet 43 (p. 223), he appropriately locates it on the beach of the ocean of egotism from which he is emerging. The Love which he buries is as much self-love as it is the ideal love represented by his starlike wife. Meredith has brought us to this scene of sonnet 43 by way of the image of helplessness at sea in sonnet 40, and so the pattern of imagery contributes to a theme of spiritual death and burial; there is also perhaps a strong suggestion that the wife's suicide at the end is a vehicle for expressing the husband's ending of an old life of delusion and his preparation for renewal in a new life of reality. Thus, in its last three sonnets, the poem concludes with a series of scenes on a beach. The seashore is an appropriately symbolic conclusion because it is a boundary between two contrasting regions; the husband is left on this boundary, balanced between opposing modes of being. It is to this point that the poem's symbolic structure has brought the husband in his spiritual development. At last, ironically, marriage seems most possible, and so the husband and wife briefly glimpse again what once was their youthful hope. She makes the sacrifice necessary to free him from the old ideals, leaving him to begin again upon a more secure basis. That new life cannot be as secure as the land itself, however, or it will petrify, and it cannot be left to drift or drown in the ocean depths; it is a faint, thin edge of light created by a complex process of "ocean's force" cast "upon the shore" at midnight. This image, with which Meredith concludes the poem, is strikingly appropriate for rendering the situation of the surviving husband: he is the soul whose health is a function of a true marriage between natural desire and natural restraint.

Marriage is false and dangerous if it sets out like a ship gliding over the depths of passion and guided by heavenly lights. From the opening of *Modern Love*, the husband compares his disastrous marriage with a shipwreck (4, p. 184). The joys of the past have all been lost, as though spilled like treasure from a wreck at sea (16, p. 196). When husband and wife pretend that theirs is a happy marriage, they float and shoot like ephemerids over the dangerous depths (17, p. 197). When he feels boldly that he can direct his own ship, the husband admits in sonnet 20 (p. 200) that he might be wrecked, but he will not lay the blame on the devil. Despite their efforts to direct their marriage, he and his wife drift apart from one another, until they are "league-sundered by the silent gulf between" (22, p. 202). When the husband asks rather pathetically in sonnet 31, "What's my drift?," he is being more than cute, since he is drifting spiritually and emotionally from any true line of direction. He is experiencing the disorientation necessary for him to be free from illusion, but the experience is still painful and confusing. He thinks he can escape the pain by choosing to love another (his Lady); and so when he discovers his wife's misery, he tells her somewhat cynically that she might find happiness if she will but "take ship" and cast out on her own (34, p. 214). That is what he tries when he takes a mistress, but he soon discovers that he has merely compounded his misery because he has duplicated his earlier mistake of idealizing passion; realizing this in sonnet 40 (p. 220), he finds himself "helplessly afloat," not knowing what to do nor where to go (expressed by that popular Victorianism, "whereto . . . strive?"). This is the disorientation that follows the wreck of the ship of marriage, but it is a disorientation necessary to educate his soul, even to purge his ego in the waters of passion and to toss it ashore for appropriate burial.

ONE OF MEREDITH'S MOST IDEALISTIC POEMS of desire is one of his earliest, "Love in the Valley," which might be thought of as exemplifying the husband's youthful ideal of love for his wife in *Modern Love*. In the process of demythologizing love and marriage, Meredith wrote several poems on the naturalness of passion, but few so ironic and even cynical as "The Nuptials of Attila," which describes the consequences of trying to marry brutal passion with alien beauty. During the last decade of his career, still preoccupied with the themes of love and duty, marriage and balance, passion and restraint, Meredith wrote a group of poems in which he attempted to define most clearly what the nature of reality is in a world emancipated from the illusions of superstition; these poems are

"The Sage Enamoured and The Honest Lady," "The Vital Choice," "With the Huntress," "With the Persuader," and "The Test of Manhood." The last three were published under the collective title of *A Reading of Life*, a title quite appropriate for what Meredith proposed to do throughout his career.

The speaker of Meredith's "Love in the Valley"[39] is like the speakers in Rossetti's "Last Confession" and in "Jenny": all three desire to possess a girl but none wishes to mix sexual lust with spiritual affection. Rossetti's characters are products of their maker's own self-division and self-doubts, causing them to be portraits of intensely anxious souls near despair. Meredith's speaker is anxious about his success in wooing his maiden, but he is not self-conscious to the degree Rossetti's is. The lovesick swain of Meredith's poem has found the happy valley where his desire can be unreservedly identified with his duty to marry. Having had the opportunity to read of the husband's disillusionment with starlike love-ideals in *Modern Love*, we should be alert for symptoms of idealism through the star-imagery in "Love in the Valley." But since there is little evidence of irony in this poem, it would be an error to read it as if Meredith himself did not sympathize with his protagonist's idealism.

Whether or not Meredith sympathized, we should read the poem with sympathy both for the speaker and for his desire for the country girl. She is alive with nature, filled with the same vibrant beauty as the squirrel, the swallow, and the dove; she is sweet with the sweetness of all the lovely flowers; and she is bright with the light of all the heavenly stars. It is indicative of the speaker's desire to possess the girl, rather than to share life with her, that in his first view of her she is passive, asleep, unconscious of any claims upon her. He is jealous of her, uncertain of her interest in him, and insecure about his ability to court her successfully. He approves of the mother's wish that her daughter marry and increase love without care; surely this is a projection of the speaker's own attitude, that he might marry the girl, "tame" her recklessness, and create yet more life out of their love. We should not ignore the situation he imagines, in which the mother "tends" the girl, "tying up her laces, looping up her hair." This way of imagining his beloved leaves the speaker open to the kind of judgment that Wendell Stacy Johnson makes when he says that "the speaker's emotional response to his chaste mistress is ambivalent. . . . The wooing and sexual winning of a girl are considered a way, not only of changing her, of destroying her virginity, but actually of trapping her, of destroying her freedom."[40]

That the speaker's possessive desire has the sanction of the girl's mother (and so of family) is clear from the fourth stanza. He does not quite trust her primitive and innocent nature to choose its own best interest (otherwise he would not worry about the girl's inability to "read [his] worth"). Mothers are the best allies of aspiring husbands, and both are secure in their faith that marriage is the natural as well as the supernatural destiny of all young maidens. The speaker sees the girl as "one bright star" in "the bridal Heavens"; and the entire cosmos is a joyful marriage of heaven and earth, the sun and the sky, the day and the darkness:

> Happy, happy time, when the grey star twinkles
> Over the fields all fresh with bloomy dew;
> When the cold-checked dawn grows ruddy up the twilight,
> And the gold sun wakes, and weds her in the blue.
> Then when my darling tempts the early breezes,
> She the only star that dies not with the dark!   [p. 282]

Marriage is the natural conclusion to a natural process, and there is no disparity between his desire for the girl and his duty to continue the process of procreation. The speaker may doubt his ability to satisfy such large demands of nature, but he has no doubt that he is supposed to make the attempt and that the girl is supposed to yield finally to his effort.

Trouble for the lover of "Love in the Valley" will come when he tries to sustain his view of the girl as an object, a passive ideal of innocent beauty set like a star in the distant heavens. Marriage will require him to sacrifice his egoistic desire for possession and to accept his wife as a faulty mortal like himself, with few, if any, starlike attributes. Such innocent desire for possession as we find in this speaker can remain innocent only as long as the girl whom he desires is kept at a distance, like the star to which she is compared. Once she becomes available for the possession, the lover becomes a destroyer, not only of her but of himself, as long as he approaches her as either an animal or an angel. Such is the experience about which Meredith writes in "The Nuptials of Attila."[41]

Attila's career of destruction and carnage has been a rape of the earth, which has lain beneath his power like a woman. Meredith's poem opens with an image which characterizes this typical state of affairs: "Flat as to an eagle's eye/ Earth hung under Attila." (1, p. 162). His warriors anticipate his marriage consummation as though it were, or should be, yet another rape of the earth's goods: "Eagle, eagle of our breed, / Eagle, beak the lamb, and feed!" (5, p. 164). But this time, Attila, for some reason unknown to his followers, gives no sign for carnage; he seems remote from his customary self, restraining his and his men's capacity to such an extent that they devise various ways of exciting his old lust for violence. They hope he will be renewed by this marriage with the girl Ildico; indeed, Attila himself hopes for new life from this union. She

169

"was seized to make him glad and young" (14, p. 168), and for that reason the Huns could cheer, as they would cheer for any "beauty brought to yield" to the demands of brute power.

When Attila stopped the fighting to marry Ildico, he clearly desired more than her body—he wanted to renew himself by feeding upon her life. Whatever else marriage might be to a Hun, for Meredith's audience it was a sacramental tie of enormous value and not something to be taken lightly. What better way to illustrate the bankruptcy of the common notion of marriage than to force an imagined view of the nuptials of one of history's most infamous monsters, Attila the Hun? And what greater irony could be imagined for such a marriage than that his consummation of desire should also be his literal death? Ildico was to be sacrificed to his passion, but instead she made him a sacrifice to her duty. He was the fierce eagle, and she the sly cat. We do not know for certain, as the Huns do not want it to be known, whether she killed Attila or whether he died during the rites of marriage. John Lucas thinks this uncertainty is the key to the success of the poem which, according to Lucas, suggests the "fearful unknowableness about love and in particular sexual passion." Lucas underemphasizes, if he does not simply miss, the irony of the episode; and he typically belittles Meredith's skill, saying that while this "is a strange and compelling poem, and a deeply disturbing one," it is so "partly . . . because it seems to have come from something deep inside the poet that he hardly knew how to handle or control." It is inadequate to suggest, as Lucas does, that the mystery of Attila's death "can be fitted to the theme of social duty—Attila shouldn't have slipped back into a private life."[42] This is not the point of the poem at all.

If Attila was the scourge of God, as he believed himself to be, the Hun was no willing ally of nature. His attack upon the earth might have been in the service of a vengeful God, but his nuptials with Ildico prove to be the revenge of a sly Nature. The final dominant image of the poem is the thawing of the Danube in a springtime of hope. Nature triumphs in the end, bringing the dissolution of Attila's empire, a necessary phase in the process of breaking down the old to prepare for the new. His marriage was a renewal, but not of the sort he imagined, for it brought on the first phase of nature's next cycle of evolutionary development (29, p. 179). The individual actors, both Attila and his bride Ildico, are reduced to their appropriate insignificance by the concluding simile that compares news of the Queen with a leaf disappearing into the thawing Danube river. The enormous, destructive ego of Attila was "led forth," by "passion on one hand" and "Destiny" on the other (15, p. 169), to this marriage which would be its destruction. Meredith's poem illustrates his growing conviction that human happiness cannot be achieved as long as brutal passion is not restrained by a willing sacrifice of the ego; if that sacrifice is not willingly offered, Nature secures it at the cost of order, for individuals and for whole societies of individuals. (This is a theme Meredith worked out most elaborately in his *Odes in Contribution to the Song of French History*.)

"The Sage Enamoured and the Honest Lady"[43] is a comic romance in five parts, narrated in a convoluted, broken-backed style that exasperates many readers of Meredith's poetry (and prose). However, the style contributes to the meaning of this poem because it records a sensibility upon which nothing is lost and for which everything can be rendered imaginatively. If there is a single most telling charge to be leveled, it is that the poem and its narrator are too imaginative, overworking language to render a common scene into cosmic significance. It is, as G. M. Trevelyan suggests, "a poem to which there is no close parallel in literature,"[44] though a short story by Henry James might contend for comparison.

The action, feelings, and thoughts of the two characters are reflected by a narrator who finds in them a meaning of uncommon value. The action is played out in a dialogue between an "older" man, called "the Sage," and a younger, "fallen" woman whose "honesty" leads to a genuine marriage of their souls. However, to call the action a dialogue is somewhat misleading because we do not hear the actual words of the two characters; instead, we hear the narrator telling us what the two are saying. Nobody talks like this, and Meredith does not expect us to believe it. He is squeezing out of a melodramatic situation all of the essential reality that he can. By dividing the dialogue into five parts, he has produced the effect of conventional dramatic development, which comes to a climax in section 3 with its sentimental picture of the outcast woman redeemed by Love; there is a reversal of fortune when her story is met with silence in section 4, and a triumphant conclusion in section 5 when the Sage and the Lady are spiritually married in a Meredithian version of the wedding march from Wagner's *Lohengrin*.

In this poem, a civilized courtship is conducted to its glorious conclusion because the woman is honest about her natural being and because the man is graciously and courteously understanding; she rises in honesty, he condescends in courtesy, and they find one another on the same level, a blending of Nature and Reason. Her honesty removes his "cloak of dignity," and his understanding clears away her "fleur de luce" (p. 24). Through this example of the Sage and the Lady, the poem teaches the lesson of "how the wits and passions wed" (p. 26). Meredith here shows a version of successful "modern love" in which the experienced mind appreciates honest passion, clearing out from between them the misleading fictions constructed by a masculine ethos of power posing as reason.

The essential form of the poem follows the process of clearing away these fictions, closing the gap between two souls, and removing the barriers of artificiality between the two basic forces of the universe—feminine desire and masculine duty. The separation of these forces is a metaphysical fault which requires redemption for human tranquillity, and marriage is a metaphorical means of securing that redemption. The woman is typical of most women, who are caught "between man's laws / And Nature's thirst, . . . soul from body torn" (p. 20); her yearning desire is a command of Nature, but the fictions of the masculine ego have prevented her from obeying that command, leaving her "torn in two" (p. 22). She is the pathetic victim of the "atheist gloom" which "count[s] Nature devilish" and "accept[s] for doom / The chasm between our passions and our wits!" (p. 25). This chasm is a fiction, a myth of misunderstanding and ignorance which not only divides bodies from souls, men from women, and passion from restraint, it also sets the divided values into conflict against one another; this "strife" produces "the double conscience and its war, / The serving of two masters, false to both" (p. 27). Like the divided beings of Tennyson, Arnold, and Clough, Meredith's characters suffer from spiritual fractures and intellectual disorientations of dizzying proportions.

Meredith's poems propose a healing faith in Nature, but by that term he intends a complex of dynamic values which are best represented by the symbolic ritual of marriage between contradictory forces. For Meredith, as for so many other Victorian writers, "the wedding of man and woman can signify the union of the self and the world of potentiality, or of the human and the natural, or of active passion and receptive intelligence."[45] This occurs in "The Sage Enamoured" as a process of resurrecting the dead, recovering wrecks from beneath the whelming sea, and restoring the fullness of the moon to its rounded glory. These are but three of several motifs involved in Meredith's poem, all contributing to a process of uncovering, discovering, revealing, and fulfilling; for a courtship to succeed, the earth itself must be made to participate. The Lady is like an ocean whose surface reveals the slightest impression but conceals some secret deep within; when she begins to respond to the Sage's affection, her soul's action is compared to a swimmer's and her heart is sacrificed like something being drowned (p. 17). Her yearning for truth is a breath from the deep, and when she fully unveils herself to the Sage, he gives "her of the deep well she had sprung" (p. 24). She "drowns herself" for him, and he recognizes in her the "pilot-star on sea" which he had known in his youth (p. 24). After she has passed over the "bar-barous waters" separating them, their joyful union so affects her that "a new land in an old beneath her lay" as "Down under billowy vapour-gorges heaved the city" of their discovery (p. 28). Old Atlantis is dis-covered when passion and wit are united.

The discovery of a city beneath the sea is paralleled by the resur-rection of a dead body. The Lady is first introduced as a "shadow" that crosses the path of the Sage; she "drowns" her heart to save him from falling foolishly in love with her; she tells how she was one of "two drowned shorecasts" who appealed to the Court of Love when society cast her out (p. 19). But after her confession, she suffers the "punish-ment" of his silence and condemns herself as a martyr burned at the stake (of masculine egotism), but she is resurrected to a new life by her "gentle surgeon (pp. 21, 28). They enjoy the new life together in a marriage symbolized by the gold wedding ring of earth's horizon with the sky: "the hoop of gold / Rounds to horizon for their soul's embrace" (p. 27). This image brings to fulfillment the several images of the crescent moon—called at one point "a broken moon" (p. 23)—and the anticipatory image of the "nuptial ring of melody" in the first section (p. 16). No other kind of marriage deserves such a symbol of fulfillment as the golden ring here shared by the Sage and the Lady; in its crotchety way, this poem is an epithalamion to celebrate the rediscovery of what had been lost in *Mod-ern Love*, what had gone unconsummated in "Love in the Valley," and what had been violated in "The Nuptials of Attila."

In a group of his later poems, collected under the title of *A Reading of Life*,[46] Meredith sums up his thoughts on the meaning of life in a world without the security of a supernatural god. He proposes, in ad-mittedly didactic verse, that mankind is confronted with a "vital choice" between two goddesses of nature, Artemis and Aphrodite. Both are forces of great power and great value, but one without the other is insufficient for the balanced life. The artist in Meredith recognizes the intimate, or-ganic relationship between these forces, with Artemis the name for form and style and Aphrodite the name for force and content. A failure to follow both at the same time results in death both for the artist and for the man. As Joseph Warren Beach reads the collection, Artemis and Aphrodite "bear a rough parallelism with the Pain and Pleasure, the pain and lustfulness of the earlier poems. . . . Each is necessary to the good life. But neither should be followed exclusively."[47] Both goddesses, however, bear both pain and pleasure; neither can be said to represent only pain or pleasure. Meredith asks us to entertain seriously the prop-osition that not only are both "necessary to the *good* life" but to the very maintenance of life itself.

Artemis is primarily a huntress whose chastity is her freedom. She has no attachments, and so she is experienced in flight, as "one hot tide the rapturous race" (p. 186). To follow Artemis is to discover exuberant freedom, to thrill in the speed and process of life, but it is also to be always cold in body and in heart. Artemis teaches life how to dance with grace and harmony, but she also makes life the prey of her game. She is relentless in her pursuit, subduing life to her power, even destroying it for her pleasure. Men and women who follow Artemis may be "comrades, led by her," but they cannot be mates. She would give them a common authority to follow, but she would not give them the leisure to know one another apart from their obedience to her. To follow Artemis would require the two sexes to forget their differences, yes, but it would also commit them to an endless hunt without rest.

A life of chastity, of abstinence, which worships Artemis might be good training for the spiritual love called agape, and it might be excellent for developing self-discipline and bodily as well as spiritual grace. But such a life is empty, somewhat like the "cold pastoral" of Keat's ode, where life is always an anticipation, not a consummation. The warmth and the passion that are missing from the festivals of Artemis may be found by the followers of Aphrodite, whose power Meredith characterizes as that of "persuasion." Whereas Artemis makes frontal and bold attacks on her prey, Aphrodite works more subtly, insinuating herself gently into the camp of the enemy, where she works from within. She is an experience of inner force, of the subterranean power within the psyche that has been called variously the libido, the life force, the *élan vital*. She is "the stream within us urged to flood" (p. 190) until, in our overflow or outflow, we merge with all of nature. Aphrodite is a principle of plenitude, filling the void of existence and pressing all forms of restraint to the point of bursting; thus Meredith describes her as causing "our hearts for fulness [to] break," splitting veils, pressing streams to erupt, to "jet," into fountains, and bursting blossoms into full blown flowers (pp. 190–91).

But Aphrodite can torment just as much as Artemis. The follower of passion knows the torture of the appetite mocked and teased, never completely satisfied: "the rapture shed the torture weaves" (p. 191). The world of Aphrodite is filled with laughter and glee, but it can turn into "moans and sighs" too easily. She brings men and women together as mates, unlike Artemis, who makes them comrades in the chase; but Aphrodite cannot bless her couples with spiritual equality, just as Artemis cannot give hers the joys of sexual consummation. Meredith devotes much more attention to Aphrodite as the force which brings human beings together most intimately and perhaps more into accord with the laws of nature, but he presents her as a power to be restrained lest she become a destroyer of happiness. Aphrodite is an accumulating tension, under-lying the organic process of rising sexual desire as well as the motive force of the artist's fancy; but for the desire and the fancy to discover perma-nent value, Artemis with her grace of restraint must be called into alliance.

Meredith proposes, then, that "the test of manhood" lies in this crisis, when either Aphrodite or Artemis threatens to usurp the consciousness of mankind. Life is always in danger of overpopulation or sterilization, caught as it is between these two goddesses (called the "Prolific" and the "Devourer" by William Blake). Unlike Browning's protagonist who is urged to make a choice between alternative values, Meredith's is chal-lenged in continuous battle "to hold them fast conjoined within him still" (p. 201). The form of Meredith's four poems on this theme sug-gests the nature of the test: "The Vital Choice" is the thesis, followed by the two antithetical forces, Artemis in "With the Huntress" and Aphro-dite in "With the Persuader," to be resolved by the synthesis of "The Test of Manhood." This synthesis is like a battle in which an army slowly fights its way through a wilderness until it discovers a clearing with "hushed temples built of shapely stone"; the battle continues on the flanks even while the center makes this discovery of quiet peace and rever-ence. When he wishes to suggest the values of beauty and reverence, Meredith introduces the metaphor of marriage in combination with the metaphor of battle. In "With the Persuader," he had to use the marriage metaphor to suggest the way to see Aphrodite most fully: "Daughter of light, the joyful light, / She stands unveiled to nuptial sight" (p. 190). And so, in "The Test of Manhood," when the army of mankind reaches the clearing, its experience of reverence occurs during a beautiful dawn-ing, as "another sun had risen to clasp his bride." The reverence is a product of the sun married with the earth, a new earth whose song expresses the values of peace and energy, consummated at last.

The poem asks whether the reverence came from the Huntress or the Persuader, but the answer is that it comes from a "marriage" of the two in the breast of mankind. Men and women may marry under the promptings of Aphrodite and together "play the music made of two" (p. 194), but to produce a song of the earth, every person, man or woman, must unite the contrary impulses within himself. Meredith uses sexual imagery throughout "The Test of Manhood" in order to identify the process of human progress with the dynamic balancing of Artemis and Aphrodite. To "animate his race," mankind must use the gift of "pene-tration and embrace" (p. 203), while accepting from the earth the "juices" which drive, or "persuade," him through the wilderness (pp. 204–205) until he breaks through, penetrates the clearing where the Earth finds

175

at last "her man for woman" in a union of bridegroom with bride (p. 206): what causes the reverence in the clearing, then, is a ritual of marriage taking place there. The marriage which is the reward of struggle is a marriage of commitment to life as a process in natural as well as human history, a commitment that evolves through a union of love and work, of duty and desire.

6

Swinburne and Hopkins

Swinburne and Hopkins are the maverick poets of quality in the Victorian era. Both their themes and their styles are radical. In their themes, Swinburne constantly celebrates pagan desire and Hopkins consecrates his talents to heavenly duty. In their styles, Swinburne stretches sound and language in hyperbolical fashion beyond conventional meaning, and Hopkins concentrates language in economical fashion into pressure-packed images of vision. Reading Swinburne's poetry can be a relaxing experience of seduction by lovely sound; reading Hopkins's poetry is usually a nervous, sometimes anxious, experience of visionary tension. These radically different styles do not, paradoxically, alienate these poets from one another nor from audiences of good poetry, though tastes change, making one or the other more attractive at a given time. Swinburne writes in a line of British poets that would include Spenser, Shelley, and Tennyson, while Hopkins's poetical ancestry would include Shakespeare, Donne, and Keats. Each is a strong line from which Swinburne and Hopkins derive their distinctive voices of power.

While Hopkins's talent was largely hidden from most of his contemporaries, Swinburne's was operating at a notoriously white heat during Hopkins's formative years, and it is no wonder that, as Elizabeth Schneider has said, "the one contemporary writer of whose influence [on Hopkins] we can be certain, aside from Bridges, . . . is Swinburne."[1] As both Schneider and W. H. Gardner have shown, that influence was important for the development of Hopkins's special style.[2] While Hopkins could learn from Swinburne the technician, he was repelled by what he considered to be Swinburne's lack of moral principles. Hopkins continued to read Swinburne's poetry throughout his life, and so we find occasional, scattered comments on Swinburne in Hopkins's correspondence. Swin-

177

burne was important to Hopkins as much for what he was not as for what he was.

When George Meredith remarked in 1861 that he did not "see any internal centre from which springs anything that [Swinburne] does,"[3] he was referring specifically to Swinburne's prose satire, *La Ville du Policeman*, a fact which Cecil Lang reminds us has been overlooked by critics who have made the statement "a convenient peg on which to hang" indictments of *Poems and Ballads*.[4] Nevertheless, Meredith's point was a generalization made about *"anything* that [Swinburne] does," and it is a point often made by Hopkins. Specifically, Swinburne's critics could not find a moral center, a firm ground of values, or a transparent social obligation consistently maintained in his poetry; as Meredith insisted after Swinburne's death in 1909, he was a man for whom "song was his natural voice." But Swinburne's poetry seemed always to perplex even sympathetic readers like Meredith into ambivalent attitudes. Meredith exclaimed the "bawdry," "nakedness," and "naughtiness" of *Poems and Ballads* in 1866, *"but* it holds some fine stuff."[5]

Meredith's "but" is a comment typical of Swinburne's readers, who could not deny his genius even while they pointed out his "naughtiness." Hopkins was no exception, for he thought that "Swinburne's genius [was] astonishing," that he was capable of writing "a poetical dialect so ornate and continuously beautiful" that its like could probably be found in "Persian or some other eastern language." But because Swinburne did not "have any principles," Hopkins concluded that he was a "strange phenomenon."[6] Few who read his work would deny that Swinburne was an artist; but few would admit that he had any principles. It might be truer to say that Swinburne's principles were not recognized because they were not accepted. The man who maintained that "the business of verse-writing is hardly to express convictions"[7] was bound to find few in his audience fit to make comfortable judgments about his poetry.

In 1920 T. S. ELIOT CONSIDERED Algernon Swinburne still significant enough or commanding enough to devote two essays to him in Eliot's collection *The Sacred Wood*. Placing Swinburne in the company of Matthew Arnold, William Blake, and Ben Jonson, Eliot considered Swinburne's importance as a critic and as a poet. The reputation of Swinburne in both areas had perhaps already begun to decline somewhat before 1920, but Eliot's essay, damning with faint praise, probably helped to send that reputation plummeting (joining in a similar fate that of Swinburne's revered poetic master, Shelley). Eliot is thought-provoking even when he is wrong; for example, he describes the "diffuse" quality of

Swinburne's poetry as one of its "glories," but he clearly believes Swinburne might have survived better as a great poet had his poetry been more concentrated. He says,

> the words of condemnation are words which express his qualities. You may say "diffuse." But the diffuseness is essential; had Swinburne practised greater concentration his verse would be, not better in the same kind, but a different thing. His diffuseness is one of his glories.[8]

And so, with modern taste governed by such aesthetic criteria as "concentration," Swinburne's poetry has lost ground; at the other extreme of Victorian achievement, the poetry of Hopkins has gained.

Where Hopkins's poetry bears inwards, implodes, upon some point of imagistic reference (concentrating language through or toward what he called "inscape" and "instress"), Swinburne's poetry pulls apart, strains outwards, explodes, into the blank and nothingness of death and silence. For Swinburne, poetry is the capture of consciousness torn between love and death, between pleasure and pain; words themselves are caught up in the tension between these poles of opposition. The poet's conception of the nature of words may be seen in certain images he attaches to that conception—for example, in this line from *Atalanta in Calydon* which the Chorus speaks to Althaea: "For thy speech flickers like a blown-out flame."[9]

When Althaea speaks of the ill effects of love, she says that "for wise men as for fools / Love is one thing, an evil thing, and turns / Choice words and wisdom into fire and air (pp. 276–77). Words are as fire in this drama (as indeed is almost everything), caught up in the flash and fury of life impelled towards darkness and destruction. From the central image of the burning brand, conceived in a mother's dream as the symbol of her son's fate, the imagery of fire radiates, or diffuses, throughout the poetry of the drama. Apollo, god of the sun, is invoked in the prologue as one whose light will "flame above that flameless shell / Which was the moon," setting up the cosmic polarity between Apollo and Artemis, the sun and the moon; on earth Althaea is bent on opposition to Atalanta, with Meleager caught between. This is the burden of the lines spoken by the Chorus at a central point in the action:

> We are outcast, strayed between bright sun and moon;
> Our light and darkness are as leaves of flowers,
> Black flowers and white, that perish; and the noon
> As midnight, and the night as daylight hours.   [p. 306]

Fire is the way of seeing the love which defines life in the drama, which urges life, whether from the mother to the child or from the child toward the mate. When Althaea admonishes Meleager to stay away from

Atalanta, Althaea assumes that a familiar love already "burns between" herself and her son; she asks him "What dost thou, / Following strange loves?" To follow "strange loves" is to release the energies of the id without regard for civilization's various principles of order; to follow what we might call "familiar loves" would sublimate such energies into socially approved cultural activity. From a mother's point of view, to follow "strange loves" is a dangerous threat to order and tends toward destruction. Thus love, Aphrodite, is narrated by the Chorus as being born from the blood and semen of the genitals cut from Kronos by Zeus and thrown into the sea, erupting as "a mother of strife," "clothed with a burning fire" (p. 295). The image of the burning brand appears again: love is "as a brand plucked forth of a pyre" (p. 295). Indeed, Aphrodite had earlier been hailed as not only the "mother of love" but also the "mother of death."

The point about language as the fire which illuminates experience in communication becomes a comment as well about the themes and subjects of the poem; language and what language illuminates turn out to be very nearly the same thing in Swinburne's poetry. Fire is speech and love and death in the drama of *Atalanta*; when fire is contained, repressed, or nearly extinguished, it is the speech of orderly obedience (as Meleager is advised by his mother in their lively exchange [pp. 284–89]).

The love owed to mothers, to all those social institutions for whom mothers speak, sublimates passion into action that builds for society, protects it, and thus wards off the threat of cultural, if not individual, death. It is natural, then, for Althaea to extinguish the burning brand, though she will also be the means of its rekindling; she is man's fate, just as she is his origin. When fire is uncontained, given vent in speech as well as in action, it is the speech of anger and pain as well as the action of violence and death. What Swinburne has grappled with in his poetic drama is an insight later developed at length by Freud: that culture is the creative activity of sublimated sexual energy; that language is the major instrument of culture and so of sublimated sexual energy; that mothers and society encourage such sublimation; and that lovers tempt destruction in their effort to give direct expression to sexual energy.

Philip Rieff, in his book *Freud: The Mind of the Moralist*, speaks to this point when he observes that Freud's analysis of sexuality and domination led him to see that "culture" sets up definitions of sexuality which serve it in its "conspiracy" "to obtain 'the mental energy it needs by subtracting it from sexuality.' "[10] Rieff quotes from Freud's *Civilization and Its Discontents*, the English title for *Das Unbehagen in der Kultur*. The German *Unbehagen* is difficult to translate; Freud first suggested *Man's Discomfort in Civilization*, with *Discomfort* being a mod-

ernization of the German word meaning, literally, "dis-ease."[11] Rieff later
describes "Freud's basic point" on this matter as being "that human
culture is established through a series of renunciations," chief among
them being sexuality, where "the private sexual expenditure of creative
energy must be damned up and redirected toward gaining knowledge and
building artifacts to all."[12]

Life's complexities and perplexities of duties and desires are rendered by Swinburne's poetry in ways which are at once shocking to his
contemporaries and to many readers in our time, not only because he
insists on the inextricable kinship of such experiences, or concepts, as
pleasure and pain, love and death, but also—and maybe especially—because he links the relationship of mothers to sons in such obviously sexual
ways (as in this drama). The language he uses is violent, though beautiful. The brothers of Althaea describe the relationship of the sexes in
language of blood sacrifice (p. 301). Atalanta's beauty poses an alien
concept for Toxeus and Pelexippus to consider; she is chaste and unwill-
ing to sacrifice herself, her integrity, her virginity, to the ravishments of
love. Atalanta seeks to avoid the pains of love by refusing its pleasures;
for Althaea and her brothers, there is no possibility of such a separation
between pain and pleasure in love. Meleager's death will be the result
not of his attraction to Atalanta, but of Althaea's effort to prevent his
disruption of what she thinks is the natural order, that which ties her son
to her and sublimates or redirects his creative powers into social action.

The Chorus is explicit on this theme of pain mixed with pleasure in
loves sanctioned by the likes of Althaea and her brothers. The Chorus
tells how "the gods" "Put moans into the bridal measure / And on the
bridal wools a stain" (p. 305). When Meleager refers to the sexuality of
love, he speaks at first in figurative language, reflecting his habit of sub-
limating his sexual energy into channels of activity approved by his
mother, and describes the expedition of the Argonaut in quest of the
golden fleece (pp. 289–90). The entire passage is aglow with erotic energy
manifested as the adventure of sea-faring warriors; that is the kind of
activity approved by Althaea since it is no threat to her order, to her
claim on the son as hero.

But after Meleager's joint killing of the boar, with its open expression of violence in the service of the state and love for a maiden, he can
pull to the surface of his consciousness the buried metaphor of sexual
energy. He does so in a passage where he refers to his own conception
in language nearly identical to that he had used to describe the ocean
voyage of the Argonaut. Swinburne sets up an ironic tension between
the subject of conception and Meleager's dying and bidding farewell to
his mother (p. 348). Meleager dies torn between his duty to his mother,

to whom he is tied by the bitter root of love, and his fearful desire for Atalanta, whom he has just courted in an episode of bloody violence and whose attraction has aroused the cultural furies to extinguish his life. Any effort by Meleager to act with the heroic decisiveness that a tragedy entails is frustrated by his impulses divided between Althaea and Atalanta. His flaw lies in his very existence, particularly in such a world as this, drawn out in a tension of life torn between divided values. He is more the victim than the tragic victor.

Meleager is torn asunder by his conflict between his impulse to assert his individuality and his tie to his society, family, and mother. In his interesting discussion of this drama, Morse Peckham suggests that:

> *Family Relations* could well be [its] title. . . . Moreover the paradoxical character of Meleager's judgment on mothers in general and his mother in particular is found elsewhere in Swinburne's thinking, and not merely in love. It is found in his conception of God. Swinburne was no believer, and one may be reasonably certain that his judgment on God was in fact a judgment on what society, that is, mankind, uses "God" for, explanation and validation and social management.[13]

Peckham's point represents Swinburne's view of reality as one which the other Victorian poets attempted to ameliorate if not to avoid altogether, though Tennyson comes close to it in his *Idylls of the King* as does Browning in his analysis of what Guido tries to make of marriage and the family in *The Ring and the Book*; Rossetti glimpses some of the horrors of love's relationship with death in *The House of Life*, while Arnold, Clough, and Meredith devise strategies of irony to deal with such a view of reality.

The fires of passion and death and language fraught with the dangers of communication all burst forth in the central chorus of the drama. Here is expressed the major importance of the theme of language; it is the vehicle of all man's hopes and fears, as the tenuous instrument of culture that hangs always between order and disorder, between all opposing poles of values. The Chorus opens its lament on the nature of things with what amounts to its primary and ultimate complaint, on the ambiguous nature of language:

> Who hath given man speech? or who hath set therein
> A thorn for peril and a snare for sin?
> For in the word his life is and his breath,
>   And in the word his death,
> That madness and the infatuate heart may breed
>   From the word's womb the deed
> And life bring one thing forth ere all pass by,

Even one thing which is ours yet cannot die—
Death.   [p. 304]

Tennyson, in the *Idylls*, blamed the "broken word" for the failure of trust and faith in the ideal of an orderly society; Browning feared the inadequacy of language for direct communication; Arnold found the era too hurried to listen to the words which could save it; and Rossetti meditated on the paradox of the word as a dead memorial of the soul's eternity. But Swinburne goes beyond them all to brave the ultimate implications of language as an instrument of culture, as an instrument of life itself. In the word is the self as it has come to know itself, its instrument of self-consciousness; but also in the word is an instrument of peril and sin, upon which the self may falter and through which it must, in the end, die. Language is a measure of time, and at the end of speech is eternity, an eternity of silence.

AMONG THE LATEST, and generally sympathetic, published remarks on Swinburne as intended for the general reader, is an essay by Ian Fletcher, published for the British Council to replace an earlier, unsympathetic piece by Sir Herbert Grierson. Fletcher observes that

> Swinburne is not a Victorian curiosity, but a highly original poet, an exhilarating metrist; his poetry explores unusual areas of experience and his lyricism, at its best, is rich and haunting. . . .
>
> He gives voice to the dark underside of the Victorian psyche, writing of the aggressive, the cruel, even the demonic aspects of sexual love, and of the suppression or perversion of human instincts by social and religious tyrannies. . . . Readers were dazzled or repulsed by the violent rhythms or topics of his verse.[14]

Some critics, perhaps even Fletcher, affect amusement at the thought that anyone could be "dazzled or repulsed" by Swinburne's *Poems and Ballads*, but given his proper hearing, Swinburne can still dazzle or repulse. This is close to the point that Morse Peckham has been making in his several books on nineteenth-century art in general and in his remarks on Swinburne in particular. For Peckham, Swinburne was, with Richard Wagner and Oscar Wilde, a leader of art into the modern era of concern for "style and value"—a "first stage of stylism" that "involved the reconsideration of everything the objectists had looked at, but with a structured self, symbolized in aesthetic surface or style."[15] As such, Swinburne explores reality in the vanguard of those who are still inching their way out beyond the security of seventeenth- and eighteenth-century assumptions; Peckham has put it in more entertaining, and provocative, language: "Yet we must always remember that just as millions of people in Europe and America have never truly entered the Enlightenment, so millions of people have never truly left it, have never seen its weaknesses."[16]

In Peckham's analysis, the modern crisis is a crisis of consciousness, a recognition, perhaps for the first time, that values are not objective truths found in nature but are entirely subjective; instead, values are the result of speculative orientations. Peckham argues that Swinburne fashions gorgeous aesthetic structures whose beauty lures the self into an identity that can perceive the rest of experience as "meaningless, chaotic, and without value."[17] Only the beautiful aesthetic surface within which, or along which, the self momentarily abides, has any order; by its order, the rest of experience seems deranged and even terrifying. Peckham's thesis is useful to account for what is disturbing in Swinburne's art: the tension between its gorgeous sound and its frequently ugly subject matter.

Ian Fletcher has used Peckham's ideas in creating a biographical interpretation of Swinburne's art:

> [Swinburne] discovered his poetic identity through the distinction between personality and "self" trapped within personality, in his case an absurd body, without access to women. His solution was to transmute concrete being into artifice by imitation, parody, and caricature. In other words he tried to release identity by remoulding the styles of the past into an integrity that was of the surface only, and thus to achieve selfhood with the aid of tradition.[18]

While Fletcher tries to uncover psychological motives for Swinburne's art, Peckham describes the art as an epistemological tool for survival. One critic undershoots while the other overshoots the art itself.

"The Triumph of Time" is but one of several lyrical poems in *Poems and Ballads* that deals with the theme of erotic desire and its painful pleasures. The publication of that volume in 1866 caused great outcries of indignation and disgust among Swinburne's contemporaries, especially at such poems as "Anactoria" and "Dolores," both of which seem to celebrate not merely the frankly sexual experience, but the "abnormal" sexual experiences of lesbianism and sadomasochism. These poems and others like them deserve a better reception now that we have some distance from their first readers.[19] "The Triumph of Time" has fared better with readers than most of the others in *Poems and Ballads,* partly because it avoids most of the sensational themes of the others and partly because it speaks forcefully from the poet's own heart of his lost love (probably his cousin Mary Gordon).

"The Triumph of Time" opens at the crisis point of the speaker's life, when he has lost his love, and the remainder of the poem expresses his efforts to deal with that loss. There is a reason for it beginning and there is a reason for it ending as it does, Housman to the contrary notwithstanding; the reason for the beginning is the crisis and the reason for the ending is to be found in the middle—the wrestling with disappointment and the structuring of a value rescued from this loss. The literary pattern of crisis-resolution is a familiar and conventional one, especially for nineteenth-century authors; this has often been commented upon by such critics as Jerome H. Buckley, Morse Peckham, and more recently by Donald C. Stuart, who comments specifically upon the pattern as it appears in "The Triumph of Time" and "Thalassius."[20]

Stuart describes both poems as Swinburne's "evolving portraits of himself as a young artist" with strong similarities to Tennyson's "Locksley Hall" and *Maud,* Carlyle's *Sartor Resartus,* and even James Joyce's *Portrait of the Artist as a Young Man.* Stuart may be a little too enthusiastic with his comparisons, but his effort provides a welcome refreshment from many less imaginative and less satisfying readings of Swinburne's poetry. One might also compare the situation and theme of "The Triumph of Time" with T. S. Eliot's "Love Song of J. Alfred Prufrock," who also strolls along the beach, has heard voices tempting him from the sea, and, in Swinburne's words, "will keep [his] soul in a place out of sight." But Eliot's poem lacks the excitement and the exciting elements that are present in Swinburne's. It is this quality of the poem that makes so much out of loss, without grand gestures of the kind Tennyson's speakers make in "Locksley Hall" and in *Maud* and without the flair of language with which Stephen Dedalus makes his heroic decision "to forge in the smithy of [his] soul the uncreated conscience of [his] race." Swinburne's speaker has no such illusions; indeed, his poem is in part an exorcism of such illusions. Still, it has feeling and capabilities for feeling that have been sharpened and even nourished by loss. This is the quality of the poem which touched F. Scott Fitzgerald's hero in *This Side of Paradise,* where the "one poem they read over and over, [was] Swinburne's 'Triumph of Time,' and four lines of it rang in his memory afterward on warm nights. . . . Then Eleanor seemed to come out of the night and stand by him, and he heard her throaty voice."

Time in and of itself is amoral, even meaningless. One makes of it whatever meaning it has. "Time, swift to fasten, and swift to sever," binds as well as divides. It can do this because it is the medium of consciousness retained, of memory that ties the past with the present, and of speculation that transforms the past or shapes the future. Thus, the title of the poem has its ironic possibilities, for it may indicate the severing and division which time has made between the speaker and his lover's life, but it also indicates the fastening and binding of the speaker's future with his past. The speaker's triumph over time is an imaginative triumph through the use of time, until by the end of the poem he can even tease time, having mastered it. Although he ends with questions, which have to do mainly with a state of being or non-being when time is no more, the speaker manifests a power of will in his decision to withhold an answer known only to him: "I never shall tell you on earth." In this negation of "never" he challenges with his singleness of purpose the entire power of time.

He gets to this point by way of exercising his imagination, recreating the possibilities of lost time: *had* his love partaken of his life's offerings, they "had grown as gods"; *had* she "loved but" him, they "had stood as the sure stars stand." They might have found in love united the still point outside time. But what love had bound, time has severed; and so perhaps what love *has* severed, time might bind. The speaker's critical realization, discovered through his loss, is that meaning functions as a fulfillment of possibilities within the self, and time is an instrument of that fulfillment. The possibilities of love seem now to have been temptations of illusion: "For this could never have been; and never, / Though the gods and the years relent, shall be"; those are "things that are well outworn." The loss of possibilities returns him from illusions to realities: "I have put my days and dreams out of mind, / Days that are over, dreams that are done" (p. 170).

Later, in poems like "A Nympholept" and "The Lake of Gaube," Swinburne's poetry affirms the life that "feast[s] on the sun." Life can do that, however, only because it can transmute loss into gain, as in "The Triumph of Time." This poem shows us Swinburne at an early point in his career, struggling to cast out the might-have-beens, to negate illusions of comfort, and instead to confront what *is*, to affirm the realities; he will chase after no holy grails. But with lost possibilities behind him, he must explore what lies ahead. And what lies clearly before him is not very comfortable or comforting, leading him into a depth of reality just as his love had lured him to a height of illusion: "The low downs lean to the sea; the stream, / . . . Works downward, . . . / The sweet sea, mother of loves and hours, / Shudders and shines" (p. 171). In this image of the sea Swinburne found a symbol of increasing importance for him, providing him with its associations of mysterious beginnings, depth of wonders, surface consciousness and deep unconsciousness, waves of time and depths of timelessness: the sea is the mother as the sun is the father, a relationship expressed more clearly in "Thalassius" and exploited more fully in "A Nympholept" and "The Lake of Gaube." Love had taken him from this reality, far above it standing with the stars. He would take his love into this reality, where all broken things belong: "I would we twain were even as she, / Lost in the night and the light of the sea"

(p. 171). The sea teaches what life must learn: "It is not much that a man can save / On the sands of life, in the straits of time." What he can save, as a poet, is "a ruined rhyme." That may not sound like much, but he will learn something better. At this point, what the speaker does not yet realize is that life, with its waves of time, breaks everything exposed to it; what he has yet to learn is that he must not expose to the waves of time anything he treasures. Those things must be kept close, concealed.

Death is one of the realities which the clear eye discovers in the sea, but it is a paradoxical reality for the living consciousness. Indeed death is the same as love, at least in the sense that it is a temptation, sometimes a powerful lure, to escape the "coil and chafe" of life. Swinburne beautifully explores the illusion of death, where all broken things should finally rest: "I wish we were dead together to-day, / Lost sight of, hidden away out of sight" (p. 172). Strangely, though, even death is merely a concept of unrealized possibilities which can be understood, or dealt with, only in terms of living actualities. Death with love is only a dream, more emphatically it is a "sick" dream. This forces the speaker to wonder, to torment himself with possibilities once again. One question is whether he would choose his love in death, given his loss of her in life (p. 173).

Life's dream of death is only an illusion of life; death as a reality is conceivable only as a vast negation. Death as a nothingness and life as a destructiveness seem to be driving the speaker onto more and more narrow grounds of value. He realizes now that he would not even change his lost love, for to do that would destroy his present sense of her value to him. What he is left with, finally, is only himself, lost to so many possibilities now broken. He will keep intact what he is by concealing his secret self from the world of "coil and chafe"; this is the "self" preserved in structures of art, rescued from the flow of what Peckham calls "personality," from which the rest of experience is viewed as an unstable welter of chaos. In the passage beginning with the famous line, "I will go back to the great sweet mother" and ending "With lips that trembled and trailing wings" (pp. 177–79), Swinburne takes us into that "place out of sight" where the speaker's soul has been hidden. There in the depths of being, beneath the surface of consciousness, represented by sleep, the soul of the speaker undergoes a regeneration, a re-vision of himself. He rises anew, or with a new commitment to life, that marks him off as perhaps a voice of the modern soul, the self without illusion, even damned by his disillusionment, who has learned from the loss of love that no thing of great treasure can long endure.

After contrasting his own incomplete, or frustrated, quest for love with that of the medieval poet, Geoffrey Rudel ("singer in France of

187

old"), whose quest for ideal love was realized at the moment of his death, Swinburne's singer must banish all things sweet, especially "sweet music." The singer may believe that he does so in order to banish the pain of remembered pleasure, but Swinburne knows from his vantage point (which is ours as well) that the speaker banishes sweet things because they are signs of unfulfilled possibilities; and so, for him at least and for the age at most, they are untenable illusions, lost paradises with no ways back (p. 180). If the earth is the region of lost loves, where far into its interior there is the place of early happiness and where at its margins is the place of strife, then our speaker chooses to be out at sea with its depths of unconscious, but real, energies hidden from the light. He pays a high price for his new residence in reality—that price being grandeur, joy, and uninhibited expressiveness.

He has been wounded and he vows never to be wounded again. He will

> . . . go [his] ways, tread out [his] measure,
> Fill the days of [his] daily breath
> With fugitive things not to treasure,
> Do as the world doth, say as it sayeth.

He keeps one last secret unto himself, and that preserves the last bit of his integrity from the onslaught of time:

> Come life, come death, not a word be said;
> Should I lose you living, and vex you dead?
> I never shall tell you on earth.   [p. 181]

Stuart is probably right when he says that "The Triumph of Time" is only Swinburne's first and not his most successful effort to transmute loss into gain, into art; Stuart believes that the poem shows us Swinburne's speaker as having "simply gained the freedom that makes art possible." The poem does bring the speaker to a state of divided consciousness, concealing the precious deeply within and revealing himself at the surface as though there were no depth to conceal. That may not be very much "freedom," but it is a stage beyond the illusions of freedom promised by love and death. Somewhat like Meleager, the speaker of "The Triumph of Time" is torn between the desire of the inner self and the duty of the outer self; but he, unlike Meleager, has found a way to survive.

SURVIVAL WITH DIGNITY, and sacrifice with dignity, are both difficult to accomplish in this problematic world which, even with its conflicts and counter-truths, is still preferable to all the illusions of freedom from it. In his next significant work, *Erechtheus* (1876), Swinburne turns

188

again to Greek sources to express the dark ironies of life trying to accommodate itself to the realities of such a world.[21] This drama is a powerful indictment of duty as a sterile marriage with death, and if it is Swinburne's "greatest work," as Jerome McGann has one of his critics say, it cannot be for the reason "Kernahan" gives: "The great moral of the play [is] that human life is an act of service, a disposal of the self to other things and persons." Self-sacrifice is a witness to the importance of what "Kernahan" calls "law—a vast, organic order made manifest with all the passion of disciplined music." While McGann's method does not commit him to the view of one of his critics, he seems prepared to support "Kernahan's" view, for he has another critic, "Thomas," say that "*Erechtheus* is a play of much passion and power . . . [which] is ultimately transformed into a sense of awe and wonder." Again, "Thomas" praises the play for its "unfathomably beautiful law."[22] Both "Kernahan" and "Thomas," if not McGann, have been betrayed by their praise of law, as order and discipline, into a misreading of this important drama.

On the other hand, Douglas Bush, noting the play's main theme of self-sacrifice and public duty, deplores its "lack of drama in the plot [which] is heightened by lack of dramatic verisimilitude in details and in the poetic style." So heavy is the theme of duty in the play that Swinburne (again, according to Bush) could hardly save it "from being a death-mask if it were not combined with his passion for the Italy of Mazzini."[23] This is a very strange way to describe *Erectheus*, unless the critic is unsure of his judgment. However, Bush may be closer than McGann's critics to the truth of *Erectheus*, for what Bush cannot reconcile is Swinburne's love of liberty with this play which calls for sacrifices of the self to the order of social and natural law. It may be necessary to make an appeal, as Bush implies, to the larger context of Swinburne's life and work in order to rescue this play from readings that would have Swinburne applaud "unfathomably beautiful law."

The beauty is there, but it is in the irony—not in the law and order. Passion and desire are sacrificed, but in a context of sorrowful dismay, which the reader increasingly must feel as the drama unfolds. Chthonia's farewell to her mother (pp. 390–92) is heavy with sorrow and rich with feeling, for she loves life and regrets death. She goes to her death with dignity because she accepts her doom, and she consoles her mother with words of love and glory. Bush says that "the impulse to skip is more frequent and irresistible" in *Erechtheus* than in *Atalanta*, but how anyone can read Chthonia's beautiful speech and not be moved by the courage of the speaker is beyond aesthetic understanding. Chthonia is no more certain than anyone else in this drama why she should sacrifice her life, "still green with flowerless growth of seedling days / To build again

189

[her] city." Swinburne arranges Chthonia's speech to contrast the light and life of a young girl's summer with the heaviness, cold, and restraint suggested by the city for whose sake the girl must sacrifice herself: Athens is a place with "firm walls," "stones," and "girdlestead"—all of which need the blood of this girl "to help knit [her] joints," "to knead the stones together," and to "fasten" "the band about" her to make her "inviolable." We cannot help but be moved by the pathos of this sacrifice, as we must be moved by the irony of Chthonia's remark that "for such end / The Gods give none they love not."

Chthonia tells her mother that she willingly goes to her death, and could do so even with a "heart that leaps up," except that she regrets leaving behind a vacancy of desire for her mother. She says her heart "flags, and falls back, broken of wing, that halts / Maimed in mid flight for thy sake and borne down." She must leave behind "the places where [she] played," the bed where she slept, and the children she never bore. All posterity may praise her and her mother for this sacrifice of her virgin life to the cold god of death, her only bridegroom. Chthonia ends her farewell with a request that death come to her to "make me now gently, tenderly take home, / And softly lay in his my cold chaste hand." The pathos, or irony, of this request is a striking denial to all those critics who can find in the play no feeling or passion. Chthonia's plea for a gentle, tender, and soft union with death, her bridegroom, contrasts starkly with the violence sung by the Chorus, for death is not to be gentle and tender for anyone. Nor will Chthonia's death be completely explicable to herself, however much she and her parents may rationalize it. She goes silently, and so with dignity, to her death; however, she also goes blindly:

> A silent soul led of a silent God,
> Toward sightless things led sightless; and on earth
> I see now but the shadow of mine end,
> And this last light of all for me in heaven.   [p. 392]

What is most Swinburnian about this scene is its love of life, its love of the warmth and light of the sun, not its resignation to death. The magnificence of Chthonia's death is measured by her love of life, and the strength of her will to duty is measured by her sacrifice of such great desire. She and all others in the drama can accept the horror of her sacrifice only as a ritual of marriage with death, for marriage promises not only harmony but also new life. This particular marriage, however, is a bitter Swinburnian ritual that may palliate but cannot obviate the necessity of death, that "strange" bridegroom who makes virgins of us all.

All manner of things are "strange" in *Erechtheus*, not the least of which are the various marriages and the will of the gods. Erechtheus himself is the offspring of a strange marriage, being a child of the Earth because he was born from the semen that fell upon the ground while Hephestus was unsuccessfully trying to rape Athena. This virgin goddess would not yield to the desires of any god or man, but she did take care of the child that came out of Hephestus's seed. And so Erechtheus was, and was not, the child of Pallas Athena, whose city he governs and for whom he will give up not only the life of his daughter Chthonia but also his own life. Like Atalanta, Athena insists upon her virginity, an identity not to be compromised or violated by anyone; also, like Althaea, she calls for her ("foster") child to sacrifice himself on behalf of the state— Athena is even more demanding than Althaea, for she wants a self-sacrifice in the death of Chthonia as well. Athena, who refused desire, insists on unconditional, absolute duty from the citizens of her city. If she is to be worshipped, she must be obeyed without reservation, and to obey Athena is to sacrifice all desire in return for her austere protection.

The play is rich with the ironies of such worship, for it sets the intellectual but austere freedom of Athena in frequent juxtaposition with the glowing warmth and light of being in the sun of Apollo (as well as with the more obvious overwhelming, chaotic power of Poseidon's ocean). The tension of the play lies in the values represented by Athena and Apollo, for in their differences is the poet's real problem. Swinburne is not troubled by the argument that Athens and its freedom deserve any sacrifice to preserve them from the threats of natural chaos, for with that argument he concurs; it is this concurrence that gives the drama its superficial calm. What drives the drama, however, is its undercurrent of unrest, of "strangeness" marking the mysterious conflicts between Apollo and Athena.

The obvious drama involves the relationships, and set speeches, of Erechtheus, Praxithea, Chthonia, and the Herald of Eumolpus; the force, or undercurrent, of anxiety at all the strange things in this world is given voice by the Chorus. This is not unusual for Greek drama, of course, but it would be unusual if Swinburne, who was most of all a lyric poet, did not use the poetry of the Chorus to render most fully his own imaginative perspective on this drama of events he did not invent. In other words, the poetic complications of the drama are revealed in the moods, judgments, and observations of the Chorus, over which the poet had more control, rather than in the play's events, over which the poet had little control. This is as it should be, for Swinburne accepted the realities of existence, just as he could accept the story of Chthonia's sacrifice for Athens; but he did not accept those realities without protest, without pain and questioning. It is "reality" that is "strange." The will of the gods in the drama is one factor in the set of realities that the poet protests and questions.

The Chorus represents a long and sophisticated protest against an existence in which the human soul is humbled, if not humiliated, by the power of gods. Seen from this perspective, the play is not at all unlike the younger Swinburne's poetry; it develops its choral lyrics in response to this cry which we hear during the first speech of the play, when Erechtheus pleads with his mother Earth, asking "what have we done" to bring on "this timeless curse?" In his great ignorance of why things are as they are, Erechtheus knows only this:

> how the soul runs reinless on sheer death
> Whose grief or joy takes part against the Gods.
> And what they will is more than our desire,
> And their desire is more than what we will.
> For no man's will and no desire of man's
> Shall stand as doth a God's will.   [p. 359]

Like Job in his affliction, Erechtheus cannot understand why he, who has never "chid with [his] tongue or cursed at heart for grief," should have to suffer or why his city should be endangered. Erechtheus is a man who does his duty above all things, and his duty is the maintenance of his city. This tamer of horses has inherited from his father, Hephaestus, the "cunning" of art through discipline. For all his self-discipline and authority over animal and human life, Erechtheus still must suffer and suffer. It is not true, as he seems to imply, that the "soul runs reinless on sheer death" only when it "takes part *against* the Gods"; it will run "on sheer death" whether or not it takes part against the gods.

This is one of the strange things contemplated by the Chorus, which often represents action and judgment in terms of marriage. The most glorious marriage celebrated in this drama is the marriage of the Earth and the Sun; that should be the model for all human marriages, but far too often the most common marriage is a marriage with death. The joy of true marriage is a result of aesthetic and intellectual freedom, and thus should the mythic relationship between Apollo and Athens be celebrated. The grief of a false marriage is a result of bondage either by the aesthetic (Apollonian) or by the intellectual (Athenian) to forces of death and destruction. When Athena refused to bear the child of Hephaestus except by proxy, as it were, she set the model for tragedy, the very tragedy here enacted. Aesthetic desire cannot long be denied by intellectual duty without dire consequences for both. Hence the Chorus is doomed to sing songs that mingle the "joyful and sorrowful," the sweet and the bitter (p. 419).

The ecstatic song of the Chorus that celebrates the primal marriage

192

of the Sun and the Earth, is the model by which we are to measure all other marriages. We hear this song just after Chthonia has left the scene for her death, praying for Athens that it shall live a "life as the sun's is above" (p. 399). Chthonia's departure for the darkness of death evokes a hymn to sunlight, to all the vitality that thrives beneath the sun. Athens is not only the city of Athena, but it is the place of union between the Earth and the Sun; and as such Athens is a symbol of perfect marriage. The Chorus sees in this city a harmony of all love:

> None of all is lovelier, loftier love is none,
> Less is bride's for bridegroom, mother's less for son,
> Child, than this that crowns and binds up all in one;
> Love of thy sweet light, thy fostering breast and hand
> Mother Earth, and city chosen, and natural land.   [p. 399]

The children of this place are flowers of earth and sunlight. Apollo quickened the earth with his love:

> the stroke of the shaft of the sunlight that brought us to birth
> Pierced only and quickened thy furrows to bear us, O Earth.
> With the beams of his love wast thou cloven as with iron or fire,
> And the life in thee yearned for his life, and grew great with desire.
> [p. 400]

These children of the earth and the sun (Athenians) are products of mutual desire:

> Such desire had ye twain of each other, till molten in one
> Ye might bear and beget of your bodies the fruits of the sun.
> And the trees in their season brought forth and were kindled anew
> By the warmth of the moisture of marriage, the child-bearing dew.
> And the firstlings were fair of the wedlock of heaven and earth;
> All countries were bounteous with blossom and burgeon of birth.
> [p. 400]

Any kind of marriage other than this will produce "strange children and changelings" (p. 401). To recover such a harmony of earth and sun, death is no sacrifice but a blessing, to be faced as a part of the life process itself. And so, well might the Chorus celebrate the sacrifice of Chthonia as a ritual of seedtime.

But Chthonia is no seed; she is still a blossom, in the bloom of her life. Hence the tragedy, the strangeness of an existence in which ripeness is not all and birth is tantamount to death. Human nature is a victim of some great divorce, as the opening of the play suggests. Erectheus prays to his mother, Earth, for some divine protection, knowing but not understanding why he must sacrifice his daughter (at the behest of Apollo's oracle). Immediately following the appeal by Erectheus, the Chorus calls upon the Sun to witness the conflict now erupting between Earth and Ocean, whom the Sun itself has "lightened and loosed" "from the lord-ship of night." To what avail does the Sun quicken "with vision his eye that was veiled" or freshen "the force in her heart that had failed" (p. 360)? If the product of vision and freedom is chaos and death, then it is better to be blind and a slave. This is a time when "strange hunters are hard on us, hearts without pity" (p. 361), members of the Chorus say, waiting to hear what Apollo's oracle pronounces, waiting "with hopes that falter." They turn from Apollo to Athena, she who was "not born of the womb, nor bred / In the bridenight's warmth" (p. 362). The Chorus appeals to Apollo and Athena to reunite as the Sun and the Earth to protect the city of human freedom:

> O earth, O sun, turn back
> Full on his deadly track
> Death, that would smite you black and mar your creatures,
> And with one hand disroot
> All tender flower and fruit,
> With one strike blind and mute the heaven's fair features.   [p. 362]

The Chorus wants no more marriages with death, such as those that have already visited the house of Erechtheus: when Boreas filled "the night with his breath" and seized Oreithyia with "a love like death"; when "Love's self" like "a bridegroom beloved of the morning" appeared in the form of Apollo to ravish Creusa; or when Cephalus drove Procris upon "the point of her own spear." Love has brought no happiness and no joy to Athens, for these have not been true marriages.

The mockery of marriage, a shade of Hymen, is the subject of the next choral song, after Erechtheus has announced the doom of the oracle. The Chorus addresses Night as the "mother" and Death "for the father" of such "sorrow" as this news from Erechtheus: "From the slumberless bed for thy bedfellow spread and his bride under earth / Hast thou brought forth a wild and insatiable child, an unbearable birth" (p. 369). After Praxithea speaks of her resignation before the oracle that dooms her daughter, the Chorus sings of that first mock marriage with a child of Erechtheus, when Boreas seized Oreithyia:

> A God, a great God strange of name,
> With horse-yoke fleeter-hoofed than flame,
> To the mountain bed of a maiden came,
> Oreithyia, the bride mismated,
> Wofully wed in a snow-strewn bed,
> With a bridegroom that kisses the bride's mouth dead.
> [p. 377]

The god of the North Wind mocked Oreithya's prayers with derision when he sprang "on the spoil of his desire" (p. 378). He carried her away "from the bosom of earth as a bride from the mother, / With storm for bridesman" (p. 379). That "marriage" has brought no good to Athens; indeed, Boreas is sometimes seen as one who helped Eumolpus carry out his attack upon Athens. Why, therefore, should the loss of Chthonia to a god, to the god of death, be any more auspicious?

This is the burden of the Chorus's "new song younger born" to mourn "now a younger grief":

> Who shall teach our tongues to reach
> What strange height of saddest speech,
> For the new bride's sake that is given to be
> A stay to fetter the foot of the sea. . . ?   [p. 379]

The Chorus is rightfully uneasy about the will and desire of the gods, even the oracle of Apollo, that "bitter and strange . . . word of the God most high" [p. 384]. They interpret Chthonia's death as a marriage ritual, but it will not be celebrated without "anguish of heart" which they feel as they watch her move toward her strange "bride-feast" (p. 388). Chthonia sees herself as a "spouseless bride," and so does the Messenger who describes her death: "the maiden stood, / With light in all her face as of a bride / smiling," and "brighter than a bridal veil / Her hair enrobed her bosom" (p. 402).

The Chorus continues perplexed, singing of "strange new tongues" and "strange children," while the Messenger speaks of "strange tears"; this is the atmosphere surrounding Chthonia's death and its aftermath, when Erechtheus meets Eumolpus in the great battle of Athens with the sea. When Ocean assaults Earth in this battle of the elements, the Chorus sings one of its most powerful lyrics (pp. 404–12), for in this event lies a climactic conclusion to false marriages, when the earth's children are assaulted or enslaved, as they have been in the past. Here we have Swinburne's apocalyptic promise of better things to come, but first there must be a great violence and spilling of blood, as in false marriages. Fearing that blood cannot purify guilt, the Chorus watches the sky darken and then hears the "song of death" that fills the air before the battle: "What bride-song is this that is blown on the blast of thy breath?" (p. 406). The "young-sun" had awakened and leaped into day "laughing," from his "bride-bed of dawn." But on the same day the wind blew in the terror from the north to darken Athenian skies. The Chorus prays to Apollo as the sun who can ward off wrath and restore the light of vision to their dark land: "O, lift up the light of thine eye on the dark of our dread" (p. 410). In their fear they are filled with "desire of [his] eye." Their dread of the darkness is increased by the news that Erechtheus has been slain by Zeus himself.

The land remains in darkness, covered by ignorance and guilt, even after the death of Eumolpus and the rescue of Athens from the power of the sea. The Chorus feels the weight of the "blood-red hand," knowing that "rain shall not cleanse it" and that they must live "in the world without sun" (p. 420). But Athena enters to promise that all will now be well for them, not only calming the "winds of the air" to a soothing calm and the storming ocean to a quiet heart, but also calling the sun to spring forth again, for the glory of this free city. While Praxithea gives thanks that her grief can be outweighed by her "joy to be made one in will / With him that is the heart and rule of life," the Chorus still feels that "the shadows of past things reign" (p. 420) so much that it can give thanks in the last lyric of the drama only in terms of "the darkness of change on the waters of time" (p. 424). These death fires may serve, ironically, as a light into the dawn of a new day, when again the Chorus can find its way into "the old garden of the Sun" (p. 393) where life and light prevail.

IN HIS TRILOGY OF PLAYS based on the life of Mary Stuart, Swinburne dramatizes a life of passion ever struggling to escape the fetters of public duty and thereby to "make life durable" for herself. Mary Stuart was a woman of "passionate and high-spirited defiance" who "cared much" for her "freedom of will and of way."[24] Swinburne believed that she exhibited the virtues of courage, personal loyalty, and gratitude to friends and that Elizabeth displayed the complementary virtues of public courage and public duty. Mary was lacking in the qualities that made Elizabeth a powerful and successful monarch, but Elizabeth was lacking in the qualities that made Mary Stuart a powerful and attractive woman. While Swinburne so obviously wished (particularly in the third play) to set these two women against one another as examples of opposing virtues, of personal desire and public duty, he was more interested in the development of private and personal desire in the character of Mary Stuart.

The highly unsuccessful reign of Mary Queen of Scots is dramatized through the three plays, beginning with her affair with Chastelard, moving to her marriage with Darnley, her relationship with David Rizzio and his murder, his complicity in the murder of Darnley, her marriage with Bothwell, and then her imprisonment and execution by Elizabeth. Swinburne shows how impossible it was for Mary Stuart to reconcile her passion of desire with her political duties; she is a manifest example of the urge to marry these sometimes conflicting virtues into a unity of balance and harmony. Swinburne illustrates through her career how perilous the Victorian ethos can be for a person with the emotional and intellectual resources of Mary Stuart. Her tragedy is also her triumph, for what she loses is merely the order of politics while her gain is the integrity of her personality.

In *Chastelard* (1865),[25] Mary Stuart marries Darnley and executes her lover. Both her marriage with Darnley and her execution of Chastelard are gestures of regard for the order of her kingdom. However, she does not disregard her inner life of the spirit, represented by her dreams and her desire for Chastelard. Her marriage with Darnley is only an empty form, bringing no grace of itself (p. 56). Her actual marriage is with Chastelard; this true marriage is brought about first as dancing (pp. 37–38), then as sleeping (pp. 40, 47), and finally as feasting (pp. 58–59, 99–100, 110). Mary Stuart becomes a divided being in this first drama; she sacrifices her passion for Chastelard in order to maintain her obligation to Darnley and the kingdom. Ironically, though, her kingdom drifts into chaos while her passion finds fulfillment when she visits Chastelard in his cell on the eve of his execution. Feeling "a bride-night's lustiness," Chastelard greets his queen as a Venus feeding upon his blood (pp. 109, 110) while she comes to him for "a little of his blood / To fill [her] beauty from" (p. 59). Thus, Chastelard's death becomes a sacrifice to maintain Mary Stuart's passion, to sustain her spirit of individuality, even while she must continue to act out her empty life of public duty. She dares to "let fame go" in order to "save love and do [her] own soul right" (p. 100).

She courts public disaster with her ferocious pursuit of Lord Bothwell for whom she is willing not only to let her fame go but even to destroy the kingdom itself. Swinburne's dramatization of Mary Stuart's relationship with him in *Bothwell* (1874) is, despite its ponderous length, an occasionally superb piece of writing.[26] In this play, Mary Stuart becomes as a fire that grows upon the wind of controversy, rising to such intensity that when she merges in desire with Bothwell they become as God (pp. 314–15). Darnley is the empty formality that the Queen conspires to destroy, and Bothwell is the inspiration that excites her to defy all the world around her. She becomes Antony to his Cleopatra (p. 128) in that it is she who is willing to lose the world for his love. Together they become a terrific energy, tantamount to nature concentrated in storm-like fury: she a ravaging fire and he a forceful wind. They are the restless activity of souls united in fulfillment and unrestrained in desire, ironically achieving in themselves the peace which John Knox maintains can be found "in the full fire and middle might of wrath" (pp. 208–10).

The Queen asks her husband, Darnley, how it is possible for anyone

197

to live "in such times honourably or safe, / When change of will and violence mutable / Makes all state loose and rootless?" (p. 238). Her question implies the answer that no one can; certainly, there can be no honorable life in the sense that honor is public fame, which in turn depends upon the self sacrificed for the sake of public order. She had compromised her true honor when she married Darnley for the sake of the state; to restore her own integrity, Mary Stuart yoked her will with Bothwell's strength to eliminate Darnley and to free herself to become perfect in desire. She tells Bothwell that she has

> the more need
> I purge me now and perfect my desire,
> Which is to be no more your lover, no,
> But even yourself, yea more than body and soul,
> One and not twain, one utter life, one fire,
> One will, one doom, one deed, one spirit, one God;
> For we twain grown and molten each in each
> Surely shall be as God is and no man.   [p. 315]

To purge herself of all distractions, to free her will of all stately trammels, is Mary Stuart's aim in killing Darnley and thus, in effect, killing her fame (or her dependence upon it for honor) and annihilating her public duty. She will be true to herself alone, uniting her desire with Bothwell's and so together perfecting their desires to become "one and not twain, one utter life, one fire." She takes on a "wifehood well nigh done with duty now" (p. 344) when she kills Darnley and marries Bothwell; together they "are past the season of divided wills" when "[their] deed alone [they] live by" (pp. 344, 360–61, 362). The Queen murders duty and deifies passion to find the inner peace which is denied the kingdom; when her subjects rebel to separate her from her lover, they merely strip her of the self which she has already destroyed. At the end of the play, Queen Mary has become, in fact, only Mary Stuart, exiled and alienated from the land she never loved. Stripped of the self which divided her will, she is paradoxically stronger in exile than she ever was in her own kingdom.

Just as she must learn in *Bothwell* what true duty is—the liberation of self as desire—in *Mary Stuart* (1881), she learns what true marriage is.[27] Through the three dramas, Swinburne shows the education not only of a famous (or infamous) queen whose best lesson is in how to be a woman, but perhaps more importantly he shows the education of a soul, any soul, learning to find its fullest expression in a world of frustrating conflicts. Swinburne's royal heroine thrives upon social chaos and lonely exile: Mary Stuart has hardly a thought for Bothwell after they are separated. She does not need him any longer, for whatever he brought to her she has now made a part of herself. Each of her marriages has helped to define more clearly her own character, revealing to her at each step what she could—and what she could not—do without to discover her identity. Each marriage has had an element of the false in it, and so each has had to be dissolved by one means or another. Even the marriage with Bothwell has had to be if not dissolved, then transcended, for it would have become a shackle to Mary Stuart's essentially free spirit.

Bothwell brought her fulfillment, helped her to perfect her desire, but he could not complete the integration of a will that had for so long been divided: Mary Stuart still must learn that duty cannot be forever disregarded, cannot be totally eliminated, without leaving a crippling mark or wound. She has to learn that perfect desire requires its own duty, a duty to itself, as it were, in which marriage between passion and action accomplishes the most complete expression of self which is possible in this life. Such a complete action is possible only in the final, absolute marriage with death. From the first, Mary seems destined to act out the ritual of marriage with death; in her dream of dancing with Chastelard, "clothed in black with long red lines and bars / And masked down to the lips" (*Chastelard*, p. 38), she has anticipated her end, when she will be "brought home" "like a bride" to mount the scaffold for her execution (*Mary Stuart*, pp. 471–74). She meets her bridegroom, death, like a bride on fire with desire:

> And now they lift her veil up from her head
> Softly, and softly draw the black robe off,
> And all in red as of a funeral flame
> She stands up statelier yet before them, tall
> And clothed as if with sunset. [p. 474]

The frequent associations of her love with death throughout the three dramas has insistently prepared us for this climax to Mary Stuart's life. She has learned that a life of passion requires many sacrifices, not the least being the sacrifice of those men whose souls have fed her passion; as she says to Mary Beaton, "man by man, . . . they perish of me" (p. 439). Finally, she realizes that her desire is for something more than the lives or loves of men (p. 437), it is for an absoluteness of passion which is the self fulfilled. Through her character, Swinburne has dramatized the terrible struggle of a soul at war with most of the constraints of duty, pressing its claims for satisfaction upon all who come in its way, and rising through the shambles it has helped to create to become, somewhat like the phoenix bird, a spectacle of beauty mixed with death. Mary Stuart was a striking failure as a monarch, but she was a stunning success as a woman: as Drury says to Paulet, "She shall be a world's wonder to all time" (p. 425).

IN 1880, AT THE AGE OF 43, when he published "Thalassius" in *Songs of the Springtides*[28] (and after he had been "rescued" from near-death by his friend Theodore Watts), Swinburne had achieved the perspective that allowed him to understand his relationship to his art, a relationship he describes in the poem. He had behind him the many experiences of life that constitute the triumphs of time, but throughout all these experiences there was at least one constant: his devotion to the beautiful artifacts of language. His art was what really rescued Swinburne; Watts would probably not have been at hand had Swinburne's poetry not attracted him in the first place. Swinburne had created beauty out of such different experiences as lust for fatal ladies (*Poems and Ballads, Atalanta in Calydon*), desire for political freedom, laments for lost leaders (*Songs Before Sunrise, Songs of Two Nations*), and delusions of order in nature ("A Forsaken Garden"). He could then, in "Thalassius," review his life of the spirit as a mysterious birth from the Ocean, making its appearance in its dawn of consciousness as a foundling on the shore, cared for by a foster-father instilling in him an ambition for the "high things" of "Liberty," "Love," "Hate," "Hope," and fear (pp. 290, 292, 293, 294).

Stuart has argued that these lessons of the "high song" taught by the foster-father are "conventional values" which must be corrected by the unconventional values associated with the "dread lady" who lures the poet-child into orgies of the flesh. At least on this point, Stuart allows his analogy with D. H. Lawrence and Wallace Stevens to take him too far from the total lesson of the poet-child in "Thalassius"; the values of the foster-father are not so much unlearned as supplemented by the experience of the flesh. The spirit is made more complete, given a ground of realization for the values learned in the abstract. If anything, the frenzied abandonment to fleshly pleasure has helped to make more valuable the lesson previously taught.

It may be true, however, that the old "conventional" values, which are made to seem so abstract by the entanglements of flesh, can never again be as valuable as once they were; they are equivalent to the lost love of "The Triumph of Time." The poet-child has been sundered from his innocent past by the "dread lady," and he escapes, exhausted, into a sleep of deep consciousness, again echoing the return to the sea in "The Triumph of Time": "and his eyes gat grace of sleep to see / The deep divine dark dayshine of the sea" (p. 301). Here again is rebirth, revision, and this time there is no doubt about the conclusion, as there may have been in "The Triumph of Time": "He communed with his own heart, and had rest." In the light of such passages as this, and others that celebrate the joy of song's birth, it is difficult to follow Meredith Raymond's argument that the poet *loses* his soul, or must be willing to lose it, twice—once to Apollo and once to mankind.[29] Throughout the first two-thirds of "Thalassius," the experience of the poet-child has been one of cumulative knowledge, with nothing really lost except innocence and ignorance. Nor is there a loss when the poet has come home again and finds his true father, Apollo, whose fire enters the poet to identify the poet with Apollo. He becomes Apollo on earth, the incarnation of light and music: "Being now no more a singer, but a song," worthy of the blessing that Apollo then bestows upon him.

Swinburne now knows himself for what he is and knows what cannot be changed in him; he is now as secure in his identity as was William Blake from the moment of that awful illumination recorded in *Milton*, when Blake became the incarnation of Milton's spirit joined with the great archetype of all artists, the Zoa Los. Swinburne makes as subtle, though not as powerful, a statement as Blake did in distinguishing the artist as singer from the artist as song; the first will always live in self-division like the speaker in "The Triumph of Time," like the man of mere talent with no commitment, or like the man of genius with no audience. The other is secure in his integrity, his word is the thing it names and his song is the consciousness that knows all things in itself. This man *needs* no larger audience than himself, though he knows that his audience is all time and all places measured by his father, Apollo. This Apollo assures him in his benediction that closes the poem:

> "Because thou hast kept in those world-wandering eyes
> The light that makes me music of the skies;
> Because thou has heard with world-unwearied ears
> The music that puts light into the spheres;
> Have therefore in thine heart and in thy mouth
> The sound of song that mingles north and south,
> The song of all the winds that sing of me,
> And in thy soul the sense of all the sea." [p. 303]

That Swinburne would write a poem based on the story of Tristram and Iseult seems to have been inevitable, given his strong interest in the force of passion and love's debt to death. His *Tristram of Lyonesse* (1882) has the marks of an epic effort; it was to be the high achievement of a poet blessed by Apollo.[30] And, indeed, *Tristram of Lyonesse* sometimes rises to a high poetic achievement. It records many of the themes and subjects with which Swinburne was concerned between 1865 and 1882, including the theme of passion as fate, the subjects of marriage and of the development of the artist, and the symbolic imagery of the sun and the sea. When Tristram and Iseult fall so deeply in love that they are spiritually united for eternity, they repeat in a finer tone the relationship of Mary Stuart and her lover Bothwell. Swinburne is able to examine yet

again, as he did in the drama, the dynamics of a relationship in which
identities are lost in a union of desires; in this story, however, he is able
to explore the consequences of desire fulfilled, not at the expense of public duty (as in *Bothwell*), but rather without the sanctification of insti-
tutionalized marriage. Ironically, this classic story serves as a vehicle for
examining the failure of formalized marriage to unite individual desire
and selfless duty.

Not only does the story reexamine the subject of marriage, but it
also restates Swinburne's interest in using the imagery of the sun and the
sea to narrate either the development of the artist (as in "Thalassius") or
of the mature consciousness (as in "The Lake of Gaube"). The plunge
into the water, which occurs at crucial points in both "The Triumph of
Time" and "Thalassius" and which constitutes the form of "The Lake
of Gaube," is a major episode in *Tristram of Lyonesse*. In part 8, "The
Last Pilgrimage," before his final battle, Tristram swims in the sea as
though he were renewing his strength at the mysterious source of all life.
His contact with the water is, in imagery of sexual consummation, a ritual
enactment of divine or cosmic processes:

> And from his heart's root outward shot the sweet
> Strong joy that thrilled him to the hands and feet,
> Filling his limbs with pleasure and glad might,
> And his soul drank the immeasurable delight
> That earth drinks in with morning, and the free
> Limitless love that lifts the stirring sea
> When on her bare bright bosom as a bride
> She takes the young sun, perfect in his pride,
> Home to his place with passion.   [pp. 142–43]

Tristram is the fierce energy of the sun, almost Apollo himself, plunging
into the receptive waters of the sea. He brings to the limitless freedom
of the sea a strong measure of discipline, a sense of mission and purpose
which characterize duty and moral obligation. When Swinburne compares Tristram to Achilles, bathed in divine light as he shouts from the
ramparts in book 18 of the *Iliad*, we are to remember that Achilles chose
the short life of fame for love of his friend Patroklos, and when he returned to the battle he knew himself to be a dead man. The association
of Tristram leaping into the sea with Achilles returning to battle helps
Swinburne to portray Tristram as a hero who is willing to give up much
of the world for the sake of love and duty. Death is to be the climax of
desire united with duty, and so the hero's preparation for his last battle
is appropriately described as a marriage of the primal elements.

Marriage as duty is so empty that any body will do; thus Mark can
be easily duped into thinking that he slept with Iseult when Brangwain

slipped into his bed under cover of "the nuptial dark" (p. 61). And marriage as desire alone is suffocatingly self-destructive; thus Iseult of Brittany pines with desire which, going unfulfilled, enlarges to monstrous proportions until she is turned into a fiend, unleashing forces of destruction. When two souls are united by a blending of desire with duty, Iseult with Tristram, they become the entire cosmos harmonized without constraint by time or space, and their union is a song of nature:

> And all that hour unheard the nightingales
> Clamoured, and all the woodland soul was stirred,
> And depth and height were one great song unheard,
> As though the world caught music and took fire
> From the instant heart alone of their desire.
> ["The Queen's Pleasance," p. 71]

Tristram's constant willingness to serve, assisting King Mark, King Arthur, or, finally, Ganhardine, shows his capacity for subordinating himself to another, for restraining his desire and fulfilling the desire of another. Swinburne shows us a Tristram capable of responding to duty (unlike the Tristrams of Tennyson and Arnold) and thereby made stronger by his union with Iseult, who brings to him the power of limitless passion. Their fate is to be lost to the world but not to one another, for like so many other Victorian heroes and heroines, they find perfect marriage only when they die: "There slept they wedded under moon and sun / And change of stars" ("The Sailing of the Swan," p. 167). When their tomb is overwhelmed by the flooding ocean, "peace they have that none may gain who live, / And rest about them that no love can give" (p. 168); they have become the power represented by the sea and the sun, the source and the aim of all life driven by desire and directed by duty.

Swinburne's singers learn to triumph over death and time by learning to fulfill their private desires in dreams and visions, even at the risk of losing a public identity. Their triumphs come through the songs of Apollo, the intensity of whose light is all the more illuminating for having risen from the depths and the darknesses of the sea, mother of both life and death. Intensity of identification with the light, as with the song, will indeed "make life durable." It is this increasingly Apollonian quality which Georges Lafourcade notes when he says that "after 1880 the pessimism which had been a marked feature of Swinburne's inspiration tended to grow lighter; . . . his view of life became tinged with a mild form of optimism."[31]

DISCUSSING "A NYMPHOLEPT," Jerome McGann has insisted that we distinguish the perception of Pan, the god in or of the forested earth,

203

from the landscape itself and what McGann prefers to call "the visionary maiden."[32] He argues that "the reality of fear is not annihilated, it is metamorphosed . . . when Swinburne looks into the visionary eyes"; the metamorphosis is a change from fear to desire to delight, according to McGann. This all seems helpful, especially the identification of the vision as feminine (justifying the title as "caught by the nymphs"), but McGann does not go far enough. In his essay on "Ave Atque Vale," he describes Swinburne as becoming more Apollonian as he grew older, and so McGann might have been expected to connect what happens in "A Nympholept" with Swinburne's devotion to Apollo, but he does not. The key section occurs in those stages of the speaker's metamorphosis through fear, desire, and delight, and it is at those points that we should focus our attention. We shall see that there is an analogy between the poem's rapture of noontime vision and what in "Thalassius" had been the poet's rapture of becoming not a "singer but a song." Both poems testify to the poet's ability to make life clear and to make it durable because it can be seen so distinctly by the light of the visionary imagination: the man's desire is the poet's duty.

That something creative is in process in "A Nympholept" is clearly indicated by the imagery of sexual union through which the first section of the poem sets the scene.[33] "Sharp" "shafts" of sunlight penetrate the woodland shades, softly melting the shadows (and it should be noted also that we are immediately given some hint of the creative powers of this light that also destroys—it destroys darkness—when it is compared with the arrows from "the string of the God's bow," for this could only be Apollo, certainly not Pan); "winds fan" across the "face of the warm bright world" with a "creative . . . invasive power" (here Pan is identified as the source of the wind, its "breath"); the Sun's light and the Earth's breath shall mix creatively to produce the visionary experience. Then comes the lovely passage of stanza 3. Later the "silence trembles with passion," the "twilight quivers and yearns," and the woodland, like a woman yearning for her lover, "palpitates" with desire.

One strange and somewhat confusing aspect of the poem is that the experience of sexual union which is used to explain the process of imaginative vision is not clearly broken down into one beloved and one lover, as, for example, it would be if the earth were the feminine and the sun the masculine or a woodland nymph the feminine and a woodland satyr (Pan) the masculine. Instead, the woods with their soft shades are both feminine earth and the poet himself; notice how it is the speaker whose sensibilities are invaded when the palpitating woods are approached by Pan, whose breath comes "fierce in the tremulous maidenhair" (p. 71). The speaker is the palpitating woods of earth, as stanza 8 makes clear.

"The naked noon is upon" the speaker when the sun's rays pervade, invade with light "unmerciful, steadfast, deeper than seas that swell" (p. 72); but surely this is not the might of Pan possessing the woodland speaker. There are two lovers as there are two referents for the feminine beloved; the two lovers are Pan and Apollo, in a wildly delightful, creative mixture of wind and sunlight pressed upon a trembling earthly spirit.

At first the speaker recognizes only Pan as the lover (pp. 72–74). But is Pan really "all" as his name implies, the only lover whose love celebrates the live earthly being? If so, the poem should end with the eighteenth stanza, and that would be enough to communicate what Kerry McSweeney says the whole poem is designed to project: a "clear and 'steadfast' perception of the world around him."[34] Clear perception may be sufficient to serve the scientist, but it is only the first requisite of the singer.

After passages of troubled questioning whether Pan is the only god of man and earth, the speaker begins to wonder, "What heart is this, what spirit alive or blind, / That moves thee?" Pan is wedded to "change," to mutability, and as a lover is most unreliable, faithful only in spring and summer and less so in autumn and winter. There must be another lover, the "light and the life in the light," whose "spirit" moves even the life of Pan. The answer had been hinted at earlier, even as the speaker identified Pan as the coming lover:

> the star
> We call the sun, that lit us when life began
> To brood on the world that is thine [Pan's] by his grace for a span,
> Conceals and reveals in the semblance of things that are
> Thine immanent presence, the pulse of thy heart's life, Pan.
> [p. 73]

The second lover, Apollo, sheds the light that reveals the presence of the first lover, Pan.

The speaker's recognition of the second lover comes in the most ecstatic stanzas of the poem, beginning "What light, what shadow, diviner than down or night, / Draws near?" (p. 77). The experience is so unique, so intense, that it rules itself out as an ordinary perception; it seems to be a dream, but, as the poet keeps reassuring himself, he is not asleep. This is the most awake moment possible for human perception, and in this moment he is seized, enraptured, a "nympholept" seized by his vision; he unites with the earth, fulfilled of its joys, perhaps recognizing that it has its being through him even as he has his being through it. He is at one with the heart as the lover with his beloved or even as the singer with his song; but still the consciousness of separate being remains, as though following consummation, indicated by the question of "No more?" There is still a final consummation, perhaps the ultimate one, for human consciousness: identification of the light with the vision of consciousness itself. The poet asks, addressing his vision made possible by the sun:

> My spirit or thine is it, breath of thy life or of mine,
>   Which fills my sense with a rapture that casts out fear?
> Pan's dim frown wanes, and his wild eyes brighten as thine,
>   Transformed as night or as day by the kindling year.   [p. 80]

The separation of consciousness, the shadows of time and change, the divisions of all life—including the division between the singer and the song—are all annihilated in the visionary light, as the poem emphasizes in its concluding lines:

> for the shadows that sundered them here take flight;
> And nought, is all, as am I, but a dream of thee.   [p. 81]

The dreams are the ordinary experiences of shadowed life, the interceptions or blurrings of vision, which contain all lesser perceptions, down to the very last of perceptions, the least dream of light's vision, death.

To emphasize the power of light and intense vision, with which the poet identifies his very life, "The Lake of Gaube" celebrates the sun as "lord and god, sublime, serene," in its fiery light the poet's spirit not only survives but even thrives, like the legendary power of the salamander, with whose flamelike beauty Swinburne compares his own spirit which dives into the dark waters of the lake.[35] This poem is a literal triumph over time, for in it Swinburne returns from the twilight to the noontime of his life. His dive into the lake is a dive into his past, which is recovered with all its noontime freshness; when he dives into his past, he finds the vision that awaited the diver upon his return to the light:

> And swiftly and sweetly, when strength and breath fall short and the
>   dive is done,
> Shoots up as a shaft from the dark depth shot, sped straight into sight
>   of the sun.   [p. 201]

As PAUL MARIANI HAS OBSERVED, "Except for Bridges, Patmore, and Dixon (with all of whom he corresponded), Hopkins seems to have followed *no* contemporary poet as closely as he did Swinburne."[36] Even when he was reading no other "modern" works, Hopkins made a point in 1888 to read the latest poem by Swinburne. He told Dixon that he "read very little modern poetry, however [he] read [Swinburne's *Locrine*]."[37]

As much even as Tennyson, Swinburne was for Hopkins a significant voice of his age. Many of the things in his era to which Hopkins objected were to be found in Swinburne's works and reputation: "a strain of conventional passion, kept up by stimulants," the "barbarous" practice "of greatest this and supreme that," an absence of "thought and insight."[38] Hopkins objected most to the immorality of modern poetry. He blasted Swinburne and Hugo as "those plagues of mankind," but in the same context he includes even Milton, who was "a very bad man" because he broke "the sacred bond of marriage" and encouraged others to do the same.

Hopkins's belief in the sanctity of marriage was not the only strong tie between himself and his Victorian brethren. He wrote to Bridges in 1879 that he found in Bridges's poetry most of what he missed in the poetry of Tennyson, Swinburne, and Morris—that is, "point of character, of sincerity or earnestness, of manliness, of tenderness, of humour, melancholy, human feeling."[39] This is a considerable indictment, and it may simply reveal how easily Hopkins could exaggerate the praise of his friend's work, but it also illustrates Hopkins's own reliance upon conventional Victorian catch-phrases as substitutes for serious literary criticism. It is ironic that he should indict Swinburne and the others for a lack of "manliness" since not many years afterwards, in 1881, Hopkins joined Dixon in condemning Kingsley's "bullying" kind of masculinity; in fact, Hopkins learned from Swinburne to call that kind of blither "the stink."[40] This same letter indicates that Hopkins had, on at least one occasion, actually heard Swinburne read his poetry. Apparently it was a memorable enough experience that Hopkins recalled a line from Swinburne's recitation, a line which has not been discovered in Swinburne's writings: "where the Thames had laid the mud low."

Despite his belief that Swinburne lacked a moral center to his vision, Hopkins could not deny the beauty and power of the poetry that communicated Swinburne's vision. Hopkins told Baillie in 1867 that it was "impossible not personally to form an opinion against the morality of a writer like Swinburne,"[41] suggesting that Hopkins had to struggle with something in himself that preferred to ignore the question of morality altogether. In his letters of the next two decades, Hopkins increasingly tends to ignore the question of morality in Swinburne's poetry, concentrating instead on its style. In 1880 Hopkins told Bridges that Swinburne did not have "style," though he had, like Tennyson and Morris, an "individual style." A year later, Hopkins admitted to Dixon that however strange Swinburne might be, "his poetry seems a powerful effort at establishing a new standard of poetical diction, of the rhetoric of poetry."[42] Swinburne's poetry, however, was too "archaic" to represent "a perfect style"; for a poet to find "a perfect style," he must use "the current language heightened, to any degree heightened and unlike itself, but not . . . an obsolete one."[43] Hopkins's judgment that Swinburne used archaic or obsolete language, and so failed to find a "perfect style," was consistently maintained throughout Hopkins's lifetime. However, he did mellow in his insistence that Swinburne and others should measure up to the standard of style which seemed "perfect" to Hopkins.

Swinburne's poetry always held a strong attraction for Hopkins, even a lure or trap for the younger poet. Hopkins struggled mightily to escape Swinburne's trap, and perhaps some of the strangeness of Hopkins's own poetry is a result of his swerve away from the influence of Swinburne. At any rate, in 1883 Hopkins wrote Patmore that Swinburne's poetry was "strong" "in flow, in the poetical impetus, and also in richness of diction." And in 1886, Hopkins commented to Dixon that Swinburne's style was "extraordinary" for its "music of words and the mastery and employment of a consistent and distinctive poetic diction, a style properly so called." Swinburne's is "a poetical dialect so ornate and continuously beautiful" that Hopkins speculates that only Persian poetry might be comparable. For all his years of resistance, Hopkins still cannot overcome the lure of Swinburne's beautiful style. His only resistance is to exclaim (somewhat lamely) that "words only are only words."[44] Hopkins would not want to admit that Swinburne's beautiful words were anything more than "words," for that would expose his religious imagination to an assault by Swinburne's (perhaps more) powerful nihilistic imagination. In his last recorded comment on Swinburne, Hopkins tells Bridges that Swinburne's poetry "is all now a 'self-drawing web'; a perpetual functioning of genius without truth."[45] Hopkins was, in 1889, a man filled with a fear of the silent darkness growing about his spirit, while Swinburne was writing poetry of bizarre happiness and affirmation, invoking Apollo as his inspiration. Clearly Swinburne wove a beautiful web which Gerard Manley Hopkins had difficulty escaping—if, indeed, he did.

Besides his interest in Swinburne's style, Hopkins betrays in his own early poetry a strong interest in some of the same subjects he found in Swinburne's poetry. Hopkins was just as fascinated as Swinburne (though not as notoriously) with subjects of painful death, violent destruction, and masochistic pleasures; Hopkins resorted to imagery of blood, violence, struggle, pain, and pleasure throughout his career in poetry. This aspect of Hopkins and his poetry has been analyzed by Michael W. Murphy, who concludes that "the violent imagery represents a sublimation of a strong sado-masochistic element in Hopkins' personality."[46] Murphy's is the kind of gratuitous comment that used to be made about Swinburne, but whether or not it is true about either poet, the fact remains that both used this kind of imagery throughout their poetry. For an audience which had for generations fed upon the imagery of Christianity, there might be little shock in a poetry which accommodated itself to the Christian dispensation, and so Hopkins seems to have escaped the kind of horrified criticism with which Swinburne was commonly dispatched.

Both Swinburne and Hopkins demonstrate through their art that individual desire is a force of imagination, of the self in the process of realizing itself, of consciousness becoming conscious of itself; both poets learned to express desire in forms appropriate to themselves. For Swinburne, those forms celebrate the claims of an absolute entity, ever flowing and never finally defined, underlying both life and death. Such a celebration horrifies, though it may fascinate, Hopkins, whose poetic forms are struggles to contain desire, to define the self within limits so demanding that to transgress them would be to court absolute destruction. Both Hopkins and Swinburne attempt to rescue and affirm the individual self, though each pursues his own course. Swinburne's duty is to release the self as insatiable desire, and Hopkins's desire is to discover the way to his necessary duty—a perfect sacrifice of self in a perfect style.

When Hopkins discusses the "perfect style," he hints that it is a form of self-sacrifice, in which the poet yields his identity to some utter otherness that Hopkins calls "classical" and "modern" at the same time.[47] The process of "heightening" the "current language" to achieve this "perfect style" is analogous with a heightening of the spirit to enact the sacrifice of Christ. The key word here is *heighten*—that is, raising the self and the language to a pitch of duty that demands everything, including even life. The process is a surrendering to the mastery of a force (or form) that is unknown and sometimes terrifying. Hopkins's wrestling with language is tantamount to the soul's wrestling with God, and his achievement of style is his spiritual as well as his artistic duty.

Early in his career, Hopkins composed a sensuously luxurious poem which he called "A Vision of the Mermaids."[48] This poem links Hopkins with others of his contemporaries, like Arnold and Tennyson, who also resorted to legends of mermaids to embody their themes of (sexual) desire rising from the depths to spread a rosy glow of imagination over the world of the senses. The structure of Hopkins's poem employs an interesting strategy to communicate its vision. It opens and closes with its focus upon a rock which lies close enough to land so that when the sea is low it can be seen; the speaker swims out to it, observes a rose-lovely sunset, notices a crowding of rose-islands around his rock, looks closer and sees that they are mermaids, watches them sport in the water, and hears their sorrowful song just before the evening dissolves in darkness and he "steals away" from the rock to return to "the stirless bay." For the young Hopkins, then, the beauty of the earth is a feminine loveliness which attracts and even tempts the speaker to his doom.

Hopkins's speaker is secure on his rock, while all the rest of the creation flows around him, circles him, crowds and gathers to his vision. The speaker's vision is protected from serious encroachment because it is grounded upon a solid foundation; from that grounding he can look up into—and beyond—the sky to catch "Keen glimpses of the inner firmament." The mermaids are children of "father Sea," yearning with sadness for the realms of the sun, while he is a privileged being, able to pass to and from the depths of the sea and the depths of the sky. His ability, however, is a function of vision only, not a function of total, or spiritual, being. Hopkins's speaker may be safe from the lure of the mermaids, but his memory is haunted by the one time when he saw them and heard their song. The poem echoes the predicament of Coleridge's "Kubla Khan," inspired by a vision of a singing maiden to create a poem lamenting the loss of the vision. Hopkins's poem strikes a pose of compromise, betraying little of the anxiety of Coleridge's; for Hopkins, the middle region of his vision, safe on the rock or back in "the stirless bay," is sufficient for inspiration. He will not sacrifice his hope for the light of heaven and so feels no need to resist the lure of the mermaids. He will not, therefore, plunge into the depths of the ocean, and he cannot (yet) rise to penetrate the "inner firmament" for a vision larger and more permanent than "keen glimpses."

This poem shows us a "safe" position, safe when measured by the more risky plunges of imagination taken by Tennyson, Arnold, and Swinburne, all of whom will risk the loss of their visions in their courtship of sea depths. Hopkins's speaker is, however, not entirely safe, for his glimpse of the inner firmament is contingent upon the cooperation of the sun, the clouds, and the wind; his security on the rock is also contingent—upon the withdrawal of the tide. All seems finally concealed beneath a "veil"—the mermaids, the sky, the ocean, and the rock itself all are covered by a film, a veil—and then, when the poem ends, the entire scene is covered over by a veil of darkness. Surrounded by this process of events, just as he is surrounded by the ocean, the speaker is very much a passive agent whose only significant action is to swim out to and back from the rock. There such a vision is possible, but no happiness attends the visionary, who not only senses a sorrow that cannot be relieved but who, in stealing away, betrays a sense of some guilt for his vision. He is punished by the refusal of the vision to return.

The sorrow heard in the song of the mermaids is a sorrow of unsatisfied yearning, and it is no wonder the speaker recognizes it, for his is a similar song. This poem does not relieve the longing, nor does it make any promises of relief. The speaker does not yet know himself well enough to recognize that he is the source of the sorrow he hears in the mermaids' song. In "Continuation of R. Garnett's *Nix*" Hopkins's speaker knows immediately the sorrow of the mermaid. The speaker is a woman whose identity has been stolen and who has been made a prisoner by the Nix. While imprisoned in a "crystal grot" (as explained in Garnett's poem), the speaker in Hopkins's poem imagines the scene of her lover's seduction by the Nix posing as herself. The Nix has taken the blonde hair and blue eyes of the speaker, attributes which might be recovered by the speaker if she could but reach certain rocks which lie "not so far outward in the sea." Hopkins thus returns to the image of the rock in the sea to represent a power of security; in this poem the speaker is not willing, however, to attempt to reach the rocks: "I dare not taste the thickening salt, / I cannot meet the swallowing main." By refusing to enter the sea waters, she virtually abandons her lover to the Nix. Thus, Hopkins's poem splits her identity between the fair and the dark side; her dark side is triumphant in the struggle for identity. The passion of desire triumphs over the will for release from desire.

Speakers whose conditions leave them yearning for release are frequent in Hopkins's early poetry. In "Il Mystico," the speaker tries to exorcise the demons of "sensual gross desires" from himself so that his spirit can soar freely to penetrate the thin "veil that covers mysteries." "One of the Spies" sent by Moses to scout the Promised Land is left behind in the wilderness to die, because he lost heart for the journey. Hopkins adopts the character of the Spy and expresses his desire to return to Egypt, land of refreshing waters. God dooms the weak-hearted Israelites to years of wandering and dying in the desert, while they, like this Spy, dream of returning to the rich valleys of Egypt, even if their return comes at the price of their freedom: "We desire the yoke we bore, / The easy burden of yore." In contrast to the dry, hot sterility of the Spy's desert suffering, the suffering of "Pilate" for his own special weakness occurs in a scene of cold, hard sterile rocks and ice. In his fragments of a soliloquy by Pilate, Hopkins expresses the horrible pain of the man who not only denied the divinity of Christ but allowed Him to be murdered. Pilate must suffer through endless repetitions of his error, wishing to escape his guilt by dealing himself the same punishment he allowed others to inflict upon Christ.

The ocean of mysterious beauty and yearning desire is withdrawn from the landscapes of both "A Soliloquy of One of the Spies" and "Pilate," leaving those speakers isolated among burning sand or stony shadows. They are in predicaments of their own choosing—they have refused to do their duties. Hopkins is suggesting through these early poems and fragments that a man's soul, his spirit, his selfhood, should be grounded upon a solid footing of duty, however dangerous and distant, and that that footing can be reached only after a struggle, after an exorcism or repression of his "sensual gross desires." These desires are wide and deep as the ocean, as seductive and beautiful as mermaids, but also, finally, as bitterly sterile as scorched or frozen deserts. A life spent pursuing the satisfaction of fleshly desires would be about as fruitless and disappointing as the life of an alchemist who has given all his energies to the effort to transform base metals into gold.

Hopkins imagines the mental state of one of those ancient alchemists in his poem, "The Alchemist in the City." The Alchemist's pursuit of a hopeless dream, to transform the ugly pot into beautiful gold, is a hope of transforming the base into the ethereal. This sorrowful poem gains additional poignancy if we read it as a forecast of the late Hopkins. The poet here seems to foresee the dangerous futility of so much of his own life's interest as an artist of the beautiful. All his skill and all his craftsmanship will be, at best, only a mockery and, at worst, his damnation, if it is applied to the wrong ends. The Alchemist spends his last days looking out his window, wishing he were free from the city with all its "making and melting crowds" that pass by without knowing him. He chose to cast himself upon this busy task of making gold and now he no longer has any choice: he must continue what he now knows to be an empty, even a foolish, ritual. Like so many of Hopkins's early speakers, the Alchemist yearns for an escape to more certain values (including a place among "rocks where rockdoves do repair") and away from the place of uncertainty, the place of "making and melting."

St. Thecla, in the poem by that name, also yearns to escape. She is preparing for her marriage when she hears Paul preach the virtue of continence. She does not react in any way except to sit and listen. Hopkins concludes the poem on an ambiguous tone: Thecla is "forced . . . from the spot" where she is sitting to hear Paul preach. Who forces her is not altogether clear and what she is forced to do we are not told. The poem is unfinished, but we know from the legend that Thecla left her family to follow Paul to Rome where she suffered the martyrdom that earned her sainthood. Hopkins's interest in her is typical of his early thematic interests: the sacrifice of fleshly desire for spiritual duty. The poem opens with an image of the hourglass whose sand chokes "sweet virtue's glory" as a process typical of the action of time covering the memory of ancient heroes and heroines such as Thecla. However, the image is also an indication of Hopkins's usual attitude that processes of the flesh are impediments to the progress of the spirit. In his own acts of imagination, the poet can liberate Thecla's memory from the bondage of history. By describing Paul as a "true Bellerophon," Hopkins seems intent upon constructing a metaphor that will allow him to identify Paul as a power of imagination. If Paul is a "true" rider of Pegasus, then he may serve as a model for all poets who wish to ride Pegasus to heaven.

THE WAY TO HEAVEN IS NOT EASY, as both St. Paul and Gerard Hopkins discovered. After breaking a long silence with his great poem *The Wreck of the Deutschland*, Hopkins returned again and again to themes and images of wrecks, storms, stresses, pain, darkness, and sacrifice. *The Wreck of the Deutschland* celebrates Hopkins's first magnificent consummation of his poetic talent in a union of his visionary desire with his spiritual duty. The *Deutschland* is almost an epithalamion, a "spousal verse" of union between Hopkins and his God, between the martyred nun and her Savior, Jesus, and between Hopkins and the nun. These three "marriages" unite souls with God and thus manifest the sacramental function of marriage, a process of learning to submit to a mastery which is also a mercy. Hopkins's version of this process is a particularly violent one, but even under "normal" circumstances, true marriage of the spirit with God may be a wrecking of the flesh.

Part 1 of this poem is a confession of submission to assault. Though the assault proves to be a benevolent one, perhaps not even an assault at all, it was nevertheless suffered with much dread and pain. The spirit of the speaker has resisted, in Jonah fashion, the will of God, and so before he can perform his duty to God, he must be mastered by God, for whom it is fair to use all the weapons at His command, including fear and pain. Dreading the attack of God, the speaker was "almost unmade" by the "touch" of his assailant; God, like Zeus, ravishes human souls in the form of lightning, but Hopkins's God adds a quaintly English touch by using a "lashed rod" to strike "terror" into his victim. In his flight from God, the speaker whirled, flashed, drifted, and finally subsided, "steady as a water in a well" before recognizing in the "pressure" of his pursuer a valuable gift, "Christ's gift."

Underlying the rhythm of this flight-pursuit is a pattern of sexual assault, and surely this contributes to the special power of Hopkins's poem. After ravishment, the victim adores his attacker and discovers that God "is both a Master and a Lover."[49] Hopkins presents this spiritual assault as a fleshly consummation, imagined in its climax by the feminine soul of man:

> How a lush-kept plush-capped sloe
> Will, mouthed to flesh-burst,

> Gush!—flush the man, the being with it, sour or sweet,
> Brim, in a flash, full!—Hither then, last or first,
>   To hero of Calvary, Christ's feet—
> Never ask if meaning it, wanting, warned of it—men go.   [stanza 8]

He has been possessed by God, and now he eagerly submits to the will of God. The soul is not only ravished, it is enslaved. In the excitement of surrendering to an overwhelming force, the speaker has lost his autonomy. Hopkins's vision of union with God has no place for compromise; the self must yield totally and absolutely, leaving no shred of desire for anything but to do the will of God. The phenomenology of this act is so alien to the liberal tradition of most English literature of the nineteenth and twentieth centuries that one must wonder at Hopkins's skill in capturing audiences from this tradition. The first part of *The Wreck* recounts, from the liberal perspective, the humiliating and dehumanizing enslavement of a soul by fleshly power. All of the means of capturing the soul are means of flesh, first pain and then pleasure; the opening stanza summarizes these means as a fastening and binding of flesh and bone, a shaking of flesh and bone ("almost unmade"), and then a touching "afresh." In the end there can be no desire left but to "adore" the Master whose mercy is boundless (stanza 10).

When looked at in these terms, the first part of the poem is an unnerving denial of freedom and dignity. But Hopkins wants his poem to tear away the false mask of freedom and dignity that conceals from the liberal vision the truth of nothingness and darkness without God. The inevitable arrival of Death cannot be concealed, and to His nothingness and blackness all must submit. That is the true indignity, and against that fact Hopkins cries out with all his talent. A man is either a slave to nature and death or he is a servant of God; there is no middle way. To choose not to do the will of God is sometimes impossible, as the first part of *The Wreck* shows us, though the soul will try and will try with all its strength. When the conquest is finished, the victim is an adoring servant whose dignity comes from his desire to serve. He no longer has any real choice (if he ever did) between selfish desire and selfless duty.

Part 2 of the poem narrates the same process of assault, but in this section the assailant is Death and the savior is the Bridegroom called for by the nun for "the consummation of her mystical marriage."[50] We are to recognize in this part of the poem that dignity of flesh is a rag-and-bone shop for purchase by death. There is no desire beyond death itself worth expressing, unless it is the desire for a hero to trample down the monster Death. No man is strong enough, either alone or in union with any number of other men, to rescue mankind from death; he might as well attempt to quell such a storm as the one that destroyed the Deutschland. One man, of many, attempted heroically to combat the ravages of the storm:

> One stirred from the rigging to save
> The wild woman-kind below,
> With a rope's end round the man, handy and brave—
> He was pitched to his death at a blow,
> For all his dreadnought breast and braids of thew:
> They could tell him for hours, dandled the to and fro
> Through the cobbled foam-fleece. What could he do
> With the burl of the fountains of air, buck and the flood of the wave?
>
> [stanza 16]

Here is the true humiliation of man, to be "dandled the to and fro / Through the cobbled foam-fleece." Such an absurd spectacle of puny flesh, grotesquely humorous, victimized by a monstrous nature, contrasts sharply with the "tall nun" who "rears herself" through the "storm's brawling" to call upon "A master, her master." While there can be no self-mastery in nature strong enough to rescue dignity through death, there can be, and there is in the vision of this poem, a strength to defy nature, to submit to being mastered, and to look through death. The Tall Nun calls, mysteriously, for her master to come to her; it is mysterious because she seems to be calling for Death even while she is surrounded by death, but in truth (in the truth of Hopkins's vision, at any rate) she is calling for the same mastery from which the speaker of part 1 was fleeing. The terms chosen by the speaker to understand what happened to the Tall Nun are terms very like those he used to describe his own soul's ravishment by God: they are terms of sexual consummation.

The Tall Nun was calling for something the speaker finds difficult to understand or to explain. "What did she mean?" he asks; was she calling for "lovely Death" or for the martyrdom ("for the crown") of heroic death? The answer is not that she wished to secure the comfort of "the jay-blue heavens" or "moth-soft Milky Way." It was not in her mind to reach out for "the heaven of desire." The Tall Nun was already filled to the brim with the being of Christ; there was no room in her vision for anything else except His absoluteness. She called to him as if he were her lover, as if he were "her hero bride-groom coming to take her home."[51] She opened herself to him for his utter possession:

> There then! the Master,
> *Ipse*, the only one, Christ, King, Head:
> He was to cure the extremity where he had cast her;
> Do, deal, lord it with living and dead;
> Let him ride, her pride, in his triumph, despatch and have done with
> his doom there.
>
> [stanza 28]

The speaker can understand the Tall Nun's experience as something like, if not the same as, his own earlier experience of being possessed by God. Because she gave herself so completely to her lover, Christ, He had "glory of this nun"; on the other hand, the speaker, who resisted his attacker, God, found "glory in thunder" (stanza 5) after his conquest. They all participate in the glory of fulfillment, the perfect satisfaction of desire: the speaker in living and the Nun in dying.

When he interrogates his heart for feeling such "glee" at the thought of what happened to the Tall Nun (stanza 18), the speaker feels "touched" again, as he had been when God touched him "afresh" (stanza 1). The contemplation of her death has recreated for him his experience of finding glory in God's conquest. His contemplation—or perhaps better, meditation—"make[s] words break from [him] here all alone" (stanza 18). His heart, in the act of "uttering truth" will repeat, will participate in, the call of the Tall Nun for her lover, Christ, who is the "master" of herself and of the speaker. Both call upon Christ as God to become their master, to lord it with them both, "with living and dead" (stanza 28). In stanza 30 the speaker questions Jesus, as earlier, in stanza 18, he had questioned his own heart, for the heart conquered by God is Jesus and so cannot help "uttering truth." The Tall Nun "conceived" Christ in the word of her call, but her word was the "Word," the same "Word" uttered here by the poet himself out of his own "heart-throe, birth of a brain" (stanza 30). Together, then, the Tall Nun and the poet-speaker gave birth to Christ, as Hopkins puns upon the paradox that Christ was both the Father and the Son of his Mother.

As the artist whose responsibility it is to utter truth through words that make up the "Word," Hopkins could well be pleased with this poem, for in it he has found his way to identify his desire with his duty, and he has accomplished it through a meditation upon the death of a heroic woman. His voice actually becomes her voice, a process which is compared in the poem to helping her conceive and give birth to the truth of Christ. The poet-speaker functions as her lover would, ecstatically husbanding the imagination of salvation. He ends his poem with a double invocation, to Christ, "new born to the world," and to the Tall Nun, newly dead to the world; he calls for yet another possession, another conquest, "upon English souls" (stanza 35). His call for the new-born Christ to return as Britain's King stirs the same mythic waters from which Tennyson summoned his Arthur; both Hopkins and Tennyson express a yearning for some powerful, all comprehending symbol of authority to give direction and shape to a lost peoples' whelming desire. This new-born King should be, as Hopkins's poem here so describes him, a "prince, hero of us, high-priest," and he should bring light and warmth to barren hearths (hearts) at the same time that he disciplines (as a Lord would master) the multitudes, the "throngs" of Englishmen. England should open her heart to the return of her Lord—as Guinevere should have to Arthur, as the Tall Nun did to Christ—or England will be attacked by the glory of God as was the speaker; his final lines in the poem express the poet's hope that England's reunion with her Master will be a royal marriage, not a "hard-hurled" assault. As Wendell Stacy Johnson has recognized, this reunion is a "hope for a birth, or a re-birth that is to wed men, as it were, to God."[52] The suffering and sacrifices of the Tall Nun and the poet-priest are the dowry bestowed upon the anticipated bride, England.

Of the poems and fragments which Hopkins composed during the period following *The Wreck of the Deutschland,* the poem that readily invites comparison is "The Loss of the Eurydice." It is not much like *The Wreck* except that its subject is a shipwreck; however, it bears a similar burden for finding meaning in human disaster. The earlier poem could focus upon the redemptive action of faith in the Tall Nun's submission to Christ's mastery, but "The Loss of the Eurydice" cannot find such a focus. The human actors of this poem are driven asunder not only by the ocean's storm but also by the twists of English church history, for England lost the true faith and so her English souls are doomed at death when they do not find the way back to truth. They are strong in their capacity to be virtuous, witness these dead sailors, but virtue and duty to false gods or heretical dogmas are insufficient to save souls. This poem is an elegy for the lives of so many lost in the wreck of the Eurydice, and it is an elegy for the loss of true faith in modern Britain.

Without true faith, the natural being of mankind may be lovely and strong for life, but that will not take the soul through death to a more lovely and stronger spirit. This poem puts the lie to nature, which in its beauty is a terrible lure to destruction: "And you were a liar, O blue March day." The ship was looking in the wrong direction, for while the bright blue lay before it, there was a black storm cloud moving in from over the land. When the storm hit, the men were helpless; when Hopkins quotes the cry of " 'All hands for themselves,' " he surely intends the continuing irony of the fate in store for Protestant heretics from Mother Church. These men can do nothing "for themselves," and especially can they do nothing with their "hands." They are in the hands of God; rather, they are *not* in the hands of God. Each of the men Hopkins chooses to describe—Marcus Hare, Sydney Fletcher, and one nameless corpse—is an example of the futility of merely natural power.

The utmost virtue that Marcus Hare could muster in this time of his despair is a "drive for righteousness" and refusal to swerve from his duty;

he could not, however, call for Christ as did the Tall Nun. Marcus Hare chooses not to serve time and does his duty as best he sees it, but he goes with his ship into absolute darkness. Sydney Fletcher leaps from the sinking ship, gives himself up to the stormy waters, fights against death, and is pulled from the sea by another ship; whether his rescue is a salvation seems unlikely, given the general tone of irony in the poem. Hopkins indicates little hope for the soul of this rescued man when he comments that in the joy of his rescue, Fletcher "lost count what came next, poor boy." The rescue of Fletcher is framed by the example of Hare's desperate duty and "one sea-corpse cold" taken on board. This picture of "lovely manly mould" as an example of "the best we boast our sailors are" becomes an ironic coda to the vignettes of Hare and Fletcher, for all the sailors are typified by this dead man. He "is strung by duty, is strained to beauty," as Hopkins puts it in one of his strongest lines of irony in the poem, for here is the relic of a heart-rending loss:

> Leagues, leagues of seamanship
> Slumber in these forsaken
> Bones, this sinew, and will not waken.   [ll. 82–84]

This young man, one of those who lay "asleep unawakened" before the wreck, now lies stretched upon a bed from which he "will not waken." The cry of the poet is the lament of the priest who cannot save a lovely and beloved soul from eternal sleep. He ends his elegy with a prayer to Christ, knowing that souls in hell cannot be redeemed but hoping to awaken "souls sunk in seeming" from their doomed careers. The tension of the poem is a wringing of beauty out of priestly duty. "The Loss of the Eurydice" is no celebration, as is *The Wreck of the Deutschland*; instead, it is a poet's beautiful lament for the loss of natural virtue to natural disaster.

Hopkins's generous responses to the beauties of nature constitute one of his characteristic distinctions and also mark him as a poet of the high Victorian era when few writers could escape the influences of Wordsworth, Carlyle, and Ruskin. Like his literary brethren in England, Hopkins's perception of natural beauty was a function of an ethical or, more emphatically, of a religious sensibility. Hopkins was, like Wordsworth, "fostered alike by beauty and by fear." *The Wreck of the Deutschland* and "The Loss of the Eurydice" are fosterlings of fear; at the same time, however, Hopkins was composing poetry that witnessed his more gentle fostering by the "beauty" of nature. This appears in the fragment of "Moonrise" (composed in 1876) and in a group of sonnets composed during the summer of 1877, including "God's Grandeur," "The Starlight Night," "Spring," "The Windhover," and "Pied Beauty." These poems, which have been much commented upon, are testimonies to Hopkins's spiritual as well as aesthetic awakening. They are successfully fashioned designs which balance and unify the stresses of desire and duty that often clashed within the poet's sensibility. These poems are products of a period in Hopkins's life which Carlyle might have called "The Everlasting Yea"—when Hopkins discovered the "open secret" of God's grandeur in the world about him. Without the presence of God brooding "with warm breast" "over the bent World," however, all this beauty would be, like the duty of the sailors lost in the wreck of the Eurydice, an empty irony.

Those sailors never woke from their spiritual slumber and so were lost in the fell darkness. Hopkins displays in the poems of this time just how much value there is for those who awaken. His poems are designed to wake his reader to fresh discoveries, as he found for himself in the lovely fragment of "Moonrise" when he "awoke in the Midsummer not-to-call night" to receive "the prized, the desirable sight" from which his slumber had divided him. Like God's grace, this light of the moon came "unsought, presented so easily" for the soul lost in the darkness of his mortality. But once awakened—whether rudely as in *The Wreck of the Deutschland* or gently as in "Moonrise"—the soul is all alive in wonder and ecstasy to the prize of nature. "The Starlight Night" is a bursting out of natural beauties, a cornucopia of beauty the plenty of which scatters to reveal "the spouse Christ." The poem is a form of wedding song, celebrating the homecoming of the spouse whose arrival excites all of nature into an explosion of light. This bursting forth of nature in spring and summer is a manifestation of the creative power of God working through nature, as though Christ, the bridegroom, were taking joy in his bride.

These sonnets are Hopkins's "spousal verse," as Wordsworth described his own "Home at Grasmere." Even "The Windhover" is something of a "spousal verse," addressed to "Christ our Lord" whose lively virtues are manifested in the windhover's flight. Here though, the prize is yet to be gained, and again the poet emphasizes the necessity of submitting to "the mastery of the thing." Awakening and discovering are redemptive acts of perception, and they purchase gifts of great (and gentle) value, but they are not entirely painless. To be awakened by "moonlight" is a rare phenomenon; nature asleep usually requires a stronger stimulus, especially during a time of darkness. But like the Pope in *The Ring and the Book* or the poet in *In Memoriam*, Hopkins discovers that even the smallest spiritual light shines bright with meaning against the darkness. Crossing that threshold of consciousness, however rude or violent, takes one into the "morning," into the presence of a master whose

219

creation is a palace of dazzling beauty. Hopkins, at this time of his life, has awakened, gained admission to the place, bent his spirit to serve, and sings to please his Lord in the "kingdom of daylight."

On 23 September 1877, Hopkins was ordained a Jesuit priest and soon afterwards began his duties working among the people. His beautiful sonnets celebrating the presence of God in His natural creation were composed mostly during the summer immediately preceding his ordination, suggesting the high pitch of keen anticipation for the climax to his training in God's service. Just after the ordination and after he began his priestly duties, Hopkins found he had little free time for composing poetry; however, he managed to write a few poems, some of them his "sweetest" (as Hopkins himself might say), mainly on themes connected with his duties among the parishioners. This small group of poems includes three which show Hopkins at work as a priest bringing God to mankind, administering the Sacraments of Holy Communion, Holy Matrimony, and the Last Rites. In these poems Hopkins serves God and man, making "hallowed bodies" out of the fallen bodies of mankind.

In the summer of 1879 he administered a "Bugler's First Communion." The poem is a charming example of how pleasing it is to be of service, to bear the yoke of duty lightly when it is beneath the mastery of God, whose "too huge godhead" can so humble itself that it can reside even in the "leaf-light housel" of the Host. That the priest can carry God, even work the magic of consecrating the Host so that God manifests Himself, is an exhilarating notion; when the bugler boy asked ("begged") for the gift of Communion, the priest reacted as a loving, doting mother might: "Forth Christ from cupboard fetched, how fain I of feet / To his youngster take his treat!" Hopkins represents his duty as something he took keen pleasure in doing, serving out a "treat." But mixed with this pleasure is also an apprehension that the boy, being mortal, might "rankle and roam / In backwheels" even though he "seems by a divine doom channelled." The note of apprehension that creeps into the poem's otherwise cheerful service is peculiar, for it voices a doubt that the Host will be effective. When the priest asks that he not see the boy again because he does not wish to risk disappointment, the priest betrays the beginning of a terrible doubt—about himself, not about God. And when he ends the poem with a "plea" that his "pleas" not go "disregarded" in Heaven, he compounds the mystery of the poem; his service to God, to this boy, has turned from sweet cheer to anxious pleading.

Does the priest here show any of the signs of doubt that will later become giants of despair? That is anticipating too much, probably, but "The Bugler's First Communion" does suggest that Hopkins fulfilled his service not only with alacrity, but also with jealous fear that his charge might wane if not become inefficacious. His priesthood is his duty, his sign of submission to do the will of God and bear his grace for others; his battle, insofar as he is a soldier of Christ, must be with Satan, not with God Himself, although Hopkins is more likely to wrestle with God in his poetry. Even in the "Bugler," he concludes with an image of "adamantine heaven" against which he sends his pleas to "brandle . . . with ride and jar." Hopkins's priest is almost an outsider, helping others into Heaven while he is left to wander about in the wasteland of errant spirits. As long as he can keep close to the beauties of nature, Hopkins seems satisfied that he is close to God, but when the natural landscape begins to darken, to recede into the background of his spiritual duty, Hopkins increasingly betrays a growing anxiety that he may be left in the darkness.

When he performs a marriage ceremony and composes a poem for the occasion, "At the Wedding March," Hopkins again sounds like an outsider to God's grace. Paul Mariani interprets the third stanza as voicing Hopkins's marriage as a priest with God,[53] but there is little evidence for this in the poem. The first stanza wishes "honour" for the groom and a fruitful womb for the bride, now that their bodies have been hallowed by the sacrament of matrimony. Hopkins does not represent marriage as a ritual of reconciling duty and desire; instead, he assumes that marriage is, indeed, a sacrament through which God's grace operates, creating new life, but also bringing into the lives of the married partners "dear charity." This is the point of the second stanza, that marriage brings "comfort" because it brings God's gift of love, "divine charity," through this couple's submission to His will that "fast bind[s]" them together. The last stanza, therefore, marks the great virtue of the marriage sacrament here made available to this unnamed couple: marriage is a "March" of God's grace, locking and binding hearts and bodies to His will, triumphing over flesh and time to bestow the gift of immortality. We may wish, as Mariani suggests, that Hopkins's tears of joy are for his own gift of immortality, but the poem seems to say only that this particular way to God's gift is through a marriage of the sort which the priest has just administered. He is not the beneficiary—the newly married couple is.

With his poem "Felix Randal," on the occasion of administering the Last Rites, Hopkins elegizes the death of the "hardy-handsome" blacksmith to whom the priest had earlier "tendered" "our sweet reprieve and ransom." The opening line tells us that the priest had been expecting news of the death, for the man had been "pining, pining" for a long while. The priest has done all he can, his "duty [is] all ended" with the news of death, and the only reason for his asking the questions he does in the first stanza must be to know if the soul of Felix Randal is at rest in the bosom of God. Even in this lovely poem, Hopkins cannot un-questioningly celebrate the efficacy of the sacraments he has administered. The great need of all mankind, whether the bugler boy, the newly wedded couple, or Felix Randal, is "comfort," and in particular the com-fort of knowing that they are bound "fast" by the "divine charity" of God. Hopkins's duty as a priest is to assist with that binding; the dying man has been broken and disordered by sickness, and it is the duty of the priest to mend him. But how to mend one who is doomed to the utter disorder of death? The poet is the maker of order, but as priest he must submit to the belief that there is meaning in this humiliation to fleshly order. No wonder the poet asks, for the priest, if his "duty [is] all ended." The poet cannot yield his interest entirely to the will of God, giving up at the point of death; he must reestablish some order to this scene of disorder. Surely Hopkins wished he could emulate, as priest and poet, working at his own "grim forge," the figure of Felix Randal.

BETWEEN 1879 AND 1885 HOPKINS worked at the composition of a verse play based upon the death and resurrection of St. Winefred. There are four pieces of writing associated with this play: first, a dialogue between Winefred and her father, Teryth; second, a monologue by St. Beuno describing the healing virtues of St. Winefred's Well; third, "The Leaden Echo and the Golden Echo (Maidens' Song from St. Winefred's Well)"; and fourth, a monologue by Caradoc, spoken just after he has murdered Winefred. This is the probable order of composition for these pieces, with only "The Leaden Echo and the Golden Echo" considered to be in complete enough form not to be a mere fragment. Nevertheless, these writings constitute a remarkable, even startling, development in Hopkins's canon. When read in the order in which they would have appeared as parts of a completed drama (excluding "The Leaden Echo"), they reveal an interesting conflict of wills—the will to master versus the will to be mastered—with a resolution in terms of the "natural super-natural." As drama, the pieces do not cohere, they are merely fragments; however, when read as experiments, in the order of their composition (including "The Leaden Echo"), they display Hopkins's development, moving from a poetry of celebration through a poetry of internalized de-bate and toward a poetry of anxiety, even despair. (Some kind of pattern has been noticed by most critics of Hopkins's development, though not all agree on what that pattern is, of course.) *St. Winefred's Well* is par-ticularly useful for discovering Hopkins's changing emphases, if not his changing values.

In the fragment of dialogue between Teryth and Gwenvrewi (Winefred) we discover an innocent sounding girl, keenly excited for news about the arrival of her uncle, Lord Beuno; she has little to say in the scene (and nothing to say in the two other fragments), but we know her character from the monologues of her father, her uncle, and her murderer. From her father, who delivers a monologue (or rather, a soliloquy) just after Winefred exits to prepare a room for their guests, we learn that his authority over his daughter is a mix of the father (sternness) and the mother (affection). Winefred has learned to submit to his authority in a gracious and loving manner, preparing her for a later role of submission to God. Teryth, like God, mixes his duty as a father with his affection as a mother (in the quaint manner of assigning emotion to the female). Besides revealing the heroine's charming innocence of proper subordination, this first fragment performs two other functions. One is to identify in the character of "mastery" a mix of qualities, as shown here in Teryth, including duty as authority and affection as possession. If authority is exercised without affection, it can deteriorate into mere rationalization; if authority is not exercised and yields all to affection, character becomes mere appetite. Teryth maintains the proper balance, though he feels the temptation to yield one to the other in his final words. Another function of this first fragment is to associate Winefred with flowers, "sweet bines," "this bloom, this honeysuckle," whose harvesting the father (as gardener?) dreads.

The next two fragments of the drama juxtapose a soliloquy by Caradoc with one by St. Beuno. Caradoc enters after having just murdered Winefred; he is stunned at first (reminding us of Milton's Satan in the opening of *Paradise Lost*), shocked by the spectacle of his late deed. His recovery from the shock is a marvelous reversal of psychology, for he not only overcomes his temporary paralysis but triumphs in an assertion of his will to power. His words are punctuated frequently with references to himself as the center of all existence, demanding like God that all become subordinate to his will, but his mastery is most unlike God's as it is most unlike Teryth's: Caradoc, like Browning's Guido, justifies his deed as an act of duty to the law that protects his own integrity, his own pride. Virtue, then, is valor, and right is resolution. His act of violence has been a necessary action of the will to power. Caradoc, again like Teryth, questions within himself a "weakness" to affection, calling his attraction to the beauty of Winefred (she was "time's one rich rose" in this otherwise "darksome world") a weakness of the flesh. Rather than dismiss the importance of his affection (or put it into balance with his duty, as does Teryth), Caradoc magnifies it into an outrageous assertion of desire that is never satisfied:

> To hunger and not have, yét   hope ón for, to storm and strive and
> Be at every assault fresh foiled,   worse flung, deeper disappointed,
> The turmoil and the torment,   it has, I swear, a sweetness,
> Keeps a kind of joy in it,   a zest, an edge, an ecstasy.
>   [*St. Winefred's Well*, act 2, ll. 55–58]

Rather than balance, or temper, his will to power with affectionate regard, Caradoc murders in himself the "softer," the "feminine" emotions
and dooms himself (again like Guido or Milton's Satan) to a life of
despair.

In the last fragment, the soliloquy by St. Beuno, the flower that
Caradoc had destroyed is reborn, a bursting forth of life in all the forms
of springtime beauty, especially as a freshly flowing stream of water with
healing virtues. This is the miracle of rebirth for all of nature as well as
for Winefred, who has been restored to life after her violent death. The
conflict of wills between Caradoc and Winefred (though not dramatized)
seems to have been resolved in favor of Caradoc, the will to power and
possession; but Hopkins cannot leave it thus, for his was to be a tragedy
ending in the despair of Caradoc and in the death of Winefred. The
proof of the resurrection, the testimony of current grace, lies in the renewal of life after death in all of nature, as in this springtime beauty
described by St. Beuno. Nevertheless, nature has suffered a grave wound,
as did Winefred, and all her creatures, including man, must search for
healing waters of faith. St. Beuno catalogs the faults and miseries of mankind needing to fulfill desires, quench thirsts, and exercise weakened or
paralyzed faculties, all of which can be done by pilgrimages to this water
of St. Winefred's well, the place of God's mercy and miracle of His
making.

When read in this manner, Hopkins's fragmentary drama is a triumph of faith. However, when read in the order of its composition
(including "The Leaden Echo"), it tells a somewhat different story. Then,
one moves from the happy innocence of expectation in Winefred and the
pride of paternal authority in Teryth, to the joyful praise of God's mercy
and miracle of life in nature uttered by St. Beuno, to the piece later titled
"The Leaden Echo and the Golden Echo." This was to have been a kind
of chorus in the drama, and as such it might well have prefigured the
drama's resolution of lost mortal beauty into the recovery of all beauty
through God's mercy. But as an expression of Hopkins's own experiences
during this period of his life, this poem witnesses his growing debate
with himself as a poet celebrating natural beauty and as a priest condemning mortal error.

The "leaden echo" is fleshly beauty falling into despair of survival
(voicing the thoughts of Caradoc, simplified), and the "golden echo" is a

promise of someplace where beauty survives all mortality. The last eleven lines of this poem are not, however, as confident as the first part of the passage that is devoted to "the golden echo." The trust that "while we slumbered" in our mortality, there is a place where we wake and wax in beauty, is almost undercut by the next line, a question: "O then, weary then why should we tread?" If the "golden echo" is right, and the message is clearly hopeful, then why still do we feel "so haggard at the heart, . . . so fagged, so fashed, so cogged, so cumbered?" The only answer is that "care" is "kept" out there, up there, somewhere, "yonder." This is an answer of the High Victorian, in the spirit of Tennyson's Ulysses or King Arthur, Arnold's Scholar-Gipsy, and even Swinburne's Tristram: all pursue a distant goal, always receding with the horizon, leaving the process of pursuit as the only meaning that is certain. Hopkins's poem ends, almost weakly pathetic, in the echoing of "yonder." It is an uncertain consolation for so much certain pain.

Perhaps it is better to cut off the weakness of uncertain hope, the feminine side, in one's self as Caradoc does. The fragment of *St. Winefred's Well* containing Caradoc's soliloquy is the last piece Hopkins composed for this story. It is a startling performance when considered as the conclusion to the work-in-progress: in it Hopkins puts into the mouth of a murderer much of what is matter for his own (confessional) poetry of the same period in his life. The man whose celebration of natural beauty as evidence of God's presence and God's fecund love becomes the man who could not find God in the darkness, like Tennyson's King Arthur at the end of his mystic reign. Caradoc presents a possible reaction to the darkness, a reaction much like Guido's in his second monologue or like Mary Stuart's in the dramas by Swinburne.

One might defy all that is, even "this darksome world," with his single self, choosing "henceforth / In a wide world of defiance [to live] alone" (act 2, ll. 38–39). His assault and murder of Winefred is thus an affirmation of his own worth "in a wide world of defiance," constituting a murder of part of himself as well as a murder of another human being. His only duty is to himself and his only desire is to maintain his desire as a force of possession. Caradoc reenacts the role of Achilles when Achilles learns of the death of Patroklos; like Achilles, Caradoc would destroy all the world to make a place for himself. But Achilles knew a duty to divine superiors and subordinated his mighty wrath to the design of Zeus; Caradoc cannot do this because he knows of no such design. When we read Caradoc's speech as a voicing of Hopkins's own thoughts and feelings at the time, we are astonished and moved by the intensity of the temptation to despair. Hopkins had heard the "golden echo"; he had faith that like his own alchemist in the city, he could turn the lead into gold; and he kept moving "yonder" until here he has arrived, like Browning's Childe Roland, at the dark tower where dark forms surround him, to watch while he battles with himself.

The descent of darkness is a major event in one of Hopkins's best poems from his later work, "Spelt from Sibyl's Leaves," a Victorian version of the conventional ode or hymn to evening. In it, Hopkins strikes a pose like so many earlier English poets who addressed evening (Milton via Collins and Wordsworth); unlike his predecessors, however, Hopkins does not find in evening any of the compensatory relief that is customary. Instead, his poem is a death chant, watching while darkness covers the sky to become an enveloping tomb, encompassing nature and man. The event is a signal that "earth her being has unbound"; nature is disintegrating, yielding her beautiful order of unity in variety, losing all her "dapple," which "is at an end, as/tray or aswarm." The "self" is driven in upon itself, "steeped and pashed," separated from the "dapple" of nature by the whelming darkness. All that lovely variety of natural beauty is disappearing, and we can hear the melancholy tones of a man lamenting the loss of his love. Hopkins revelled in the loveliness of nature, seeking there the satisfaction of his aesthetic desires. Early in his career, he discovered the loveliness and pursued it without total satisfaction because he had not yet made a connection between his aesthetic desires and his religious duties (Carlyle and Ruskin to the contrary notwithstanding); in the middle years of Hopkins's career, he made that connection more often than not and celebrated it in some of the happiest poetry of the Victorian era; that happinesss began to fade into the austerity of lean duties which he pursued with severe self-sacrifice in his later years, bringing into his poetry a tone of sorrowful farewell to natural loveliness, of desperate resignation to all-devouring death, and of ironic detachment from all earthly desires.

"Spelt from Sibyl's Leaves" begins, then, as an unwinding, unbinding of earth's "skeined strained veined variety," and seems to fall apart under the pressure of "earnest" evening in a process that overwhelms the speaker with an increasing sense of separation and isolation. The sestet of the poem turns upon the image of the "beakleaved boughs dragonish" that announces a last judgment when the old dragon will be set loose to destroy the world. Darkness, death, and the old dragon are all one, and that one must drive all life to the crisis of profound choice between good and evil, leaving no possibility of compromise or plea of ignorance. The unwinding suddenly becomes a rewinding "upon, all on two spools," whereupon all the threads of existence are stretched after being divided between "two flocks, two folds—black, white; right, wrong." The poet who so loved the luxurious plenty of color and form in nature and who thought he found God in all of it has been disabused of his error; for here on the eve of destruction, he is torn apart, himself "dismembering" in the process of facing up to a terrible choice between "black, white; right, wrong," all that is left of, or all that underlies the appearances of, nature's plenitude. We hear, indeed, in the sounds of the poem itself Hopkins's own "thoughts against thoughts in groans grind."

The sorrowful farewell to natural, or "mortal," beauty that begins "Spelt from Sibyl's Leaves" becomes an agonizing recognition that beauty's variety has been a confused mixture of only two basic and contradictory strands between which one must choose. The richness and royalty of nature is an illusion. This discovery plunges the poet into pits of disappointment, if not despair. Imagery of unwinding/winding, slackening/twisting, and wringing/wrestling appears often in the poetry of the last five years of Hopkins's life. The tension of these poems is a function of further sacrifice and greater submission as the poet moves further from his spousal verse of 1877, further from his happy love for nature, and closer to his last sacrifice—of life itself. The last poems are exercises in submission to spiritual duty, to a command for utter sacrifice, which for a poet means giving up not only his love for nature but even his art itself. Duty to God is even more demanding than Hopkins imagined in *The Wreck of the Deutschland.*

His temptation to yield all to despair is the subject of "Carrion Comfort." His refusal to comfort his flesh is the same as sacrificing worldly beauty, the most important comfort he has known throughout his poetry. Of course, it would be comforting to know that God approves of his work, either as a poet or as a priest. His being has gone slack, somewhat like the slackening process of the earth unbinding herself during the evening of "Spelt from Sibyl's Leaves." But unlike that poem, "Carrion Comfort" makes a defiant choice; it is not hung between the "two spools" of "right, wrong." Here the choice is between, at last, living and dying, and the poet who celebrates mortal life cannot destroy himself any more than the priest who celebrates immortal life.

The relationship between the speaker and his pursuer in "Carrion Comfort" echoes the relationship described in part 1 of *The Wreck of the Deutschland,* but in the earlier poem the chase ended in a love embrace, a happy recognition, a joyous submission. In that earlier poem also, the Master makes, binds, and touches afresh after almost unmaking His victim, but in this poem the antagonist wrings, bruises, and threatens to devour. The sestet here speaks of gaining some value from the experience of wrestling, of being beaten and trod down, as though the self (soul) were the "grain" being separated from the "chaff" during harvest; but that occurred in the past, during "that night, that year / Of now done darkness." (We note that Hopkins increasingly questions his own fertility in his last poetry, as though he suspects his "grain" may be no better, after all, than "chaff.") In "Carrion Comfort" Hopkins performs a trick of perspective, as he did in "Felix Randal," withdrawing from the present crisis (of the opening) to a vision of the past when things were better (in the sestet). He seems, however, to be questioning his earlier celebration of submission, when he "kissed the rod" and "stole joy." Should he not have cheered himself as "hero" instead of/or as much as he cheered his triumphant adversary? Left alone in the dark, the speaker concludes his review of his past with an explanation usually interpreted as an admission that he should cheer now just as he once did when he realized that God was his adversary. But his explanation might instead be an appalling recognition that he will not choose God even after recognizing Him. That is not a popular conclusion, but it must be considered, especially in light of the time shifts within the poem, where the conclusion occurred in the distant past and the opening is occurring in the present, when he can choose very little, pathetically realizing that less and less is possible: "hope, wish day come, not choose not to be."

The darker his world becomes, the more mysterious and intimidating does his God become for Hopkins. And his world is becoming darker because the poet is driven by his religious duty to make greater and greater sacrifices of his worldly values. What had been "an isle of roses" in "A Vision of the Mermaids," then a "world's splendour and wonder" with a "dappled-with-damson west" in *The Wreck of the Deutschland*, or a place with "azurous hung hills" revealing the majestic shoulder of God in "Hurrahing in Harvest" has become in "Carrion Comfort" a "wring-world" with "turns of tempest." Whether Hopkins is in religious doubt will continue to preoccupy the critical camps, but surely there is much evidence to show how darkling his world has become. In these last poems his strategy of design is to acknowledge the fragmenting of nature, the dissolving of color, the disappearance of pied variety, and then to confront the starkness of what remains; the poems sing out with great hurt, for the poet has found such great satisfaction from his love affair with nature. His divorce from nature and courtship of God prove to be not as delightful and pleasurable as a dream of courtly love.

Most of Hopkins's last poems (with the notable exception of "That Nature Is a Heraclitean Fire") are composed in a style as austere as his vision of life was becoming. Rarely do these poems gush with lovely sounds and imagery; they do not roll with the enthusiasm of his earlier work. Severity of style communicates severity of vision in such poems as "No worst, there is none," "I wake and feel the fell of dark," and "To seem the stranger lies my lot." All three describe increasing alienation, retreat, and maybe even abandonment. In "To seem the stranger," Hopkins expresses his theme of estrangement as a painful parting from his family and his native country, to which is now added the "third remove" to Ireland, a "remove" that suggests an estrangement also from God Himself, for heaven has, along with the rest of Hopkins's world, become "dark." Indeed, "dark heaven's baffling ban" is paralleled with "hell's spell," both of which frustrated his creativity, his heart's wisest word.

Choosing to begin his sonnet on estrangement with a listing of his "Father and mother dear, / Brothers and sisters," Hopkins has catalogued the plenitude of nature's fertility which is portrayed as the human family bound together by marriage; he next describes his love for England as a romantic courtship for a "wife / To [his] creating thought"; and he draws near his end with an image of his own breeding heart that heaven and hell conspire to thwart. He chose not to marry and father a family; he courted all England (as a people and a place of nature's beauty) with little or no success; and now his spiritual Father has disappeared into darkness, as distant as his earthly father and as unheeding as his beloved England. His "hoard" of wise words accumulates though it says nothing for lack of listeners, but he will create despite all adversities.

In an unfinished poem he sent to Robert Bridges in 1885, Hopkins tried to write something that would appeal to a popular audience, "a patriotic song" for English soldiers that begins, "What shall I do for the land that bred me." Its main theme is the desire to serve one's native country in whatever way possible and with whatever talent one possesses. The connection of this theme with "To seem the stranger" is clear, but in this unfinished poem Hopkins has not resigned his hope of communication. And while the poem is not complicated by Hopkins's spiritual torment, it shows that he had not abandoned England even if he chose to follow God into "dark heaven." The poem is a simple expression of "duty," but it contains a line pointing the way for Hopkins's final artistry: "Immortal beauty is death with duty." This provides a clue for appreciating what Hopkins turned to when he left the service of "mortal beauty." When he asks the question, "To what serves Mortal Beauty?" in the poem by that title, he marks his turn from nature's pied beauty; but in the answer provided by the poem, Hopkins reveals the way he chooses to get through the consequent darkness.

That way is—simple sounding enough—"merely meet it" and penultimately, "leave, let that alone." Such is the partial answer to the question what to do with "Mortal Beauty." This sonnet follows a pattern of images typical of Hopkins's work: from a question of *service*, to an operation of *mastery*, concluded with an epiphanic *flashing*. As long as one does no more than "glance" at the beauty of mortality and not get caught in a "gaze out of countenance," he may preserve the only value of such beauty: to keep alive a consciousness of something "better," the meaning of all "good," which is "God's better beauty, grace." Hopkins is his own best witness to the danger of mortal beauty, for his constant struggle has been to free himself from aesthetic attachments, from his desire for mortal beauty. He must pass beyond desire, beyond mortal beauty. When he tells us "merely [to] meet it . . . then leave, let that alone," he points a way to his last stance, ironic detachment. For him to serve well, he must master his desire for mortal beauty, except for the flash of "self" that makes up the "world's loveliest." It must be the flash of other selves, however, for Hopkins knew the greatest danger lay in his own self-awareness; he struggled to lose himself in a flash of grace, but his own flash has nearly disappeared in his last poems. "To what serves Mortal Beauty" concludes with the ultimate answer of "Yea, wish that though, wish all, God's better beauty, grace." The tone is wistful, even defiant, combining "Wish . . . wish" with "yea . . . though." If God's beauty is (only) "better," then mortal beauty is "good," and one might not need to detach himself from it, instead wishing for it and everything else.

Such a conclusion is weakly compromising when compared with the intense and courageous statements in the other poetry Hopkins was writing at the same time. We know that at the end Hopkins's best poems are poems of sacrifice, both of the world and of himself. This one indicates his continuing hunger of imagination for worldly beauty, which he almost masters with his understatements of merely meeting it and letting it alone.

This same yearning desire underlies his attempt to write a marriage song for his brother Everard in 1888. The "Epithalamion" is a glance backward to his own "summertime joys"; its exuberance, its "sudden zest" in the loveliness (even seductive loveliness) of natural things recalls Hopkins's earlier, summertime poetry in style and subject. In this poem, as in "To what serves Mortal Beauty," he concludes his (suggestively) fragmentary effort with a gesture of detachment: "Enough now; since the sacred matter that I mean / I should be wronging longer leaving it to float." "Enough now" is a call of his duty, away from his desire. But Hopkins cannot finish the poem, which trails off with some lame comparisons between "the delightful dean" and "wedlock" between the river's water and "spousal love." It is a strange comparison to make, since the water has been a scene of community bathing, of "boys from the town / Bathing." That is hard to picture as a vehicle for comparing "spousal love," especially from Hopkins. The poem is rather an embarrassment of riches, of mortal beauty from which Hopkins attempts to gather "God's better beauty, grace"; but it does not work, and Hopkins knows it. The flash of nature he gazes upon threatens to disintegrate his duty.

The only way for Hopkins is to let all that alone, divorce his duty from his desire, and accept his own motto that "immortal beauty is death with duty." Such a motto could be ironic, even bitter, for it suggests an identity between duty and death; and coming from a person who had a boundless zest for mortal beauty, such an identity does not much enhance the quality of immortal beauty. Ironic or not, the motto is written upon the banner under which Hopkins wrote his last two completed poems, "The shepherd's brow" and "To R. B." They are his farewell to dangerous mortal beauty. The opening of "The shepherd's brow" echoes the sublime force and terror of his earlier poetry, such as *The Wreck of the Deutschland*; and so the "shepherd" is himself just as he was when he could discern the will of God in earthly terrors and natural catastrophes. The shepherd is also that in himself which imitates Christ, the pastor, and so Hopkins as priest can acknowledge the "glory" as well as the "horror and the havoc" in heaven's "forked lightning." The dual function of heaven's lightning, implied by its "forked" feature, introduces a theme of profound divisiveness: the "giant groans" and "towers" of angels are contrasted with the "brittle bones" and "gasp[s]" of "baby" man. Hopkins contrasts the absurdly human with the "majestical" angels—even those angels who fell to become demons. Lurking behind all mortal beauty is the hovering shadow of a majestical fallen Angel whose groans are, ironically, the gasps of fallen man. The poem pictures the world of man twisted by the fall of angels: hence, the breath of mankind is a *"memento mori"* and the poet's breathing is a process of dying ("I that die these deaths"); the inflated pride of fallen angels is the blazoned boldness of creatures who "void with shame"; and that is the poet's urge to "feed this flame" of self-identity. The way to deal with mortal beauty is to recognize its diminished capacity, and so Hopkins outlines the absurd, scoffs at human pretentiousness, including his own, and looks at himself in the "smooth spoons" of his last sonnets.

Hopkins looks at himself on the reverse side of the "smooth spoon" in his last sonnet, "To R. B." Here, the "Man Jack" and his "hussy" are exchanged for a father and mother, as Hopkins concludes his work as an artist with a poem whose texture is dominated by the paramount Victorian symbolic image—the family. In the "winter world" of his imagination, Hopkins tells Robert Bridges that his "father" has died. And it is significant that Hopkins identifies the function of fathering with "fine delight," a close equivalent to the "desire" of other Victorian poets. In Hopkins's case this desire has been a force or tendency in himself for celebrating the loveliness of God's natural world and also for championing the justice and mercy behind all dangers of mortal beauty. As such, desire is "the fine delight that fathers thought," engendering "immortal song" upon the "mother" of the mind. But now, Hopkins admits to Bridges, his mind is barren and there is no hope for new life because his mind is a "widow." Like Swinburne, then, Hopkins ends his career as a son of Apollo, "sweet fire the sire of muse," but Hopkins's father has died and with him has died the summertime joys of artistic creativity. Hopkins's only remaining beauty is the "immortal beauty [of] death with duty," as Apollo yields everything to an all-demanding Christ-Jehovah.

7
Elizabeth Barrett Browning and Oscar Wilde

There is between two great love affairs that took place during Queen Victoria's reign an equally great leap of sensibility, one that has left its mark deep in the history of modern British literature. Elizabeth Barrett's elopement with Robert Browning on 19 September 1846 is a famous affirmation of the power to marry duty and desire into a single motive for living; on the other hand, Oscar Wilde's trial, conviction, and imprisonment for two years, beginning 25 May 1895, on account of his love for Lord Alfred Douglas, constitute an infamous denial that there can be any other publicly acceptable symbol for uniting one's duty with one's desire. Elizabeth Barrett Browning's poetry celebrates the liberating power of love and marriage, triumphant over the extreme (though classic) obstacles put in her way by her father; this was a myth to which she held, long before she met Robert Browning, and so her elopement with him was a "miracle" of myth becoming reality. By the end of the century, Oscar Wilde attempted to write poetry that celebrated the same romantic myth, but his poetry is notoriously derivative, a mere echo of his immediate predecessors. Wilde's "truth" was to "lie" about the myth of the "happy English home"; and in that, he increasingly excelled as a comic dramatist, although he did not lose hope entirely that one's duty could find some, perhaps new, way of joining with one's desire.

WHEN WILLIAM WORDSWORTH DIED IN 1850, some of Elizabeth Barrett Browning's admirers thought she should become England's poet laureate. That such a notion could be taken seriously (as indeed it was) suggests the high esteem she commanded at that time. But since the end of the nineteenth century, she has been less fortunate, for one hears very little about this fine poet from twentieth-century literary critics. The silence has been more damning even than the judgment of Hopkins, who had little praise for the poetry of either Elizabeth or Robert Browning, calling them "the scarecrow misbegotten Browning crew." Hopkins citicized one of Robert Bridge's poems by accusing it of being "Browningese." Begrudgingly, however, Hopkins did admit that "the Brownings are very fine in their ghastly way." He felt that they were among those who, like Tennyson and Swinburne, did not have "style, except individual style or manner."[1]

Not surprisingly, Swinburne's estimate of her poetry differed sharply from Hopkins's. Swinburne was most enthusiastic, saying in a letter to John Nichol that "she is the greatest woman that ever lived, except Sappho and Deborah! I know no fourth poetess like them."[2] That was in 1857, and he did not change his opinion more than forty years later when he wrote in a preface for *Aurora Leigh* that "she was a great woman and a great poet."[3] Swinburne highly praised *Aurora Leigh*, which in 1857 he called "her greatest work" and later remembered as a great literary occasion: "The advent of *Aurora Leigh* can never be forgotten by any lover of poetry who was old enough at the time to read it."[4] But Virginia Woolf deplored the fact that by 1932 readers had forgotten not only *Aurora Leigh*, but Elizabeth Barrett Browning herself, remarking that "fate has not been kind to Mrs. Browning as a writer. Nobody reads her, nobody discusses her." Virginia Woolf also praised *Aurora Leigh* for its complex challenge to aesthetic sensibility as "a masterpiece in embryo," flawed but commanding interest and inspiring respect nonetheless.[5]

With the recent increase of interest in women and women's studies, we might expect to see an appreciative discussion of Elizabeth Barrett Browning's poetry by one of our fine literary critics, but Patricia Meyer Spacks in *The Female Imagination* ignores her and her work. Perhaps Elizabeth Barrett Browning finds no place in the book because she did not write prose, to which the study is limited, but surely hers was a "female imagination" in many of the senses that Spacks's book suggests. There was for Elizabeth Barrett Browning, just as for Anaïs Nin, an "equation between writing and freedom," and her poetry, like "eighteenth- and nineteenth-century novels," rests "on the assumption that marriage will provide [a] sufficient outlet for a woman's energies." But her imagnation is "female" enough to "allow at least subterranean challenges to the vision [of marriage that she appears] to accept."[6] Finally, although Ellen Moers does not omit Elizabeth Barrett Browning from her study of *Literary Women* (indeed she calls Mrs. Browning and George Sand "positively miraculous beings"), Moers errs in her enthusiasm by saying of *Aurora Leigh* that "it is *the* feminist poem."[7]

It was not, however, as a feminist poet that Elizabeth Barrett's early reputation was established in the mind of the Victorian public. It was rather as a skillful maker of the popular romantic and religious poems that were included in her first two published volumes of original work, *The Seraphim, and Other Poems* (1838) and *Poems* (1844).[8] Not all the poems in these volumes are in the same thin vein of sentimentality that marks "The Young Queen" or "The Romaunt of the Page"; even in these early poems there are signs of her mature imagination—"lively and secular and satirical," as Virginia Woolf described it.[9] Certainly there is a lively inventiveness even in the first volume's title poem, *The Seraphim*, a short drama in two parts with an epilogue. Its "action" consists of a continuous dialogue between two seraphim, Ador and Zerah, who are the last of the angels to depart heaven for earth where they must witness the crucifixion of Christ, the "woe" of God.

Part 1 of *The Seraphim* records a struggle by desire to resist duty. If Zerah (as desire) cannot learn to sacrifice his place next to God, to descend to witness human suffering in the spectacle of Christ's Passion, then Zerah will know only the form, the appearance, of duty, not its reality: "Not for obeisance but obedience, / Give motion to thy wings!" Ador tells him (1.106). The angels' desire to please God had always been identical with their duty to do His will, but in this crisis of the earth's history, that identity is, if not actually threatened with division, at least under stress of unusual proportions. We are told that all the angels but these two have gone upon their sad mission with alacrity, leaving behind them their "golden harps":

> And the golden harps the angels bore
> To help the songs of their desire,
> Still burning from their hands of fire,
> Lie without touch or tone
> Upon the glass-sea shore.   [1.5–9]

Theirs is a "high instinct of worshipping" (1.31), a quality which even in withdrawal from heaven leaves behind "pulses in the air / Throbbing with a fiery beat" (1.36–37). Heaven is a place and a condition of being, where music and fire are attributes of love as desire and worship. Zerah, like all the others, must learn to keep his desire identical with his duty, and his temptation to separate them is the essence of this little drama. Should he attempt to return to God's presence, Ador tells Zerah, he will lose all his "being's strength" in the "ecstatic pain" of God's mourning Love; he will lose his voice of song, be "God-stricken to seraphic agony" (1.87). Zerah's only function, even as it is his only reason for being, is to love to obey. Realizing this, Zerah recovers his integrity with his assertion that God's "will is as a spirit within my spirit, / A portion of the being

I inherit. / His will is mine obedience" (1.110–12). Immediately Zerah trembles into the bright essence of his being: "a flame all undefiled through."

Contemplating the complex picture of God as man, of man as heart and man as clay, Ador is moved to exclaim in wonder why man with his "holy Heart's devout law-keeping" cannot exist without so much blood streaming (1.281–87). Ador turns to Zerah, challenging him to do his duty in at least witnessing this spectacle of divine suffering:

> Are ye unashamed that ye cannot dim
> Your alien brightness to be liker him,
> Assume a human passion, and down-lay
> Your sweet secureness for congenial fears,
> And teach your cloudless ever-burning eyes
> The mystery of his tears?   [1.294–99]

This is the final thrust of argument, as Zerah yields completely, becoming strong in his courage to give up his selfish desire, to swim "away from [his] inward vision," and to become one with the tendency of God's love that bears him along the same way as all the rest of God's creation: "One love is bearing us along," as Ador says to end the first part.

As imagined in part 1 of *The Seraphim*, angelic desire without some kind of test, such as the one imagined here, can seem to be little more than mere selfish indulgence, animal instinct without animal limits. But, when we are shown how such pure desire, loving the warmth and light of God, can be stretched if not separated by a duty that takes it away from its inertia of instinct, then we may begin to perceive something of the nature of a desire that cannot be differentiated from a duty. Only angels, seraphim, know it entirely, however; and their challenge in this drama, ironically, is to imagine the alien experience of mankind, where differentiation and division are all too common and where ambivalence and ambiguity are natural functions of being. Part 1 thus focuses upon the definition of heavenly desire as duty; part 2 focuses upon the complement of heavenly duty as desire.

Whereas in heaven no effort is required to worship in love, for that is a state of light, warmth, and music, on earth such worship requires great effort, for that is a state of darkness, cold, and silence. This is what is most striking to the two seraphim when they make their descent. They quickly discover that what keeps this world together is the strictest kind of duty, silent obedience to natural law, broken only when the creation mourns the death of God. When Christ hangs crucified, he gives himself up to death, the sign of submission to mortal nature; in this submission is perfect duty, self-sacrifice, yielding the vital self to the silence and darkness of mere matter, to be hurled about with all the rest of inarticulate nature. This is such an extreme from heavenly desire that the seraphim have great difficulty in comprehending, but when they learn that Christ has desired his death, has moved in love through obedience to this humiliating conclusion, they can better appreciate the virtue that is instinctive to them but difficult for mankind.

The poet brings into focus the weeping mother of Christ at the foot of his cross, a novel experience for angels to view. Weeping is alien to angels, as it is to the merely physical creatures. Those who are capable of weeping, mankind, are those alone who can know "creature-duty" (2.389). A "woman's hoarse weeping" may be worth more "in God's ear" than the clear music made by angels (2.508–511). In the sorrow and compassion that weeping signals is the power to unite spirit and matter in human experience, and so the mother weeping for her murdered son is especially a sign of selfless love that unites duty, as a creature, with desire, as a spirit. Indeed, when the mother weeps, "dumb matter grows articulate / And songful seraphs dumb" (2.430–31).

In this man-god submitting himself to the indignity of death the seraphim see a terrible beauty—"a passion which is tranquil" (2.618)—at work. To their own joyful music of fiery adoration, the angels must henceforth add the "passion-song" of mankind: "blend / Both musics into one" (2.658–59). To recover love through duty in such dark silence is a wondrous thing to angels, accustomed as they are to "infinite love." It is a "double bliss" to discover the infinite through the finite, to join the desire for God with the duty of sacrifice. The silent weeping of mothers for their dead sons is a human sign of divine sorrow, the sorrow of God for his dying Son, the sorrow of Christ for his own executioners. It is "the love and woe being interwound" that most perplexes the angelic visitors (2.742), for they are accustomed to unconditional love without any need for sacrifice.

In her epilogue, the poet returns us to the human perspective, where it is as strange to imagine seraphic being as it was for angels to imagine human being. We are returned to light in the epilogue, finishing as we began with music, light, and warmth, except in the end we are in "the common light of this day's sun" on a "summer's day" rather than in the "fiery heat" of heaven's "glow." Or, maybe Elizabeth Barrett wants us to feel that the two modes of light are now made the same by the power of Christ's Passion. What is certainly the same is the poet's human sorrow, identified with the mother suffering at the foot of her son's cross. In asking that angels forgive her for daring to imagine their view of the Crucifixion, the poet emphasizes her song as a form of weeping. What she can add to angelic music, that form of "lips" "burning" in heavenly desire, is the human music of sorrow. Together, heavenly desire and human duty may admit her into the midst of the angels, "to hear [their] most sweet music's miracle (2.1046).

The ingenius quality of this poem is its ironic perspective, but that same quality may be the most natural for Elizabeth Barrett to adopt. She seems to know that her imagination is angelic, perhaps too angelic for human sufferance. This poetic drama attempts to work out some of the internal stresses, perhaps some self-doubts, of her imagination, suffused as it is by the rosy glow of heavenly desire in which God is all love. To overcome a natural inclination to be at rest in one's place of happiness (as Zerah is shown to be in the first part of the drama) requires a vigor of imaginative effort which marks Elizabeth Barrett's early poetry. This is a virtue of her art, that it strives to imagine the otherness of existence, to confront, accept, and attempt to resolve the ambiguities and divisiveness of earthly being. The most ironic quality of her early poetry is that it seems to have to work to imagine the unhappy, to leave heaven behind while overcoming a certain fear of earth, with all its darkness and ominous silence.

Marriage as a rescue from loneliness, if not a rescue from earthly darkness itself, is a constant theme of Elizabeth Barrett's poetry, long before she herself was to be so rescued. In two other poems of the 1838 volume, "The Soul's Travelling" and "Sounds," she sets up contrasts of irony between marriage and funerals, not in the Blakean sense of "the Marriage hearse" but rather in the Biblical sense of Christ's parable that likens the kingdom of heaven unto a marriage feast from which those not properly dressed are cast into outer darkness (Matthew 22). While sitting somewhat apart from the street in a city, the poet describes in "The Soul's Travelling" how she watches "the great humanity which beats / Its life along the stony streets" (ll. 2–3). In the midst of that procession, she sees "the black-plumed funeral's creeping train, / Long and slow . . .

> Creeping the populous houses through
> And nodding their plumes at either side,—
> At many a house, where an infant, new
> To the sunshiny world, has just struggled and cried,—
> At many a house where sitteth a bride
> Trying to-morrow's coronals
> With a scarlet blush to-day.   [ll. 45–54]

She imagines herself flying from the din of the city into the green shadows of surrounding nature. But she discovers how inadequate nature is for satisfying the human heart alone: "O fair, fair Nature, are we thus / Impotent and querulous / Among thy workings glorious?" (ll. 189–91).

It is vain to leave the city for nature if the reason is to be happy, for that kind of happiness is possible only for angels. Although the poem does not directly say so, flight from the city is the same as joining the funeral train, leaving behind the life promised in the newborn infant and in the bride, who blushes today but tomorrow wears a crown.

That Elizabeth Barrett is more akin to her seraph Zerah than she is to the blushing bride is made very clear in "Sounds," where she hears the child

> . . . shouting at his play
> Just in the tramping funeral's way;
> The widow moans as she turns aside
> To shun the face of the blushing bride
> While, shaking the tower of the ancient church,
> The marriage bells do swing.   [ll. 48–53]

Through all the sounds of life, she hears the voice of God speaking in her soul to "look up to heaven" and realize that only He is "the end of love! give love to *Me*!"; this same voice tells her to "seek none other sound" than "the droppings of My victim-blood" (ll. 129–33). The tension of her soul is well represented by her own contrast between this sound, this voice of God, and her love of "the songful birds and grasses underfoot" (l. 127). The poet may not, in fact, hear "the voice of God" which she searches for in the last stanza (l. 137) as long as she, like the widow, "turns aside / To shun the face of the blushing bride." That is the hard lesson of the spirit that seeks to find meaning in nature by fleeing the life of the city, and it is, we may suspect, the nearly unacceptable lesson of a maiden Elizabeth Barrett.

In the most ambitious poem of her 1844 volume, Elizabeth Barrett further explores the theme of loneliness. *A Drama of Exile* works a conventional subject in a popularly Victorian way, taking the story of Adam and Eve after their exile from Eden and making it into a hymn to married love. While the verse technique of the poem shows greater skill than most of the 1838 poems, the subject and theme of *A Drama of Exile* are disappointing echoes of Byron, Shelley, and, of course, Milton. The first two scenes are little more than preparations for the epithalamic and apocalyptic last scene, showing the triumph of Christ and the blessing of earth's first married couple.

Scene 1 highlights an encounter between Gabriel and Lucifer. One thematic function here is to show how far Lucifer has fallen from the standard of duty. When Gabriel laments the ruin of his fellow angel,

Lucifer scornfully responds that he has at least chosen his ruin, for his glory lies in his will, "not of service." He acts as he does because he is "volitient, not obedient" (ll. 91–92). In one of the better passages of the drama, Lucifer declares that his being cannot be measured by the constraints set upon it by the nature of God's universe:

> What if I stand up
> And strike my brow against the crystal-line
> Roofing the creatures,—shall I say, for that,
> My stature is too high for me to stand,—
> Henceforth I must sit? Sit *thou*!
> GABRIEL: I kneel.   [ll. 107–111]

Lucifer's will to defy all limits, all laws, is his satanic desire to break down those limits, those laws, into a wild chaos of darkness and death. What Lucifer cannot perceive, or refuses to accept, is the principle of duty, a principle which contains within it just as much freedom of will as does his own notion. Duty as a gesture of kneeling is not only charged with more spiritual meaning than the mundane, or even domestic, gesture of sitting to keep from hitting one's head on the ceiling, but duty as kneeling bears with it an admirable exercise of free will. Kneeling gives beautiful form through restraint of power to an action which would otherwise be formless, an expense of destructive energy that breaks through the "crystal-line."

In contrast, Eve "drops heavily / In a heap earthward" when she and Adam appear in the second scene. This will be a typical scene in the drama: the unbearable guilt of the woman who first sinned in the world, who allowed her selfish desire to undermine her duty to God. As far as Adam is concerned, Eve is a gift from God, for "without her use in comfort" existence would be merely a "full desertness" (ll. 486, 487). Eve feels "renewed" by Adam's love for her; he describes her as his "crown" of being in exile; he, who had been king in Eden and who lost his crown there, has in Eve a happy substitute in exile. Through the metaphors of the crown and the nightingale, Eve gathers meaning in the drama as the bearer of paradisal values out of Eden. Adam tells her that she is his "Eden full of birds" (ll. 495).

What Adam and Eve must recover is their Edenic sense of duty as service, as a form of desire held under control and directed to selfless ends. When the Spirit of Inorganic Nature describes how God had fashioned all things "for use and duty" that they "Might shine anointed with his chrism of beauty" (ll. 1058–59), it makes a mistake of nature: "use" is but one function of "duty," and in the sense of physical nature it is a use without choice, without passion or desire. The Spirit of Organic

Nature makes a similar mistake when it asks why it should suffer the same corruption as Adam and Eve, wondering what it has done that nature "should fall from bliss as [they] from duty?" (l. 1157). Nature, whether inorganic or organic, cannot comprehend the sense of duty as a human obligation made special by its capacity for mistakes.

Lucifer falsely conceived natural law, divine justice, as little more than mechanical "use" and senseless restraint. Because of his own "blind desire" (l. 851), he scorned all limits and attempted to "drive up like a column erect"; he repeats to Adam and Eve the point he made earlier to Gabriel in scene 1 that he refused to stoop "to service at the footstool" (l. 1407) and sought "to transpierce / And overtop" those limits which have caused anguish and "petty griefs" for the human couple. Lucifer's exile, imitated *in petto* by Adam and Eve, was the ironic consequence of his having overshot himself, not only "transpiercing" nature, but also striking "out from nature in a blot" to become an "outcast," "mildew," a "leper," and finally the senseless dust itself (ll. 1382–89). At the end of the drama, a Chorus of Angels forecasts for Adam and Eve the Last Judgment, when Christ will become a Tamer of "the horse of Death"; the Chorus tells how that horse, as once had Lucifer, will stream its "blurting breath" "up against the arches of the crystal ceiling," but the horse will be led forth "calmly" to the Throne of God, where it will be made "Meek as lamb at pasture, bloodless in desire" (ll. 2173–84). Between the "blind desire" that drove the Morning Star in its service to Lucifer and this last lamblike desire of defeated death is a stretch of terrible history, during which Lucifer has nearly destroyed the original identity of love and service by separating the meanings of desire and duty into blind force, or instinct, and senseless restraint, or tyranny.

While nothing remains for Lucifer except the dust of annihilation, the laws of nature can be redeemed to their original function, as Christ explains: "without this law / Of mandom, ye would perish." He commands nature's laws to become "servants in pleasure, singers of delight" to man, just as "angels are to God" (ll. 1802–1803). The presence of mankind brings to nature a saving power of imagination, for, as Christ says, man will "extend / Across [nature's] head his golden fantasies / Which glorify [nature] into soul from sense" (ll. 1811–13). In rectified obedience, the Earth Spirits "promise milder duty" to mankind (l. 2011). Nature will therefore learn to yield itself in service to mankind, as men should learn to live "for others' use," to become "duty-laden" (ll. 1621–22).

Between the senseless, or blind, desire of Lucifer and the instinctual, blind, duty of nature, Adam and Eve must learn the important connecting link—call it love or service or worship or marriage. Whatever it is called, it accomplishes the wonderful, though necessary, transformation of duty into desire and desire into duty. Eve learns to understand that she, like Lucifer, had attempted to rise through the crystal limits, and that that has resulted in her present exile, wandering "beneath the roofless world" of a nature almost blind in its mechanical force. Eve feels overwhelmed by grief for what she has lost. She was once the "helpmate and delight" of Adam as well as "the lady of the world, princess of life (ll. 1303, 1238). In exile, the most important titles that Eve can bear are "woman, wife, and mother" (l. 1837). Christ commands Adam to fulfil his "office" as a "man" and "bless the woman" Eve (ll. 1823–24). This Adam does in his address to her as "Mother of the world" whose "lofty uses" and "noble ends" can be summed up in those names of "woman, wife, and mother." Eve can "rise" from her post-Edenic guilt to bear, with her husband and children, new joys into the world, where her love "shall chant itself its own beatitudes." Her greatest reward will be "a child's kiss" (l. 1868), just as the greatest gift to mankind will be the child Jesus (ll. 1959–66). Eve accepts these new tasks and this blessing by her husband, Adam: "I accept / For me and for my daughters this high part / Which lowly shall be counted" (ll. 1897–99).

The "noble work" of Eve as a "woman, wife, and mother" will have its full share of suffering and sorrow, as Adam makes clear during his speech of "blessing." Among those sorrows will be the "tyranny" of husbands, those with "larger bones / And stronger sinews" (ll. 1865–66). Elizabeth Barrett here anticipates one of the points made in Tennyson's *The Princess*, but she does not go further to foresee a time when the woman can join with the man to become "thought in thought, / Purpose in Purpose, will in will," as the Prince dreams for Princess Ida. Indeed, there are few occasions throughout her career when Elizabeth Barrett Browning transcends this ideal of her *Drama of Exile* in which the woman best redeems herself, best recovers "the name of Paradise" and "the memory of Edenic joys" (ll. 1881–82) by wearing with humility the "crown" that Adam sets upon her head (ll. 1874–75). Her "crown" is pointed with suffering all the pains of "womanhood," but so is it rounded with the glories of "woman, wife, and mother."

Elizabeth Barrett's notion of marriage as the "crown" of womanhood is the forming theme of her poem on the occasion of Queen Victoria's wedding in 1840. This poem, "Crowned and Wedded," was included in the 1844 poems along with *A Drama of Exile* and several ballads narrating various courtships, romances, and weddings. Victoria in her marriage "doth maintain her womanhood" and learns thereby that "fairer goeth bridal wreath than crown with vernal brows" (ll. 36, 38). All her subjects should "Bless the bride" rather than "God preserve the queen" (l. 46). Prince Albert should "esteem that wedded hand less dear for sceptre than for ring, / And hold her uncrowned womanhood to be the royal thing" (ll. 57–58). While this poem is hardly a triumph as art, it is clearly a statement of something important to Elizabeth Barrett before and after her own marriage. It was a nice accident of history that Victoria could become queen of England and so by her marriage typify, if not symbolize, the great hope of her subjects (including many poets) that domestic order is political order because both derive from the divine order made possible by the sacramental power of marriage.

Elizabeth Barrett was not always so sure of this, or at least she sometimes examines situations that frustrate—if they do not deny—the efficacy of the ideal of marriage. Her ballads of 1844 helped to make her a popular and famous poet in her lifetime, and it can be no accident that these ballads are monotonously preoccupied with weddings, whether happy or unhappy. The fantastic tale of "The Romaunt of the Page," improbable as it seems in narrative, is not so improbable as a theme expressing an ideal of marriage. This story of a "knight of gallant deeds / And a young page at his side" shows how important it is for a wife to keep her place in the home while her husband takes his in the world of action. The page, it turns out, is in fact that very wife, now serving her knightly husband in disguise. She tests him with a story of her ("his") "sister" who pretended to be a page to her knightly husband; the knight's reaction is that he would forgive his wife for doing such a thing, but "evermore / [he] would love her as [his] servitor / But little as [his] wife" (ll. 228–29). The "page" volunteers to stay behind to hold up the Saracens while the knight rides ahead (not knowing the page's intentions); she agonizes that she has "renounced her womanhood, / For wifehood" (ll. 272–77). We are asked to accept this equation between "womanhood" and "wifehood," both of which are sacrificed when the wife joins her husband in the field of battle (where she will, in disguise, lose her life because she feels she has indeed "renounced" wifehood by renouncing her "womanhood"). Such an ideal of marriage, although it is set in a medieval tale of the crusades, does not, in fact, unite duty and desire as much as it distinguishes (in terms perceived by Arnold and Clough) two duties and two desires which are kept in their places by a delicate balance of convention.

THERE ARE FEW who don't know anything about the Barretts of Wimpole Street; many people know something about Robert Browning's courtship of Elizabeth Barrett. But unless we read their love letters, we cannot appreciate the drama, the wit, the pain, and the beauty—as well as the love—that absorbed this famous couple between 10 January 1845 and 12 September 1846. The first date marks the beginning of their correspondence, when Robert Browning wrote of his love not only for Elizabeth Barrett's poetry (that "fresh strange music" with its "true new brave thought"), but also of his love for her: "I do, as I say, love these books with all my heart—and I love you too."[10] Some twenty months later, on a Saturday, these two great poets were secretly married in St. Marleybone Church, London. A week later they left England for Italy, where they would make their permanent home for the remainder of Elizabeth Barrett Browning's life.

This is a familiar story in its outlines, and to read their love letters is, as their editor says, like reading a work of fiction.[11] Looked at in another way, these letters provide a model for understanding how the Victorian spirit pressed for a union of head and heart through the efficacy of marriage; more specifically, Elizabeth Barrett's correspondence with Robert Browning contains a dynamic education in the identification of duty with desire through marriage. Midway through their courtship, she wrote this to Browning:

> Then I will confess to you that all my life long I have had a rather strange sympathy & dyspathy—the sympathy having concerned the genus *jilt* (as vulgarly called) male and female—and the dyspathy the whole class of heroically virtuous persons who make sacrifices of what they call "love" to what they call "duty."[12]

The record of her relationship with Browning confirms the basic truth of this confession, for once Elizabeth Barrett discovered her love for Robert Browning there was never any hesitation on her part to define that love as her primary duty. She was therefore, as she says in this same letter, quite "free from anxiety" even though she had yet to contend with that older "duty" to her father.

In the beginning of their correspondence, most of the expressions of love and desire come, naturally, from Browning; he must learn to contend with Elizabeth Barrett's insistence upon her duty to her father and family. Then, in what amounts to a turning point, he convinces her that, after she has admitted her love for Browning, her real duty is to herself; and from that point on, Elizabeth Barrett no longer has "two duties" even though she continues to have "two affections" to the very end. Her letters begin to show an increasing willingness to express her complete love for Browning, her desire for him and for his love, and her amazed joy for their marriage, when she will have a "right" "openly to love" and to hear "other people call it a duty."[13]

At first, the only desire she will admit to Browning is her desire for success as an artist. By that she means that she wishes for the fulfillment of the "idea" in her mind when she writes, but too often there is a chasm between "the thing desired & the thing attained." This could leave her in a state of despondency, "if the desire did not master the despondency." He responds that he also is exacting as a critic, but he playfully suggests that if his own audiences' "duties of appreciation" were as forward in their regard for his work as he is for her's, he would "be paid after a fashion." At this stage in their relationship, "duty" is always something owed to others, as she reveals when she tells Browning that her life of ill health and seclusion have taught her the value of "the duty of social intercourse," a notion Elizabeth Barrett will maintain throughout her life.[14]

But definitions of duty and desire sharpen with the increasing seriousness of their relationship. As her father, Edward Barrett Moulton-Barrett, begins to assert himself, Elizabeth Barrett begins to confide to Browning some of the problems that he was causing for her. Speaking of her father, she explains, "He simply takes it to be his duty to rule, & to make happy according to his own views of the propriety of happiness—he takes to be his duty to rule like the Kings of Christendom, by divine right." Although she betrays some sarcasm in this remark, she tries to explain that it is more the fault of the "system" than of her father, whose affection she always trusts. "After all," she says much later, "he is the victim. He isolates himself—& now and then he feels it . . . the cold dead silence all round, which is the effect of an incredible system." She explains how her father accuses her of being "undutiful" when she expresses her wish to travel to Pisa for her health, how he will not acknowledge the "sacrifice" she is willing to make when she chooses not to be "undutiful." Browning retorts with this very sensible advice: "You are called upon to do your duty to yourself." He tells Elizabeth that if she finds it difficult to be true to herself, to her affections, rather than to her father, then that is a measure of her real duty to herself: the decision must be "difficult, or how were it a duty?" he asks. The easy thing would be to say it is her duty to obey her father's tyranny. Browning concludes with a "dream" of their marriage, when he might enjoy the privilege of her company quite as freely as any of her brothers or even her father.[15]

While Browning's one "desire" is to be acceptable to her, Elizabeth Barrett's response is to assure him that she has no problem any longer with knowing what is her true duty. He tells her that he desires her "more earnestly than [he] ever knew what desiring was, to be" hers, that his love for her is "but an earnest desiring to include [her] in [him]self," and that he is "desirous of any opportunity of serving" her. She admits that she must choose between "two affections," one for Browning and one for her father: "It is not my fault if I have to choose between two affections,—only my pain: & I have *not* to choose between two duties, I feel . .

since I am yours" (emphasis added). She tells him that his only duty is to himself as a poet, for poets "have stricter duties thrust upon them." Over and over she insists that Browning must put his art ahead of his love for her, and that sometimes causes him some pain and misunderstanding. But one year after their correspondence began, she announces to him quite clearly that her affection is identical with her duty to him alone: "I look to you for my first affections & my first duty."[16]

The burden of her letters to Browning is now an expression of her love for him. She tells him that his "love has been to [her] like God's own love, which makes the receivers of it kneelers." She sees more clearly that her father's notion of duty has deteriorated because it has become disconnected from the sympathy of love: "After using one's children as one's chattels for a time, the children drop lower & lower toward the level of the chattels, & the duties of human sympathy become difficult in proportion. And (it seems strange to say it, yet is true) *love*, he does not conceive of at all." She is grateful to Browning for rescuing her from this condition of "chattel" with his "divine love" that has drawn her "back into life." Now she has so many "wishes" that "they recoil back on [her] in a spring-tide . . flow back, wave upon wave." Thus has he awakened in her a great desire for life.[17]

She begins to discuss the subject of marriage, reporting how her friend Mrs. Jameson had suggested that there should be a "septennial marriage act" that allows the partners to decide whether to continue their marriage every seven years. Elizabeth Barrett protests: "I like Mrs. Jameson, mind!—and I like her views on many subjects—*Ex*clusive of the septennial marriage act, though." Because marriage is the seal of love for Elizabeth Barrett, there can no more be a dissolution of its power than a denial of God's love for his creation; anything else would "be based upon nothingness." She insists that Browning consider their relationship a freedom to love, not a duty to acknowledge obligation; when she thinks he has written only because he thinks he is supposed to, she tells him that she "seem[s] to hear the rattling of the chain all this distance." She wants love from him, not obligation: "I am not over-particular, I fancy, about what I may be loved for. There is no good reason for loving me, certainly, & my earnest desire . . . is that there should be by profession no reason at all." If he must have a reason to love her, let it be for something so trivial as that he loves her for her shoes. Truly, any *reason* for love becomes a condition and a compromise, which she denies.[18]

To be bound by reason is to make marriage into a bondage for both. She begins to express her fear that Browning not base his love for her upon some reason, or some duty. "Oh, I understand perfectly," she playfully warns, "how as soon as ever a common man is sure of a woman's affections, he takes up the tone of right & might . . & he *will* have it so . . & he *won't* have it so." Such is the "system" she has noticed in her own father's behavior, and so has she long remembered a conversation she once heard when she was a child: "I heard two married women talking. One said to the other . . 'The most painful part of marriage is the first year, when the lover changes into the husband by slow degrees.' " And most of all Elizabeth Barrett does not want her lover, the poet, to become "a common man," a "husband." Thus she is happy with their secret marriage for more than one reason: not only will it put off a confrontation with her father, but by it they can avoid the whole "system" of public marriages that is deadening to genuine affection. Referring to the upcoming marriage of her cousin, she exclaims, "Do you know, the pomp & circumstance, the noise & fuss & publicity of this marriage of theirs happen just in time to make me satisfied with 'quite the other principle' as you said. . . . So barbarous a system it is, this system of public marriages."[19]

Browning must understand that he is not to be compelled by the conventions of this barbarous "system of public marriages" any more than they are to be compelled to marry according to its expectations. He is to be the "lord of the house-door-key, & of [his] own ways," but so is she to share that atmosphere of freedom, as she goes on to say, teasingly, "so that when I shall go to Greece, you shall not feel yourself much better off than before I went."[20] Finally, she protests that most "public marriages" are merely formal commitments to a certain duty, regulating the exploitation of women as chattel, as wives: "When women are chosen for wives, they are not chosen for companions—that when they are selected to be loved, it is quite apart from life," she observes.

> Men like to come & find a blazing fire & a smiling face & an hour of relaxation. Their serious thoughts, & earnest aims in life, they like to keep on one side. And this is the carrying out of love & marriage almost everywhere in the world—& this, the degrading of women by both.[21]

To choose a spouse, even if it is to love, is all wrong if it is "quite apart from life." The substantive must be *love*, which is free of reason; the condition may be *duty*, which follows from or is identical with the love, becoming "dutiful affection." And so, with marriage being the seal of God's love in which duty to one's self is duty to God, Robert Browning can tell Elizabeth that her duties are "to God & [her]self," while she can confess that her love for him *is* her love for God: "You only!" she exclaims in her last letter before their elopement, "As if one said *God* only."[22]

THE IDEAL OF A ROMANCE made real by marriage informs these love letters, which in turn provide the setting for the famous, although little studied collection, *Sonnets from the Portuguese*. Imagination as erotic desire gives these forty-four sonnets a warmth and color that we rarely find in major Victorian poetry. There is a significant pattern of thematic development holding the sonnets together in sequence; it is evident mainly when we approach them after having read Elizabeth Barrett's earlier poetry and her letters to Robert Browning. In these sonnets, erotic desire becomes divine love, a point of great importance, for in her earlier poetry Elizabeth Barrett usually celebrated the sanctioning of eros by God. Now it is love who is god, rather than God who is love. Adding to the drama of these sonnets, to their breathless excitement of discovery, is the reversal of an earlier symbolic image: the Shadow of God (in *The Seraphim*), usurped by the shadow of Satan (in *A Drama of Exile*), here becomes the Light of Love. While *Sonnets from the Portuguese* does not become an epithalamion, it is throughout a hymn to earthly love and as such gives us one of the best possible insights into the poet's conception of desire.

The sequence opens forcefully, even dramatically, with a scene of the speaker drawn "backward by the hair" by "a mystic Shape." Because her life had been often crossed by shadows of life's sorrow, she instinctively thinks she has been seized ("in mastery") by Death, the last shadow. But she is delightfully, ironically, wrong, for she has been seized by Love. The image of the woman drawn backward by her hair invites an interpretation of strongly sexual power at work, but more importantly it shows how Elizabeth Barrett Browning recognizes the ironies of misidentifying Love as Death. She is taking us from the edge of her speaker's grave to a new life made possible in this power of love. This "mystic Shape," coming quietly up behind her, seizing her for life, has no definite form or identity; he is too much a stranger to have even a name. Imagery of fire and light help to explain this shape, illuminate it, and define it for both the speaker and the reader. Out of the dust and ashes of her life, which she casts at the feet of this "mystic Shape," the speaker discovers "red wild sparkles" that "dimly burn / Through the ashen grayness" (sonnet 5); this image of desire bursts into scorching fire until it can be seen clearly that "love is fire" (sonnet 10).

The light and heat of her passion contribute to the speaker's growing acceptance of her worthiness to be loved; she is learning that there is "nothing low / In love" (sonnet 10). The first form of identification for her mystic Love is that he is royal—a prince and then a king; he is a "princely Heart" (sonnet 3), "noble" "like a king" (sonnet 16) who has set a "crown" upon her head (sonnets 12, 38) so that she can join him "on a golden throne" (sonnet 12). While the poet uses a metaphor of the lover as musician and singer in a way that reinforces the metaphor of prince and king, the associations of royalty are common to both (sonnets 3, 4, 26). This royal power has overwhelmed the speaker, who considers herself too lowly for his attention. He properly belongs in a palace rather than in her poor house with its broken casements and poor latch, but he has crossed "the threshold of [her] door / Of individual life" and so bent low to be with her (sonnets 4, 6). The relationship outlined by these metaphors is cut from the Cinderella pattern (reinforced by the imagery of ashes in sonnet 5). The miracle of the speaker's transformation into a princess, in sonnet 12, keeps her in a state of awe and wonder to the very end of the sequence, when her "pilgrim's staff" bursts into "green leaves" at her lover's sight (sonnet 42). Not only is she rescued from the grave, but her "life's lower range" has turned from dust and ashes into "fresh Spring," when her very thoughts are a "greenery" and her heart a garden of flowers the year around (sonnets 23, 21, 29, 44). The princely lover has stooped to enter her lowly house, lifted her from her ashes, led her forth into a springtime life, and takes her to "another home" (sonnet 25).

Emphasizing his role as saviour, the speaker describes her lover as her redeemer (with echoes, of course, of Christ). He might have begun, in his "mystic Shape," as something of a rapist, but in his "conquering" he proves "lordly" while "lifting" her "upward"; this the speaker understands when she tells us that she is like "a vanquished soldier [who] yields his sword / To one who lifts him from the bloody earth" (sonnet 16). To submit to love, to serve with desire, is to "rise" from "this drear flat of earth" (sonnet 27). She now realizes that her lover has not only raised her but also liberated her from her "chains" of grief and dreariness (sonnet 20) and rescued her from behind the "prison-wall" of her loneliness (sonnet 41). By these deeds, she knows him not only as her "new angel" (sonnet 42), but by the holiest of names, God Himself.

Elizabeth Barrett does not come easily to this identification, nor does she do so without some hesitation and qualification. But only God could perform such miracles as she has witnessed in herself by this love, and finally she must acknowledge Him as her lover. From "mystic Shape" to royal musician to princely courtier and liberating soldier: these are the stages of identity through which the power of love has come for the speaker. The poet admits that all of her earlier poetry had been but "visions" and that her music had grown "silent" until her lover appeared in her life, becoming the reality that her visions had only "seemed" to be (sonnet 26). Such a large reality could not be measured by the human soul alone. She is close to this ultimate identification in sonnet 20, where she compares her lover's absence and her own anxieties during his absence to the doubts of atheists "who cannot guess God's presence out of sight." Then, in the exhilaration of gratitude for having been rescued from dreariness, she exclaims in sonnet 27 that she had "looked for only God, [and] found *thee!*" In sonnet 33, comparing herself to the child who stops her "innocent play" when her name is called by those loved ones who now are dead, she asks that her lover's name now be heir to that of God Himself. Finally, in sonnet 37, she recognizes fully "all that strong divineness" that attaches to his "sovranty." It is no wonder, then, that in sonnet 43 she cannot count all the ways she loves him, for his attributes are infinite and his identity fills all dimensions to "the ends of Being and ideal Grace," high and low, past and future.

To submit, then, is to conquer, and to be ravished is to be made royal. This truth of paradox is the essence of genuine love, when desire becomes worship and sense becomes soul. One of the most frequent metaphors of the sequence is the lover as musician, or singer, and by this metaphor Elizabeth Barrett Browning has most consistently explored the right relationship of the lovers. At first, he is "chief musician" and she a "wandering singer" who passes through the darkness outside palace walls wherein he entertains nobility (sonnets 3, 4). When her "minstrel-life" grew "weary" with "the burden of a heavy-heart" (sonnet 11), he ap-peared with his "antidotes / Of medicated music" (sonnet 27) to restore her to health, to a new vigor of imagination witnessed by these very sonnets. His service to her has summoned her to become his servant; sonnet 17 suggests that his art should be devoted to all mankind, while her own will be devoted only to him. His music made her old "visions," her old songs, seem unreal; he becomes the realization of her ideal sung about in former times (sonnet 26). She will become his instrument of music, imperfect though she might be (sonnet 32); nevertheless, because he is a master musician, he can make sweet music from even so "defaced" an instrument. Her final tribute to their love, in the pattern of this metaphor, occurs in sonnet 41, where she describes herself as a musician in a prison; many listened while pausing briefly to hear her "music in its louder parts / Ere they went onward" to do the world's business, but he, her poet-lover, heard her "voice's sink and fall," heard her entirely, and dropped his own "divinest Art" at her feet to better listen to her music. In this pause of mutual appreciation, this willingness to lay down one's own interests and to attend to another soul's great need, lies the essence of mutual desire as genuine love and redemptive power.

As her sometimes vapid love poetry of 1838 and 1844 acquired warmth and conviction in *Sonnets from the Portuguese* during her court-ship, Elizabeth Barrett's "political" poetry acquired strength and deter-mination after 1846 when she became Elizabeth Barrett Browning and moved to Italy. Her poetry occasioned by those exciting years in Italy, including *Casa Guidi Windows* (1851), *Poems Before Congress* (1860), and the *Last Poems* (1862), has been criticized for being disloyal (at worst) or naive (at best); but it often shows a maturity of style, a toughness of mind, and a complexity of emotion that belie such criticism. Surely one of her most underrated poems is *Casa Guidi Windows*, a work which sometimes has the ring of Robert Browning's poetry but which finally achieves a unique sound of its own. Although part 1 was composed three years before part 2, the work is an aesthetic unity. This unity is, in part, a result of the tone that is developed by the speaking voice of a person who looks out her windows upon a Florentine street, describes what she sees there, has seen there, and hopes to see there. Underlying this tone, adding melody to the poem's harmony, is a theme of happiness which the speaker hopes for Italy (and, it is fair to think, which Elizabeth Barrett Browning has discovered with her husband and, after his birth in 1849, with their son).

Part 1 is, as the poet describes it, "an exultant prophecy" which is "dropped" in part 2. Part 1 begins appropriately as a "meditation and a dream" evoked by the song of a child who had passed beneath the poet's windows the preceding evening, a song of *"bella liberta."* Italy certainly had the beauty, in her history and in her art, but it did not have the liberty. The poet pays tribute to Italian history and art, but in doing so she berates all those now living who cannot detach themselves from the corpse of the past, who cannot turn from the tomb to live in the temple. Italy is itself a child, merely singing of liberty; the country needs to turn the ideal of its art into the reality of its life. Like this child whose song the poet has just heard, the land and its people are still in training, learning to walk: "By mother's finger steadied on his feet" (1.12). Some of Italy's singers, however, insist on treating her as a "childless . . . widow of empires," even a shameful harlot, or a "Cybele, or Niobe," or "sweet, fair Juliet" (ll. 22–23, 23–26, 32, 40), self-murdered for innocent love. But the speaker will have none of that: "Of such songs enough, / Too many of such complaints" (ll. 40–41). She would have her readers go to the so-called tomb of Juliet at Verona, and there it would be found to be "void" (1. 42), as empty as Christ's own tomb. But Juliet never existed, she was only an "image" that "men set between themselves and actual wrong," deluding themselves with their own fantasies.

Italy lives in a way that Juliet never did; rather, Italy should be able to live in the reality with as much life as Shakespeare gave to the vibrant and beautiful Juliet. Imagination (or, as Elizabeth Barrett Browning will later identify this power, desire for a clear purpose) is what is needed—an imagination acting on real events at the present time, and perhaps this poem is itself such an activity. Using her open windows as a frequent image throughout the poem, the poet thrusts them on us as symbols for vision, for new vistas and outlets upon reality. In the central passages of part 1, a "thousand windows" are opened, with Casa Guidi windows but a part of a large scene of vision (l. 478). This section of the poem describes the great procession in Florence when the Grand-duke permitted "the citizens to use their civic force / To guard their civic homes" (ll. 460–61), for which those citizens have staged this parade in celebration. The poet looked out upon streets and piazzas flooded "with a tumult and desire" (l. 453): "hands broke from the windows" (l. 483), then "a cloud of kerchiefed hands" rose through "the murmuring windows" (l. 491), and along the streets "babies leapt / Right upward in their mother's arms" (ll. 528–29). These, and others, were signs of great passion, "tumult and desire," which the poet took for true symbols of a new energy, a new life in the people. Her faith was given substance by the final scene of the episode, a scene at the end of the parade when the Duke "drew / His little children to the window-place / He stood in at the Pitti" (ll. 557–59). This was a sign that "Right and Law" stood together, "each in reverent awe / Honored the other" (ll. 538–40). The relationship of the Duke and "his little children" with the people, filled with desire "to guard their civic homes," brought together two sets of values that heretofore had been widely separated as are "men from humble homes and ducal chairs" (l. 552). Elizabeth Barrett Browning gathers from the scene a promise of a new era, not unlike her own British Victorian one, in which the nation is a happy family, where the "desire" of the people for "Right" can be married with the "duty" of the leaders for "Law."

It is exactly this virtue of "duty" that much of the poem is designed to celebrate, in part 1 at least. The poet feels some confidence in the Duke, not only because he has shown himself to be a family man, but also because she "like[s] his face"; he shows himself "careful with the care that shuns a lapse / Of faith and duty" (ll. 564, 569–70). His willingness to identify himself in a window with his children shows that he values fatherhood highly; and fatherhood is a sacred trust of duty by governors every bit as much as it is by husbands. When the duty of the governor unites with the desire of the people, "popular conscience" rises from "popular passion" and they "announce law / By freedom" (ll. 742–43, 715–16). The poet's dream, then, is for a freedom that is the law, in which "thinkers" will take "the place of fighters" (ll. 727–28); this can happen when "thought" "pioneers / All generous passion" (ll. 770–71). Therefore, what the people need is some direction for their "tumult and desire," and it is the duty of their leaders to become "teachers": "Rise up, teacher ! here's / A crowd to make a nation!" (ll. 772–73). The remainder of part 1 is a call for such a teacher, a deliverer, a hero who can turn "popular passion" into "popular intellect" (ll. 1093–94). This may sound like Thomas Carlyle (or any number of others whose works could not escape the influence of that Victorian prophet), but it certainly marks Elizabeth Barrett Browning as a Victorian with a strong British faith in education as well as, or perhaps for the sake of, domestic happiness. Whether or not Carlyle had much to do with her way of putting such matters, she had from personal experience all the guidance she needed to feel that this way was appropriate for Italians as well as for the British: that experience could be Christian (with Christ as king and teacher) or Protestant (with education supreme) or domestic (with father as governor and teacher) or marital (with husband as any of the former) or even poetic (with the poet as teacher [ll. 1090–1100]).

She calls out for this heroic teacher to do for all of Italy what the Duke has done for Florence, and more: "But the teacher, where?" Among other possibilities, he might be one who keeps "house" like other peasants, "with inlaced / Bare brawny arms about a favorite child, / And meditative looks beyond the door" (ll. 823–26). If such a person should rise to answer the call, this would not surprise Elizabeth Barrett Browning; what would surprise her would be an answer by a pope, for popes have too much to overcome to do their proper duty by the common people of Italy. The pope "sits in stone and hardens by a charm" (l. 1037), and though he is a holy Father, he is no father who can show his children like the Duke at the window in Florence. For a pope to become the "deliverer" would be a miracle, but she would accept him whatever he might be, "pope or peasant," as long as he is "a man" (ll. 1052, 1035). This man must show to the Italians what the poet and her husband have found in Italy: that the very mountains "live in holy families," that their own Vallombrosa is a "paradise" made "divine to English man and child" by the poetry of John Milton (ll. 1131–63). The Brownings have found this paradise in Italy (ll. 1172–84) because of their love for one another and because their imaginations have been taught by Milton's poetry. It is their turn to inspire their readers to heroic endeavor, possible to those who believe that "the world shows nothing lost" when one keeps his "post / On duty's side" (ll. 1210, 1212–13); the "true success" is in the "daring" (l. 1215).

This challenge to her readers only seems "a dream" to the poet when she thinks back on it from the vantage point that opens part 2 of *Casa Guidi Windows*. Not that she no longer believes that "true success" is in the "daring," but events have proved to her that there was too little "daring" in the gestures of those parading Florentines, so there was no true success. This second part is a bitter confession of misinterpretation, but it is a determined affirmation of the poet's continuing faith in the need not only for a heroic deliverer who will do his duty by his people, but also for a genuine desire by the people for their own deliverance. This second part of the poem is in some ways a more complex analysis of political reality than Elizabeth Barrett Browning is usually given credit for. It may be less enthusiastic, more self-critical, and more analytical than the first part, but it is strongly emotional, as Juvenalian satire, disappointed and yet, finally, optimistic. The complexity of the analysis may anticipate a comparable complexity found in *Aurora Leigh*, where desire (or passion) cannot so easily be assigned to only one of the partners in a marriage (whether domestic or political) and duty (or intellect) to the other. Part 2 of *Casa Guidi Windows* still holds to an ideal of political happiness as, at least, something not unlike domestic happiness, but the poem now insists that there must be a greater emphasis on the *duty* as well as the desire of the people and the *desire* as well as the duty of the leaders.

Italy has not only failed to achieve its political "manhood," it has gone back to sleep, as "little children" do when they "sleep upon their mothers' knees" (ll. 14, 10, 12). This image of children on mothers' knees will occur again at the end of the poem, transfigured by the poet's imagination to become a symbol not of failure but of hope. *Casa Guidi Windows* is framed by such an image, from the opening of part 1 with a child singing, to the opening of part 2 with that child asleep, to the closing of the poem with a child smiling for its mother's happiness. Before she can see that smile, however, the poet undergoes an anguish of bitter disappointment and scornful outrage that will produce some of her most powerful poetry.

The power is a product, first, of measured self-scorn:

> But we, who cannot slumber as thou dost,
> We thinkers, who have thought for thee and failed,
> We hopers, who have hoped for thee and lost,
> We poets, wandered round by dreams, . . .   [ll. 16–19]

Like the messenger who brings back the news of Troy's defeat to cheer Clytemnestra, the poet has in part 1 been "cozened" with hope that "sorrow [is] ended" (ll. 20–23). Now she must narrate the tragedy of "this Atrides' roof." The image of the "lintel-post / Which still drips blood" marks another distinction of part 2: its sharp, symbolically functional imagery. The dripping blood nearly blinds the hero, Mazzini; blood has "splashed" on his brow from heroes who have died beside him (ll. 538–39). In counterpoint to the imagery of the dripping blood of heroes is the "smooth olive-leaf" worn by the Austrian soldiers who return the Grand-duke to Florence; this olive leaf, covered by dust, mocks at peace even while it sheds Italian heroes' blood. One of the most powerful images in the poem is that of a garden worm cut by a spade:

> You kill worms sooner with a garden-spade
> Than you kill peoples; peoples will not die;
> The tail curls stronger when you lop the head:
> They writhe at every wound and multiply
> And shudder into a heap of life . . .   [ll. 340–44]

The image is startling, especially when we consider that the worms are not only people but also "God's own vitality" (l. 345); it is worthy of Edward Taylor or Emily Dickinson (who admired Elizabeth Barrett Browning's poetry).

It is through such imagery that the poem works out its turmoil of pain and hope. The mockery of the olive-leaf in soldiers' helmets causes the poet to cry out with indignation at what the "hollow world" calls "peace" (in a tone that anticipates Tennyson's *Maud*). If, as this world says, war is peace, then, the poet retorts, peace is war. The "peace" of the hollow world is the peace of gibbets, dungeons, chains, and starving homes (ll. 384–98); if there can be "no peace which is not fellowship / And which includes not mercy" (ll. 399–400), then the "faint of heart of [her] womanhood" prefers "the raking of guns across / The world" (ll. 406, 401–402). The peace of a hollow world not only mocks at itself, but it cuts out the heart of the family that achieves its happiness at the cost of human suffering. Such peace is not worthy of the hearth beside which it sits "in self-commended mood," keeping "at home" while the world outside is filled with anguish (ll. 408, 412).

One of the most important images for the developing pattern of part 2 incorporates this one of a "hollow world" with its mockery of peace. Out of the "tumult and desire" that throbbed through part 1 has come a complex new view of the world in part 2. Here the scene has disintegrated into "a universe that breaks / And burns" (ll. 194–95), a "hollow world," then a "busy" world, a "Fair-going world" that hawks its hollow wares while "the poor / . . . sit in darkness when it is not night" (ll. 577–78, 625–26). In such a "fair-going world" (which, with its imagery of disintegration anticipates Robert Browning's "Fifine at the Fair"), wearing masks and changing masks is a normal activity: "the mime / Changed masks, because a mime" (ll. 240–41), but the mimes brought "tragedies"; the breaking universe seems to have as little meaning as the changing tides, "as smooth / In running in as out" (ll. 241–42), churning human bodies indiscriminately with sand and pebbles:

> And now, the seaweeds fit
> Her body, like a proper shroud and coif,
> And murmurously the ebbing waters grit
> The little pebbles while she lies interred
> In the sea-sand.   [ll. 684–88]

This is the "memorable grave" of Garibaldi's wife, who died "at her husband's side" and now scorns "the hissing waves" just as then she scorned "the whistling shot" (l. 679). She died a hero's death, and "her little babe unborn" died with her. But this image becomes for the poet a sign of hope, even "triumph," because from these heroic Dead "be seeds of life" that will "let out the Spring-growth / In beatific green" (ll. 663, 665); then it will be seen that "earth's alive" and "new springs of life are gushing everywhere" (ll. 765, 762).

That sprig of olive leaf, after all, was green even if it was covered with dust. Before she can see the green, the poet has to blow away the dust, and this is what she does in venting her anger at both the Florentine people and the Grand-duke. She had "believed the man was true" when she saw him "among his little sons" that glorious day of the parade (ll. 65, 93), but now she knows that that was all a show, a mime, to which she responded all too enthusiastically, perhaps because she is "a woman," one who "felt [her] own child's coming life" while she watched those children with their father, the Duke (ll. 95–96). She was deceived, and now she repents, sighing while she bows her soul (ll. 58–63). The first half of part 2 is, structurally, a review of the parade through Florence which was celebrated in part 1, but here it is shown to have been all a mimicry, when people paraded in costume but lacked conviction. This scene echoes Carlyle's *Sartor Resartus* as well as his *French Revolution* in its stripping away of hollow masks and showy ornaments of clothing, even while the people protest that they were doing their duty; the poet has them say,

> "You say we failed in duty, we who wore
> Black velvet like Italian democrats,
> Who slashed our sleeves like patriots, nor forswore
> The true republic in the form of hats?"   [ll. 148–51]

They defend their cowardice by saying it was their "duty" to stay with their "wives and mothers" (ll. 173–74), to keep their shops open and their farms going; no wonder the poet sees it all as "a fair-going world."

But she will not condemn the people for their false notions of duty; if "desire was absent" (l. 203) so that all that tumult was merely a show, it was the result of a failure in leadership. How can there be any desire when there is no cause, where there is no knowledge of the end for which "courage and patience are but sacrifice" (l. 197). The teacher has not appeared to show the people how to "discern true ends" (l. 22) so they can make "full use / Of freedom" (ll. 232–33). The teacher, it may turn out, cannot be a father. At least, when the Grand-duke returned with his Austrian soldiers, he did not come back "like a father" "to pardon fatherly those pranks / Played out" earlier (ll. 269–77). Either the "dear paternal Duke" (l. 251) betrayed the image of paternity, or else the image itself is not appropriate to the heroic teacher. He at least did not even merit the "noise" of boys shouting out in "a callow voice" (ll. 269–73); instead, he was met by "sentient silence" from a people who "had learnt silence" through suffering (ll. 366, 358). The poet's own thoughts in this second part articulate the feelings of all those people who have "wept and cursed in silence" (l. 356).

She must give them voice, but she cannot shout with the exultation that informed part 1. Not only is "sentient silence" more appropriate because of the discipline of disappointment, but also because she is now a mother who cannot awaken her sleeping infant. This circumstance, first outlined in lines 293–98, not only defines well the tone of the second part as disciplined passion—"sentient silence," when a mother tries not to disturb her sleeping baby with her angry denunciations—but it also conditions the way the mother's thoughts are worked out to a hopeful conclusion. We may see it developing from that earlier reference to her belief in the Grand-duke because she had "felt her own child's coming life," to this situation where she protects her sleeping child from "the world's baseness" (l. 297), on to the later picture of Garibaldi's wife dying a hero's death while "she felt her little babe unborn / Recoil, within her" (ll. 680–81). By this point, it becomes clear to the speaker that she must not betray her own function as a mother even if grand-dukes and popes betray theirs as fathers. A mother is like the earth itself; her womb of life gives forth the human future even from the tombs of the heroic dead: "These Dead be seeds of life." And so that her poetry not be misconstrued as "nothing but death-songs" (l. 730) like those she had criticized in part 1, Elizabeth Barrett Browning concludes her poem with a celebration of the "new springs of life" that rush over all things, in a vision of her child bathed in sunlight.

Earlier, because she was disgusted with the sight of the Grand-duke and his Austrian soldiers, the speaker ordered that the Casa Guidi windows be shut:

> But wherefore should we look out any more
>   From Casa Guidi windows? Shut them straight,
> And let us sit down by the folded door,
>
> . . . .
> I have grown too weary of these windows. [ll. 425–27, 430]

In the diminished light of her apartment, she would "veil" her "sad-
dened" face, and so, in effect, turn away from the reality that she has been
describing. Looking within has forced her to focus on her child, however,
and this is dramatized by the beautiful scene that closes the poem, for the
sunlight cannot be kept completely out:

> The sun strikes, through the windows, up the floor;
> Stand out in it, my own young Florentine,
>   Not two years old, and let me see thee more!
> It grows along thy amber curls, to shine
>   Brighter than elsewhere. Now, look straight before.   [ll. 742–46]

It is a scene of naturalistic apotheosis, a scene of infant glory, concluding
with a hope for the future that children represent when they are "lifted
high on parent souls" (l. 769). Her final picture of the smiling child like
an angel leaning "inward to the Mercy Seat" verges on the Madonna-
Child painting by Cimabue (described in part 1, ll. 332–51), except that
here the speaker is the mother and her own child is the divine one.
Reality has displaced art to inspire the living. This (Pompilia-like) transfiguration at the end of the poem concentrates the Christian symbol of
the Holy Family into a pre-Raphaelite picture of the holy in common life.

THE HAPPY GLOW of the concluding scene in *Casa Guidi Windows*
reappears in the opening scenes of *Aurora Leigh* (1856), Elizabeth Barrett
Browning's masterpiece. This narrative poem in nine books opens with
an Italian setting for a handsome family of Italian mother, English father,
and their little girl, Aurora Leigh; the poem will close in the same Italian
setting, after much time has passed in England and in France, with a
picture of another family, though it is a much more complex family than
any yet described in a poem by Elizabeth Barrett Browning. There is a
mother and a child, but no father; there is a bride who had tried all her
life not to be a bride; and there is a groom who all his life has searched
for a way to make himself acceptable to his beloved. The difference between the family that opens the poem and the family that closes it not
only is a measure of the distance Elizabeth Barrett has come in her life
and poetry, but it is in several ways a measure of the complication in the
symbolic force of the family as a metaphor in Victorian poetry and
drama.

One very revealing line from part 2 of *Casa Guidi Windows* anticipates a major theme of *Aurora Leigh*: addressing the "Magi of the east
and of the west" who barter their hollow wares in the busy "Fair-going
world" of the "gorgeous Crystal Palace," the poet asks why there is "no

help for women sobbing out of sight / Because men made the laws?" (ll. 638–39). The bitterness of this question betrays the poet's bias as a "feminist" who would write what has been called "*the* feminist poem." *Aurora Leigh* takes as one of its leading themes the plight of women trying to fulfill themselves as human beings in a world where "men [have] made the laws."

However "feminist" the point of view might be, the poem is not feminist in the twentieth-century sense. If the view of Mr. Smith, the young "German student" whose conversation with Sir Blaise Delorme in book 5 is reported by Aurora Leigh, were also the view of the heroine or of the poet, then well might we call this "a" if not "*the* feminist poem." Mr. Smith, representing the progressive young, with smart ideas from their German educations in higher criticism, touts the time when "prejudice of sex / And marriage law" will be relics of the past (5.705–706). Sir Blaise, a spokesman for the older generation, scoffs at such a notion, believing that such a circumstance of "general concubinage" would lead to "a universal pruriency" (5.726, 727). Sir Blaise champions the ideal of "our fathers," who,

> when they had hung
> Their household keys about a lady's waist,
> The sense of duty gave her dignity.   [5.686–88]

A woman's duty, in the world of Sir Blaise, is to hold the "household keys" about her waist and to keep "her bosom holy to her babes." This is the duty of all who are true to "the church,—and by the church [he] mean[s], of course / The catholic, apostolic, mother-church" (5.746–47).

Aurora Leigh herself is on the side of neither Sir Blaise, with his "duty," nor Mr. Smith, with his end of the "marriage-law." She does not subscribe to the kind of duty which Lord Howe describes when he speaks of a certain John Eglinton: "He likes art, / Buys books and pictures . . . of a certain kind; / Neglects no patent duty; a good son" (5.881–83). This John Eglinton sent a letter via Lord Howe for Aurora Leigh, but she refuses to open it for she will do nothing to encourage the man, who has a reputation she does not savor: John Eglinton may be "a good son" who "neglects no patent duty," but he is "good" "to a most obedient mother," whom he dominates outrageously. Such a man as John Eglinton represents the worst kind of "duty" that Aurora Leigh has discovered, rigid formality. Between that version and Mr. Smith's, she would choose Mr. Smith's; however, up to this critical point at Lord Howe's party, her life (as represented in this poem) has been a long and sometimes painful education in duty, both its true and false forms.

The first half of the poem is, indeed, such an education, balanced in

the second half by an education in desire. When she overhears Sir Blaise
talking about the duty of women whose dignity comes from their responsibility as wives and mothers, Aurora Leigh may not be able to sympathize, for that is the very role which she has refused to accept for herself
when she declined Romney's proposal. Nevertheless, at this midpoint of
the narrative, she is going through a painful reexamination of her soul,
when she will have to admit that she may have been wrong not to have
become such a woman whose "sense of duty gave her dignity."

While Aurora Leigh is no advocate of free love, or "universal pruriency," she is an advocate of freedom for women to be themselves, loved
or not. Since her arrival in England at the age of thirteen, she has been
surrounded by persons who believe it is a woman's duty to marry and
serve. Her first encounter with such a view was when she first met her
father's sister, who took Aurora into her care not without some reservations; Aurora's aunt hated the Italian woman who was Aurora's mother:

> And thus my father's sister was to me
> My mother's hater. From the day she did
> Her duty to me (I appreciate it
> In her own word as spoken to herself),
> Her duty, in large measure, well pressed out,
> But measured always.   [1.359–64]

This is the kind of duty which would become odious to Aurora Leigh,
but it is also a consequence of Aurora's misinterpretation of English
manners, "well pressed out, / But measured always," like the land itself,
"a nature tamed / And grown domestic" (1.634–35). It will take Aurora
a long while to adapt to the English landscape as a scene of beauty, and
it will take her even longer to learn to appreciate the value of a duty
"well pressed out."

There *is* value in measured obligation, though not in the kind
which Aurora thought she saw in her aunt. We must keep in mind, first,
that Aurora saw her aunt as her "mother's hater" and, second, that much
later Aurora will admit that her aunt knew more about Aurora's heart
than Aurora herself did. In the meantime, however, the aunt represents
for Aurora Leigh all those things about England that seemed repressive,
spiritless, and merely useful. These were the qualities of life from which
Aurora's father had been rescued by his love for the Italian girl:

> My father was an austere Englishman,
> Who, after a dry lifetime spent at home
> In college-learning, law, and parish talk,
> Was flooded with a passion unaware,
> His whole provisioned and complacent past
> Drowned out from him that moment.   [1.65–71]

Aurora's view is that Italy and her mother brought new life to her father, "a sacramental gift / With eucharistic meanings" (1.90–91). Freedom, spontaneity, passion, and spirituality are the values she associates with Italy and the parents buried there.

Her aunt has, however, a very different view of the matter. She had loved her brother truly, but she had, with just as much passion, hated Aurora's mother as the woman "who had fooled away / A wise man from wise courses, a good man / From obvious duties" (1.342–44). The child cannot know what makes the aunt feel this way; it is much later before Aurora understands that her father sacrificed his property to marry the Italian girl, and by an eccentric entail, Aurora would have no legal rights to claim any of the English properties of her father's family. Equally eccentric, from her point of view, was the arrangement by her father's cousin for Aurora to be engaged to Romney Leigh, the heir to that property.

All of that seems so heartless, so rigid and "well pressed out" in English style that the word *duty* would have negative meanings for Aurora most of her life. She learned to adapt, nevertheless, to England—in its social order as well as in its natural beauty. For Aurora discovered the passion of "truth" in poetry soon after her arrival at her aunt's house, and that kept alive her spirit which seemed to have been left behind with the dead in Italy. Nourished in her imagination by the power of poetry, she was able to accommodate the demands of her "outer life" with the needs of her "inner life"; she learned to reduce "the irregular blood to a settled rhythm" (1.1057–60). Poetry was, therefore, her rescue from spiritual death, and as long as it truly did inform her "outer life" with an "inner life," poetry would be Aurora's primary interest.

When she was twenty years old, on her birthday in June, Aurora's cousin Romney asked her to become his wife. Again, Aurora cannot accept his proposal for what it is intended, or at least she believed he was merely asking her to join him in a great social cause, good enough in itself but insufficient for her as a woman and insufficient for mankind because of its emphasis on merely physical needs. Romney could not choose words any more likely to raise Aurora's resistance to his proposal than these: "I ask," he says, "for life in fellowship / Through bitter duties" (2.354–55). One of these "duties" must include a commitment to "help" the "social strait" of their time, with its "long sum of ill"; he has told her that his very being draws him "to this duty" (2.324). Romney's idea of duty is that it requires one's commitment to social improvement, and his proposal of marriage includes a joint commitment between husband and wife "for life and duty" (2.375). After Aurora refuses him, he asks if he was so wrong as to believe that love "generates the likeness of itself /

Through all heroic duties?" (2.424–25). He wonders if he was wrong to appeal to her as a woman capable of such "heroic duties" when he might have wooed her as a courtly lover in medieval romances. He thought he was complimenting her as a person, rather than insulting her as a workmate.

But Aurora cannot see Romney as a whole person, one with a heart and soul as well as an estate and a will to serve the poor. She tells him that she has not seen evidence of real love in all of England, not enough "to make a marriage with," for she is thinking of her father's and mother's marriage. Possibly Romney could have won Aurora's heart if he *had* wooed her in romantic fashion. Aurora does not admit this, of course, because her need is to preserve as much of the Italian spirit as she can, for that is her defense of her father's life. We may know this, as readers, but she does not know it on that day in June when Romney proposed marriage. What she heard him say was that she would become merely another instrument of social reform:

> "What you love
> Is not a woman, Romney, but a cause:
> You want a helpmate, not a mistress, sir,
> A wife to help your ends,—in her no end."   [2.400–403]

We should not jump to the conclusion, as probably we do when we read the poem the first time, that Aurora Leigh would refuse Romney even if he made his proposal in different terms. The agony of her life, as it is the main burden of the poem's narrative, is to review this proposal, to discover that she was terribly wrong in her reaction to Romney. She rejects him, and chooses art instead, for the artist must "not barter . . . the beautiful for barley" (2.474–75).

When her aunt discovers that Aurora has rejected Romney, she is indignant. Again she attacks Aurora's mother, who, she says, "must have been a pretty thing, . . . / To make a good man, which my brother was, / Unchary of the duties to his house" (2.619–22). The aunt makes a terrible mistake in telling Aurora that the girl's future well-being depends on the good will of Romney to honor the marriage agreement made by Romney's father. This only reinforces Aurora's belief that Romney has asked her to marry him for the sake of "duty," but now duty in the even more degrading sense of condescension and pity for her as a poor relation. Aurora says that if she married him now, she could not call her soul her own, "which so he had bought and paid for" (2.787). Of course, when Romney tries to include a "gift" of considerable money in the small estate left by her aunt, Aurora could not possibly accept. Romney tells her that his "duty" forces him to "trouble" her "with words" that would arrange for her financial security (2.1001), but again he could not choose any worse word to recommend his offer. He cannot understand how his position is being misunderstood by Aurora, or he would use the word *duty* less often when talking with her. The word finds its way into his last words to her before she leaves for her work as poet; while she sings her "happy pastorals," he will go to do his work among the poor and oppressed, being careful that he will "miss / No reasonable duty" (2.1200).

To this point, then, "duty" is what is "reasonable," "measured," "domestic," "useful," and even "heroic." For Aurora, the word has come to mean all that "provisioned and complacent past," that "dry lifetime" of "learning, law, and parish talk," that her father gave up when he was "flooded with a passion unaware." As an artist, she vows to keep that passion alive, to inform the outer life with an inner life of spirit, keeping "up open roads / Betwixt the seen and unseen" (2.468–69). Underlying her idea of art as "a special, central power" that transfixes "the flat experience of the common man," that lifts the flatness to a passion and an ecstasy, is an idea of marriage as a transfiguration, a "sacramental gift / With eucharistic meanings," as she had described her parents' marriage. By trying to unite "natural things / And spiritual" into "a perfect cosmos" in her art (7.763–64), Aurora is modeling herself after the priest who administers a sacrament through art. She will increasingly describe her art in terms of marriage, gradually discovering that even in her own life "art is much, but Love is more" (9.656).

Before Aurora has any chance of understanding herself and all her needs, she must be further educated in duty and, as a complement, in marriage. It is the thematic function of Marian Erle's role in the narrative to help Aurora Leigh discover another dimension to the meaning of marriage and duty than she knows from her aunt, Romney, and her parents. Narratively, Aurora encourages the marriage of Marian with Romney as still another way to justify her decision not to marry Romney herself; that would protect her from her own doubts just as her art does. In the course of this effort to support Marian's marriage, Aurora learns that there can be marriages without any duty at all, for that is the kind of marriage that must have existed for the parents of Marian Erle. If anything bound that couple together, it was brute passion, with no spirit of obligation, no measure of restraint. Later, Marian will serve to show that there can be, indeed, an independent and fulfilling life for a woman without marriage at all.

Aurora learns from Marian the example of duty as service, as a passion for others. When Marian told how she awoke to a new world in the hospital where she went after fleeing from her mother, she remembered especially the atmosphere of "equal care for each," and she was "astonished" with the "order, silence, law" she observed around her (3. 1111–12). For Marian it was an experience equal to that of taking "sacrament, / Half awed, half melted" (3.114–15); she had not been used "to so much love as makes the form of love / And courtesy of manners." This is what Aurora needs to realize for herself, that there can be a duty that is a "courtesy of manners," not merely a measure well pressed out. When Marian left the hospital, she went back to "daylight duties" (3.1140), after "soul and flesh were reconciled," in part because Romney discovered her in the hospital and helped her find work as a seamstress. By this, Aurora is learning that, indeed, the body needs attention of the kind that Romney devoted himself to providing, as his duty. When Marian went out to sit by a dying girl's bedside, she was "content /With duty" as a mere feat of holding "the lamp of human love arm-high" (4.44–46).

Such total giving of one's self is something new for Aurora, at least new in the form that she discovers it in Marian Erle. Aurora had interpreted Romney's proposal first as a purchase of her labor, then as a contract for her soul; but now, anticipating the kind of marriage he might have with Marian, Aurora is able to imagine something different, where self-sacrifice by English wives for their husbands would much exceed even that literal sacrifice of wives on the pyres of their dead husbands in India: "the woman's duty by so much / Advanced in England beyond Hindostan" (4.201–202). This is not attractive to Aurora at this point, but it does represent a modification of her earlier view of English wives. By the end of the poem, we understand why Marian could not be a wife for Romney, but she herself realizes it soon enough to stand him up at the altar (with some encouragement by Lady Waldemar, of course). Marian tells Aurora that she knows she is "much fitter for his handmaid than his wife" (4.228), and this is close to the truth, for that is the way Marian thinks of herself in relation to Romney. Therefore, she has just as wrong a reason for marrying Romney as Aurora believed Romney had for wanting to marry her.

Aurora, doing what she can to help this marriage along, congratulates herself for having "done a duty" (4.313); but she "felt tired, overworked." The work is, ostensibly, her writing and her support for Marian, but Aurora is suffering the first of many fits of depression (almost anxiety attacks), which occur whenever she seems close to losing Romney forever. "This marriage somewhat jarred; / Or, if it did not, all the bridal noise" was "scarce [her] business" (4.445–60). On the surface of things, Aurora regrets not having realized that Lady Waldemar would interfere with Marian, but we must wonder if something in Aurora would not *let* her realize anything that might have prevented Romney's marriage with Marian.

Aurora is increasingly unhappy, even as she matures in her art. Romney had told her on that June day that "all success / Proves partial failure" (2.267–69), and now several years later, she is learning how right he was. Knowing that "poets should / Exert a double vision," she thinks that she is not succeeding: "I still see something to be done, / And what I do falls short of what I see" (5.344–45). This middle book of the poem is heavy with Aurora's strange sadness (5.399, 410, 579–80). She speaks of her art as if it were a man, a mate, even a child (5.398–421). She imagines all her readers who may praise her "heart of passionate womanhood," but who do not realize how dreary it is for her "to sit still, / On winter nights by solitary fires" (5.429–51). No wonder she cries out, in the face of success with her art: "If this then be success, 't is dismaller / Than any failure" (5.433–34).

She tries to fill the great hollow of her life by going to Lord Howe's party, but that makes her even sadder (5.580). There she, first, overheard the conversation between Mr. Smith and Sir Blaise Delorme; then she heard that Lady Waldemar was to marry Romney; and finally Lady Waldemar tormented her with little anecdotes about visiting Romney at his place in Shropshire. Aurora goes away from the party determined to leave England and return to Italy via Paris. When she reaches home, she loosens her clothing as if she were trying to escape from herself:

> And I breathe large at home. I drop my cloak,
> Unclasp my girdle, loose the band that ties
> My hair . . . now could I but unloose my soul!
> We are sepulchred alive in this close world,
> And want more room.   [5.1037–41]

Now she begins to run from something in herself, something she does not want to admit, her desire for Romney, and so it is ironically appropriate that she return to Italy where she has strong associations with desire and passion: "And now I come, My Italy, / My own hills!"

The last books of the poem, which narrate the rediscovery of Marian (now with a child), Aurora's return to her home in Italy, and Romney's pilgrimage to join her there, are all steps toward educating Aurora in desire. She has spent her life knowing that body and soul must be joined to complete a person, but she still has been unable to accomplish in herself what she seems to have brought off in her art. Her vision has been too narrow, just as Romney had accused her of being long ago, or so she is gradually telling herself in the second half of the poem. Elizabeth Barrett Browning wants us to realize that Aurora is molding herself to fit the pattern that will be most acceptable, or most complementary, to Romney, even while she is fleeing him and his supposed marriage to Lady

Waldemar. At any rate, she now tells herself that mankind is wrong to be shocked at "nature's falling off":

> We dare to shrink back from her warts and blains,
> We will not, when she sneezes, look at her,
> Not even to say 'God bless her'? That's our wrong;
> For that, she will not trust us often with
> Her larger sense of beauty and desire,
> But tethers us to a lily or a rose
> And bids us diet on the dew inside,
> Left ignorant [of] the hungry beggar-boy.   [6.178–86]

Now she can "pray" for "the poet and philanthropist / (Even I and Romney)" to "stand side by side."

She finds Marian an unwed mother, helps her and the child as a way of paying Romney's debt to Marian. Aurora agonizes that somehow she might have "saved the man" from the Lamia, the devil, Lady Waldemar (7.186ff), but since she did not (she believes), she must suffer along with Marian. Aurora writes a letter to Lord Howe to tell him Marian's story, hoping that Lord Howe may be able to stop Romney's marriage; while she writes, she feels weary and sad (7.268–69). Then she writes to Lady Waldemar, telling her that if she has married Romney, she should be "his faithful and true wife." The amazing point about this letter is to be found in Aurora's way of defining what a "true wife" is for Romney:

> I charge you, be his faithful and true wife!
> Keep warm his hearth and clean his board, and, when
> He speaks, be quick with your obedience;
> Still grind your paltry wants and low desires
> To dust beneath his heel.   [7.344–48]

If this is the way she will interpret her own role as his wife, she is indeed a long way from being an ideal heroine for "*the* feminist poem."

However, we must note the reference to "paltry wants and low desires." Only a woman such as Lady Waldemar would have to be this kind of "true wife." Presumably, someone with higher desires and richer wants would be a different kind of "true wife." Aurora is such a person (if she could only admit it to herself); because she cannot, she is near madness thinking about Romney's marriage with that devil, Lady Waldemar. While taking the train to Italy, she is obsessed with the sound of "marriage-bells": they "must be loud" for her to hear them through the "roar of steam." She feels as if she "stood alone i' the belfry, fifty bells / Of naked iron, made with merriment / . . . All clanking" at her "until [she] shrieked a shriek [she] could not hear" (7.395–406).

In the quiet beauty of the Italian countryside, Aurora recovers her poise, thinking over her life and now admitting some difficult and painful truths. She now admits that she "was foolish in desire / Like other creatures" (7.1267–68); and like the ravens when "they cry for carrion," she also cried for "offal-food." Looking out at the darkening valley before her, she imagines herself looking at

> Some drowned city in some enchanted sea
> Cut off from nature,—drawing you who gaze,
> With passionate desire, to leap and plunge
> And find a sea-king with a voice of waves.   [8.34–44]

She feels as if she has plunged, looks up, and sees her king: "There he stood, my king!" (8.59–61). It is Romney, of course, who has come to Italy to do his duty by Marian, though as he himself admits, such a duty will be a strain: "to wed here, loving there, becomes / A duty" (8.1059–60). Marian, like Aurora so many years before, rightly rejects marriage for such reasons, though she does it "like a saint" (9.188).

During the evening of Lord Howe's party, Lord Howe told Aurora that "a happy life means prudent compromise" (5.923), something she could not have accepted at the time. But now, after the crisis of despair over Lady Waldemar and Romney, after her own admission that she, like the ravens, has a great desire for the flesh, and after discovering that "art is much, but Love is more," she is finally ready to admit that Lord Howe's advice is appropriate for her. Aurora tells Romney that she "forgot / No perfect artist is developed here / From any imperfect woman," which is what she now believes herself to have been and to be at this moment ending the poem (9.647–49). Romney has already admitted his faults, asked forgiveness from Marian and from Aurora, and paid a terrible price by his blindness (a matter of questionable taste for the poet, however symbolic it may be). He is all too ready to be Aurora's husband. She, on her side of it, subordinates art to marriage, though art still has its place: "Art symbolizes heaven, but Love is God" (9.658). Romney proposes that after God's love comes "the love of wedded souls" which "presents that mystery's counterpart" (9.882–83). Together they have found, by a route much more painful and circuitous, the same "sacramental gift / With eucharistic meanings" that Aurora's father found when he came to Italy many years before.

The painful way has been a dark journey of the soul for both Aurora and Romney. She has traveled her way through a spiritual darkness and he a physical darkness, each way appropriate to the sufferer's fault. Romney's is more melodramatic and dramatically ironic; Aurora's is more poetic. After she rejected Romney's proposal, her aunt told Aurora that she "is groping in the dark, / For all this sunlight" (2.585–86). Later, after she met Marian in Paris, Aurora says of herself: "I cannot see my road along this dark; / Nor can I creep and grope, as fits the dark, / For these foot-catching robes of womanhood" (7.148–50). That this darkness is her own passion of desire to which she is blind, wilfully blind, becomes clear to her in the last scenes of the poem. Just before she took her "plunge" to find her "sea-king," she

> sat absorbed amid the quickening glooms,
> Most like some passive broken lump of salt
> Dropped in by chance to a bowl of œnomel,
> To spoil the drink a little and lose itself,
> Dissolving slowly, slowly, until lost.   [7.1307–11]

The imagery of dissolving in a drink not only anticipates her plunge into the enchanted sea of desire, but it echoes an earlier passage describing marriage:

> where we yearn to lose ourselves
> And melt like white pearls in another's wine,
> He seeks to double himself by what he loves,
> And makes his drink more costly by our pearls.   [5.1077–81]

In the ecstasy of her new-found bliss, after she and Romney have declared their love for one another, Aurora praises the darkness and their love:

> O ecstasy
> Of darkness! O great mystery of love,
> In which absorbed, loss, anguish, treason's self
> Enlarges rapture, —as a pebble dropped
> In some full wine-cup overbrims the wine!   [9.815–20]

The pearl dissolved in the wine, marriage as sacrament, duty dissolved in desire—these are the ingredients for a new heaven where Love is God, seen in the blind eyes of Romney at the end of the poem; this is an allusion to Revelation 21, which begins with the New Jerusalem "coming down from God out of heaven, prepared as a bride adorned for her husband."

Like Swinburne, by whom he acknowledged he was much influenced, Oscar Wilde greatly admired the poetry of Elizabeth Barrett Browning, comparing her with Sappho: "Of all the women of history, Mrs. Browning is the only one that we could name in any possible or remote conjunction with Sappho." She was the "one great poetess" that "England has given to the world." Wilde admired her poetry for "its sincerity and its strength." Even when her work seemed rugged, it was "deliberate":

"she refused to sandpaper her muse," he remarks in his approval that she was always an artist, even "in her very rejection of art."[23] His enthusiasm for *Aurora Leigh* knew little restraint; he wrote to William Ward in 1876 that it was "much the greatest work in our literature."[24] Comparing it "with *Hamlet* and *In Memoriam*," Wilde applauded its "intensity."[25] All three works expressed for the young man important formulations of his own aesthetic yearnings to keep clear and distinct the dutiful claims of the world from his heart's desires; thus he praised Elizabeth Barrett Browning as "the wisest of the Sibyls, . . . for she realised that, while knowledge is power, suffering is part of knowledge."[26]

Elizabeth Barrett was rescued from the indefinite longing and unfulfilled desire that marked her early poetry; she was taken from the prison of duty to her father, and when she became Mrs. Robert Browning, she found that her desire for her lover was her duty to herself. The poetry she wrote during her courtship and after her marriage is marked by a strength of conviction that married love and domestic order embody sacramental and divine love. Her art was her service to the order of that love, and her poetry drew its strength from her belief that marriage indeed unites duty and desire. Wilde's early enthusiasm for her and for her poetry was understandable for a young man who admired both her personal and aesthetic courage, but he lacked many of her convictions and sometimes he mocked the ideals to which she had devoted her life and art. But when he did so, he was mocking something in himself; there were, in Wilde's life and in his art, destructive forces that no conventions could long contain. His writing shows all the strains of a myth breaking apart.

Marriage would be his great subject; his genius was for comic satire, and the great tradition of comedy was especially a tradition of bringing human affairs into the order of courtship and marriage. But Wilde's drama betrays a certain indifference to the convention that calls for a happy ending celebrated by the rites of Hymen: his plots are often quite dull, well-made things. What makes his drama work is the spirit of anti-marital wit with which he often endows his dandies and his dowagers. His comic spirit is nearly always on the side of the cynics or the nihilists; his plots are usually on the side of the idealists or the romanticists. Rarely could he bring off a union of the two, and rarely do his marriages convince us that duty has become the same thing as desire.

In *Lady Windermere's Fan* (1892) there is a scene in act 3 that captures this point of Wilde's constant dislocation.[27] A group of dandies has gathered in the rooms of Lord Darlington, one of the wittiest of the group, when he exclaims that "we are all in the gutter, but some of us are looking at the stars."

DUMBY: Upon my word, you are very romantic to-night, Darlington.
CECIL GRAHAM: Too romantic! You must be in love. Who is the girl?
LORD DARLINGTON: The woman I love is not free, or thinks she isn't.
CECIL GRAHAM: A married woman, then! Well, there's nothing in the
world like the devotion of a married woman. It's a thing no mar-
ried man knows anything about.   [p. 112]

Later Dumby consoles Darlington by telling him, "In this world there are
only two tragedies. One is not getting what one wants, and the other is
getting it. The last is much the worst, the last is a real tragedy!" (p. 114).
This scene captures much of the predicament of Oscar Wilde's writing.

In his poetry Wilde is, like Lord Darlington, giving us the "romantic" view: "Some of us are looking at the stars." What his poems and
tragic drama frequently express is the lesser "tragedy" of "not getting
what one wants," while his comic drama concentrates on the "real tragedy" of "getting it." The poems he published in his volume of 1881 are,
with the exceptions of "Impression du Matin" and one or two others, far
too derivative to warrant much critical attention, but they reveal the
young man's yearning desire to escape, or transform, the ugly world of
his time and place.[28] While we hear (too often) the very words of Keats,
Wordsworth, Swinburne, and Matthew Arnold when we read these
poems, we recognize the reason these poets were so important to Wilde:
they also had yearned to escape or transform the ugliness of modern life.
Wilde's favorite motif, and sometimes it was his speaker's mask, he took
from Keats: Endymion yearning for the moon. "The Garden of Eros" is
spoken by "the last Endymion" who refuses to "lose all hope / Because
rude eyes peer at [his] mistress through a telescope!" (p. 51). His faith in
the power of art to transform the world into mythic beauty is a part of
"The Burden of Itys," where he maintains that the music of Philomel
could so "vex" the "sylvan quiet" that "Endymion would have passed
across the mead / Moonstruck with love" (p. 94). When he writes, in
disgust, "On the Sale by Auction of Keats' Love Letters" (p. 252), Wilde
characteristically describes Keats as an Endymion who "wrote / To one
he loved in secret, and apart."

But sometimes Endymion and his moon goddess are united in desire.
"Panthea" imagines that the moon always come forth "fresh from Endymion's arms," and when that happens romance comes to break up "the
gaudy web of noon" (p. 185). In "The Garden of Eros" Cynthia "loves
the lad Endymion" and hides herself with him while the Sun "leaps from
his ocean bed in fruitless chase / Of those pale flying feet which fade
away in his embrace" (p. 45). Even when Endymion seems to satisfy his
longing, someone else is imagined as having been cheated out of satisfaction: whether the Sun, as in "The Garden of Eros" and "Panthea," or

270

the speaker of "Endymion," who calls, innocently, upon the moon to be her "lover's sentinel" and watch out for Endymion, whom she loves. Ironically, in a turn of recognition that anticipates the later cynicism of Wilde, the speaker of this poem condemns the "false moon" for having seduced the "young Endymion" from her warm "lips that should be kissed!" (p. 112). Even if Cynthia "loves the lad Endymion" (p. 45) or will "strip off her misty vestiture / For young Endymion's eyes" (p. 145), she retains "her most ancient, chastest mystery" (p. 51) from her cold silver beauty set at a great distance from human desire.

Wilde's lovers yearning with heavenly desire lack the definition that struggles with duty would give them, the struggles some of Elizabeth Barrett's early poetry of sentimental romance contain. Because the lovers are alive with passion, not frozen in art, they have not the form that allows one to meditate on their meaning, as the speaker does in Keats's "Ode on a Grecian Urn." They are figures in search of form, lacking the self-assurance of the characters in works by Swinburne and Browning. The many echoes that we hear while reading Wilde's poetry become a din, a chaos of beautiful sounds that haunt the poet's imagination. He is trying to put his past together, picking pieces from great English poetry that did not fail the modern spirit, such as "The Ode to a Nightingale" and "The Scholar-Gipsy" in "The Burden of Itys," or "Ode: Intimations of Immortality" in "Panthea" and "Humanitad." Wilde knows what his problem as a poet is:

> 'T is I, 't is I, whose soul is as the reed
>   Which has no message of its own to play,
> So pipe's another bidding, it is I,
> Drifting with every wind on the wide sea of misery.
> ["The Burden of Itys," p. 97]

Not only do these poems yearn for beauty, but they also long for a "message," an ideal that will keep life from growing colorless. Because there is no message, no living ideal, it is difficult to follow Pater's advice "to burn with one clear flame" and at the same time to "stand erect / In natural honour," following the advice of that other Oxford master, John Ruskin. The life of Wilde, like his poetry, seems to have been torn between the ideal of desire he learned from Pater and the ideal of duty he learned from Ruskin. For none of the three writers could these two ideals be brought together in the form of marriage.[29]

ONLY ONCE IN "THE GARDEN OF EROS" does the poet refer to a marriage, when he promises to sing "how sad Proserpine / Unto a grave and gloomy Lord was wed" (p. 45). To be wed by Hades rather than by

Hymen is the usual fate of Wilde's tragic lovers who yearn with desire for the infinite. In this poem, Eros is the "Spirit of Beauty" invoked by the poet to recover for England the same loveliness that ancient Greece once knew. England has had wonderful poets lately, including Keats, Shelley, Swinburne, Morris, and Rossetti, "but they are few, and all romance has flown" from the present time (pp. 46–51). While he has been speaking, the poet has not noticed the passage of the night, and when the morning comes, he resigns himself to a colorless dawn, in lines that anticipate Eliot's "Prufrock": "Come let us go, against the pallid shield / Of the wan sky the almond blossoms gleam" (p. 53). The landscape is silent and the sky is wan, but because he has been able to imagine something better (with the help of some great English poets) during the night, the speaker goes foward with some energy of renewed hope: "the air freshens," but still, "soon / The woodmen will be here," and nagging reality dogs his determined hope.

"The New Helen" tries to learn a lesson from Swinburne (especially "The Triumph of Time") and make of the poet a "servant of the sun" (p. 76). At first the speaker wonders why Helen has come to "walk our common earth again" when her glory lies all in the past, or "in those fields of trampled asphodel." But then the poet admits his devotion to her "flame of passion"; even if he has "lost all hope and heart to sing," he will be satisfied if he can merely kneel in her temple. Because she incarnates "the gladsome sunlight," to love her is to love the sun, that "red rose of fire." The "new Helen" is, then, the light of love, who has "come down our darkness to illume," to rescue all those "wearied with waiting for the World's Desire" (p. 77).

While "the new Helen" can become the "pale woman" who "loitered beneath the gas lamp's flare, / With lips of flame and heart of stone" ("Impression du Matin," p. 101) or the "love [that] passed into the house of lust" and left the dawn to creep "like a frightened girl" ("The Harlot's House," pp. 249–50), such transformations are rare in the 1881 volume of Wilde's poetry. Three of his most ambitious poems from that volume are "Charmides," "Panthea," and "Humanitad," all of which attempt to keep Helen from turning into a harlot.

"Charmides" does this by very unlikely means, although the narrative has some of the charm we might expect from a story by Walter Pater. The strategy here is to make a boy love a cold and chaste statue of Athena, then to reverse the situation (a frequent device in Wilde's writing) so that a chaste maiden (a dryad) loves the cold corpse of the boy Charmides; after both the maiden and Charmides are dead, a miracle allows passion to follow them into death, where marriage finally becomes possible for this otherwise unfortunate pair. Charmides's desire for the statue of Athena is perverse if we must read it as anything less than a metaphor; otherwise, it is clear that when "his lips in hungering delight / Fed on her lips," Charmides is the incarnation of all life's desire for beautiful truth or, in particular, of all artists' yearning for fulfillment in divine beauty (as even Aurora Leigh realized, to her great pain and then to her great happiness). When Charmides slipped into the unguarded temple of Athena to press "his hot and beating heart upon her chill and icy breast," he was asserting "his passion's will" (pp. 124–25) upon that divine form.

When he fled from his strange love, Charmides seemed to be a thing divine to those who saw him resting in the forest. He had to pay the price with his life for the night of divine love, but when he saw Athena come for him, he "laughed loud for joy," and then he "leapt from the lofty poop into the chill and churning foam" (p. 132). Athena punished him because of his "ardent amorous" idolatry, but his passion was not utterly doomed to waste unsatisfied. His body was found by a wood-nymph, who could not distinguish death from life any more than she knew the joys of consummated love. Again, in the episode of part 2 an unimaginative reading would be disgusted by the necrophilia of the wood-nymph, who lay beside the corpse, "thirsty with love's drouth," "played with his tangled hair, / And with hot lips made havoc of his mouth" (p. 137). Dreaming of their "bridal bed," she urges the dead boy to rise from his sleep and flee with her away from her Queen, Diana. But the wood-nymph, like the boy, is doomed to die from the power of a goddess. She died not knowing "the joy of passion, that dread mystery / Which not to know is not to live at all" (p. 146).

Venus rescued the pair from the cold of death by praying to Proserpine to "let Desire pass across dread Charon's icy ford" (p. 149). Proserpine, "whose beauty made Death amorous," heard the call of Love and let into "the loveless land of Hades" the power of Eros so that Charmides could "slay" the maidenhood of the wood-nymph even in the land of death. It is only in Hades, however, that passion can walk "with naked unshod feet / And is not wounded" (p. 152), for anywhere else, the wounds are the necessary effects of passion and desire, as both Charmides and the wood-nymph discovered. The problem that Wilde's poem explores was doubtless a real one for him, as it was for his hero, Charmides, but his solution is half-hearted, perhaps even a parody of Rossetti or Swinburne. When Wilde cries out that there is no need to try "to pipe again of love" as he begins to describe the union of Charmides and the nymph, the poet is close to smiling at himself, exclaiming "Enough, enough, . . . Enough" (pp. 151–52).

"Enough" re-echoes in "Panthea," where the speaker chides his love with desiring more from life than the beauties of nature's sights and sounds: "Enough for thee, dost thou desire more? / Alas! the Gods will give nought else from their eternal store" (p. 184). The poem is a celebration of the universal goddess of beauty in nature, imitating what Wilde takes to be Wordsworth's pantheism to affirm a non-Wordsworthian hedonism as a sufficient philosophy of life. This poem's "intimations of immortality" come from Walter Pater, or at most from John Ruskin, rather than from Wordsworth, however. The speaker rejects any attempts by his love "to waste this summer night / Asking those idle questions" about the meaning of existence; there were no satisfactory answers in ancient times, and now "man is weak; God sleeps: and heaven is high" (p. 187). The whole of life is contained in a single line: "One fiery-coloured moment: one great love; and lo! we die" (p. 187). The poet cannot "live without desire," insisting that "to feel is better than to know" (p. 183). Like Charmides, the speaker of this poem pursues beauty with passionate devotion: "Have we not lips to kiss with, hearts to love and eyes to see!" (p. 183). He is also like Charmides in his disrespect for "great mysteries" (p. 132); he is weary of religious consolations and silent, selfish gods.

The love that transcends death at the conclusion of "Charmides" is invoked in "Panthea" as the only consolation, the only meaning, for mankind that desires more. When the speaker vows to "walk from fire unto fire, / From passionate pain to deadlier delight" (p. 183) at the opening of the poem, he anticipates the aesthetic religion which he outlines in the second half of the poem. Charmides and his wood-nymph become one in a sexual embrace after death, and all mankind becomes one with nature in the great last embrace of death: "We are resolved into the supreme air / We are made one with what we touch and see" (p. 187). Man unites with nature in the "sacrament" of death, for it is not only the "young bridegroom" who knows the meaning of marriage: "the earth / Not we alone hath passions hymeneal" (p. 189). It is this thought that makes the poet's "heart leap up," to know that "we shall not die, / The Universe itself shall be our Immortality" (p. 191).

In his tragedies, Wilde suggests a similar philosophy when he brings his lovers to blissful deaths in hymeneal passions or conducts their suffering through ritual marriages with death (that faintly imitate Swinburne's drama). In his comedies, he reverses things somewhat, pointing out the living death of most marriages and celebrating Eros as the god of cynics and dandies; love will be for life and its pleasures, while marriage usually dooms one to pain and spiritual death. Like Wordsworth, Wilde in his poetry saves his spousal verse for the wedding with nature—for example, in "Humanitad"—where again he pieces together lines and images from several of Wordsworth's poems. Just as in "Panthea," where Wilde asserts a philosophy of feeling to rescue the world from its weariness and despair of meaning, in "Humanitad" he points to the springtime as a promise of relief from the universal listlessness afflicting most men in the winter world of the nineteenth century: "With the first warm kisses of the rain / The winter's sorrow breaks to tears, / And the brown thrushes mate" (p. 208). That is the time when "wantons love" and Nature becomes a "Bride" (pp. 210, 211).

Loving nature, the balm of "Panthea," is in "Humanitad" a consolation of the past which the poet cannot recover now that he is older: "There was a time when any common bird / Could make me sing in unison, a time / When all the strings of boyish life were stirred" (p. 211). He requires something more than boyish delight. Now he rejects the philosophy of death, which "is too rude, too obvious a key"; and so does he reject love, "that noble madness" from whose "sweet ruin" he must run away (p. 213). He will, like Charmides, devote himself to Athena, that goddess of cool detachment and chaste wisdom, from whom he may learn the lessons that Matthew Arnold had been teaching: how to become "self-poised, self-centred, and self-comforted / To watch the world's vain phantasies go by with un-bowed head" (p. 215). Athena is not, however, sufficient; Wilde admits he cannot "live without desire" and he cannot abide "Science" even if it could "draw the moon from heaven" (p. 215). What he yearns for is the equipoise that only Wordsworth among the poets seems to have acquired in modern art:

> that pure soul
> Whose gracious days of uncrowned majesty
> Through lowliest conduct touched the lofty goal
> Where Love and Duty mingle!   [p. 217]

But Wilde cannot find that "pure soul" anywhere in his own time; the nearest he could get to a recent ideal that mingles "Love and Duty" is Mazzini, who made a "Bride of Liberty."

Wilde's enthusiasm in this poem for the Italian cause of freedom not only links him with Swinburne, Rossetti, and the Brownings, but it suggests for his speaker a new solution to life's perplexities. It is better not to marry nature and better not to look to the past for ideals that keep life from growing colorless; instead, he will look for "the God that is within us" (p. 224). It is the freedom of the Italian patriots that inspires the poem's conclusion, not the patriotism nor the politics. To keep the soul from being torn apart by duty to country and duty to others, and still to keep desire alive, a person must be free "to make the Body and the Spirit one" (p. 225). He will strive to observe "with serene impartiality / The strife of things," and yet he will not withdraw from the strife itself; his comfort must come from "knowing that by the chain causality / All separate existences are wed / Into one supreme whole" (p. 225). His new ideal is a "governance" of his life "through which the rational intellect would find / In passion its expression" and "mere sense" "lend fire to the mind" (p. 225). "Humanitad" concludes with an image of man as "self-slain Humanity" coming down from the bloody cross of "the new Calvary" (p. 227, 228). It is an event symbolizing the speaker's new-found religion of compassionate detachment, and Wilde never entirely abandons it—indeed, he elaborates it in *De Profundis*.

MANY OF THE SAME CONCERNS and problems that preoccupy Wilde in his poetry reappear in his tragedies, beginning with *Vera, or The Nihilists* (1881), running through *The Duchess of Padua* (1883), and finding their most satisfactory resolution in *Salomé* (1891). During this period of his career, Wilde discovered an aesthetic position for himself, although it was not exactly an aesthetic philosophy. He learns to go beyond duty and desire, and even on beyond marriage; he carries forward the aesthetic gospel of Arnold and Swinburne in that same spirit of comedy that Carlyle brought with him from the mountain. What Wilde gives back to his literary fathers is their cant: Carlyle's cant of duty, Arnold's cant of high seriousness, and Swinburne's cant of desire. But what he preserves is the energy of the comic spirit, present in lively abundance throughout the writings of the Victorian sages. Here was his function: to laugh away the dross of Victorianism.

Before he realized his vocation as a breaker of idols, Wilde tried his hand at making drama in the tradition of tragic romances. He set his earliest attempt in czarist Russia, where a group of "nihilists" assassinate the Czar as a first step in their program of Communist revolution.[30] The play shows how Wilde almost lets his comic spirit escape the form he has chosen, for the character who gets the best lines is Prince Paul, the rakish dandy responsible for administering some of the worst abuses against the people of Russia. This play, like *The Duchess of Padua* (where the cruel Duke has the wittiest lines), illustrates the truth bemoaned at the beginning of the century by Shelley in these lines from *Prometheus Unbound*:

> The good want power, but to weep barren tears,
> The powerful goodness want: worse need for them.
> The wise want love; and those who love want wisdom;
> And all best things are thus confused to ill.   [1.625–28]

It is repeated after the end of the nineteenth century by W. B. Yeats in his "Second Coming": "The best lack all conviction, while the worst / Are full of passionate intensity," so that "Mere anarchy is loosed upon the world" and "The ceremony of innocence is drowned."

When Wilde chooses as the problem of *Vera* how to create a government of nihilists, he is not confusing means for ends; he is trying to represent the confusion of his times. He wears his most authentic mask when he has Prince Paul say, "One is sure to be disappointed if one tries to get romance out of modern life" (p. 222). Wilde tried to do that in his poetry, and he was among the first to be disappointed with his work. In this play he shows how the idealists are the romanticists, who are either mocked or destroyed for their idealism. The nihilists lack the wit to survive with integrity, for how they can aim for the establishment of a better government while advocating nihilism is the ultimate paradox; when Vera yields her nihilism to the authority of romantic love, she pays the price with her life. Wilde wants us to believe that the Czarevitch, as Czar, can resolve the contradictions that plague the time, for that character is both a nihilist in his ideals and a power in his office. He scatters his enemies with wit and with power. But when last we see him, he is on his knees before a woman.

In this last scene, the new Czar has told Vera that he has kept his crown in order to "lay at [her] feet this mighty Russia." He wants Vera to marry him and rule Russia "by love, as a father rules his children" (p. 253). Vera has more sense at this point than does her paramour, for she answers that she is "a Nihilist. I cannot wear a crown" (p. 255). He offers to give up his crown for her love, so that together they can "live amongst the common people" and he can "toil for [her] like the peasant or the serf" (p. 256). To stop his mad idealism, Vera ironically turns the tables on the Czar, kills herself, and forces him to remain the Czar of Russia; when she throws out the bloody dagger, she keeps the Czar from killing himself and at the same time makes the conspirators think she has assassinated the Czar. Vera's love for the Czar triumphs over her duty to obey her oath to the conspiracy and her vow to revenge her brother's suffering, but Wilde has made her triumphant desire identical with her duty to the aims of both the nihilists and her brother: political freedom. The way the dramatist brings this about is to marry Vera with death; thus Wilde saves the Czar from the restraints of marriage at the same time as he affirms the value of the family as the model for political order. Although it is not exactly what Prince Paul means, the Prince is close to this truth when he says that "a family is a terrible incumbrance, especially when one is not married" (p. 214).

There is much talk of duty in this play, but such talk is conspicuously absent from the dialogue of the ruling aristocrats, especially in act 2 where the old Czar holds a council of state that in its form echoes, but mocks, the meetings of the conspirators in acts 1 and 3. The Czar's council reveals that what the nihilists ostensibly aim for already exists: a nothingness behind the façade of order. The most important symbol for that order is the family, with the Czar as the "little father" and Russia as "mother" Russia. But when marriage and family produce children who turn upon their parents, those parents, like the Czar in this scene, renounce their progeny and the institution of marriage itself: "A plague on all sons, I say! There should be no more marriages in Russia when one can breed such Serpents as you are!" (pp. 202–203). Shortly afterwards, the "little father" is assassinated by one of his "children," the nihilist Michael.

The central feature of the nihilists' code is abolition of the family and restraint from marriage. The prologue gives us a picture of contentment with family life, as the peasant Peter Sabouroff encourages the peasant boy Michael to marry his daughter Vera, who "has got too many ideas" in her head to suit her father; she should marry and take her proper place as wife and mother. Peter thinks a person should do his duty and not think too much about it, which is what his son has done by going off to Moscow to study law: "What does he want knowing about the law," Peter exclaims; "let a man do his duty, say I, and no one will trouble him" (p. 120). Michael sees no conflict between learning the law and doing one's duty, for "they say a good lawyer can break the law as often as he likes"; therefore "if a man knows the law he knows his duty"—which is, we take it, to break the law "as often as he likes" (p. 121). Michael has the makings of a nihilist.

Colonel Kotemkin, who shares some of the same prejudices that old Peter himself admits to, tells Peter that it is dangerous for Vera to know how to read and write. Not only women, but the peasants, should keep their lowly place in the scheme of things: "Till your fields, store your harvests, pay your taxes, and obey your masters—that is your duty" (p. 128). When Vera proudly asks "who are our masters," the Colonel tells her that is the very kind of question that caused his prisoners to be taken to the mines. Events will prove that intelligence, education, and will are indeed dangerous to the order of the state but even more dangerous to the welfare of the individuals who exercise them. When Vera recognizes her brother among the prisoners, she receives from him a piece of paper which contains the address of the nihilist headquarters and the oath of nihilism: "To strangle whatever nature is in me; neither to love nor to be loved; neither to pity nor to be pitied; neither to marry nor to be given in marriage, till the end is come" (p. 135). Later, when Prince Paul joins with the nihilists (a group with which he already had much in common), he reads in their creed that "the family as subversive of true socialistic and communal unity is to be annihilated," a sentiment with which the Prince heartily concurs.

The "creed" of the conspirators is "to annihilate," and their "duty" is "to obey" (pp. 139, 209). The emptiness of "duty" is well illustrated by the relationship Michael has with one of the Czar's Imperial Guard: he tells the nihilists that he "will wear the uniform of the Imperial Guard, and the Colonel on duty is one of us" (p. 157). That way Michael can slip into the palace to kill the Czar. Later, after the assassination, he was able to escape because "the Colonel on duty was a brother, and gave [him] the password" (p. 217). And so, of course, the new Czar is quite right to tell his Colonel that he has "no need" of the guards who stand "on night duty around the palace" (pp. 248–49). Where there is no desire, there can be no duty, and the uniforms are mockeries of the authority they represent.

The creed to annihilate and the duty to obey might well be the motto for *The Duchess of Padua*, for in this play the hero, Guido Ferranti, vows to assassinate the Duke of Padua in revenge for his father's betrayal by the Duke.[31] Again, Wilde pits this vow of duty to annihilate against a surging passion of erotic desire, and again the dramatist reconciles these forces through a parody of marriage. The world of this play is not much different from the world of *Vera*, for Wilde is actually commenting on his own world through these exotic and remote settings. When the Duke uses the Church to teach his citizens that their proper duty is obedience to his authority, that is Wilde's view of his England; when the Duchess deplores the condition of women as the "chattels" and "common slaves" of their husbands, that also is Wilde's view of his England; and, prophetically for his own life, when he shows us the casuistry of judicial courts, he shows us the essence of a corrupt judicial system that served order and death before love and life.

Exactly like the nihilists, Guido forswears "all love of women," taking only "vengeance" as his "bedfellow" (pp. 33–34). Moranzone has impressed upon Guido the importance of not allowing love to interfere with his duty, but immediately after making his vow of vengeance, Guido sees the Duchess of Padua and falls in love with her. The problem of the play is quickly revealed; the drama is even more clearly focused on marriage than was *Vera*. For Guido's friend Ascanio, desire is merely an appetite, best understood as the hunger of "a widow" "for a husband" (p. 5); this attitude (the same as Prince Paul's in *Vera*) is shared by nearly everyone in the play. The appearance of a handsome young man causes the Duke to warn his friends to "look to [their] wives" "when such a gallant comes to Padua" (p. 25). The irony is, of course, that it will be his own wife who falls victim to Guido's desire, and the Duke will become the "wreck" of "passion." But then, the Duke did not have a real marriage with the Duchess, any more than he had with his "last duchess"

(p. 54). The Duchess has found it a difficult assignment to be the kind of wife that the Duke expects and commands. He tells her that she "will sit at home and spin," that "the domestic virtues / Are often very beautiful in others," but he is not to be bound by the same constraints as she (p. 80). The Duchess feels alone "and out of reach of love," like most wives whose "very bodies [are] merchandise," not much better than the woman she once noticed who "walked with painted lips, and wore / The mask of pleasure" (pp. 55–56).

Moranzone tells Guido that "we are all animals at best, and love / Is merely passion with a holy name" (p. 97). This Guido will not accept, for he is one of Wilde's idealists; like Aurora Leigh, Guido maintains that "love is the sacrament of life," that love "is [God's] image, holds His place," continuing, "When a man loves a woman, then he knows / God's secret, and the secret of the world" (p. 98). Therefore, when Guido confesses his love to the Duchess, he tells her that what makes Raphael's Madonnas "divine" is that "they are mothers merely" (p. 64). Guido has much in common with the Czarevitch, Lady Windermere, and Mrs. Arbuthnot of *A Woman of No Importance,* all of whom subscribe to Mrs. Arbuthnot's belief that "marriage is a sacrament for those who love each other" (p. 165).[32] Whether in the comedies or in the romantic tragedies, Wilde's characters of this kind require the education of experience to correct their notions of love and marriage; they need to learn the lesson that "experience is the name everyone gives to their mistakes," as Dumby maintains in *Lady Windermere's Fan* (p. 117).

Soon after his declaration of love for the Duchess, Guido has his first such lesson in experience. The Duchess kills the Duke and swears to Guido that she "did it all for [him]." She says she "will serve [him] / Like a poor housewife, like a common slave" (p. 113). This does not sound like the proud Duchess lamenting the plight of wives throughout the land, but neither does Guido sound like the moon-struck lover when he pompously tells her that "there is no love where there is any guilt (p. 118). What Guido cannot accept into his scheme is that the Duchess has allowed her desire for him to wreck her duty to her husband and so to wreck Guido's ideal of love as a sanction for marriage. Now it is the Duchess's turn to be educated by her mistake, for she now sees that "when men love women / They give them but a little of their lives, / But women when they love give everything" (p. 120).

The mistakes are not over, and the lessons are not finished for this pair, as the two final acts show. The Duchess revenges Guido's betrayal of their love by accusing him of murdering the Duke (thus making it seem that Guido has fulfilled his earlier vow of duty) and allowing him to stand trial in act 4; there she sits as the representative of the law and all duty to the law that upholds the order of the state. It is her turn to pontificate to Guido, wearing her trappings of duty with all the zest of Robert Browning's Guido Franceschini:

> This is no common murderer, Lord Justice,
> But a great outlaw, and a most vile traitor,
> Taken in open arms against the state.
> For he who slays the man who rules a state
> Slays the state also, widows every wife,
> And makes each child an orphan.   [p. 153]

The Duchess, of course, is condemning herself by her own words. The emptiness of the form to which she appeals here is made clear by her encounter with the Court Usher as she attempts to leave the courtroom. The Usher tells her,

> In all humility I beseech your Grace
> Turn not my duty to discourtesy,
> Nor make my unwelcome office an offence.
> The self-same laws which make your Grace the Regent
> Bid me watch here: My Liege, to break those laws
> Is but to break thine office and not mine.   [p. 168]

She has doomed herself by her own standard, the same standard Guido holds to—that marriage is a sacrament of divine love that upholds the order of the state.

The final act, a dungeon scene, shows that favorite device of the Victorian stage: the repentant woman pleading for forgiveness. Wilde does the same thing here that he had done in *Vera*, making Guido fall at his lady's feet begging *her* forgiveness. Now they have both walked through "the red fire of passion" (p. 194) and have passed beyond the limits of duty as they earlier understood that word. They engage in a dialogue that approaches Wagner's *liebestod* of Tristan and Isolde in its intense wedding of love with death. The Duchess drinks the poison meant for Guido, agonizes in Emma Bovary fashion, and hallucinates that she and Guido are together for their marriage; when she hears the death bells tolling, she hears their "wedding-bell" (p. 206). For his part, Guido willingly chooses to accompany his love to their "narrow wedding-bed" in the grave (p. 203), saying that "it is enough for us."

The conclusion to *The Duchess of Padua* is a frenzy of emotion, fulfilling Moranzone's prediction that Guido's "undisciplined nature" would "wreck itself on passion." It is also a silly conclusion because it tries to affirm, without conviction, a cliché that Wilde's later dramas will deny, *with* conviction: that the duties of life can become eternal commitments of desire for one person alone. While he never completely suc-

281

ceeded, Wilde sought, after *The Duchess of Padua,* to get rid of the
humbug, the mythic trappings, of both duty and desire; he tried to find
a new definition for human identity in a world where "there is no knowledge of anything," as the Fifth Jew puts it in *Salomé:* "It may be that
the things which we call evil are good, and that the things which we call
good are evil" (p. 145).[33]

Certainly the "good" of marriage has become an "evil" in *Salomé;*
Herod has married his brother's wife, and their marriage is "not a true
marriage" not only because it is incestuous but, more importantly for
Herod, because it is "sterile." Certainly it is "a marriage that will bring
evils" (p. 160). There is no sacrament in this marriage, apparently without desire and increasingly without much duty. Against the background
of this sterile marriage, Salomé mixes desire with death in a much more
convincing manner than we have seen in Wilde's previous works. She
defines her desire, first, as an appetite of the flesh and then as an assertion
of the will. She tells the soldier that she "desire[s] to speak with"
Iokanaan, and then she tells him that she *"will* speak with him" (p. 120).
Her interest in the prophet increases with his refusal to yield to her
temptation. Her desire for him is similar to Charmides's for Athena:

> He is like a thin ivory statue. He is like an image of silver. I am
> sure he is chaste, as the moon is. He is like a moonbeam, like a shaft
> of silver. His flesh must be very very cold, cold as ivory. [p. 126]

She frankly tells him that she is "amorous of [his] body" (p. 128), that
she not only desires his mouth (p. 130) but *"will* kiss [his] mouth"
(pp. 131, 132).

Iokanaan betrays no interest in Salomé's temptation, condemning
anyone who gives "herself up unto the lust of her eyes" (p. 124). He says
that he does "not desire to know who she is" and leaves her yearning
without satisfaction. When she looks with lust into his eyes, she sees only
terrible black holes, "like the black caverns where the dragons live" (p.
125). She sees death in his eyes, death for him and for herself. Iokanaan
is a personification of duty, as immovable to desire as Moranzone had
hoped Guido would be in *The Duchess of Padua;* but Iokanaan will, as
duty, be sacrificed to lust, a power greater than his own in the world of
this play. He merely fascinates Salomé, but he frightens Herod and
angers Herodias.

Herod comes onto the scene confused by his desire: "Bring me—
What is it that I desire? I forget. Ah! ah! I remember" (p. 142). He is
lusting for Salomé, but he diverts himself somewhat with trivial wants for
wine and fruit. When he asks Salomé to dance for him, she teases him:
"I have no desire to dance, Tetrarch" (p. 157). Herodias tries to discour-

age him, but he dismisses her as a person of no consequence, a sterile wife (p. 159). This accusation is near to madness, for Herodias is, as she insists to Herod, the mother of Salomé; he *will* not hear her—telling her, "Peace, woman! I say that you are sterile" (p. 160). His desire for Salomé has given him a motive for breaking his bond with Herodias. He tells Salomé he will give her whatever she desires, and so she dances for him.

Herod, ironically, has a sense of honor which guarantees that Salomé will have her desire for Iokanaan's head even though that wish conflicts with Herod's own desire. When Salomé makes love with the severed head of the prophet, wooing it like the wood-nymph with Charmides, she devours it with thirst and hunger, asserting a desire that cannot be appeased and a passion that cannot be quenched. She is not only a force of blind desire but also a force of dark destruction. Herod is disgusted by this creature whose will he has unleashed: "She is monstrous, thy daughter; I tell thee she is monstrous" (p. 181). His existence is now completely enveloped in darkness, as much by his own will as by circumstance and culture: "I will not look at things, I will not suffer things to look at me," Herod exclaims. "Put out the torches! Hide the moon! Hide the stars! Let us hide ourselves in our palace" (p. 182). He orders his guards to kill Salomé, thus putting out *that* torch; he pulls back into the darkness of his own pit, refusing to look up for any stars. Thus in concluding this play, Wilde has completed the task of annihilation that he began with *Vera*, so that he may begin his work of satire without any idealistic commitments.

BETWEEN 1889 AND 1891, WILDE PUBLISHED three essays in which he developed some of his mature ideas on art and morality: "The Decay of Lying," "The Critic as Artist," and "The Soul of Man under Socialism."[34] These essays provide clues for understanding the direction of his thought and art as it would be worked out in the comic dramas he composed between 1892 and 1895. "Art," we come to understand, is the means whereby "the desire for expression . . . can be attained," and "the desire for expression" is "the basis of life" (pp. 40–41). "Duty," on the other hand, as most people commonly understand that word, is usually enjoined upon us as a matter of "self-sacrifice": "philanthropists and sentimentalists . . . are always chattering to one about one's duty to one's neighbour" (p. 185). Too many people have mixed these terms, supposing that "the desire for expression" can somehow be the same as "duty to one's neighbour"; the main point of Wilde's essays is to insist that "the sphere of Art and the sphere of Ethics are absolutely distinct and separate." When these spheres are mistaken for one another, "Chaos has come again" (p. 198). From the point of view of ethics, art is a lie; from the point of view of art, ethics is a bore at best, death to the imagination at worst. A champion of Matthew Arnold's creed of "disinterestedness," Wilde calls for the critic to separate these spheres, that being the "duty" of criticism.

Because "the duty of imposing form upon chaos does not grow less as the world advances," criticism is needed now more than ever, when calls to other kinds of duty have been rendered absurd and unnecessary by discoveries in science; "by revealing to us the absolute mechanism of all action," science has freed us "from the self-imposed and trammelling burden of moral responsibility" (p. 179). "Duty" will take care of itself, but art as the means of self-expression, and so of individualism, must be kept free from that "trammelling burden of moral responsibility." Let science and duty have truth, and leave lying to art; since they are separate spheres, no one should object. The critic needs to "revive the old art of Lying" which has nearly been crushed beneath the increasing burden of moral responsibility. Wilde is the "critic as artist" in his essays; in his comic dramas, he becomes the artist as critic, separating duty from desire, ethics and morality from art and self-expression. Nothing could be more threatening to the ideal of marriage which, seeking to identify the two realms as one, merely "confuses" them.

"Art is the most intense mode of individualism that the world has known," Wilde tells us in his "Soul of Man under Socialism" (p. 300). When the critic separates art from ethics, he is helping to establish "Socialism," whose "chief advantage" is that it relieves us "from that sordid necessity of living for others" (p. 273) and "lead[s] to Individualism" (p. 276). "Socialism annihilates family life," Wilde admits; "With the abolition of private property, marriage in its present form must disappear," he warns. But "this is part of the programme. Individualism accepts this and makes it fine" (p. 292). When socialism can annihilate family life, it will "help the full development of personality" (p. 292), and thus it will free the self to express itself, that basic desire of life, "scientifically speaking" (p. 2). Marriage, property, and family require continuous self-sacrifice, killing self-expression, turning the soul away from being and becoming to doing and using (p. 182). "Property not merely has duties, but has so many duties that its possession to any large extent is a bore" (p. 278), and boredom is a sure killer of desire, of those "impossible desires" which make us "follow what we know we cannot gain" and so keep life in a constant process of becoming and of self-expression (pp. 180, 182).

The critic's proper desire is "to exercise influence," but he should concern himself not with influencing the individual (that is merely "chattering to one about one's duty to one's neighbour"), but with influencing "the age, which he will seek to wake into consciousness, . . . creating in it new desires and appetites" (p. 209). Keeping open possibilities for "constant change" the critic will find "true unity" for himself and make it possible for others at the same time (p. 197). This is the true freedom of being, in the process of always becoming, expressing itself in its appropriate sphere of mind, of intellect, whose essence is "motion" and "growth" (p. 197). By separating the self from the world of science—with its determinism, materialism, property, nature, truth, and duty—art makes for the freedom of the mind, the genuine "energy of life" (p. 40). That is why "in literature mere egotism is delightful" (p. 100). Egotism in ethics is tedious, "for the egotist is he who makes claims upon others," but "under Individualism people will be quite natural and absolutely unselfish" (pp. 328–29); and "art is the most intense mode of individualism that the world has known" (p. 300).

The most important work of the critic is to separate the spheres of ethics and art, self-sacrifice and self-expression, doing and talking, intellect and matter; he must leave to science the sphere of truth, but let criticism alone to work in the sphere of lying. When "lying for its own sake" (which is art) is cultivated and encouraged in a society, then that society can become civilized. Wilde was a critic attempting to civilize society, and to do that he touted the only heroism he thought appropriate to the needs of his time—the heroism of the liar, the "lost leader" of Victorian Britain. "Society sooner or later must return to its lost leader, the cultured and fascinating liar. . . . He is the very basis of civilised society" (p. 29).

The artist as critic and liar is Wilde's version of the comic spirit, taking joy in its inconsistency, its "constant change," intellectual motion, and doing nothing. The key to understanding the comedy of Wilde is to recognize how thoroughly dualistic his world is, for he most outrageously accepts, even affirms, the duality of human existence: the body is one thing, and the mind another. When one's body makes claims upon one's mind, the result is deadening tedium and dull work of duty; when one's mind makes claims upon one's body, the result is more depressing and disappointing as the claims are more successful, for this is the sphere of passion, limitless desire for possession. It is better to keep the mind separate from the body; and only those marriages which keep women's laws separate from men's laws have any chance of succeeding, for only such marriages acknowledge the truth of human experience as a radical duality.

IN HIS COMEDIES, then, Wilde does not always aim by his wit to annihilate the confusion called marriage; sometimes, he allows for the possibility of a marriage based upon distinction and clarification. When society and marriage allow mental freedom and bodily satisfaction, then society is civilization and marriage is an art. Before that can be possible, however, people must be rescued by painful criticism from their bondage to one another and sometimes from their bondage to themselves; if they have surrendered their intellectual freedom, they are more absurd and less responsive to art's liberating comedy. Those who bind their minds with notions of duty, idealism, doing, and sacrificing are the persons who have lost themselves in the "everything" of, paradoxically, materialism; their bondage is their belief that reality is objective, fixed, and ordered by inhuman laws of determining constraint—they crucify without compunction. The heroic liar, resurrected by criticism, presents another possibility by sorting out the realms of being; his "larger vision" allows a place for desire, realism, talking, and egoism that expresses itself in the "nothing" of intellectual freedom.

Lady Windermere's Fan (1892) shows how tragic marriage can be, even in a comic world, because this play is about the bondage of marriage, where the dowdies of the world tyrannize the dandies. In *An Ideal Husband*, Mrs. Marchmont, quoting Mrs. Cheveley, tells Lord Goring, "London Society was entirely made up of dowdies and dandies"; Lord Goring, a dandy himself, accepts that division of society, but turns the tables by suggesting that "the men are all dowdies and the women are all dandies."[35] Lord Goring is right for the world of *An Ideal Husband*, because there, roles are wildly exchanged—and so absurdly confused. In *Lady Windermere's Fan*, the dowdies clearly run the show despite the good efforts of Lord Darlington, the only genuine dandy.

The lesser dowdies, Lady Plymdale and the Duchess of Berwick, define their roles as wives who "have a perfect legal right" to "nag" at their husbands "from time to time" in order to make their "existence" as wives quite clear (p. 23). A husband for their kind of marriage is "the odd trick," as Darlington puts it. To the dowdies, husbands are merely useful; if they seem to be attentive to their wives, they "become a perfect nuisance," and so certain kinds of women, like Mrs. Erlynne, "are most useful" to the dowdies—they help to keep husbands under control. "They form the basis of other people's marriages" (p. 66). The best marriages are, therefore, those in which the husband appears to pay no attention to his wife: "The world has grown so suspicious of anything that looks like a happy married life" (p. 57). By this standard the marriage of Lord and Lady Windermere is about to become more successful because it is about to become very unhappy. Lady Windermere is the major dowdy of the play. She fits well into the London society of Lady Plymdale and the Duchess of Berwick, but Lady Windermere does not really know how to play the game yet. She has noticed how "London is full of women" who "look so thoroughly unhappy," but she thinks it is because they "trust their husbands." She vows that she is "not going to be one of them" (p. 58). Of course, by refusing to trust her husband, she will make him into the "odd trick" and try to tyrannize him, exactly like the other dowdies.

Lady Windermere is undergoing a painful learning process in the play, but she never becomes a female dandy. Lord Darlington tries to liberate her, to change her costume from dowdy to dandy, but she has neither the courage nor the wit to make the change. She even admits it herself, and then her own mother tells her the same thing when Mrs. Erlynne "saves" her from perdition in act 3: "You haven't got the kind of brains that enables a woman to get back. You have neither the wit nor the courage" (p. 100). In the world as it is constituted, a woman such as Lady Windermere had better make the best of marriage as bondage. The Duchess of Berwick and Lady Plymdale are too stupid to know they are in worse bondage than are their husbands; they are like the jailers always tied to their prisoners. When Lady Windermere chooses not to trust her husband, she strengthens her own bondage in a similar manner.

Both Lord and Lady Windermere are willing to make a sacrifice for their marriage: ostensibly it will be themselves, but really Mrs. Erlynne, who becomes the scapegoat of the social order. Lady Windermere insists to Lord Darlington that life is not "a speculation. It is a sacrament. Its ideal is love. Its purification is sacrifice" (p. 17). This is an interpretation she never repudiates, although she has an opportunity to test it when she decides to leave her husband. What she really means is that marriage is a sacrament that sacrifices others for its own ideal existence. When she tells Mrs. Erlynne that "we all have ideals in life," Lady Windermere thinks she is saying that her mother's ideal has preserved her own integrity; but as Mrs. Erlynne and the audience know, that ideal does not exist any more than the uncompromising integrity that Lady Windermere affects.

Mrs. Erlynne says, indeed, that "ideals are dangerous things. Realities are better" (p. 145). Mrs. Erlynne is a female dandy whose intellectual and bodily freedom are purchased at the cost of consistency—a sign of her individualism. She "will not consent to be the slave of [her] own opinions" ("The Critic as Artist," p. 197). Realities may be better than ideals, but not for Lady Windermere. Mrs. Erlynne knows how to play the game of survival, but she knows her daughter does not; and so she does not deal in truth with those who cannot handle it. When Lady Windermere offers to do her "duty" and tell her husband the "truth" about Mrs. Erlynne's "sacrifice" the evening before, Mrs. Erlynne stops her: "It is not your duty—at least you have duties to others beside him" (p. 148). She can invoke the sacred words to guide her daughter to the only happiness her daughter can know. When she gets Lord Augustus after all, Mrs. Erlynne shows the world how capable a person she really is. Lord Windermere congratulates Lord Augustus, "Well, you are certainly marrying a very clever woman"; and Lady Windermere, doing the same, says "Ah, you're marrying a very good woman" (p. 155). But neither Lord nor Lady Windermere knows *how* clever, nor in just what sense, nor how *good* Mrs. Erlynne really is.

The only person in the play who has the courage and the wit to match Mrs. Erlynne's is Lord Darlington, but not even he has the command of circumstances that she has. He is too much a part of the scheme to handle all the reality she manages. Nevertheless, Lord Darlington is the only man in the play who can lay genuine claim to being a dandy. That role is possible for him not only because he has wit and knows that his freedom lies in his ability to talk and do nothing, but also because he is not married. Outside the limits of the play, we know that he comes dangerously near to losing his freedom when he tempts Lady Windermere to elope with him. He tells her early in the play that "life [is] too complex a thing to be settled by these hard and fast rules" that she lays down in her uncompromising fashion; but Lord Darlington is kept free from the full complexity of the life that Mrs. Erlynne knows. When he tells Lady Windermere to "be brave! Be yourself!" he is saying perhaps more than he knows (p. 71). Lady Windermere can only be the self she has modeled from the "ideal" of her mother—a false ideal; she cannot be the self that her "real" mother presents to the audience. If she could, Lady Windermere might be a proper wife for Lord Darlington.

But in the world of *Lady Windermere's Fan*, the only realized dandy is a woman. Lord Darlington would merely become Lord Windermere if he were to marry Lady Windermere. His integrity is secure only as long as he remains the "romantic," always in love with a woman who does not love him, a "last Endymion" in the "gutter" of London society (pp. 112–14). It is not until his last two comedies that Wilde can conceive of a marriage between dandies; until then, their doom is to be always in love but never married. That same "cynical" reading of society prevails in *A Woman of No Importance* (1893) which is, if anything, even more cynical than *Lady Windermere's Fan*. The trick here is to be always in love without *falling* in love and becoming a sacrifice upon the altar of idealism. Lord Illingworth is the strong dandy of *A Woman of No Impor-*

tance. He is the masculine version of Mrs. Erlynne, just as Mrs. Arbuthnot is the feminine version of Lord Darlington. And just as in the earlier comedy, neither Lord Illingworth nor Mrs. Arbuthnot is completely free from the bondages that confuse duty with desire. He knows the value of intellectual play, of wit, telling Mr. Kelvil that "the intellect is not a serious thing, and never has been. It is an instrument on which one plays, that is all" (p. 24). But when Lord Illingworth tells Mrs. Arbuthnot, at the end of the drama, that she had once been for him "the prettiest of playthings, the most fascinating of small romances" (p. 189), he betrays his weakness, even his bondage.

Attached as he is to property (with all its "duties"), Lord Illingworth confuses ethics and aesthetics when he makes a person into a "plaything" and believes that "nothing is serious except passion" (p. 24). While Kelvil "never regarded woman as a toy," he is not as well off as Illingworth because Kelvil regards woman as "the intellectual helpmeet of man in public as in private life. Without her we should forget the true ideals" (p. 28). Kelvil takes all life too "seriously," reducing intellect to the role of public duty, something Lord Illingworth certainly will not be caught at. He attempts to educate his son Gerald to understand that "women represent the triumph of matter over mind—just as men represent the triumph of mind over morals" (p. 112). To maintain this "triumph," Lord Illingworth explains, a man must never marry: "One should always be in love. That is the reason one should never marry" (p. 115). When Lady Hunstanton discovers Lord Illingworth and Gerald together, while they are discussing these matters of love and marriage, she does not know how well she has helped to give a new definition to the word *duty* when she says to Illingworth, "I suppose you have been telling our young friend, Gerald, what his new duties are to be" (p. 116). She is equally ignorant of the irony she creates when she tells Mrs. Allonby later that "it would do [Lord Illingworth] a great deal of good" to be in "a happy English home" like the one those two dowdies think they see in Mrs. Arbuthnot's house; the irony operates when we recall that Lord Illingworth has told Mrs. Allonby that "all influence is bad, but that a good influence is the worst in the world" (p. 151).

Lord Illingworth has devoted himself to always being in love and so to keeping his spirit of desire constantly alive. He has managed to outmaneuver the "good influence" of "a happy English home" until now, when he is dangerously near to sacrificing himself for the sake of his son. When he proposes to marry Mrs. Arbuthnot, he insists that he does not do it for the sake of any such duty as Gerald has called for: "I don't admit that it is any duty of mine to marry you. I deny it entirely" (p. 183). His proposal is motivated only by his desire to "leave [Gerald] his property. . . . What more can a gentleman desire in this world?" (p. 178). Lord Illingworth's willingness to sacrifice himself is a measure of his faith in the importance of a particular form of desire—"a desire to see life," as he put it earlier (p. 108). But Illingworth cannot completely separate that desire from the public sphere of property and reputation. He has not, consequently, succeeded in "the triumph of mind" over matter, however much he may think he has triumphed "over morals." It is fitting that he should propose marriage to Mrs. Arbuthnot.

And it is equally fitting that she should refuse his proposal. For Mrs. Arbuthnot is a dowdy in the clothing of a dandy. In fact she makes a dandy with a dowdy appearance. Like Mrs. Erlynne, Mrs. Arbuthnot exists apart from the superficialities of social duty and material welfare, but unlike Mrs. Erlynne, Mrs. Arbuthnot did not choose her independent status nor does she ever forget the faults of the past, the faults of others. For her everything is serious, especially passion. When she rejects Illingworth's proposal, she explains that she is motivated by not one but "two passions": her love for Gerald and her hate of Illingworth. "They feed each other," she explains. She believes "all love is a tragedy," and in so believing she is a fitting character in Wilde's comically absurd world. She succeeds where Illingworth fails in educating their son, for Gerald becomes a victim upon the altar of marriage.

Mrs. Arbuthnot explains to Gerald that she will not and cannot marry his father because "marriage is a sacrament for those who love each other" (p. 165). She perceives life as a gutter filled with sin, where "God's house is the only house where sinners are made welcome" and where one spends his time "in Church duties" (p. 168). She explains to Gerald her idea of love (mixed as it is with hate) when she tells him that "it is my disgrace that has bound you so closely to me. It is the price I paid for you—the price of soul and body—that makes me love you as I do" (p. 169). The irony of her statement lies in her confession that she has paid for his love with her soul as well as her body, and so she has nothing to give either Gerald or Illingworth. For her to marry anyone would, indeed, be a mockery, but that is something Gerald cannot understand. He insists over and over that his mother "must marry" Illingworth, telling her, "It is your duty" (p. 169). Believing this, he is a willing husband for Hester Worsley.

BECAUSE HESTER WORSLEY HAS LEARNED that she was wrong in maintaining that "the sins of the parents should be visited on the children," she might be capable of further education and might promise a liberating marriage with Gerald. That she *might* is further hinted by her willingness to make little of her "riches" by sharing them with her husband. She will have far to go from her earlier insistence that there should be only one law for both men and women; her American idea of equality before the law threatens to maintain the insidious confusion of spheres of truth, leveling all life to a single standard of duty and doing. Finally, there are no hopeful marriages in *A Woman of No Importance* as there are in *An Ideal Husband* and *The Importance of Being Earnest*.

An Ideal Husband (1893–95) shows us two marriages, one already made but threatened, the other a promise for the future. With the promise of marriage between Lord Goring and Miss Mabel Chiltern, Wilde for the first time in his comic dramas brings forward a marriage of intellectual liberation. The marriage of common bondage and confusion between Sir Robert Chiltern and Lady Chiltern is a study in contrast; Sir Robert is a study of desire, but desire for the wrong thing—power—while Lady Chiltern is a study of duty, but again in the wrong way—sacrifice. By the end of the play, a resolution of differences is suggested and the confusion of values is discriminated: the Chilterns show us a marriage proper to the sphere of ethics, while Lord Goring and Mabel Chiltern show us the hope for a marriage proper to the sphere of art.

Mrs. Cheveley, a literary descendant from Mrs. Erlynne via Mrs. Arbuthnot, is the character whose presence makes possible the sorting out of marriages and the distinctions drawn among duties and desires. Mrs. Cheveley has wit and courage, but she attempts to influence persons rather than to enlarge the vision of "the age." Her desire is not for self-expression, but for the possession of things. She is a liar, not in art but in ethics; and she is a dowdy without peer in Wilde's comedies, for she uses marriage as her means to manage others, the worst kind of "absolute mechanism." Mrs. Cheveley is a force for corruption because she confuses art and ethics; she is the Salomé of the comedies because of her insatiable desire for power. She tells Sir Robert that "politics are my only pleasure" (p. 17).

Sir Robert Chiltern is most vulnerable to Mrs. Cheveley's weapons because he represents the world of power for which she hungers. Sir Robert tells Lord Goring that he had been seized by a great "desire for power" at the time he sold the government secret: "My ambition and my desire for power were at that time boundless" (p. 82). Lord Goring knows at the play's end that Sir Robert's desire for power is not and cannot be completely satisfied, that "power is his passion" (p. 230). In one sense, Lady Chiltern is completely wrong when she tells Sir Robert that "power is nothing in itself. It is power to do good that is fine" (p. 64); the application of power "to do good" is "fine" in ethics, but as far as Sir Robert's own identity is concerned, the power in itself is the source of his energy—it is his version of "amour de l'Impossible," his "passion," as Lord Goring says. Power is the closest Sir Robert can come to self-expression. Indeed, had he retired from public service, as Lady Chiltern desired him to do (she says, "It is his duty"), Sir Robert "would lose everything" (pp. 229, 230).

In the beginning of the play, Sir Robert is a dowdy in politics because he pretends to be better than his neighbors—he believes that "a political life is a noble career" (p. 18), which it might be for someone who knows himself and understands his motives better than Sir Robert does. He needs to be educated, and he is—by Mrs. Cheveley, who shows him that politics is also "a clever game . . . and sometimes it is a great nuisance" (pp. 17–18). Because Mrs. Cheveley understands the importance of games and the need for masks, she is a dandy in petticoats; she tells Sir Robert that "well-dressed women" "represent the irrational" (p. 16), and she tells Lord Goring that "a woman's first duty in life is to her dressmaker" (p. 170). When Mrs. Cheveley goes on to claim that "no one has as yet discovered what the second duty is" she is deceiving herself, for the genuine dandy knows that the "second duty" is to the self or to nothing at all.

The genuine dowdy is Lady Chiltern. Her character helps us to understand what Wilde means in "The Critic as Artist" when he has Gilbert say "that the desire to do good to others produces a plentiful crop of prigs," but at the same time "the prig is a very interesting psychological study, and though of all poses a moral pose is the most offensive, still to have a pose at all is something" (p. 184). As everyone in the play recognizes, Lady Chiltern is something of a prig—the dowdy of ethics. Mrs. Cheveley remembers Lady Chiltern from their schooldays: "She always got the good conduct prize" (p. 14). To maintain that pose, however, costs Lady Chiltern a good deal. For her to be able to say to her husband that "it can never be necessary to do what is not honourable" (p. 64), she must believe in unreality, in what she calls "ideals," which she loves more than she loves people. When he is about to topple from his pedestal of ivory, she "saves" him, pleading with him not to fall: "Oh! don't kill my love for you, don't kill that!" (p. 65). Sir Robert "saves" her love by risking the loss of the one thing that gives his life meaning, his political office.

Lady Chiltern's "mania for morality," as Mrs. Cheveley calls it (p. 46), nearly destroys her husband and their marriage. When Sir Robert tells Lord Goring that he feels "like a man on a ship that is sinking," that "the water is round [his] feet, and the very air is bitter with storm," he does not realize the important connection between what he has just said and his next words: "Hush! I hear my wife's voice." Between Mrs.

Cheveley and Lady Chiltern, Sir Robert is indeed at the center of a storm. He will need all the "strength and courage" he can muster to make his way out of this. Ironically, he does not have the same strength and courage he had years ago when he yielded to the temptation to sell a government secret. He tells Lord Goring that "there are terrible temptations that it requires strength, strength and courage, to yield to" (p. 83). If he had made the "rational compromise" (p. 65) he intended to make in order to protect his office from Mrs. Cheveley, he would have shown that same kind of "strength and courage." Instead, he yielded to his wife's ideal of honor and risked losing everything.

Sir Robert and Lady Chiltern cannot save themselves from one another any more than they can save themselves from Mrs. Cheveley. They live too much in the world of things and ideals, seeming opposites but identical in their rigid demands and tyrannical abstractness. Sir Robert is a great speaker, but his talk is for others; he learns how important it is for himself as well. Lady Chiltern is a great chatterer about duty to others, and so she learns that she must stop her husband from doing his "duty," from sacrificing himself to her ideal of him. Their teacher is Lord Goring, who declares that "it is the growth of the moral sense in women that makes marriage such a hopeless, one-sided institution" (p. 142). He is the dandy who saves the Chilterns and thereby saves for the nation a fine and useful politician.

Lord Goring has all the credentials of the critic as artist. He "love[s] talking about nothing," he tells his father, because "it is the one thing [he] knows anything about" (p. 27). This the most blissful circumstance of intellectual freedom, an insight Lord Goring shares with Socrates, that man so wise because he was so ignorant. Lord Goring sees right through the philosophy of power that Sir Robert learned from the Baron. When Sir Robert tells Lord Goring how "luxury was nothing but a background, a painted scene in a play, and that power, power over other men, . . . was the one thing worth having," Lord Goring calls it "a thoroughly shallow creed" (p. 81). This he can say because he, along with Oscar Wilde, knows that power over the world is bondage to the world and that the only joy is in the untrammeled existence of self-expression. The only power that counts for him is the power of charity, which he tells Lady Chiltern "is the true explanation of this world, whatever may be the explanation of the next" (p. 101).

When Lord Goring tells Lady Chiltern that "women are not meant to judge [men], but to forgive us when we need forgiveness," again he is making his point about the need for charity. But then he adds that "a man's life is of more value than a woman's. It has larger issues, wider scope, greater ambitions. A woman's life revolves in curves of emotions.

It is upon lines of intellect that a man's life progresses" (pp. 228–29). This will not endear Lord Goring to the women's liberation movement of any century, but it expresses in conventional terms an important element of Wilde's belief that spheres of value must be kept separate, not confused, in marriage or politics just as in art and morals. This requires, indeed, a largeness of vision that few are capable of glimpsing, much less of maintaining. But if the distinctions are maintained, then Lord Goring's point about sacrifice might be better understood: "We men and women are not made to accept such sacrifices from each other. We are not worthy of them" (p. 229).

The one person in the play who can share this vision with Lord Goring is Mabel Chiltern, for she keeps spheres of activity separate very well. She has the wit to make her a fitting Beatrice for Goring's Benedict. She tells him that her "duty is something [she] never [does], on principle. It always depresses" her (p. 205). And after she accepts his proposal of marriage, she tells Goring's father that she does not want her husband to be "an ideal husband. . . . It sounds like something in the next world" (p. 238). In this world she prefers that he "be what he chooses." As for herself, she wants to be "a real wife to him." Although Lord Caversham seems satisfied with this "common sense" answer, we should not be so naive as he to think that "a real wife" means a "common wife." The stress should be put on *real*, not on "wife." But in the end, everybody is happy (except Mrs. Cheveley, of course). The wits are united with one another, and the workers are kept together. Lord Caversham, who had told his son it "is your duty to get married . . . You must get a wife, sir" (p. 145), points persuasively to the marriage of the Chilterns as a model to be imitated: "Look where your friend Robert Chiltern has got to by probity, hard work, and a sensible marriage with a good woman" (p. 145). In the end, it is Caversham's own son who takes the Chilterns toward a better marriage—through the art of doing nothing and talking about everything.

The Importance of Being Earnest (1894–95) may be a "trivial comedy for serious people," as its subtitle indicates, but it is also a serious comedy for trivial people, as its themes suggest.[36] In the world of "serious people" the most trivial persons are dandies and do-nothings, and since the play is about dandies and do-nothings, it is trivial to the serous but serious to the trivial. In its farcical action and witty dialogue, we are admitted back into the garden where talk is everything and action counts for little. The only serpent in this garden is a reverend canon, for he is indeed, as Miss Prism says, "a womanthrope," who holds by "the practice of the Primitive Church which was distinctly against matrimony" (p. 83). Miss Chasuble is herself a much deteriorated descendant of Lady Windermere et al., because Miss Chasuble is a dowdy prig of intellectual pretensions who has high respect for "duty and responsibility" (p. 68). She and the reverend canon deserve one another more than either of them knows. In the garden at Woolton perfect marriages are possible, for in that place the myth of Ernest Worthing can become real—it cannot be killed off even for the sake of Dr. Chasuble and Miss Prism. In Wilde's dream world at Woolton, irony is romance, myth is reality, and the great liars learn the importance of being Ernest, if not earnest. The wealth of this garden is such that it can accommodate the luxury of two marriages of liberation, pushing into the background (or back into the city) all those marriages of bondage which have been exposed in Wilde's previous comedies.

The most important qualities of the dandy—that is, wearing masks and changing them often—are combined with the most important qualities of the critic as artist—self-expression and charity—to make the two couples of this comedy into models of acceptable marriage. Even the marriage-broker of the plot, Lady Bracknell, is brought round to celebrate these light-hearted marriages. Algernon has a high tone of "moral responsibility" in his relationship with his manservant, Lane, whose view of marriage is very "demoralising" (pp. 3–4). But once in the country (Bunburying, but posing as Ernest Worthing), Algernon abandons his mask of morality, telling Jack that his "duty as a gentleman has never interfered with his pleasures in the smallest degree" (p. 99). Jack Worthing wears his mask of Ernest in town and Jack in the country, for he "has to adopt a very high moral tone" in his position as guardian to Cecily Cardew: "It's one's duty to do so." He has done a nice job of carrying off this pose, for Miss Prism considers him without equal among those who have "a higher sense of duty and responsibility" (p. 69). But in his role as Ernest Worthing, Jack is able to escape all that "sense of duty"; his success in this role can be witnessed by his answers to Lady Bracknell's questions about his qualifications for marrying Gwendolen. He tells her that he "know[s] nothing" and derives his income from investments, not land. Both answers please her enormously, especially the latter: "What between the duties expected of one during one's lifetime, and the duties exacted from one after one's death, land has ceased to be either a profit or a pleasure" (pp. 41–42).

To "know nothing," be unattached to property, capable of changing identities behind masks, including the mask of duty—these are nice credentials for the two men of the story. But they belong not only to the men; Gwendolin and Cecily display equally strong credentials. Gwendolin is a dandy with a vengeance, asserting that "the home seems to [her] to be the proper sphere for the man. And certainly once a man begins to neglect his domestic duties he becomes painfully effeminate, does he not?"

(p. 117). But immediately she turns that about to admit that while she might not "like that," still "it makes men so very attractive." She threatens to "rescue" her Ernest from Cecily, considering it her "duty to rescue him at once, and with a firm hand" (p. 123). She believes in the inequality of the sexes and affirms the distinction of spheres of value. Gwendolen tells Cecily that "it is obvious that [their] social spheres have been widely different" (p. 124), and later Gwendolen tells Algernon that it is "absurd to talk of the equality of the sexes" (p. 152). Her powers of discrimination, which are fine enough "never [to have] seen a spade" and to commend men for their heroic self-sacrifice, their willingness to undergo the ordeal of christening, show that Gwendolen is an artist: "The object of Art is not simple truth but complex beauty. . . . Art itself is really a form of exaggeration; and selection, which is the very spirit of art, is nothing more than an intensified mode of over-emphasis," as Wilde has Vivian say in "The Decay of Lying" (pp. 23–24).

Cecily is also an artist for the same reasons. She, like Gwendolen, carries her diary with her and uses it to fullest advantage; she may be an even more practiced liar than any of the others, for she even lies with gusto to herself when she writes in her diary—artful lying for its own sake. Cecily also appreciates the sanity of insincerity, like a good dandy; she has noticed how her guardian "is so very serious! Sometimes he is so serious that I think he cannot be quite well" (p. 67). Miss Prism, dull as usual, responds by saying that Jack "enjoys the best of health." Both would agree with Lady Bracknell, who maintains that "health is the primary duty of life" (p. 29), but each would supply a different definition of what constitutes that health: in the world of duty and material things, health is merely physical; but in the world of art and intellectual things, health is a state of free imagination. Cecily has a free imagination, and she uses it with vigor in her meeting with Gwendolen; preparing to battle for Ernest, Cecily throws aside her "shallow mask of manners" (p. 124) and puts on her mask of crude frankness. She, like the three other dandies, can pass freely from one pose to another in her constant energy of spirit.

While Lady Bracknell may not change masks with as much alacrity as Cecily Cardew, Lady Bracknell is not above the strategy of changing positions when circumstances warrant. She knows how to live with Algernon's Bunburying, keeping that character in his mythic place, dead or alive. She is pleased with men who "know nothing," for it shows that they have escaped the dangerous effects of a British education (p. 41); she is equally pleased with those who keep their income safe from property. What she cannot tolerate is bad taste, of the kind that Jack betrays when he tells her he was "bred in a hand-bag." That displays "a contempt for the ordinary decencies of family life" (p. 47), which reminds her of "the worst excesses of the French Revolution"—the most infamous confusion of values that Europe ever knew. Although marriages may breed eccentricity, as it did in the father of Jack and Algernon, that does not discredit marriage—in Lady Bracknell's eyes, at any rate.

It is difficult at times to read *The Importance of Being Earnest* without thinking that Wilde is making an elaborate joke against heterosexual marriage; Bunburying, and women with firm hands who are attracted to feminine men whose place is properly in the home, may add up to a sign of the fig, a final commentary on Victorian duty that subordinates individual desire to corporate welfare on the model of "the happy English home." We do not need to think this to appreciate the play for its gaiety of good humor, but it would not be out of place. The author of a very moving letter to Lord Alfred Douglas (first published as *De Profundis*) surely would not mind. In it Wilde says, "If life be, as it surely is, a problem to me, I am no less a problem to life. People must adopt some attitude towards me, and so pass judgment both on themselves and me."[37]

Notes

CHAPTER 1: INTRODUCTION

1. *The Duties of Man and Other Essays*, trans. Ella Noyes, Thomas Okey, and L. Martineau, ed. Bolton King, Everyman's Library (London, 1894), p. 66.
2. Ibid., p. 60.
3. *The Wives of England, Their Relative Duties, Domestic Influence, and Social Obligations* (London, 1843?), p. 32.
4. Ibid., p. 162.
5. "Explosive Intimacy: Psychodynamics of the Victorian Family," in *The New Psychohistory*, ed. Lloyd de Mause (New York, 1975), p. 50; Kern is quoting from and describing a marriage manual by the American phrenologist O. S. Fowler, *Love and Parentage Applied to the Improvement of Offspring*, published in 1846.
6. *The Four Loves* (London, 1960), p. 17.
7. Kern, "Explosive Intimacy," p. 30.
8. "Virginibus Puerisque," in *The Works of R. L. Stevenson*, 26 vols. (London, 1922), 2:12.
9. C. G. Jung, "Marriage as a Psychological Relationship," in *The Book of Marriage*, arr. and ed. Count Hermann Keyserling (New York, 1926), p. 353.
10. *The Playwright as Thinker: A Study of Drama* (New York, 1946), pp. 67–68.
11. Patrick J. Smith, *The Tenth Muse: A Historical Study of the Opera Libretto* (New York, 1970), p. 285.
12. Theodore Fenner, *Leigh Hunt and Opera Criticism: The "Examiner" Years, 1808–1821* (Lawrence, Kan., 1972), p. 3; Fenner is quoting, in part, Donald Jay Grout, *A Short History of Opera* (New York, 1947), pp. 4–5.
13. Sigmund Freud, "The Most Prevalent Form of Degradation in Erotic Life," in *On Creativity and the Unconscious: Papers on the Psychology of Art, Literature, Love, and Religion* (New York: Harper Torchbooks, 1958), p. 183.

14. *Love in the Western World*, trans. Montgomery Belgion (Philadelphia, 1940?), pp. 261–62.
15. Ellis, *Wives of England*, p. 155.
16. Ibid., p. 18.
17. Program notes for the recording of *Alceste* by the Paris Philharmonic Orchestra and Chorus conducted by Rene Leibowitz, libretto by Calzabigi, French version by du Roullet, English version translated from the French by Herma Briffault (New York: Oceanic Records, 1952).
18. *Mozart and Beethoven: The Concept of Love in Their Operas* (Baltimore, 1977), p. 140.
19. "Marriage as a Sacrament," *The Book of Marriage*, p. 500.
20. Singer, *Mozart and Beethoven*, p. 139.
21. Lewis, *Four Loves*, p. 148.
22. *The Magic Flute, Masonic Opera*, trans. Herbert Weinstock (New York, 1971), p. 98.
23. *Opera as Drama* (New York: Vintage Books, 1956), p. 123.
24. Singer, *Mozart and Beethoven*, p. 112.
25. *The Great Operas of Mozart: The Magic Flute* with German text, English version by Ruth and Thomas Martin (New York, 1941), pp. 382, 383. All quotations of *The Magic Flute* are from this edition to which page numbers in the text refer.
26. *The Other Victorians: A Study of Sexuality and Pornography in Mid Nineteenth-Century England* (New York, 1966), p. 26.
27. Mazzini, *Duties of Man*, p. 75.
28. "Introduction," *Fidelio or Wedded Love* (London, 1938), p. xiv.
29. Ernest Newman, *Seventeen Famous Operas* (New York, 1954), p. 260; Newman does not agree with those who so argue.
30. Program notes for the recording of *Fidelio* by the Philharmonia Orchestra and Chorus conducted by Otto Klemperer, Angel Records 3625/C1; the translation is by William R. Gann. All quotations from *Fidelio* are from this translation to which page numbers in the text refer.
31. Freud, "The Most Prevalent Form of Degradation," p. 186.
32. *Love and Will* (New York, 1969), pp. 29–30.
33. Rollo May's terms; ibid., pp. 204–205, 218.
34. *The Notebooks of Samuel Taylor Coleridge*, ed. Kathleen Coburn, 3 vols. (Princeton, N.J., 1957–73), vol. 3, *1808–1819*, note entry 3699.
35. Ibid., text entry 3699.
36. Ibid., text entry 4006.
37. Marcus, *Other Victorians*, p. 23; George Bernard Shaw, *The Quintessence of Ibsenism* (1913; reprint ed., New York, 1957), p. 34.
38. *Notebooks of Coleridge*, text entry 4272.
39. Marcus, *Other Victorians*, p. 27.
40. De Rougemont, *Love in the Western World*, p. 261.
41. Bernhart, "Marriage as a Sacrament," p. 493.
42. De Rougemont, *Love in the Western World*, p. 299.
43. Martin Cyril D'Arcy, *The Mind and Heart of Love: Lion and Unicorn, A*

Study in Eros and Agape, rev. ed. (Cleveland, Ohio: Meridian Books, 1956), p. 337.

44. "The Sufferings and Greatness of Richard Wagner" (a speech written for the fiftieth anniversary of Wagner's death and delivered on February 10, 1933, at the University of Munich) in *Freud, Goethe, and Wagner* (New York, 1937), p. 101.

45. Francis Fergusson, *The Idea of a Theater: The Art of Drama in Changing Perspective* (1949; reprint ed., Garden City, N.Y.: Anchor Books, 1953), p. 86.

46. Bentley, *Playwright as Thinker*, p. 74.

47. "Nietzsche *contra* Wagner," in *The Case of Wagner*, trans. J. M. Kennedy, in *The Complete Works of Nietzsche*, ed. Oscar Levy, 18 vols. (1909–13; reprint ed., New York, 1964), 8:65.

48. Fergusson, *Idea of a Theater*, pp. 104–106.

49. *Librettos of the Wagner Operas* (New York, 1938), p. 313; translator unknown. All quotations from *Tristan und Isolde* are from this translation to which page numbers in the text refer.

50. *The Oxford Ibsen*, ed. and trans. James Walter McFarlane, 8 vols. (London, 1960–77), 5:282. All quotations from *A Doll's House* are from this translation to which page numbers in the text refer.

51. Shaw, *Quintessence of Ibsenism*, p. 56.

52. *Marriage and Morals* (London, 1929), pp. 115, 13, 26.

53. George Bernard Shaw, *Complete Plays, with Prefaces*, 6 vols. (New York, 1962), 3:648. All quotations from Shaw's plays are from this edition to which volume and page numbers in the text refer.

54. T. S. Eliot, *The Complete Poems and Plays: 1909–1950* (New York, 1952), pp. 225–93. All quotations from Eliot's works are from this edition to which page numbers in the text refer.

55. Russell, *Marriage and Morals*, p. 240.

56. *Love Declared: Essays on the Myths of Love*, trans. Richard Howard (New York, 1963), p. 161; originally published in French as *Comme Toi-Meme*.

57. May, *Love and Will*, p. 95.

58. W. S. Gilbert, *The Savoy Operas*, 2 vols., Introduction by David Cecil, Notes by Derek Hudson (London, 1962), 1:187, 261. All quotations from Gilbert's librettos are from this edition to which volume and page numbers in the text refer.

59. Lionel Trilling, describing Freud's *Civilization and Its Discontents*, in *Sincerity and Authenticity* (Cambridge, Mass., 1972), p. 151.

Chapter 2: Tennyson

1. *Either/Or*, trans. David F. Swenson and Lillian Marvin Swenson, 2 vols. (Garden City, N.Y.: Anchor Books, 1959), 2:5–157.

2. Wendell Stacy Johnson, "The Theme of Marriage in Tennyson," *Victorian Newsletter* 12 (Autumn 1957):6–10, discusses marriage as Tennyson's ideal of harmony rescuing the self from loneliness.

3. For a seminal study of this subject, see Lionel Stevenson, "The 'High-Born Maiden' Symbol in Tennyson," *PMLA* 63 (1948):234–43; for a follow-up study, see Clyde de L. Ryals, "The 'Fated Woman' Symbol in Tennyson," *PMLA* 74 (1959):438–43.
4. J. C. Mays, "*In Memoriam*: An Aspect of Form," *University of Toronto Quarterly* 35 (October 1965):22–46.
5. *The Language of Tennyson's "In Memoriam"* (Oxford, 1971), p. 112.
6. "*In Memoriam*" (1936), reprinted in *Critical Essays on the Poetry of Tennyson*, ed. John Killham (New York, 1960), pp. 207–15.
7. *The Poems of Tennyson*, ed. Christopher Ricks (London, 1969), pp. 1038–39, headnote.
8. *The Collected Works of Walter Bagehot*, ed. Norman St. John-Stevas, 12 vols. to date (London, 1965–), vol. 2, *The Literary Essays*, p. 184; Bagehot's comments originally appeared in the *National Review* 9 (October 1859): 386–94.
9. Sir Charles Tennyson, *Alfred Tennyson* (New York, 1949), p. 491.
10. *The Fall of Camelot: A Study of Tennyson's "Idylls of the King"* (Cambridge, Mass., 1973), p. 6.
11. *On the Poems of Tennyson* (Gainesville, Fla., 1972), pp. 109, 133–34.
12. *The Deserted Stage: The Search for Dramatic Form in Nineteenth-Century England* (Athens, Ohio, 1972,) pp. 96, 97.
13. References to the text of *Becket* are taken from *The Poetic and Dramatic Works of Alfred Lord Tennyson*, Cambridge Edition (Boston and New York, 1898), pp. 659–708.
14. Jerome Hamilton Buckley, *Tennyson: The Growth of a Poet* (Cambridge, Mass., 1961), p. 166.

CHAPTER 3: BROWNING

1. William Barrett, describing the careers of Kierkegaard and Nietzsche, in *Irrational Man: A Study in Existential Philosophy* (Garden City, N.Y.: Anchor Books, 1962), p. 13. I am much indebted to this work for my discussion in this chapter of Kierkegaard's "stages"; see especially pp. 149–76.
2. References to the text of Browning's poems are from the ten volume Centenary Edition, *The Works of Robert Browning*, ed. F. G. Kenyon (London, 1912).
3. The major works in which Kierkegaard elaborates his terms are *Either/Or* (1843), *Repetition* (1843), *Fear and Trembling* (1843); they are summarized in *Stages on Life's Way* (1845). Besides Barrett's chapter in *Irrational Man*, I have drawn upon two other studies of Kierkegaard for my discussion: James Collins, *The Mind of Kierkegaard* (Chicago, 1953), and George Price, *The Narrow Pass: A Study of Kierkegaard's Concept of Man* (New York, 1963).
4. E. LeRoy Lawson, *Very Sure of God: Religious Language in the Poetry of Robert Browning* (Nashville, Tenn., 1974), p. 25.

5. "Aesthetic Validity of Marriage," *Either/Or*, 2:5–157; see also Collins, *Mind of Kierkegaard*, pp. 76–77, and Price, *Narrow Pass*, p. 73.
6. Lawson, *Very Sure of God*, p. 128.
7. Otten, *Deserted Stage*, p. 9.
8. Ibid., pp. 7–8.
9. Ibid., p. 11.
10. Quoted in W. Hall Griffin and H. C. Minchin, *The Life of Robert Browning*, rev. ed. (Hamden, Conn.: Archon Books, 1966), p. 75.
11. *Browning's Experiments with Genre* (Toronto, 1972), p. 59.
12. *The Variance and the Unity: A Study of the Complementary Poems of Robert Browning* (Athens, Ohio, 1973), p. 184.
13. *Focusing Artifice*, pp. 43–44.
14. Hair, *Browning's Experiments*, p. 60.
15. King, *Focusing Artifice*, p. 48; see also W. David Shaw, *The Dialectical Temper: The Rhetorical Art of Robert Browning* (Ithaca, N.Y., 1968), p. 52.
16. *Browning* (London, 1972), p. 44.
17. Ibid., p. 46.
18. F. G. Kenyon, "Introduction," *The Works of Robert Browning*, 4:vii–x.
19. *Browning's Characters: A Study in Poetic Technique* (New Haven, 1961), p. 130.
20. King, *Focusing Artifice*, p. 27.
21. *Stages on Life's Way*, trans. Walter Lowrie (Princeton, N.J., 1940), p. 400.
22. "For passion never blinds you but makes you all the more clear-sighted. You then have forgotten your despair and all that commonly weighs upon your soul and thought, the accidental contact you have established with a person engages your attention absolutely." *Either/Or*, 2:204.
23. Price, *Narrow Pass*, p. 194.
24. Ibid.
25. Ibid., pp. 169, 173, 177.
26. Ibid., pp. 180, 189.
27. The following comment from *Stages on Life's Way* provides a useful gloss for understanding the Pope's intention: "The religious healing consists on the contrary in transforming the world and the centuries and the successive generations and the millions of contemporary men to an evanescent distraction, in transforming jubilation and acclaim and aesthetic hero-worship to a disturbing distraction, the notion of being 'finished,' to juggler's illusion, so that the only thing remaining is the individual himself, the single individual, placed in his God-relationship under the rubric: Guilty?/Not guilty?" (p. 418).
28. *The Disappearance of God* (1963; reprint ed., New York: Schocken Paperback, 1965), pp. 85, 86.
29. *Either/Or*, 1:98, 101, 105.
30. Ibid., p. 79.
31. *Das Unbehagen in der Kultur* (1930), translated as *Civilization and Its Discontents*, vol. 21 in *The Standard Edition of the Complete Psychological*

Works of Sigmund Freud, ed. and trans. James Strachey, in collaboration with Anna Freud, 24 vols. (London, 1955–74); see especially 21:138–45. Freud summarizes his thesis: "When an instinctual trend undergoes repression, its libidinal elements are turned into symptoms, and its aggressive components into a sense of guilt" (p. 139).

CHAPTER 4: ARNOLD AND CLOUGH

1. Walter E. Houghton, The Poetry of Clough: An Essay in Revaluation (New Haven, 1963), p. 226.
2. Michael Timko, Innocent Victorian: The Satiric Poetry of Arthur Hugh Clough (Athens, Ohio, 1963), p. 9.
3. G. Robert Stange, Matthew Arnold: The Poet as Humanist (Princeton, N.J., 1967), p. 290.
4. William A. Madden, Matthew Arnold: A Study of Aesthetic Temperament in Victorian England (Bloomington, Ind., 1967), p. vii.
5. "On the Modern Element in Literature," The Complete Prose Works of Matthew Arnold, ed. R. H. Super, 11 vols. (Ann Arbor, 1960–76), 1:19, 20, 28.
6. The Letters of Matthew Arnold to Arthur Hugh Clough, ed. Howard Foster Lowry (London and New York, 1932), p. 97.
7. Miller, Disappearance of God, p. 223.
8. The Poems of Matthew Arnold, ed. Kenneth Allott (London, 1965), p. 138 n.
9. Letters of Arnold, to Clough, November (15, 22, or 29?) 1848, p. 95.
10. "Conclusion" to Literature and Dogma, in Prose Works of Arnold, 6:409–11.
11. The translation is by C. Day Lewis, The Aeneid of Virgil (1952; reprint ed., Garden City, N.Y.: Anchor Books, 1953), p. 125.
12. "Matthew Arnold's Tragic Vision," PMLA 85 (January 1970):112.
13. "Arnold's 'Empedocles on Etna,'" Victorian Studies 1 (1958):326–32.
14. Arnold's Poetic Landscapes (Baltimore, 1969), p. 198.
15. Stange, Matthew Arnold, p. 263.
16. Matthew Arnold (1939; reprint ed., New York: Meridian Books, 1955), p. 123.
17. "Arnold's Balder Dead," Victorian Poetry 4 (Spring 1966):69.
18. Mary W. Schneider makes an important point that "Clough was more than a pastoral poet, as Arnold knew, but he is remembering the Clough he knew and the days of their early friendship"; see "Orpheus in Three Poems by Matthew Arnold," Victorian Poetry 10 (Spring 1972):41.
19. Letters of Arnold, to Mrs. Clough, Oct. 2, 1868, no. 60, p. 160; to Clough, dated after Dec. 6, 1847, no. 5, p. 63; to Clough, July 20, 1848, no. 18, p. 86.
20. Ibid., to Clough, June 7, 1852, no. 39, p. 123; to Clough, Sept. 23, 1849; no. 32, p. 110; to his mother, Nov. 20, 1861, no. 57, p. 157.
21. Ibid., to Clough, Feb. 12, 1853, no. 42, p. 129; to Clough, June 7, 1852, no. 39, p. 123.
22. Ibid., to Clough, June 7, 1852, no. 39, p. 123; to Clough, Feb. 12, 1853, no.

42, pp. 128, 129; to Clough, dated after Dec. 6, 1847, no. 5, p. 63; to Clough, dated after Sept. 1848–49, no. 24, p. 97; to Clough, Sept. 23. 1849, no. 32, p. 109.

23. Ibid., to Clough, Sept. 23, 1849, no. 32, p. 111; to Clough, Feb. 12, 1853, no. 42, pp. 129, 130; to Clough, Sept. 6, 1853, no. 48, p. 142; to Clough, July 5, 1861, no. 57, p. 155.

24. Ibid., to Clough, dated after Dec. 6, 1847, no. 5, p. 63; to Clough, July 20, 1848, no. 20, p. 86; to his mother, Nov. 20, 1861, no. 57, p. 158.

25. *The Correspondence of Arthur Hugh Clough*, ed. Frederick L. Mulhauser, 2 vols. (Oxford, 1957), to T. Burgidge, July 21, 1844, 1:131.

26. Timko, *Innocent Victorian*, p. 8.

27. *Correspondence of Clough*, to T. Arnold, July 16, 1848, 1:215.

28. Ibid., to Blanche Smith, Jan. 1852, 1:301.

29. The text for Horace's *Epode* XVI, l. 37, is from Horati Flacci, *Opera*, ed. Edward C. Wickham and H. W. Garrod (Oxford, 1901), no pagination.

30. *Correspondence of Clough*, to C. E. Norton, December 9, 1853, 2:470.

31. *Arthur Hugh Clough* (New York, 1970), p. 59.

32. References to the texts of Clough's poems are from *The Poems of A. H. Clough*, ed. H. F. Lowry, A. L. P. Norrington, and F. L. Mulhauser (Oxford, 1951).

33. Johnson, *Sex and Marriage*, p. 80.

34. *Correspondence of Clough*, to J. C. Shairp, Feb. 20, 1848, 1:200–201.

35. Timko, *Innocent Victorian*, p. 149.

36. Ibid., p. 138.

37. Houghton, *Poetry of Clough*, p. 124.

38. Timko, *Innocent Victorian*, p. 152.

39. Houghton, *Poetry of Clough*, pp. 206–207.

40. Ibid., p. 160.

41. Timko, *Innocent Victorian*, pp. 166–67.

Chapter 5: Rossetti and Meredith

1. *Letters of Dante Gabriel Rossetti*, ed. Oswald Doughty and J. R. Wahl, 4 vols. (Oxford, 1965–67), to William Allingham, Nov. 29, 1860, no. 353, 1:384.

2. Oswald Doughty, *A Victorian Romantic: Dante Gabriel Rossetti*, 2nd ed. (London, 1960), p. 273.

3. *Letters of Rossetti*, to William Allingham, August 1863, no. 507, 2:492.

4. *Dante Gabriel Rossetti: His Family-Letters, with a Memoir by William Michael Rossetti*, 2 vols. (London, 1895), 1:235; hereafter cited as *Rossetti: Letters and Memoir*.

5. Hoxie Neale Fairchild, *Religious Trends in English Poetry*, 6 vols. (New York, 1939–68), vol. 4. *1830–1880: Christianity and Romanticism in the Victorian Era*, p. 404.

6. *Rossetti: Letters and Memoir*, 1:405.

7. *Letters of Rossetti*, late July or Aug. 1853, no. 119, 1:150.

8. Ibid., between December 1854 and Jan. 18, 1855, no. 193, 1:234.
9. Ibid., June 16, 1866, no. 682, 2:600; the lines quoted are from fn. 2 which cite the words of William Michael Rossetti.
10. Ibid., from the text of Rossetti's letter.
11. Ibid., to Alice Boyd, March 15, 1870, no. 947, 2:817.
12. Ibid., to William Davies, March 16, 1881, no. 2435, 4:1857, 1858.
13. With the exception of *The House of Life*, all quotations from Rossetti's poetry are from vol. 1 of *The Collected Works of Dante Gabriel Rossetti*, ed. William M. Rossetti, 2 vols. (London, 1886); page numbers for this volume are noted in the text.
14. David Sonstroem, *Rossetti and the Fair Lady* (Middletown, Conn., 1970), p. 194.
15. Carol T. Christ, *The Finer Optic: The Aesthetic of Particularity in Victorian Poetry* (New Haven, 1975), p. 38.
16. Sonstroem, *Rossetti and the Fair Lady*, p. 27.
17. Jerome J. McGann, "Rossetti's Significant Details," *Victorian Poetry* 7 (Spring 1969):50.
18. Richard L. Stein, *The Ritual of Interpretation: The Fine Arts as Literature in Ruskin, Rossetti, and Pater* (Cambridge, Mass., 1975), p. 148.
19. Robert N. Keane, "Rossetti's 'Jenny': Moral Ambiguity and the 'Inner Standing Point,'" *Papers on Language and Literature* 9 (Summer 1973): 276.
20. Jules Paul Seigel, "*Jenny*: The Divided Sensibility of a Young and Thoughtful Man of the World," *Studies in English Literature, 1500–1900* 9 (Autumn 1969):691.
21. Stephen J. Spector, "Love, Unity, and Desire in the Poetry of Dante Gabriel Rossetti," *Journal of English Literary History* 38 (September 1971):443.
22. All references to *The House of Life* are from *The House of Life: A Sonnet-Sequence*, ed. Paull Franklin Baum (Cambridge, Mass., 1928); sonnets are identified in the text by their numbers, as established in this edition.
23. Johnson, *Sex and Marriage*, pp. 88–89.
24. *The Letters of George Meredith*, ed. C. L. Cline, 3 vols. (Oxford 1970), to Frederick A. Maxse, Dec. 1861, no. 130, 1:121.
25. *Letters of Meredith*, to W. C. Bonaparte Wyse, May 31, 1861, no. 101, 1:85.
26. Ibid., to Dante Gabriel Rossetti, June 8, 1870, no. 450, 1:418.
27. Ibid., to Dante Gabriel Rossetti, Nov. 19, 1871, no. 491, 1:458.
28. Ibid., to James Thomson, Oct. 18, 1881, no. 716, 2:641.
29. Ibid., to Theodore Watts-Dunton, Nov. 6, 1904, no. 2202, 3:1508.
30. Ibid., to William Michael Rossetti, Sept. 18, 1906, no. 2319, 3:1569.
31. Ibid., to Ford Madox Hueffer, Oct. 15, 1908, no. 2512, 3:1671.
32. Ibid., to the editor of *The Times*, April 14, 1909, no. 2553, 3:1692.
33. Ibid., to Frederick A. Maxse, Oct. 19, 1861, no. 121, 1:106.
34. Ibid., to Mrs. Janet Ross, Dec. 1, 1863, no. 256, 1:237.
35. Quoted by Lionel Stevenson in *The Ordeal of George Meredith: A Biography* (New York, 1953), p. 345.

36. "Meredith's Pessimistic Humanism: A New Reading of *Modern Love*," *Modern Philology* 67 (May 1970):345.
37. All references to *Modern Love* are from vol. 24 of *The Works of George Meredith*, Memorial Edition, 27 vols. (London, 1909–11); the sonnet numbers, and page numbers on which they may be found in this volume, are indicated in the text.
38. *A Troubled Eden: Nature and Society in the Works of George Meredith* (Stanford, Calif., 1961), p. 367.
39. The original text of "Love in the Valley," *Works of George Meredith*, Memorial Edition, 27:280–83.
40. Johnson, *Sex and Marriage*, pp. 45–46.
41. *Works of George Meredith*, 25:162–79; the section numbers of "The Nuptials of Attila," and the page numbers on which they may be found in this volume, are indicated in the text.
42. "Meredith as Poet," in *Meredith Now: Some Critical Essays*, ed. Ian Fletcher (New York, 1971), p. 22.
43. *Works of George Meredith*, 26:15–29.
44. *The Poetry and Philosophy of George Meredith* (London, 1912), p. 194.
45. Johnson, *Sex and Marriage*, p. 47.
46. *Works of George Meredith*, 26:185–207.
47. *The Concept of Nature in Nineteenth-Century English Poetry* (New York, 1936), p. 492.

CHAPTER 6: SWINBURNE AND HOPKINS

1. *The Dragon in the Gate: Studies in the Poetry of G. M. Hopkins* (Berkeley and Los Angeles, 1968), p. 49.
2. Ibid.; William Henry Gardner, *Gerard Manley Hopkins, 1844–1889: A Study of Poetic Idiosyncrasy in Relation to Poetic Tradition*, 2 vols., 2nd ed. (New Haven, 1948–49), 2:92–94; see also Schneider's essay, "Sprung Rhythm: A Chapter in the Evolution of Nineteenth-Century Verse," *PMLA* 80 (June 1965):237–53.
3. *Letters of Meredith*, to Frederick A. Maxse, Oct. 19, 1861, no. 121, 106.
4. "Introduction," *The Swinburne Letters*, ed. Cecil Y. Lang, 6 vols. (New Haven, 1959–62), 1:xviii.
5. *Letters of Meredith*, to William Hardman, ca. June 17, 1866, no. 373, 1:342 (emphasis added).
6. *Letters of Gerard Manley Hopkins to Robert Bridges*, ed. Claude Colleer Abbott (London, 1935), to Bridges, April 22, 1879, no. 59, p. 79; *The Correspondence of Gerard Manley Hopkins and Richard Watson Dixon*, ed. Claude Colleer Abbott (London, 1935), to Dixon, July 29, 1888, no. 41, p. 157; June 30, 1886, no. 34, p. 136; Dec. 1, 1881, no. 22, p. 99.
7. *Swinburne Letters*, to the editor of the *Spectator*, June 7, 1862, no. 33, p. 52.
8. "Swinburne as Poet," *The Sacred Wood* (1920; reprint ed., New York: University Paperbacks, 1960), p. 145.
9. *Atalanta in Calydon*, in *The Complete Works of Algernon Charles Swin-

burne, Bonchurch Edition, ed. Sir Edmund Gosse and Thomas James Wise, 20 vols. (London, 1925–27), 7:273. Since there are no line numbers in this edition, page numbers for this volume are noted in the text.

10. *Freud: The Mind of the Moralist* (1959; reprint ed., Garden City, N.Y.: Anchor Books, 1961), p. 164.
11. Ernest Jones, *The Life and Work of Sigmund Freud*, abridged in 1 vol., ed. Lionel Trilling and Steven Marcus (Garden City, N.Y., 1963), p. 465.
12. Rieff, *Freud*, p. 217.
13. *Victorian Revolutionaries* (New York, 1970), p. 289.
14. *Swinburne* (Harlow, Eng., 1973), p. 3.
15. *Beyond the Tragic Vision* (New York, 1962), p. 315.
16. Ibid., p. 76.
17. Ibid., p. 314.
18. Fletcher, *Swinburne*, p. 52.
19. "The Triumph of Time," in *Complete Works of Swinburne*, 1:169–81.
20. Jerome H. Buckley, *The Victorian Temper: A Study in Literary Culture* (Cambridge, Mass., 1951); Morse Peckham, "Toward a Theory of Romanticism," *PMLA* 66 (1951):5–23; Donald C. Stuart, "Swinburne: The Composition of a Self-Portrait," *Victorian Poetry* 9 (1971):111–28.
21. *Erechtheus*, in *Complete Works of Swinburne*, 7:357–424.
22. *Swinburne: An Experiment in Criticism* (Chicago, 1972), pp. 118, 126–29.
23. *Mythology and the Romantic Tradition in English Poetry* (1937; reprint ed., New York, 1963), pp. 344–47.
24. "Mary Queen of Scots," in *Complete Works of Swinburne*, 14:403, 409.
25. *Chastelard*, in *Complete Works of Swinburne*, 8:1–133.
26. *Bothwell*, in *Complete Works of Swinburne*, 8:135–387, 9:1–284.
27. *Mary Stuart*, in *Complete Works of Swinburne*, 9:287–475.
28. "Thalassius," in *Complete Works of Swinburne*, 3:288–303.
29. Meredith B. Raymond, *Swinburne's Poetics: Theory and Practice* (The Hague, 1971), p. 159.
30. *Tristram of Lyonesse*, in *Complete Works of Swinburne*, 4:23–168.
31. *Swinburne: A Literary Biography* (1932; reprint ed., New York, 1967), pp. 294–95.
32. McGann, *Swinburne*, p. 186.
33. "A Nympholept," in *Complete Works of Swinburne*, 6:68–81.
34. "Swinburne's 'A Nympholept' and 'The Lake of Gaube,'" *Victorian Poetry* 9 (1971):210.
35. "The Lake of Gaube," in *Complete Works of Swinburne*, 6:200–202.
36. Paul L. Mariani, "Hopkins' 'Andromeda' and the New Aestheticism," *Victorian Poetry* 11 (Spring 1973):46.
37. *Correspondence of Hopkins*, to Dixon, July 29, 1888, no. 41, p. 156.
38. *Letters of Hopkins*, to Bridges, Feb. 22, 1879, no. 54, p. 73; *Further Letters of Gerard Manley Hopkins Including His Correspondence with Coventry Patmore*, ed. Claude Colleer Abbott, 2nd rev. ed. (London, 1956), to Baillie, May 22, 1880, no. 136, p. 246; to Patmore, Nov. 23, 1883, no. 174, pp. 336–37.
39. *Letters of Hopkins*, to Bridges, Oct. 22, 1879, no. 64, p. 96.

40. *Correspondence of Hopkins*, to Dixon, Oct. 26, 1881, no. 20A, pp. 81–82.
41. *Further Letters of Hopkins*, to Baillie, Sept. 15, 1867, no. 127, p. 228.
42. *Letters of Hopkins*, to Bridges, Oct. 26, 1880, no. 70, p. 111; *Correspondence of Hopkins*, to Dixon, Dec. 1, 1881, no. 22, p. 99.
43. *Letters of Hopkins*, to Bridges, Aug. 14, 1879, no. 62, p. 89.
44. *Further Letters of Hopkins*, to Patmore, Nov. 23, 1883, no. 174, p. 336; *Correspondence of Hopkins*, to Dixon, July 29, 1888, no. 41, p. 156.
45. *Letters of Hopkins*, to Bridges, April 29, 1889, no. 171, p. 304.
46. "Violent Imagery in the Poetry of Gerard Manley Hopkins," *Victorian Poetry* 7 (Spring 1969):10.
47. See *Letters of Hopkins*, to Bridges, Oct. 26, 1880, no. 70, p. 111; *Correspondence of Hopkins*, to Dixon, Dec. 1, 1881, no. 22, p. 99.
48. References to Hopkins's poetry are from *The Poems of Gerard Manley Hopkins*, ed. W. H. Gardner and N. H. MacKenzie, 4th ed. (London, 1967).
49. M. B. McNamee, "Mastery and Mercy in *The Wreck of the Deutschland*," *College English* 23, no. 4 (January 1962), p. 276.
50. Geoffrey Hartman, "Hopkins Revisited," in *Beyond Formalism: Literary Essays, 1958–1970* (New Haven, 1970), p. 236.
51. Paul L. Mariani, *A Commentary on the Complete Poems of Gerard Manley Hopkins* (Ithaca, N.Y., 1970), p. 68.
52. *Gerard Manley Hopkins: The Poet as Victorian* (Ithaca, N.Y., 1968), p. 74.
53. Mariani, *A Commentary*, p. 161.

CHAPTER 7: ELIZABETH BARRETT BROWNING AND OSCAR WILDE

1. *Letters of Hopkins*, to Bridges, Oct. 26, 1880, no. 70, p. 111.
2. *Swinburne Letters*, to John Nichol, February 11, 1857, no. 7, p. 10.
3. "Aurora Leigh," *Complete Works of Swinburne*, 16:4.
4. Ibid.
5. *The Common Reader, Second Series* (London, 1932), pp. 202, 208.
6. Patricia Meyer Spacks, *The Female Imagination* (New York, 1975), pp. 315, 317.
7. *Literary Women* (Garden City, N.Y., 1976), pp. 5, 40.
8. References to Elizabeth Barrett Browning's potery are from *The Complete Poetical Works of Elizabeth Barrett Browning*, Cambridge Edition (Boston and New York, 1900).
9. Woolf, *Common Reader*, p. 207.
10. *The Letters of Robert Browning and Elizabeth Barrett Barrett, 1845–1846*, ed. Elvan Kintner, 2 vols. (Cambridge, Mass., 1969), R.B. to E.B.B., Jan. 10, 1845, no. 1, 1:3.
11. Ibid., 2:1089.
12. Ibid., E.B.B. to R.B., Feb. 14, 1846, no. 232, 1:457.
13. Ibid., E.B.B. to R.B., Dec. 12, 1845, no. 173, 1:318; E.B.B. to R.B., Sept. 13, 1846, no. 558, 2:1066.
14. Ibid., E.B.B. to R.B., Jan. 15, 1845, no. 4, 1:9; R.B. to E.B.B., Jan. 17, 1845, no. 5, 1:11; E.B.B. to R.B., March 5, 1845, no. 12, 1:35.

15. Ibid., E.B.B. to R.B., Aug. 20, 1845, no. 87, 1:169; E.B.B. to R.B., Jan. 26, 1846, no. 214, 1:422; E.B.B. to R.B., Sept. 25, 1845, no. 113, 1:211; R.B. to E.B.B., Sept. 25, 1845, no. 114, 1:213–14.

16. Ibid., R.B. to E.B.B., Oct. 14, 1845, no. 128, 1:234; R.B. to E.B.B., Nov. 21, 1845, no. 155, 1:283; R.B. to E.B.B., Nov. 23, 1845, no. 157, 1:287; E.B.B. to R.B., Dec. 12, 1845, no. 173, 1:318; E.B.B. to R.B., Dec. 30, 1845, no. 186, 1:349; E.B.B. to R.B., Jan. 15, 1846, no. 203, 1:395.

17. Ibid., E.B.B. to R.B., Feb. 23, 1846, no. 244, 1:489; E.B.B. to R.B., March 3, 1846, no. 256, 1:514; E.B.B. to R.B., May 5, 1846, no. 344, 2:680; E.B.B. to R.B., May 7, 1846, no. 348, 2:687.

18. Ibid., E.B.B. to R.B., May 7, 1846, no. 348, 2:688, 687; E.B.B. to R.B., May 11, 1846, no. 353, 2:695, 696.

19. Ibid., E.B.B. to R.B., July 4, 1846, no. 440, 2:844; E.B.B. to R.B., July 6, 1846, no. 444, 2:853; E.B.B. to R.B., July 26, 1846, no. 473, 2:901.

20. Ibid., E.B.B. to R.B., Aug. 2, 1846, no. 483, 2:923.

21. Ibid., E.B.B. to R.B., Aug. 12, 1846, no. 499, 2:957.

22. Ibid., E.B.B. to R.B., Aug. 26, 1846, no. 524, 2:1007; R.B. to E.B.B., Aug. 30, 1846, no. 531, 2:1023; E.B.B. to R.B., Sept. 18, 1846, no. 573, 2:1086.

23. "English Poetesses," in *Miscellanies*, vol. 14 of *The Complete Works of Oscar Wilde*, First Collected Edition, ed. Robert Ross, 15 vols. (1908–22; reprint ed., London, 1969), pp. 111, 110, 113.

24. *The Letters of Oscar Wilde*, ed. Rupert Hart-Davis (New York, 1962), to William Ward, July 26, 1876, p. 21.

25. Ibid.; see also Wilde to William Ward, Aug. 28, 1876, p. 25.

26. "English Poetesses," p. 114.

27. Quotations from *Lady Windermere's Fan* are taken from *The Complete Works of Oscar Wilde*, with Introduction by A. B. Walkley, 12 vols. (New York, 1923), 7:9–155; page references for this volume are indicated in the text.

28. Quotations from Oscar Wilde's poetry are from vol. 9 of *Complete Works of Wilde*, First Collected Edition; page references for this volume are indicated in the text.

29. Richard Ellman has discussed *Salomé* in terms of Wilde's relationships with Ruskin and Pater, suggesting that Iokanaan is "Ruskinism as Wilde understood that pole of his character" and that Salomé "is related to Paterism." See "Overtures to *Salomé*," in *Yearbook of Comparative Literature* 17 (1968):17–28, and in *Tri-Quarterly* 15 (1969):45–64, reprinted in *Oscar Wilde: A Collection of Critical Essays*, ed. Richard Ellmann (Englewood Cliffs, N.J., 1969).

30. *Vera, or The Nihilists: A Drama in a Prologue, and Four Acts*, in *Complete Works of Wilde*, First Collected Edition, 2:115–261; page references for this volume are indicated in the text.

31. *The Duchess of Padua*, vol. 1 of *Complete Works of Wilde*, First Collected Edition; page references for this volume are indicated in the text.

32. *A Woman of No Importance*, vol. 4 of *Complete Works of Wilde*, First Collected Edition; page references for this volume are indicated in the text.

33. *Salomé*, trans. Lord Alfred Bounce Douglas, with Oscar Wilde's approval, in *The Complete Works of Oscar Wilde*, with Introduction by Arthur Symons, 12 vols. (New York, 1923), 9:105–183; page references for this volume are indicated in the text.
34. *Intentions and the Soul of Man*, vol. 8 of *Complete Works of Wilde*, First Collected Edition; page references for this volume are indicated in the text.
35. *An Ideal Husband*, in *Complete Works of Wilde*, First Collection Edition, 5:31; page references for this volume are indicated in the text.
36. *The Importance of Being Earnest: A Trivial Comedy for Serious People*, vol. 6 of *Complete Works of Wilde*, First Collected Edition; page references for this volume are indicated in the text.
37. *De Profundis*, in *Complete Works of Wilde*, First Collected Edition, 11:64.

Index

313